Neuropsychological Perspectives on Learning Disabilities in the Era of RTI

Neuropsychological Perspectives on Learning Disabilities in the Era of RTI: Recommendations for Diagnosis and Intervention

Edited by:
Elaine Fletcher-Janzen
Cecil R. Reynolds

WILEY

John Wiley & Sons, Inc.

Library of Congress Cataloging-in-Publication Data

Neuropsychological perspectives on learning disabilities in the era of RTI : recommendations for diagnosis and intervention / edited by Elaine Fletcher-Janzen, Cecil R. Reynolds.
    p. ; cm.
   Includes bibliographical references.
   ISBN 978-0-470-22527-1 (pbk. : alk. paper)
   1. Learning disabilities—Diagnosis. 2. Learning disabled children—Education. 3. Remedial teaching. 4. Neuropsychological tests for children. I. Fletcher-Janzen, Elaine. II. Reynolds, Cecil R., 1952–
   [DNLM: 1. Child. 2. Learning Disorders—diagnosis. 3. Education, Special. 4. Eligibility Determination—standards. 5. Neuropsychological Tests. 6. School Health Services. WS 110 N937 2008]
   RJ496.L4N484 2008
   618.92′85889—dc22

                                            2007045589

Dedication

We dedicate this book to the lifetime of work in learning disabilities of Dr. James C. Chalfant whose seminal work with Margaret A. Scheffelin, *Central Processing Dysfunctions in Children*, inspired and directed the research of generations in furthering the understanding of learning disabilities.

Contents

Foreword

Sally Shaywitz

This is a book about the future—the future of education, the future of our children—and how best to integrate the advances of modern neuroscience into an educational framework for teaching all children to read, particularly those with a learning disability. The future is now, certainly the next minute and the next day; the point is the future is close at hand and the burning question is how do educators best use the 21st century tools available to provide the most effective reading instruction to all readers, typical and struggling. This book asks a series of central questions of a diverse group of researchers and educators, who not surprisingly have always interesting and not always converging perspectives. The questions are six in all, with responders asked to address at least four. The initial series of queries grapple with how to translate the avalanche of progress in neuroscience into educational actions that will advance the state of the art of diagnosing and providing effective interventions to students with learning disabilities. Accordingly, we have:

1) What do you think neuroscience has to offer laws and policies associated with learning disability determination?;
2) What do you think neuroscience has to offer the assessment and identification of learning disabilities?;
3) How will future developments in neuroscience affect how we classify and intervene with learning disabilities?

Given the extraordinary progress in understanding reading at the level of the brain itself, it is imperative that we take the next step in the process that has progressed from first doubting if neuroscience research and findings belong in the education equation to an almost giddy, glowing appreciation for the remarkable advances in the ability to "see" the brain at work to the serious questions posed in this volume of what is the most effective application of these wondrous advances. Briefly, these advances include the identification of the neural systems used in reading and how these systems differ in good and poor readers; the pinpointing of neural systems serving fluent reading and the identification of those systems used in compensation. The demonstration, for example, of decreased activation in struggling readers of the "word form" area necessary for rapid, fluent reading now provides both a target for reading interventions and a neurobiological explanation of the necessity for extra-time for dyslexic readers. Brain imaging studies suggest that there are two specific subtypes of struggling readers, one based on more inherent influences, the other reflecting more environmental influences. Of direct practical relevance, our and other neuroimaging studies demonstrate the plasticity or malleability of the neural systems for reading. Specifically they indicate that teaching matters and that the neural circuitry for reading is responsive to evidence-based intensive reading interventions—with effective instruction, the brain can change and reading can improve. Recent evidence also points to differences in the development of the neural circuitry for reading in good and struggling readers; good readers appear to develop a sound-based system while dyslexic readers develop a system that seems to be more tuned to memory.

Wow—yes, but the basic question is what does this progress mean for education. How do we most wisely use this sophisticated, new neurobiological knowledge to further education in the classroom? At its most critical level—how does the educational enterprise productively integrate neurobiological evidence into classroom and school practices.

And so, having considered the implications of the extraordinary possibilities now offered by neuroscience, the contributors are asked to consider timely, critical issues of how to reconcile these advances with current and proposed educational policies and practices. Specifically, as we consider the future of education, how do we reconcile and maximize the contributions of neuroscience, Neuropsychology, and Response to Intervention (RTI) to the development of the most accurate, efficient, and effective identification and intervention model:

1) How do you reconcile RTI as a means of diagnosis of LD with knowledge from the clinical neurosciences?;
2) What role does Neuropsychology have to play in the diagnosis of LD?; and
3) What role does Neurospychology have in designing interventions in the context of RTI?

This exceptional volume offers timeliness, relevance, and the added pleasure of the insightful responses of a range of researchers, including Alan Kaufman who provides a context and historical perspective and Virginia Berninger whose work has contributed to our new knowledge of the reading brain and who sees much benefit in, for example, the potential of RTI to inform educational policy. Other contributors, while acknowledging the potential utility of RTI approaches for example, as a *pre-intervention* strategy, also raise important questions regarding its readiness for acceptance and widespread implementation as a diagnostic tool or as an intervention strategy. Striking in this respect are the cogent, and, what I found to be, often compelling arguments made by thoughtful and highly knowledgeable contributors such as Cecil Reynolds and H. Lee Swanson, who raise serious, constructive questions about what they perceive is a less than critical examination and acceptance of RTI.

As the RTI approach rolls into schools and classrooms across the nation, it is indeed timely, in fact, essential that the kinds of questions and concerns raised in the chapters of this book are made part of an informed national discussion. Is RTI the answer to the search for the most effective strategy for the early identification and accurate diagnosis of a reading disability and for providing effective reading instruction and timely intervention services? Or is RTI more of a Trojan horse, outwardly appealing but filled with risky, unproven, and in the end, potentially harmful, practices; or, is it somewhere in-between? If RTI is problematic, are there modifications or constructive approaches to improving this model? Perspectives on each of these possibilities are well-represented in this volume. For example, Swanson reminds the reader that RTI is not a new, but rather an old, concept going back three decades and goes on to provide an in-depth discussion of the weak experimental basis for RTI. He cites the lack of controlled randomized studies of RTI's effectiveness as an identification model or as an intervention strategy; the lack of consistent (standardized), reliable and valid applications of evidence-based instruction using RTI; and the lack of a proven expert teaching model for such instruction. Swanson asks the fundamental question: What is meant by "non-responsiveness"—how is it defined and how is it measured? How this question is addressed brings with it significant, practical consequences; for example, lack of a consistent approach to determining responsiveness will identify different children and report varying prevalence rates, dependent on methods used rather than something innate within specific groups of children.

Swanson also brings to the reader's attention the lack of solid empirical support for the use of RTI as an identification model. An often stated advantage of RTI is its lack of reliance on IQ measurement and with it, the elimination of the necessity of demonstrating an IQ-achievement discrepancy. However, the question raised here asks if RTI represents an instance of just a different form of discrepancy model; here, based on discrepancy from grade level performance. A central assumption of RTI models is that intelligence is irrelevant to the acquisition of reading. Consequently, the argument goes, intelligence needn't be considered in the identification or approach to reading disability; if provided equal opportunity (high quality instruction) there will be equality of outcomes for all children. What is often not stated, but noted in this volume, are the flaws embedded within such an assumption. The reader is reminded that empiric data indicate that such equality of instruction will result in greater, not lesser, variability in educational outcomes. Equality of educational opportunity may perhaps result in equality of performance on phonological measures, but far less so on measures of reading comprehension or vocabulary. Swanson notes that while outcomes may be similar in groups of struggling readers identified as discrepant or as non-discrepant, meta-analyses indicate that verbal IQ is a significant factor in moderating the effect size or the magnitude of the difference in performance of the two groups and further, that IQ accounts for a significant amount of the explainable variance in reading. Clearly, the empiric data as to the relevance of IQ in interpreting treatment outcome is complicated and at times, contradictory; in any event far more nuanced than its detractors often present. At the least, the extant empiric evidence does not seem to support the exclusion of aptitude from assessment of response to intervention or certainly, from diagnosis of a learning disability.

An important, not to be missed, discussion concerns the role of RTI as a strategy for the identification of children as learning disabled. Reynolds, for example, asks the question, is failure to progress at the same pace as their classmates in response to "appropriate instructional methods" sufficient for a diagnosis of a learning disability. He reviews data strongly suggesting that it is not. Such an approach where a child could be labeled as learning disabled in one classroom, but not in another, "fundamentally alters the concept of disability at its very roots." Interestingly, the further argument is made that RTI is fundamentally a special case of discrepancy—here, between the response and progress of a classroom and that of an individual child. Such a context-dependent approach based on the relative progress of a child compared to a class seems to completely deny the most basic tenet and underlying concept of a learning disability as a disparity between academic aptitude and academic achievement residing *within* the individual child. Reynolds notes that implementation of an RTI model will result in the disproportionate identification of students with lower IQs (below 90) bringing with it the re-introduction of the old notion of the child who is a "slow learner." As a corollary, failure to consider aptitude, will result in a failure to identify and consequently, will ignore the needs of those students who are in the higher deciles for academic aptitude. For example, a very bright child who struggles in reading, but whose performance is close to the average level of performance of his/her classmates (who are of generally lower academic aptitude), and at the same time, excels in other academic areas, would be overlooked if an RTI model were to be implemented at that child's school. Reynolds voices concern that in this type of implementation, RTI "denies the historical concept of the specificity of a learning disability . . ." and replaces a "wait to fail" model with a "watch them fail" model. Noting the recent convergence of neurobiological and behavioral data indicating differences in processing of information in individuals with a learning disability, he expresses concern that RTI seems to ignore demonstration of a processing disorder—a key element critical to the theoretical concept and practical implementation of a diagnosis of a learning disability. These and other important concerns are raised, including the potential of the RTI model, which by-passes the assessment of the individual child, to lead to misdiagnosis and without information about a child's neuropsychological profile, to lead to mis- or inadequate treatment of a learning disability.

This represents but a small sampling of the often intense, often controversial, but always interesting and highly informative discussions to be found in the succeeding pages. Not to despair, the contributors all offer highly constructive and feasible approaches, for example, to developing improved models combining neuropsychological and neurobiological findings together with elements of RTI.

What makes this book so interesting is that here we have, brought together in one place, from a broad range of respected educators and researchers, contrasting and alternative views—views that can be compared and contrasted as the reader goes through the volume. I know that I particularly enjoyed going back and forth as I read each response, assimilating the points made by each contributor and often, a contrasting view expressed by another contributor. Fascinating, helpful, important reading—clearly a work that should be read by researchers, policy makers, and educators.

Sally E. Shaywitz, M.D.
Audrey G. Ratner Professor of Learning Development,
Co-Director, Yale Center for Learning, Reading, and Attention,
Co-Director, Yale Center for Dyslexia and Creativity
Author of *Overcoming Dyslexia,* Alfred E. Knopf, 2003

Preface

It is nearly 30 years since we began editing and writing about childhood brain-behavior relationships. When we started producing special education reference works, the field was just beginning to be defined by laws and practice guidelines and there was excitement about research illuminating what was going on in the brains and minds of children with learning disabilities (LDs). At that time, vitriolic arguments about IQ and the nature of intelligence were front and center, researchers were sure that learning disabilities were neurobiological in origin, reading curricula sought to rectify processing deficits, and the right of all children with disabilities to a free, appropriate public education that reflected individual learning needs was supported by all. In this sense, not much has changed over the years. The same could be said of today's popular discourse about learning disabilities; however, we have observed that the numerous and wondrous advances in neuroscience and neuropsychology appear to be absent from the current federal efforts to create a behaviorally oriented Response-to-Intervention (RTI) method of identifying learning disabilities. There is no doubt that, while not new, RTI is a promising method to assist children with reading problems in the early grades. Professionals who support the RTI approach to LD determination are well intentioned and tireless in their dedication to these children. Unfortunately, supporting a methodology that ignores important confounding variables (such as the common comorbidity of LD with other neurobiological disorders) defies the scientific method that binds all scientific inquiry. Intervening in the lives of unidentified children with learning disabilities without the benefit of well-constructed, standardized, norm-referenced assessment instruments ignores the inherent objectivity, fairness, and wealth of information these instruments provide. Insisting that all reading problems are remediated by phonologically based curricula and the occasional confusion of reading fluency with reading comprehension ignores many of the brain processes that bring full reading comprehension in later grades.

Ignoring neuroscience's and neuropsychology's contribution to understanding the brain processes involved in multiple learning tasks disregards a body of research literature that has a direct and important impact on policies and practice. We also believe that a disregard of neuroscientific contributions at this critical time may well expose many children who have learning disabilities and other comorbid conditions to unnecessary stress and failure. A narrow application of RTI creates LD identification by default: An unnecessary practice in the face of neuroscientific evidence of the dynamic localization of attention, executive functions, and specific areas of the brain related to reading.

This volume of work was created to illuminate the contribution of neuroscience and neuropsychology to learning disability identification. Translational research about the brain was very limited (mainly by technology) years ago when the identification of LD was formalized for the first time. This is not the case today. Translational research that seeks to take robust research results from the laboratory and reform them into classroom intervention is becoming the benchmark for evidence-based intervention. It is very important that educational professionals and policy makers understand the implications of the latest neuroscientific research because it has direct application to how we think about learning and the brain.

The authors in this book are practicing neuroscientists, neuropsychologists, clinical psychologists, and school psychologists with training in brain-behavior relationships. All of the authors bring a wealth of research and experience to their chapters. All of these authors are concerned about how the future of education will embrace neuroscientific findings.

It is questions like those found in this book that lay bare the worldviews and professional personalities of the authors. On the surface everyone is talking about the same issues. Indeed, we were worried about the possible redundancy of the text, but deep down we knew that the diverse nature of neuroscience would show the individual differences and rich experiences of our authors. If there was any doubt in the reader's mind that neuroscience and neuropsychology does not have an important part to play in current educational reform, this book will dispel that doubt. This is the statement we aimed to make, and we trusted that the process of going inside the minds of those who embrace neuroscience would be an interesting read indeed—and it is! We also want to note that we did not suggest to authors that they take a specific tact with their answers. We requested chapters of individuals from all points of view and the contributor's list indicates those who wished (or had the time) to participate.

We would like to thank all of the authors for their hard work. We asked that the manuscript be written in less than 4 months knowing full well that it would place stress on these very busy individuals. Nonetheless, they came through and created a strong and eloquent message. We would like to also thank Alan Kaufman for his sage description of the history of neuroscience and neuropsychology in the study of learning disabilities—it sets the stage beautifully. We would also like to thank Sally Shaywitz for adding her foreword to this book—we could not think of a stronger individual to lead this endeavor. We must also thank the "pit crew" at John Wiley and Sons, led by our editor Isabel Pratt, who turned this manuscript around on a dime so that the message could get out into the world in a timely manner. Elaine would like to thank her family, David, Emma, and Leif, for supporting yet another project. Cecil never tires of thanking Julia for her support and concern and continues to wish he had the same gifts to return.

Elaine Fletcher-Janzen
San Angelo, Texas

Cecil R. Reynolds
Bastrop, Texas

October, 2007

About the Contributors

Virginia W. Berninger, Ph.D., is Professor of Educational Psychology and Director of the NICHD-Funded Literacy Trek and Write Stuff Intervention Projects and the Multidisciplinary Learning Disabilities Center at the University of Washington. She is affiliated with the School Psychology (APA approved) and Learning Sciences Program.

Richard Boada, Ph.D., is a child clinical neuropsychologist on the faculty at the University of Colorado Health Sciences Center. He trained in Developmental Cognitive Neuroscience at the University of Denver with Bruce Pennington, Ph.D., and is involved in research investigating the cognitive and genetic factors underlying speech, language, and reading disorders. He is the recipient of APA dissertation, National Research Service, and Young Investigator awards. He is also a licensed speech-language pathologist.

David Breiger, Ph.D., is a clinical associate professor in the Department of Psychiatry and Behavioral Sciences at the University of Washington in Seattle and the Director of the Neuropsychological Consultation Service in the Department of Child and Adolescent Psychiatry at Seattle's Children's Hospital and Regional Medical Center. His research interests include neurobehavioral effects of brain tumors and treatments for leukemia in childhood, as well as early onset Schizophrenia.

Ronald T. Brown, Ph.D., ABPP, is a professor of public health, psychology, and pediatrics and is dean of the College of Health Professions at Temple University. He has published over 200 articles and books in the area of child clinical and health psychology. He is a past member of the National Institutes of Health Center for Scientific Review study section on Behavioral Medicine Interventions Outcome and is the editor of the Journal of Pediatric Psychology.

Jessica A. Carboni graduated with a Bachelor of Science degree from Pennsylvania State University. Jessica is currently a graduate student in the Ph.D. program for school psychology at Georgia State University.

Owen Carr, M.S., is a Licensed Specialist in School Psychology Trainee who is employed with Upshur County Shared Service Arrangement in Gilmer, Texas. He has studied both School Psychology and Neuropsychology at the University of Texas at Tyler. He has assisted with several research efforts and publications in the fields of neuropsychology and psychometrics.

Amy Nilson Connery, Psy.D., is a pediatric neuropsychology fellow at the NeuroDevelopment Center in Salt Lake City, Utah, and at the Idaho Elks Rehabilitation Hospital in Boise, Idaho.

Brian P. Daly, Ph.D., is an Assistant Professor in the Department of Public Health at Temple University. Dr. Daly is an Instructor in Health Psychology and the Director of the Temple Children's Hospital pediatric psychology clinic. Dr. Daly's research interests include interventions for children and adolescents with chronic illness, school mental health services, and resiliency factors among urban children and adolescents of color.

Raymond S. Dean, Ph.D., ABPP, ABPN, ABPdN, is currently named the George and Frances Ball Distinguished Professor of Neuropsychology and Director of the Neuropsychology Laboratory at Ball State University, where he has served in this position since 1984. He has published some 500 research articles, books, chapters, and tests. He is coauthor with Dr. Richard Woodcock of the Dean-Woodcock Neuropsychological Battery (Riverside, 2003).

Scott L. Decker, Ph.D., graduated from Ball State University with a doctorate in school psychology and specialized in neuropsychology. After completing his degree, he consulted on the development of several popular intelligence measures including the Stanford-Binet–Fifth Edition and the Woodcock-Johnson–Third Edition. Additionally, he is a coauthor of the Bender-Gestalt–Second Edition. He currently is an Assistant Professor at Georgia State University, where he teaches courses and conducts research in cognitive and neuropsychological assessment.

Sangeeta Dey, Psy.D., is a neuropsychologist and currently serves as Chair of the Child and Adolescent committee at the Massachusetts Psychological Association. She maintains a private practice in Lexington, Massachusetts, and is a staff member at the North Shore Children's Hospital. She conducts research and provides neuropsychological evaluation for children with developmental vulnerabilities, attentional problems, and learning disorders and has particular interest in understanding the neuropsychological profiles of children from other cultures.

Colin D. Elliott, Ph.D., is the author of the *Differential Ability Scales (DAS)* and its second edition, the *DAS-II*. For over 20 years he was the director of the program for training school psychologists at the University of Manchester in England. He is a NASP member and is a Fellow of APA and of the British Psychological Society. He now lives in southern California and is an Adjunct Professor at the University of California, Santa Barbara.

Steven G. Feifer, D.Ed., NCSP, is a nationally renowned speaker in the field of learning disabilities and has conducted over 150 seminars for educators and psychologists throughout North America. He has authored five books on learning disorders in children and is dually trained as both a school psychologist and school neuropsychologist. Dr. Feifer currently works as a school psychologist in Frederick, Maryland, and is a course instructor for the American Board of School Neuropsychology.

Elaine Fletcher-Janzen, Ed.D., NCSP, obtained her doctorate in school psychology from the College of William and Mary in 1993, and has been a school psychologist in the public schools and neuropsychiatric inpatient settings for the past 24 years. She has coedited and authored 14 books and reference works.

Michael D. Franzen, Ph.D., is Associate Professor of Psychiatry at Drexel University College of Medicine and Chief, Section of Psychology and Neuropsychology, at Allegheny General Hospital in Pittsburgh, Pennsylvania. He is a Fellow of Division 40 of APA and of NAN, as well as a Fellow of the Pennsylvania Psychological Association. He has published numerous scientific articles, chapters, and books in neuropsychology and serves on the editorial boards of several professional journals.

Javier Gontier, M.A., is completing graduate studies in psychology at the University of North Carolina Wilmington. He has held positions as clinical psychologist in hospitals in Chile, South America. In addition, he has held academic positions at universities in Chile as well as published in both Chilean and American journals of psychology.

Merrill Hiscock, Ph.D., is a neuropsychologist whose research interests include attention and cerebral lateralization in children and adults. He has spent many years providing clinical services to children with school problems. Dr. Hiscock joined the University of Houston faculty in 1989 and is also affiliated with the UH Center for Neuro-Engineering and Cognitive Science.

James A. Holdnack, Ph.D., is currently a senior research director with The Psychological Corporation. He completed postdoctoral training in neuropsychology at the University of Pennsylvania. As a licensed psychologist, he served children with complex medical, psychosocial, and learning disorders for the Division of Child Mental Health in Delaware.

Arthur MacNeill Horton, Jr. Ed.D., ABPP, ABPN, is the author/editor of over 15 books, more than 30 book chapters, and over 150 journal articles. He is a past president of the American Board of Professional Neuropsychology, the Coalition of Clinical Practitioners in Neuropsychology (CCPN), and the National Academy of Neuropsychology (NAN).

Steven J. Hughes, Ph.D., L.P., is a pediatric neuropsychologist, Assistant Professor of Pediatrics and Neurology at the University of Minnesota Medical School, and Director of Education and Research for the TOVA Company, publisher of the Test of Variables of Attention (TOVA). Dr. Hughes is a diplomate of the American Board of Pediatric Neuropsychology.

Alan S. Kaufman, Ph.D., is Professor of Psychology at Yale University School of Medicine and the series editor with Nadeen Kaufman of Wiley's *Essentials of Psychological Assessment* series. He has written numerous books on the Wechsler Scales and intelligence testing and is the author of several widely used assessment instruments.

Sally L. Kemp, Ph.D., holds a Ph.D. in developmental psychology with a subspecialization in Neuropsychology from Columbia University. Her 25-year career has integrated nursing, teaching, and neuropsychology practiced in a pediatric multidisciplinary setting. Research has centered on dyslexia, ADHD, and autism. Dr. Kemp is a coauthor of NEPSY and NEPSY-II.

Marcel Kinsbourne, M.D., is a pediatric neurologist who has made a variety of empirical and theoretical contributions to neurology, pediatrics, education, cognitive psychology, and philosophy. He has spent many years providing clinical services to children with school problems.

Marit Korkman, Ph.D., was clinical neuropsychologist in hospital departments for children between 1975 and 1995, researcher at national research institutes in France and in Finland, professor of neuropsychology at Åbo Akademi University from 1997 to 2007 and at University of Helsinki 2007, senior author of *NEPSY—A Developmental Neuropsychological Assessment,* and author of numerous research articles and book chapters.

Ronald B. Livingston, Ph.D., is Professor of Psychology at the University of Texas at Tyler and coordinator of the School Psychology Training Program. He is the author of numerous research articles and other publications, primarily in the areas of psychometrics and neuropsychology.

Lawrence J. Majovski, Ph.D., ABPP-CN, ABClinP, is a clinical associate professor in the Department of Psychiatry and Behavioral Sciences at the University of Washington in Seattle and the Department of Child and Adolescent Psychiatry at Seattle Children's Hospital and Regional Medical Center. He has been in private practice for 31 years and is a fellow in the American Academy of Child Psychology, American Academy of Clinical Neuropsychology, and National Academy of Neuropsychology.

Daniel C. Miller, Ph.D., is a professor in the School Psychology Doctoral and Specialist Training Programs at Texas Woman's University in Denton, Texas. He has been an active leader and presenter in state and national school psychology associations since 1992. Dr. Miller is the author of the *Essentials of School Neuropsychological Assessment* (Wiley, 2007).

Rosemarie Scolaro Moser, Ph.D., the director of RSM Psychology Center, LLC in Lawrenceville, New Jersey, received her Ph.D. in professional psychology from the University of Pennsylvania. She is a board-certified neuropsychologist (ABPN) and rehabilitation psychologist (ABPP), as well as a certified school psychologist. Dr. Moser's publication topics include learning, memory, and brain disorders, with research expertise in youth sports concussion.

Kimberly B. Oliver graduated with a Bachelor of Arts degree in psychology from Georgia State University. Kimberly is currently a graduate student in the Ph.D. program for school psychology at that same university.

Lisa A. Pass, Ed.S., NCSP, earned her Educational Specialist degree in school psychology from the University of Kansas. She has worked in the school systems in both Kansas and Alabama. She is currently a Ph.D. student at Ball State University, where she works in the Neuropsychology Laboratory.

Bruce F. Pennington, Ph.D., is a developmental neuropsychologist who has earned an international reputation for his research on dyslexia, ADHD, and autism. He is particularly interested in using genetic and neuropsychological methods to understand comorbidity among disorders, such as the comorbidity between dyslexia and ADHD. He is a John Evans Professor of Psychology at the University of Denver, where he heads the Developmental Cognitive Neuroscience program. His honors include Research Scientist, MERIT, and Fogarty awards from the National Institutes of Health, the Samuel T. Orton Award from the International Dyslexia Association, and the Emanuel Miller Lecture from the British Child Psychology and Psychiatric Association. He is also a Fellow of AAAS.

Antonio E. Puente, Ph.D., is Professor of Psychology and Director of Centro Hispano at the University of North Carolina Wilmington. He has been president of several organizations (e.g., Division of Clinical Neuropsychology of the APA; National Academy of Neuropsychology). He has published extensively in the area of cultural neuropsychology.

Cecil R. Reynolds, Ph.D., is the author of more than 300 scholarly publications and author or editor of 45 books including the *Encyclopedia of Special Education* and the *Handbook of Clinical Child Neuropsychology*. Former editor of *Archives of Clinical Neuropsychology* (11 years), he is now editor of *Applied Neuropsychology*. He is also the author of several widely used tests of personality and behavior, most notably the BASC-2 and the RIAS. He is currently a professor of educational psychology, professor of neuroscience, and Distinguished Research Scholar at Texas A&M University.

Cynthia A. Riccio, Ph.D., is a Professor, Director of Training for the School Psychology program, and a member of the neuroscience faculty at Texas A&M University. Her research interests include ADHD, pediatric neuropsychology, and learning/language disorders. She has over 50 referenced journal articles published or in press and coauthored a book on the use of continuous-performance tests in clinical practice.

Margaret Riddle, Ph.D., is a child neuropsychologist specializing in learning disorders in children. She is Director of the Developmental Neuropsychology Clinic at the University of Denver. She speaks frequently to groups of educators about the identification and remediation of dyslexia and is the author of "Dyslexia: Reading Disabilities (Assessment)" *Corsini Encyclopedia of Psychology*.

Andrew L. Schmitt, Ph.D., is an Assistant Professor of Psychology at the University of Texas at Tyler. He received his doctoral degree in clinical psychology from the University of Texas, Southwestern Medical Center at Dallas, and is a licensed psychologist in the State of Texas. Dr. Schmitt teaches courses in applied testing and neuropsychology and has numerous publications and professional presentations, primarily in the areas of dementia, psychometrics, and neuropsychology.

Sally Shaywitz, M.D., is a neuroscientist, a professor of pediatrics at Yale, and codirector of the Yale Center for the Study of Learning and Attention. She is a member of the Institute of Medicine of the National Academy of Sciences, and of the National Reading Panel, mandated by congress to determine the most effective reading programs. She has written for *Scientific American* and the *New York Times Magazine*. Dr. Shaywitz lectures throughout the country and appears regularly in national media.

Gerry A. Stefanatos, D.Phil., is an associate professor and is Chair of the Department of Communication Sciences and Disorders at Temple University in Philadelphia. He has published numerous articles in the field of neuropsychology and cognitive neuroscience. His research integrates neuropsychological/neurolinguistic approaches to the study of brain function with functional neuroimaging techniques (fMRI and ERP).

Julie A. Suhr, Ph.D., earned her Ph.D. in clinical psychology at the University of Iowa and completed postdoctoral training in clinical neuropsychology at the University of Iowa Hospitals and Clinics. She is currently an associate professor in the Department of Psychology at Ohio University, where she conducts research and supervises training of students in neuropsychological assessment.

H. Lee Swanson, Ph.D., holds an endowed chair and holds the rank of Distinguished Professor at the University of California at Riverside. He has over 250 publications in such journals as *Intelligence, Journal of Experimental Child Psychology, Memory & Cognition, Developmental Psychology, Journal of Educational Psychology,* and *Review of Educational Research;* serves on the review board of 15 journals; and is currently Editor-in-Chief of the *Journal of Learning Disabilities.*

1

Neuropsychology and Specific Learning Disabilities: Lessons from the Past As a Guide to Present Controversies and Future Clinical Practice

Alan S. Kaufman

Learning disabilities and neuropsychology have always been intertwined, even before Ralph Reitan put neuropsychology on the map in the 1950s or Sam Kirk coined the term *learning disabilities* in 1963. The history of specific learning disabilities (SLDs) is steeped in the tradition of brain damage and brain dysfunction, whether one traces the roots of SLD to the perceptual processing disorder approach of Kurt Goldstein and Alfred Strauss or to the developmental language disorder conceptualization of Samuel Orton and James Hinshelwood (Shepherd, 2001). And if the past endorses the strong relationship between SLDs and neuropsychology, that endorsement is no less powerful than the impact of present research or future applications of technology on the essential role of neuropsychology on the assessment of SLD.

The history of SLD is not a linear or chronological one but rather an uneasy amalgam of two traditions that are conceptually distinct and seemingly resistant to integration. The Goldstein-Strauss-Werner history—based initially on Kurt Goldstein's (1942) studies of the perceptual, cognitive, attentional, and mood disorders of soldiers who sustained head injuries—emphasizes disorders of perception, especially visual perception. Indeed, it is the deficit in perceptual processing that is considered the specific learning *disability* (there is no room in this model for specific learning *disabilities*). However, a different history of SLD that predates Goldstein first began

1

appearing in Europe in the 1890s with accounts of an adult patient who lost the ability to read following a stroke, though he could speak and write fluently, remember details, and understand easily (Dejerine, 1892); and accounts of a 14-year-old nonreader, Percy F.: "I might add that the boy is bright and of average intelligence in conversation. . . . The schoolmaster who has taught him for some years says that he would be the smartest lad in school if the instruction were entirely oral" (Morgan, 1896, p. 1,378). This tradition, popularized by Orton and Hinshelwood, produced an impressive literature following Dr. Pringle Morgan's 1896 account of Percy, which depicted clear-cut cases of individuals with learning disabilities specific to reading and writing (e.g., Kerr, 1897; Morgan, 1914) and later on specific to arithmetic (Schmitt, 1921). Hinshelwood (1917) believed the problem to be a congenital lesion in the left angular gyrus, which impaired the ability to store and remember visual memory for letters and words; Orton (1937) hypothesized a functional brain disorder associated with the inability of one hemisphere to become dominant over the other for handling language, but he nonetheless "accepted the notion of the origin of dyslexia in the angular gyrus region" (Spreen, 2001, p. 285). Both agreed that SLD was a function of a developmental disorder of written language.

Occasionally, neuropsychologists who write about the history of SLD blend the Goldstein-Strauss-Werner tradition with the Hinshelwood-Orton approach: "Orton's theory remained a theory until, in 1947, Strauss and Lehtinen called attention to the frequent appearance of neurological signs in learning-disabled children" (Spreen, 2001, p. 286). But usually the two traditions are treated separately.

Indeed, the two historical roots of SLD could not be more different in conception, origination, or research methodology. Yet they converge in their basic premise that neurology and neuropsychology are the keys for understanding learning problems and ultimately treating them. Even the founding fathers of the developmental language disorder approach, while relying on a field of neuroscience that was in its infancy, did not agree on the neurological causation of the problem. Yet the fact remains that, regardless of the orientation of the early SLD pioneers, and regardless of whether one's intuitive understanding of SLD is more aligned with a specific perceptual disorder or an array of specific disorders in language development, all paths to the present field of SLD come through the fields of neurology and neuropsychology.

THE GOLDSTEIN-STRAUSS-WERNER VISUAL PERCEPTUAL APPROACH TO SLD

The Goldstein-Strauss-Werner theory posited that a disorder of visual perception, along with the concomitant attentional problems, impairs learning on tasks that depend on perception and attention. Fix the perceptual disorder of these brain-damaged individuals (in a learning environment that reduces distraction and inattention), and you have fixed the learning problem (even Mental Retardation). Goldstein's student, Alfred Strauss, extended his mentor's work to mentally retarded adolescents and observed the same kinds of perceptual, mood, and learning disorders in this low-IQ population that Goldstein had found with head-injured soldiers (Strauss & Werner, 1943). These researchers attributed the disorders to brain damage and concluded that (a) there was a difference between Mental Retardation caused by brain injury and Mental Retardation that was familial, (b) brain injury produced specific perceptual and behavioral deficits, and (c) special education aimed at treating the observed perceptual and behavioral problems would be effective with Mental Retardation due to brain injury but not due to inheritance from parents. Strauss worked with an educator, Laura Lehtinen, to implement the perceptual training (Strauss & Lehtinen, 1947), emphasizing the point that remediation of learning and behavior problems worked hand-in-hand with identification of learning and behavior problems from the inception of the perceptual disorder movement.

The next logical step to extend the theory was to study children, not just adolescents and adults, and to investigate children with normal or near-normal intelligence. These studies included children with known brain damage, such as cerebral palsy (Cruickshank, Bice, & Wallen, 1957), and, intriguingly, samples of children who evidenced learning and behavior problems *but did not show clinical signs of brain damage* (Strauss & Kephart, 1955)—that moved the field forward in a dramatic way. Goldstein, Strauss, Werner, Cruickshank, and Kephart were the pioneers who established the concept of a learning and behavior disability caused by *minimal brain dysfunction* (i.e., not detectable through standard clinical procedures, but brain injury nonetheless) that was distinct from Mental Retardation.

Lehtinen's early work suggested that remediation of the perceptual disorders was feasible, and a plethora of visual-perceptual-motor training programs began to predominate in the 1960s, with names like Frostig, Ayres, Getman, Kephart, and Barsch associated with different methodologies on the same theme. However, subsequent systematic reviews of 81 research studies, encompassing more than 500 different statistical comparisons, concluded that "none of the treatments was particularly effective in stimulating cognitive, linguistic, academic, or school readiness abilities and that there was a serious question as to whether the training activities even have value for enhancing visual perception and/or motor skills in children indicated" (Hammill & Bartel, 1978, p. 371). Yet, this lack of research support did not stop the visual training in the schools and it did not slow down the movement that endorsed learning disabilities (usually known then as *minimal brain dysfunction* or *perceptual disorder*) as problems with perception (usually visual but sometimes auditory). In fact, several influential special educators who have studied SLD history (e.g., Kavale & Forness, 1995; Torgesen, 1998) believe that the Goldstein-Strauss-Werner "view influenced the definition of 'specific learning disability' in federal laws and also influenced U.S. public school practices" (Shepherd, 2001, p. 5).

THE ORTON-HINSHELWOOD DEVELOPMENTAL WRITTEN LANGUAGE APPROACH TO SLD

Like the Goldstein-Strauss-Werner approach, the Orton-Hinshelwood view of SLD had its roots in the learning problems and behaviors of adults with brain damage. Rather than focusing on war-injured soldiers, the developmental language pioneers were impressed by late–nineteenth century accounts of adults in Great Britain, France, and Germany who suffered known brain damage to specific regions of the brain and lost the ability to read—despite retaining writing and spelling skills (Shepherd, 2001). In the early part of the twentieth century, the accounts began to include children who were seemingly normal with no overt signs of brain damage, but (like the brain-damaged adults) had a specific disability in reading, writing, or arithmetic despite normal abilities in other areas of cognition and achievement. Though Hinshelwood (1895), an ophthalmologist, initially focused on acquired word blindness based on an adult patient who could not read subsequent to injury to the angular gyrus, he was impressed by Morgan's (1896) first reporting of congenital word blindness in children. He became intrigued by subsequent accounts published by physicians (including himself) of 14 cases in Europe and North America of children and adolescents with reading disorders that were apparently congenital and not due to any known brain injury (Spreen, 2001).

This accumulation of clinical cases impelled Hinshelwood (1917) to publish a widely read monograph, *Congenital Word Blindness,* that included detailed descriptions of these children, such as a boy of 12 who was brought by his mother to have his eyesight checked: "He could barely read by sight more than two or three words, but came to a standstill every second or third word. . . . [But he] read all combinations of figures with the greatest of fluency up to millions" (p. 21). And just as Sally Shaywitz (2003) insists that the diagnosis of dyslexia is no less accurate or science-based than nearly any other medical diagnosis, Hinshelwood (1917) said virtually the same thing about a century earlier—that it's fairly easy to diagnose congenital word blindness because the condition is as clear-cut and distinct as any other medical pathology.

Orton (1937) coined the term *strephosymbolia* (twisted symbols) to describe what later came to be known as *dyslexia*. He provided excellent clinical descriptions of children with reading disorders who, he observed, had special difficulty with letter and word reversals—the kinds of transpositions that suggested to Orton that these children read from right to left. He was a firm believer in thorough assessment, including the recording of extensive family and school histories and the administration of IQ and achievement tests. He was especially interested in children's performances on different areas of academic achievement to confirm his belief that children with a reading disability would score lower on reading and spelling tests than on arithmetic tests; and that children with writing disabilities would score lower on tests of spelling than on arithmetic tests. Orton did not feature disorders of mood or attention as aspects of the learning disability (as did the perceptual theorists), but he noted that many of his patients with reading disorders also had speech and motor disorders; they were predominantly male; they tended to have life-long difficulties with academic skills; and he often treated several members of the same family.

Hinshelwood (1917) limited the diagnosis of congenital word blindness to those who demonstrated the gravity of the defect and evidenced a purity of symptoms, but he excluded children who were just a bit slow in acquiring reading skills. Orton's definition was not as stringent: "Our experience in studying and retraining several hundred such cases has convinced us that they form a *graded series including all degrees of severity of the handicap*" (Spreen, 2001, p. 285).

Hinshelwood advocated assessment methods that were remarkably similar to Orton's and they both strongly favored remediation that was targeted directly at the academic problem. For example, they both emphasized a phonics approach to teaching reading, differing only in Hinshelwood's preference for teaching sound to letter correspondence versus Orton's method of teaching letter to sound correspondence (Shepherd, 2001). As with the perceptual disorder theorists, neurology was believed to be at the root of the learning problem (brain damage to Hinshelwood and failure to establish dominance to Orton). However, the brain damage or dysfunction was tied directly to the specific language disorders that the children displayed—not to a single process such as visual perception. And contrary to the Goldstein-Strauss-Werner theorists, remediation was aimed at improving the specific area of learning deficit (such as spelling or reading), not at strengthening a supposed underlying process. Both theories of the historical roots of SLD emphasized developmental disorders, but these brain-related disorders were either perceptual in nature (Goldstein-Strauss-Werner) or associated with written language (Hinshelwood-Orton)—the distinction between minimal brain dysfunction and developmental dyslexia, respectively.

SAM KIRK'S INTEGRATION OF THE TWO MODELS

Kirk (1963) coined the term *learning disabilities* when he delivered a speech to a large group of parents whose children were having school difficulties and to a smaller group of professionals with a keen interest in the topic. All were seeking a label for these children that Kirk referred to as having developmental deficits of one kind or another (which encompasses developmental disorders of both perception and written language). Kirk's label had a decided educational flavor, focusing on the nature of the problem rather than the hypothesized cause, and it was the precursor for the federal definitions and laws of the late 1960s and 1970s that proclaimed *specific learning disabilities* as a disorder that entitled special education services to anyone with an SLD diagnosis. When reading the text of Kirk's (1963) speech, it is clear that his notion of learning disabilities was more aligned with Hinshelwood-Orton than Goldstein-Strauss-Werner as he referred to "a group of children who have disorders in development in language, speech, reading and associated communication skills needed for social interaction" (p. 3). However, like the perceptual theorists, Kirk stressed that the disorder involved a processing disorder. But, unlike those theorists, he believed the processing disorders to be *psycholinguistic* in nature, not visual perceptual. He believed that these psycholinguistic disorders led directly to disorders in reading, language, and so forth—an approach that is consistent with the Hinshelwood-Orton belief that brain damage or brain organization is related specifically to written language disabilities. Kirk, however, was more consistent with the perceptual theorists regarding his model of remediation: He believed that a child's weak psycholinguistic processes (as measured by his Illinois Test of Psycholinguistic Abilities, described in his 1963 speech, but not published until 1968) needed direct remediation in order to treat a child's learning disability. Unfortunately, subsequent research on the effectiveness of psycholinguistic training yielded the same dismal conclusions that were reached for perceptual training (Newcomer & Hammill, 1976).

THE FEDERAL DEFINITION OF SLD

The definition of SLDs that was inaugurated in the Children with Specific Learning Disabilities Act of 1969 was retained in the Right to Education for All Handicapped Children's Act of 1975 and has remained intact for IDEA 1997 and IDEA 2004. The first part of this definition is as follows:

> The term "specific learning disability" means a disorder in one or more of the basic psychological processes involved in understanding or in using language, spoken or written, which disorder may manifest itself in imperfect ability to listen, think, speak, read, write, spell, or do mathematical calculations.

This definition is clearly a derivative of Kirk's approach to the disorder, but when it is related to the two separate historical roots of SLD it is unquestionably the voice of Goldstein-Strauss-Werner, not Orton or Hinshelwood. Processing disorders had no role in the notion of developmental disorders of written language.

The second part of the definition is an amalgam of the two historical traditions:

DISORDERS INCLUDED—Such term includes such conditions as perceptual disabilities, brain injury, minimal brain dysfunction, dyslexia, and developmental aphasia. (*Federal Register,* 2006)

The terms *perceptual disabilities* and *minimal brain dysfunction* are associated with Goldstein and Strauss, whereas the terms *dyslexia* and *developmental aphasia* are Hinshelwood-Orton concepts. The definition is literally built by committee, which undoubtedly accounts for much of the controversy that has hounded the field of SLD from its inception and that has grown exponentially over the past decade.

Part of this controversy concerns the need to identify a processing disorder as part of the diagnostic process (Hale et al., 2004), a mandate of the IDEA 2004 SLD definition that tends to be ignored or trivialized by those who favor a Response-to-Intervention (RTI) only approach for diagnosing SLD (e.g., Gresham, 2002). Interestingly, processing disorders are part of the SLD definition from the Goldstein-Strauss-Werner perspective, but, as noted, such disorders play no part in the Hinshelwood-Orton definition. Therefore, from a historical perspective, the necessity of identifying a processing disorder receives only mixed support.

However, with history as a guide to practice, the need for neuropsychological assessment as part of the diagnostic process receives broad-based support. Regardless of the tradition with which one identifies most closely, history is unanimous in associating brain damage, brain dysfunction, or brain organization with SLDs. Whether or not the problem is a disordered process or a kind of brain dysfunction specifically associated with reading, writing, or arithmetic, neuropsychological assessment is necessary to better understand the individual's learning disability and to treat it. Kirk did not specifically endorse the neurological basis of SLD, but he did endorse the need for assessment: "The concept of learning disability as used in education does not deny or reject a neurological deficit. . . . The major emphasis is on the use of psychological tests and/or observation for the purpose of organizing a remedial program. Such a program is . . . very dependent upon the determination of psychological abilities and disabilities" (Kirk & Kirk, 1971, pp. 12–13). Indeed, all historical approaches to SLD emphasize the spared or intact abilities that stand in stark contrast to the deficient abilities, as well as the necessity of developing a remedial program based to some extent on test results. Although the programs designed to remediate perceptual and psycholinguistic processes have not proven effective either to improve the disordered process or "cure" the learning disability, there is a growing body of neuropsychological literature that supports neuropsychological assessment both to map the areas of the brain that are associated with specific aspects of the reading process and to inform intervention (Shaywitz, 2003; Spreen, 2001).

NEUROPSYCHOLOGICAL RESEARCH AND SLD

Neurology and neuropsychology have been intimately associated with SLD for more than a century. The wealth of neuropsychological research that has blossomed steadily since the early case studies of head-injured soldiers with mood and perceptual disorders (Goldstein), and of adults and adolescents with specific reading disabilities (Hinshelwood), makes it imperative that neuropsychological assessment retain that intimate link to SLD diagnosis and treatment. However, from a historical perspective, it is also true that much of the association between brain damage or dysfunction and SLD has been by presumption and implication. The clinical cases of adults with reading disorders following known brain injury provided hard data of a link between brain damage and SLD. But the dozens of clinical reports of children or adolescents with so-called congenital disabilities were based on the assumption of central nervous system dysfunction (i.e., soft data, not hard science; Benton, 1982). As recently as a decade ago, the National Joint Committee on Learning Disabilities (1998) emphasized that SLD was intrinsic to the individual and *presumed* to be caused by CNS dysfunction. Given the behavioral orientation of the RTI movement during the first decade of the twenty-first century, it is important to ask whether the scientific data now support a hard link between neuropsychology and SLD or the relationship remains presumptive.

Initial evidence of a neurological link focused on soft signs (such as poor motor coordination, left-right confusion), which were more prevalent in SLD than normal populations (e.g., Hertzig, 1983). Though these soft signs were often criticized because they were developmental in nature and disappeared over time, data suggested otherwise: Spreen (1988), in the Victoria study of 203 children diagnosed with SLDs, showed that soft signs observed at ages 8 to 12 years persisted or even increased through age 25. Despite Spreen's findings of the stability of soft signs, this line of research proved a virtual dead end because soft signs "rarely point to specific locations in the cortex" (Spreen, 2001, p. 286). More compelling data came from autopsy studies of a total of six individuals with dyslexia (Drake, 1968; Galaburda & Kemper, 1978; Humphreys, Kaufmann, & Galaburda, 1990), which consistently showed "dyslexic brains" to differ from normal brains: "The autopsy studies showed microdysgenesis with ectopias and dysplasias bilaterally along the Sylvan fissure frontally and along the planum temporale, in the left more than in the right hemisphere" (Spreen, 2001, p. 287). However, computerized tomography (CT) studies have only occasionally supported the asymmetries reported in the autopsy studies, and have sometimes contradicted the findings, for example, when age and brain size are controlled (Schultz et al., 1994); reviews of the CT literature do not consistently support asymmetry of the plana in individuals with dyslexia (e.g., Morgan & Hynd, 1998). Another line of research suggested corpus callosum abnormalities in adults with dyslexia (e.g., Duara et al., 1991), but a review of pertinent studies indicated that the results have not been replicated across samples of individuals with dyslexia (Beaton, 1997).

Different avenues of research have explored *functional* abnormalities in children with SLDs, using positron emission tomography (PET), single-photon emission tomography (SPECT), functional magnetic resonance imaging (fMRI), and electrophysiological (EEG) techniques, an advance over the strictly *structural* abnormality approach of the CT scan studies (Bigler, Lajiness-O'Neill, & Howes, 1998; Spreen, 2001). The metabolic imaging studies have provided intriguing results based on changes in blood flow and blood oxygenation while individuals with and without dyslexia are performing specific reading tasks such as phonological processing, lexical-semantic processing, orthographic-visual processing, auditory processing, and so forth (e.g., Shaywitz et al., 1998; Rumsey et al., 1997). These studies have helped localize the brain areas involved in each aspect of reading and have identified differences in processing between normal individuals and those diagnosed with dyslexia, as well as gender differences in phonological processing. Again, different teams of researchers differ in their conclusions, in part because of different methodologies, different tasks, comorbidity, small sample sizes, and inadequate descriptions of the populations of individuals with dyslexia (Spreen, 2001). Probably the best conclusions of the burgeoning literature that has attempted to demonstrate a clear association between neuropsychology and SLDs are (a) "the neurological basis is no longer 'presumed,' although it is not always confirmed, and less specific than we would like it to be" (Spreen, 2001, p. 301); and (b) "the technological advances in imaging the brain along with examining electrophysiological and metabolic correlates of function have been impressive. Although these techniques . . . are very sensitive in detecting certain abnormal neurologic conditions, these techniques have not yielded much clinical or diagnostic utility in the assessment of the individual with a learning disorder" (Bigler et al., 1998, p. 79).

But, despite these cautions, there is much reason for optimism based on the accumulating evidence from an impressive array of studies using EEG and metabolic imaging techniques, such as the innovative studies conducted by Shaywitz and her colleagues. In their studies of normal readers they discovered clear-cut differences in how men and women read: "men activated the left inferior frontal gyrus, while women activated the right as well as the left" (Shaywitz, 2003, p.77). Of the three neural pathways for reading, their research and the imaging studies of other researchers indicated that beginning readers rely primarily on two relatively slow, analytic routes (parieto-temporal and frontal), whereas experienced, skilled readers depend on an express pathway—occipito-temporal. And when comparing good readers to dyslexic readers, Shaywitz (2003) notes: "As they read, good readers activate the back of the brain and also, to some extent, the front of the brain. In contrast, dyslexic readers show a fault in the system: underactivation of neural pathways in the back of the brain" (p. 81). Indeed, there has been widespread support from a variety of fMRI and PET scan studies to indicate that individuals with dyslexia demonstrate reduced left temporo-parietal responses relative to controls during reading tasks such as phonological processing—a finding that was first observed in adults (e.g., Rumsey, 1992; Shaywitz et al., 1998) and then verified with children (e.g., Shaywitz et al., 2002). Recent studies that utilize diffusion tensor imaging (DTI), a form of MRI, provide evidence that the integrity of the *white matter structure* of the neural pathways in the left temporo-parietal region differs for good versus poor readers, as indices based on the white-matter structure correlated significantly with reading ability (Beaulieu et al., 2005; Deutsch et al., 2005).

Also of great interest is the dramatic series of studies now underway by Sally Shaywitz, Jack Fletcher, and others—the application of brain imaging studies to directly evaluate how the neural systems used for reading respond to specific interventions (Shaywitz et al., 2004). For example, Shaywitz and her colleagues used fMRI to study poor readers' responses to the implementation of a 1-year experimental intervention program: "The final set of images obtained one year after the intervention had ended was startling. Not only were the right-side auxiliary pathways much less prominent but, more important, there was further development of the primary neural systems on the left side of the brain. . . . [T]hese activation patterns were comparable to those obtained from children who had always been good readers" (Shaywitz, 2003, pp. 85–86). These exciting, positive, educationally relevant results stand in stark contrast to the hundreds of failed intervention studies in the 1960s and 1970s that featured the training of perceptual and psycholinguistic processes (Hammill & Bartel, 1978; Newcomer & Hammill, 1976).

Specific details about Shaywitz's and other researchers' neuroimaging studies, as they apply both to diagnosis and remediation of SLD, appear throughout this volume (see, especially, the chapters by Erin Bigler, Gayle Deutsch, Jack Fletcher, Elaine Fletcher-Janzen, Jane Joseph, Byron Rourke, and Sally Shaywitz). The exciting results and implications of these studies far outweigh the inconsistencies and occasional contradictions in the CT, EEG, and imaging literature. The history of SLD is steeped in neuropsychology and neuroscience, including a diverse set of studies with the Halstead-Reitan Neuropsychological Battery by Rourke and others that consistently identified neuropsychological deficits in individuals with SLD while also distinguishing those with SLD from patients with brain damage and from normal controls (Reitan & Wolfson, 2001). The present is enriched by novel and insightful applications of neuroimaging technology to SLD diagnosis and treatment, and the future of SLD assessment should continue to embrace the essential link between brain functioning and the identification of *learning abilities* as well as learning disabilities.

REFERENCES

Beaton, A. A. (1997). The relation of the planum temporale asymmetry and morphology of the corpus callosum to handedness, gender, and dyslexia: A review of the evidence. *Brain and Language, 60,* 255–322.

Beaulieu, C., Plewes, C., Paulson, L. A., Roy, D., Snook. L., Concha, L., & Phillips, L. (2005). Imaging brain connectivity in children with diverse reading ability. *NeuroImage, 25,* 1266–1271.

Benton, A. L. (1982). Child neuropsychology: Retrospect and prospect. In J. de Wit & A. L. Benton (Eds.), *Perspectives on child study* (pp. 41–46). Lisse, Netherlands: Swets & Zeitlinger.

Bigler, E. D., Lajiness-O'Neill, R., & Howes, N-L. (1998). Technology in the assessment of learning disability. *Journal of Learning Disabilities, 31,* 67–82.

Cruickshank, W. M., Bice, H. V., & Wallen, N. E. (1957). *Perception and cerebral palsy.* Syracuse, NY: Syracuse University Press.

Dejerine, J. (1892). Contribution À l'etude anatomic-pathologique et clinique des différentes variétés de cécite verbale. *Comptes Rendus des Seances et Memoires de la Societé de Biologie et de Ses Filiales, 44,* 61.

Deutsch, G. K., Dougherty, R. F., Bammer, R., Siok, W. T., Gabrieli, J. D. E., & Wandell, B. (2005). Children's reading performance is correlated with white matter structure measured by diffusion tensor imaging. *Cortex, 41,* 354–363.

Drake, W. E. (1968). Clinical and pathological findings in a child with developmental learning disability. *Journal of Learning Disabilities, 1,* 9–25.

Duara, B., Kushch, A., Gross-Glenn, K., Barker, W., Jallad, B., Pascal, S., Loewenstein, D. A., Sheldon, J., Rabin, M., Levin, B., & Lubs, H. (1991). Neuroanatomical differences between dyslexic and normal readers on magnetic resonance imaging scans. *Archives of Neurology, 48,* 410–416.

Federal Register (2006). Vol. 71, No. 156 / Monday, August 14, 2006 / Rules and Regulations at http://www.gpoaccess.gov/fr/index.html.

Galaburda, A. M., & Kemper, T. L. (1978). Cytoarchitectonic abnormalities in developmental dyslexia: A case study. *Annals of Neurology, 6,* 94–100.

Goldstein, K. (1942). *After-effects of brain injuries in war.* New York: Grune & Stratton.

Gresham, F. M. (2002). Responsiveness to intervention: An alternative approach to the identification of learning disabilities. In R. Bradley, L. Danielson, & D. Hallahan (Eds.), *Identification of learning disabilities: Research to practice* (pp. 467–519). Mahwah, NJ: Erlbaum.

Hale, J. B., Naglieri, J. A., Kaufman, A. S., & Kavale, K. A. (2004). Specific learning disability classification in the new Individuals with Disabilities Education Act: The danger of good ideas. *The School Psychologist, 58* (1), 6–13, 29.

Hammill, D. D., & Bartel, N. R. (1978). *Teaching children with learning and behavior problems* (2nd ed.). Boston: Houghton-Mifflin.

Hertzig, M. E. (1983). Temperament and neurological status. In M. Rutter (Ed.), *Developmental neuropsychiatry* (pp. 164–180). New York: Guilford.

Hinshelwood, J. (1895). Word-blindness and visual memory. *Lancet, 2,* 1564–1570.

Hinshelwood, J. (1917). *Congenital word blindness.* London: H. K. Lewis.

Humphreys, P., Kaufmann, W. E., & Galaburda, A. M. (1990). Developmental dyslexia in women: Neuropathological findings in three cases. *Annals of Neurology, 28,* 764–774.

Kavale, K. A., & Forness, S. R. (1995). *The nature of learning disabilities: Critical elements of diagnosis and classification.* Mahwah, NJ: Erlbaum.

Kerr, J. (1897). School hygiene in its mental, moral, and physical aspects. *Journal of the Royal Statistical Society, 60,* 613–680.

Kirk, S. A. (1963). Behavioral diagnosis and remediation of learning disabilities. In *Proceedings of the annual meeting of the conference on exploration into the problems of the perceptually handicapped child,* Vol. 1, pp. 37. Chicago.

Kirk, S. A., & Kirk, W. D. (1971). *Psycholinguistic learning disabilities: Diagnosis and remediation.* Urbana: University of Illinois Press.

Morgan, A. E., & Hynd, G. W. (1998). Dyslexia, neurolinguistic ability, and anatomical variations on the planum temporal. *Neuropsychology Review, 8,* 79–93.

Morgan, B. S. (1914). *The backward child.* New York: Putnam.

Morgan, W. P. (1896). A case of congenital word blindness. *British Medical Journal, 2,* 1378.

National Joint Committee on Learning Disabilities (1998). Operationalizing the NJCLD definition of learning disabilities for ongoing assessment in the schools. *Learning Disabilities Quarterly, 21,* 186–193.

Newcomer, P. L., & Hammill, D. D. (1976). *Psycholinguistics in the schools.* Columbus, OH: Bobbs-Merrill.

Orton, S. T. (1937). *Reading, writing and speech problems in children.* New York: Norton.

Reitan, R. M., & Wolfson, D. (2001). The Halstead-Reitan Neuropsychological Test Battery: Research findings and clinical applications. In A. S. Kaufman & N. L. Kaufman (Eds.), *Specific learning disabilities and difficulties in children and adolescents: Psychological assessment and evaluation* (pp. 309–346). Cambridge, England: Cambridge University Press.

Rumsey, J. M. (1992). The biology of developmental dyslexia. *The Journal of the American Medical Association, 268,* 912–915.

Rumsey, J. M., Nace, K., Donohue, B., Wise, D., Maisog, J. M., & Andreason, P. (1997) A positron emission tomographic study of impaired word recognition and phonological processing in dyslexic men. *Archives of Neurology, 54,* 562–573.

Schmitt, C. (1921). Extreme retardation in arithmetic. *Elementary School Journal, 21,* 529–547.

Schultz, R. T., Cho, N. K., Staib, L. H., Kier, L. E., Fletcher, J. M., Shaywitz, S. E., Shankweiler, D. P., Katz, L., Gore, J. C., Duncan, J. S., & Shaywitz, B. A. (1994). Brain morphology in normal and dyslexic children: the influence of sex and age. *Annals of Neurology, 35,* 732–742.

Shaywitz, S. (2003). *Overcoming dyslexia: A new and complete science-based program for reading problems at any level.* New York: Knopf.

Shaywitz, S. E., Shaywitz, B. A., Pugh, K. R., Fulbright, R. K., Constable, R. T., Mencl, W. E., Shankweiler, D. P., Liberman, A. M., Skudlarski, P., Fletcher, J. M., Katz, L., Marchione, K. E., Lacadie, C., Gatenby, C., & Gore, J. C. (1998). Functional disruption in the organization of the brain for reading in dyslexia. *Proceedings of the National Academy of Science of the United States of America, 95*, 2636–2641.

Shaywitz, B. A., Shaywitz, S. E., Pugh, K. R., Mencl, W. E., Fulbright, R. K., Skudlarski, P., Constable, R. T., Marchione, K. E., Fletcher, J. M., Lyon, G. R., & Gore, J. C. (2002). Disruption of posterior brain systems for reading in children with developmental dyslexia. *Biological Psychiatry, 52*, 101–110.

Shaywitz, B. A., Shaywitz, S. E., Blachman, B. A., Pugh, K. R., Fulbright, R. K., Skudlarski, P., Mencl, W. E., Constable, R. T., Holahan, J. M., Marchione, K. E., et al. (2004). Development of left occipitotemporal systems for skilled reading in children after a phonologically-based intervention. *Biological Psychiatry, 55*, 926–933.

Shepherd, M. J. (2001). History lessons. In A. S. Kaufman & N. L. Kaufman (Eds.), *Specific learning disabilities and difficulties in children and adolescents: Psychological assessment and evaluation* (pp. 3–28). Cambridge, England: Cambridge University Press.

Spreen, O. (1988). *Learning disabled children growing up*. New York: Oxford University Press.

Spreen, O. (2001). Learning disabilities and their neurological foundations, theories, and subtypes. In A. S. Kaufman & N. L. Kaufman (Eds.), *Specific learning disabilities and difficulties in children and adolescents: Psychological assessment and evaluation* (pp. 283–308). Cambridge, England: Cambridge University Press.

Strauss, A. A., & Kephart, N. C. (1955). *Psychopathology and education of the brain-injured child*. New York: Grune & Stratton.

Strauss, A. A., & Lehtinen, L. E. (1947). *Psychopathology and education of the brain-injured child. Volume 2: Progress in theory and clinic*. New York: Grune & Stratton.

Strauss, A. A., & Werner, H. (1943). Comparative psychopathology of the brain-injured child and the traumatic brain-injured adult. *American Journal of Psychiatry, 99*, 835–838.

Torgesen, J. K. (1998). Learning disabilities: An historical and conceptual overview. In B. Wong (Ed.), *Learning about learning disabilities* (2nd ed.; pp. 3–34). San Diego: Academic Press.

2

RTI, Neuroscience, and Sense: Chaos
in the Diagnosis and Treatment of
Learning Disabilities

Cecil R. Reynolds

O n Monday August 14, 2006, the Office of Special Education and Rehabilitative Services (OSERS) of the Department of Education of the United
States issued 307 pages of rules and regulations for the implementation of
changes made to the Individuals with Disabilities Education Act (IDEA) as
amended in 2004 by the Individuals with Disabilities Education Improvement Act (IDEIA) of 2004 (P.L. 108-446). Notably, these 307 pages of
new rules and regulations are in the form of the Federal Register and much
closer to 500 normal book pages. These regulations may be viewed in their
entirety in the Federal Register/46549/Vol. 71, No. 156/Monday, August
14, 2006/Rules and Regulations. (The Federal register web site may be
accessed and searched for all federal rule-making at: http://www.gpoaccess
.gov/fr/index.html.) According to OSERS, this ream of rules and regulations was necessary to clarify and delineate the changes to how children
are to be identified and served through special education as children with
disabilities in public schools as made by the enactment of IDEIA. While
many changes were made to IDEA under the guise of the improvement
act of 2004, it was the changes to the sections related to identification and
intervention with children believed to have a disability associated with the
category of learning disability that prompted the current volume.

While the actual definition of a learning disability in the law changed very
little, two very key changes did occur. The first was the prohibition against
requiring a severe discrepancy between aptitude and achievement for the
diagnosis of a learning disability (although still allowing for a severe discrepancy to be considered in the determination of the presence of learning

disability), and the second was the requirement for implementation of a process known as *response to intervention* (RTI) as a mandatory component of the process of determining the presence of a learning disability. At first, many professionals in the field believed these regulations had eliminated the requirement for a comprehensive evaluation prior to the determination of a learning disability. Fortunately, Posny (2007), at that time the director of OSERS, in her invited address to the National Association of School Psychologists convention, clarified this matter and noted that "RTI does not replace a comprehensive evaluation" in the determination that a learning disability exists and that diagnosticians must use a variety of data-gathering tools and strategies even if RTI is used. According to Posny (2007), results of RTI may be one component of the information reviewed, but they are insufficient for determination of a disability.

Unfortunately, despite the length and detail of the regulations presented in the Federal Register, extremely little guidance is provided regarding the actual determination of the presence of a learning disability beyond the administrative processes that must be put into place. The federal regulations associated with IDEA apply only to schools, of course; however, the diagnosis of learning disabilities is most frequently undertaken in the public schools, and the federal rules will come to dominate diagnostic practices. Adding to this near certainty, there appears to be little consensus in the scientific literature as to specifically what criteria should be applied in the determination of a learning disability. Every individual diagnostician seems to know one when they see one (i.e., a child with a learning disability), but few can articulate any specific criteria that lead them to the diagnosis consistently. The failure to have objective, repeatable criteria that clinicians can understand and apply will lead inevitably to chaos in the field.

Prior to addressing specific questions that were posed to each of the authors in this book, I feel compelled, as have some others, to address more general issues related to the current state of learning disability determination or diagnosis. The first of these is the concept of RTI as a diagnostic method.

CONSIDERATIONS IN RTI AS A METHOD OF DIAGNOSIS OF LEARNING DISABILITIES

First of all, what is RTI? Posny (2007) tells us that "RTI is a way of screening children, early in their schooling, that can help schools and educators identify those who may not be responding to instruction—and thus may be at risk for school failure. The technique allows schools, on a school wide basis, to provide any student more intensive support—and monitor their progress—than may be typically available in every classroom." It is difficult to imagine anyone being opposed to such an intent. The Posny definition, however, provides little guidance and in this sense is much like the federal regulations. Those who have been working in the field developing the concept for many years give somewhat better guidance. For a nontechnical explanation, the words of Fuchs et al. (2003) seem reasonably clear:

In broad terms, RTI may be described as follows:

1. Students are provided with "generally effective" instruction by their class room teacher;
2. Their progress is monitored;
3. Those who do not respond get something else, or something more, from their teacher or someone else;
4. Again, their progress is monitored; and
5. Those who still do not respond either qualify for special education or for special education evaluation. (p. 159)

Many proponents of RTI (e.g., Reschly, 2005; Shinn, 2005) argue that children who do not respond to instructional methods that have been validated to be effective with the majority of children should then be considered to be children with a learning disability and moved on to a special education placement. Those in this particular camp do not see any further diagnostic evaluation or assessment as being useful either for designing instruction or determining the presence or absence of a disability. Furthermore, they argue that intelligence is irrelevant to learning to read and that it should not be considered in the diagnosis of a learning disability, because children with low IQs learn to read just as well as children at other IQ levels if given proper instruction (e.g., Siegel, 1989, p. 472).

The determination of a learning disability then would be made under an RTI model based upon a student's failure to progress at the same rate as that of other children in the same classroom, once it had been ascertained that appropriate instructional methods had been applied. Intellectual level would be ignored so long as it was above those levels generally regarded as reflecting the presence of mental retardation and no disturbance or dysfunction of any form of psychological processing would need to be considered or demonstrated. This approach also fosters the concept of *relativity of a disability* in the context of the individual classroom as opposed to the population at large. For example, Reschly (2005) argued that it was not only reasonable but a desirable and expected outcome of RTI that a child would be considered learning disabled in one teacher's classroom but not in a different classroom where the general achievement level and progress rate of other students was different. This fundamentally alters the concept of disability at its very roots. A disability is recognized as a psychopathological condition primarily associated with the individual. The RTI model focuses on the failure of a child–school interaction that is complex and modified by the overall achievement level of an individual classroom. While focusing on potential failures of the child–school interaction and seeking remedies other than special education is entirely appropriate, the latter is not a disability as traditionally understood but more accurately reflects a failure of general education to accommodate normal variations in learning.

RTI largely is touted as avoiding many of the criticisms of prior diagnostic approaches that incorporated concepts such as severe discrepancies between aptitude and achievement levels relative to age mates. In truth, RTI does not avoid many of these same problems and creates a number of specialized problems of its own.

As an approach to prereferral intervention, RTI is highly appropriate and shows great promise in promoting problem solving and the improvement of instructional practices overall. As a method/process of diagnosis of individual children, it fails on numerous points (after Reynolds, 2005):

1. RTI, being based on discrepancy from grade level (whether at the classroom, school, district, or national levels), is simply, at its root, a special case of severe discrepancy analysis that assumes everyone is of equal ability or academic aptitude, and that everyone should progress at highly similar, albeit not identical, rates. RTI advocates argue that the provision of high-quality instructional methods will bring individuals to a common level of academic achievement. This is contrary to 100 years of science associated with education, individual differences, and knowledge of pedagogical outcomes. Alexander (2007) has highlighted the assumption that high-quality, individualized instruction will result in equality of educational outcomes (meaning equivalent levels of academic achievement) as one of the great myths of education. As Alexander notes, the scientific literature is consistent in demonstrating that high-quality, individualized instruction enhances the heterogeneity of educational outcomes, producing greater variability of outcomes, not lesser (also see Reynolds, 2007). RTI as envisioned in the writings of Siegel (1989) and others (e.g., Reschly, 2005) seems to confuse equality of opportunity with equality of outcomes (e.g., see Nichols, 1978, for a still relevant, detailed explanation). Certainly everyone is entitled to high-quality instruction, but it will not produce equivalent levels of academic attainment for all children. Siegel's (1989) assertion that intelligence is unrelated to acquisition of reading is refuted not only by common sense and years of experience with children in various learning environments but more importantly by virtually hundreds if not thousands of research studies on the relationship between intelligence and achievement (e.g., see Sattler, 2001) as well as specific work aimed directly at testing such a hypothesis (Fuchs & Fuchs, 2006; Fuchs & Young, 2006) and manuals for various intelligence tests that show very strong correlations between IQs, especially verbal IQ, and reading test scores (e. g., Reynolds & Kamphaus, 2003).

RTI inevitably will suffer from the inconsistencies in measurement models that also plagued severe discrepancy analyses (e.g., see Reynolds, 1984, for a discussion of these issues). The issues in determining gain scores under RTI models are many and potentially even more complex than the issues surrounding severe discrepancy models, and many variations of how to approach such comparisons will be proffered with varying levels of mathematical sophistication—but, one can be quite certain there will be numerous applications that produce different results and identify different children under the different nonconsensual models that will be in use. Such was a common criticism of severe discrepancy analysis models, and one that is unresolved at best and potentially worsened by RTI models.

Others have noted this dire concern as well. Simply put, RTI lacks a consistent means of determining responsiveness and the application of different methods identifies different children, which was a common criticism of severe discrepancy criteria (i.e., the method is unreliable and inconsistently applied).

Fuchs, Fuchs, and Compton (2004) concluded:

> . . . alternate methods of assessing responsiveness produce different prevalence rates of reading disability and different subsets of unresponsive children. This is important because a major criticism of IQ-achievement discrepancy as a method of LD identification is the unreliability of the diagnosis. . . .

> As demonstrated in our analyses . . . different measurement systems using different criteria (all with reference to RTI) result in identification of different groups of students. The critical question is which combination of assessment components is most accurate for identifying children who will experience serious and chronic reading problems that prevent reading for meaning in the upper grades and impair their capacity to function successfully as adults. At this point, relatively little is known to answer this question when RTI is the assessment framework. (pp. 225–226)

Although these statements were published in 2004, as of this writing, the situation has not changed.

2. RTI creates ability tracking in essence whereby students with IQs below 90 certainly will be disproportionately identified as having a specific learning disability—or we will further "dumb down" the curricula. If intellectual functioning is related to learning rate or complexity (and it is), this outcome is mathematically inevitable. RTI sends forward children for identification as eligible for special education as learning disabled those who continue to perform academically below the level of classmates even after having received "high-quality instruction." This seems a throwback to the era of the old concept of the "slow learner," and it seems these children are destined to be considered disabled under current rules if RTI is in fact followed. The only conceivable way to prevent this outcome is to restrict the academic progress of children with IQs that exceed 100.

3. RTI ignores the needs of students with academic aptitude in the top 10% of the student population, in particular who are able to remain near grade level in one area while excelling in most other academic areas, and those who are held back academically due to their struggles within a specific academic domain, such as reading or math, so long as their performance is equivalent or nearly equivalent to the average level of performance in their classroom or school. While some might argue this is essentially social justice, it is not in the best interests of society to hold back the academic attainment levels of any of our youth and all should be promoted toward the highest possible level of academic attainment in each academic area. This particular flaw of RTI, as currently implemented, denies the historical concept of the specificity of a learning disability as well. To assume that a highly able student who is achieving academically at the 99th percentile in all academic areas save one—perhaps mathematics for example, where the student is performing just slightly below grade level, is doing just fine, and there is no reason to suspect a learning disability in math—is a radical alteration of the concept of a specific learning disability generally and is an issue that has not been addressed adequately in the disability literature.

4. RTI, while clearly allowable and promoted under the recent revisions to IDEA, ignores the processing disorder component of the definition of learning disability entirely. Reschly (2005), Shinn (2005), and others have argued the irrelevancy of this aspect of the definition of learning disability in the federal regulations, going so far as to argue that it not only can but should be simply ignored. The presence of some form of neuropsychological processing problem has been central to the concept of learning disability since the origins of thought concerning the disorder, even prior to it being named. Neuroscience research has documented repeatedly differences in the cytoarchitecture as well as processing in the brains of individuals with a variety of learning disorders over a period of decades (e.g., see Galaburda & Kemper, 1979; Niogi & Candliss, 2006; and Shaywitz et al., 2002). To ignore such advances in our science and to ignore the differences in learning created by these clear differences in how children with a learning disability manipulate information in the brain hardly can be seen as an advance in diagnosis or treatment of children with a learning disability.

5. RTI is a model of diagnosis by treatment failure, which has long been proven a poor model in medicine. RTI has been promulgated in part through criticisms of prior models of learning disability diagnoses as being "wait to fail" models where we do not diagnose or serve children until there is a discrepancy between their level of academic attainment and level of intellectual functioning. RTI does little to remedy this issue. In reality, children are not referred for intervention even under an RTI model until they reach problematic levels of academic attainment in a classroom—failure in this sense is denoted by the referral itself—adequately achieving students are not referred for learning problems. For children who have a learning disability, the RTI

model truly becomes a "watch them fail" model of diagnosis since diagnosis and referral to special education is then predicated on repeated assessments that show a lack of progress. There are, however, many reasons why children may not respond to academic instruction, of which the presence of a learning disability is but one explanation. RTI as a model of diagnosis does nothing to rule out any explanation or related disability beyond the receipt of poor instruction and adds nothing to the understanding of the individual child's cognitive structure or skills.

6. As alluded to previously, RTI ignores the common possibility of other problems such as emotional disturbance, Attention-Deficit/Hyperactivity Disorder (ADHD), and the like that may be responsible for the educational needs of the referred student since it bypasses the comprehensive assessment of the student, thus promoting misdiagnosis and mistreatment. There is now a substantial literature regarding evidence-based treatments for many forms of childhood psychopathology. Matching the proper evidence-based treatment with the appropriate disorder requires accurate diagnosis. As currently conceptualized, RTI fails to provide instruction that is modified on the basis of student characteristics, which is the key to true individualization of any form of intervention. RTI simply provides the same thing for everyone and ignores alternative explanations and the potential presence of any other form of disability or other pertinent student cognitive characteristics easily revealed in comprehensive neuropsychological assessments.

7. RTI promotes a one-size-fits-all approach to intervention and remediation that ignores over 100 years of research on individual differences. RTI assumes everyone learns equally well under the same models of instruction. If this were true, then RTI would not be needed to begin with. In fact, children referred for RTI and on further for potential placement in special education as children with a disability have in fact been exposed to the same classroom instruction as other children who did respond. Different models and methods of instruction are required in order for children who do not respond to common, sound classroom instructional practices to achieve at appropriate educational levels.

8. RTI assumes the regular classroom instruction provided to date has not been evidence- or science-based (i.e., that the regular education teacher does not understand instructional methods or know how to teach effectively). This is essentially the first assumption or attempt at explanation of failure under the RTI model. The assumption essentially is the teacher has failed to provide proper delivery of the curriculum. If this were true, the fact that the majority of children in the classroom are achieving would seem to be oxymoronic or otherwise inexplicable.

These issues just outlined represent serious problems not only with the implementation but also with the conceptualization of RTI as a model for diagnosing children with a disability. Until these problems are solved, proposed applications of RTI seem premature; however, RTI is now the law of the land and will be implemented despite the fact that RTI does not meet modern scientific standards of evidence as espoused by the USDOE Institute for Education Sciences in that studies of RTI have not included control groups so that placebo, Hawthorne, or other effects are controlled. Following a review of the empirical literature on RTI, with special attention to its effectiveness and feasibility, Fuchs, Mock, Morgan, and Young (2003) reached the following conclusions:

- On the one hand, a consensus grows that the IQ-achievement discrepancy should be abandoned as a marker of the disability. On the other hand, as we have tried to make clear, there is an absence of a validated replacement. (p. 168)
- More needs to be understood before RTI may be viewed as a valid means of identifying students with LD. (p. 157)

It is imperative that these issues be addressed quickly, comprehensively, and with careful attention to the measurement dilemmas, the mathematically driven outcomes of the different models of measuring responsiveness, and the conceptual basis of RTI as challenged in the previous discussions. RTI cannot be implemented with any form of reasonable consistency until these matters are addressed. For the present, however, if RTI is used to ensure the implementation of better problem-solving models and greater responsibility within the general education curriculum for the academic attainment levels of all students, and is used as a prereferral intervention to in fact determine when additional, comprehensive diagnostic information is required to rule out or rule in a disability, and not as a method of diagnosis in and of itself, nor as a means of denying children with a disability access to special education, RTI will represent an advance in general educational models.

WHAT DO YOU THINK NEUROSCIENCE HAS TO OFFER THE ASSESSMENT AND IDENTIFICATION OF LEARNING DISABILITIES?

Under a strict model of RTI as a means of diagnosis of learning disability, there are no neuroscience applications or interests. This would be a grand step backwards in the field.

Rather, under models in which children receive comprehensive evaluations, the purpose of which includes understanding brain-behavior relationships that are associated with processing of information and acquisition of knowledge, particularly from a Lurian perspective (e.g., see Reynolds & French, 2005), the neurosciences have a great deal to offer.

Shaywitz (2005) has provided an excellent, narrative summary of the essential nature of the contributions neurosciences have for not only the assessment and identification of learning disabilities but also to the development of interventions driven by student characteristics:

> Modern brain imaging technology now allows scientists to non-invasively peer into, and literally watch the brain at work—in children and in adults. Using this new technology, we and other laboratories around the world have now identified the specific neural systems used in reading, demonstrated how these systems differ in good and struggling readers, pinpointed the systems used in compensation, and identified the systems used in skilled or fluent reading. In addition, we have identified different types of reading disabilities and also demonstrated the malleability or plasticity of the neural circuitry for reading in response to an evidence-based reading intervention. These and other studies have provided a new and unprecedented level of insight and understanding about common neuropsychological disorders affecting children and adults, their mechanisms, their identification, and their effective treatment. (p. vii)

Shaywitz continues by noting the extraordinary complexity of the brain and its relationship to learning. The brain has long been known to be a dynamic organ of information processing and learning and one that constantly changes itself in response to its environment and at the same time modifies the environment in which it resides (Reynolds & French, 2005). Just as neuropsychology demonstrated many years ago that children with different neuropsychological profiles, representing or modeling brain-behavior relationships for the individual child, predicted differential response to variable pedagogical approaches, the work to which Shaywitz refers has now provided hard neurological evidence of the reasons for the effectiveness of different methods with different brains. As these methods become more and more refined, more accurate diagnoses become possible leading to more clearly targeted and refined intervention methods that are truly individualized.

The biological basis of learning disabilities has been demonstrated both through hard neurological evidence as well as through a variety of neuropsychological studies. Various subtypes of learning disabilities have been differentiated on the basis of neuropsychological test performance (e.g., Semrud-Clikeman, Fine, & Harder, 2005), and our knowledge of the subtypes continues to increase as larger samples and longitudinal studies become available. As the neurosciences, including neurology and neuropsychology, continue to refine our knowledge of the biological basis of learning disabilities, diagnostic markers can become more and more precise as well as objective. While RTI may well have a role in distinguishing children who are simply slow to acquire reading skills from those who may truly have a learning disability, it will ultimately be up to the neurosciences to distinguish between those who have a learning disability and those who do not, as well as to distinguish among those with a learning disability who will respond to which form of evidence-based instruction. Work in these arenas is already relatively advanced although much remains to be discovered and refined.

WHAT ROLE DOES NEUROPSYCHOLOGY HAVE TO PLAY IN DESIGNING INTERVENTIONS IN THE CONTEXT OF RTI?

The response to this question flows directly from the conceptual basis of the response to the preceding question. An assessment model that first eliminates individuals who respond quickly to remedial instruction in reading, as RTI may be used properly, and then moves toward comprehensive neuropsychological assessments of nonresponders, leads us directly to a model of intervention based on the assessment. Such a model has been described generally by Semrud-Clikeman, Fine, and Harder (2005), and models specific to reading provided by Joseph (2005), arithmetic by Lerew (2005), and written language by Chittooran and Tait (2005), as primary examples. Generally, these models take advantage of the strengths in children's information-processing strategies in order to teach them the skills necessary for continued academic development in such key areas as reading, writing, and arithmetic. Such models have been recommended, with evidence for their support available since the 1970s (e.g., see Reynolds, 1988).

These models represent a variation of aptitude-treatment interaction models that are dependent upon patterns of abilities and not levels of aptitude. The discussion by OSERS of the regulations for implementation of the changes to IDEA notes that aptitude-treatment interaction research has failed to produce evidence-based differentiated instructional approaches to the remediation of learning problems. This discussion, however, is simplistic in focusing on literature that is essentially devoted to looking at level as opposed to pattern of aptitudes (also see Hartlage & Reynolds, 1981; Reynolds, 1994) as those attributes would be expressed in a comprehensive assessment, most thoroughly conducted as a neuropsychological evaluation. The differentiation available through neuropsychological assessments is particularly inviting in this process since neuropsychological tests tend to have greater specificity in their assessment of cognitive processes and lesser correlations with general intelligence. Neuropsychological models are thus more aligned with ability patterns and less so with absolute levels of performance.

WHAT ROLE DOES NEUROPSYCHOLOGY HAVE TO PLAY IN THE DIAGNOSIS OF LEARNING DISABILITIES?

Ultimately, it falls to the study of brain-behavior relationships on a functional level as expressed in learning environments to define what is and is not a learning disability. While the hard neurological evidence referred to previously in the work of Shaywitz and others is clearly demonstrative of the biological basis of learning as well as learning dysfunctions, provides insights into the dynamic interplay of various regions of the neocortex when engaged in learning, and demonstrates these interplays can be changed through pedagogical as well as psychotherapeutic methods (e.g., see Cozolino, 2002), detailed information about function in the real world can only be derived through actual performance-based assessments such as are available to neuropsychologists and other psychologists engaged in comprehensive assessments. Ultimately then it will fall to such functional assessments to identify the impact of the neurobiological substrates of learning and learning dysfunctions on the individual student and allow us to identify specific patterns of strengths and weaknesses in cognitive processes that lead to evidence-linked pedagogical methods for specific children.

By linking patterns on comprehensive neuropsychological test batteries to functional neuroimaging methods, we will ultimately derive specific neuropsychological profiles that contain key marker variables associated not only with the presence or absence of a learning disability but that will drive us toward specific interventions for specific learning problems. These links ultimately may have applications in all of education and not just special education and help us overcome the many barriers to establishing a discipline and a practice of educational neuroscience in the schools. To argue, as has been done in the past, that the brain and its function has nothing to do with learning denies decades of advances in the study of brain-behavior relationships as well as hard data from studies of the cytoarchitecture as well as dynamic interaction of brain regions that differ across individuals who learn in different ways, at different rates, and through different interactions and modifications of their environments.

HOW DO YOU RECONCILE RTI AS A MEANS OF DIAGNOSIS OF LEARNING DISABILITY WITH KNOWLEDGE FROM THE CLINICAL NEUROSCIENCES?

The principal means of reconciliation of RTI and the primary application of RTI in any diagnostic role is essentially as noted previously. RTI can be used to differentiate what were characterized at one time in our educational history as essentially slow learners who will respond to more intensive instruction within a general education environment. These children are not characterized accurately as children with a disability. Rather, children who do not respond rapidly to such interventions and who are resistant to traditional pedagogical methods can then be moved to a status-comprehensive neuropsychological evaluation. RTI thus can reduce the number of false-positive referral candidates and make available more professionally trained clinicians who can see children on a timelier basis to perform accurate diagnoses and design appropriate intervention plans. RTI also may assist in the diagnosis of learning disability by making general education more responsible for general education problems and creating a spirit of maintaining in the general education classroom students who may simply be difficult to teach. Additionally, this reinforces the expectation that teachers are capable and expected to reach such students appropriately and reduces the number of children placed in programs for children with a disability simply because these children create too much of an inconvenience for the general education program. In this sense, RTI can be of great benefit to special education by reserving special education for children who have a disability and placing the responsibility for children who need minor accommodations, have motivational issues, or are simply difficult to teach squarely on the shoulders of general education. This may promote the goal of increased individualization of pedagogical methods for all children, which would also be a very positive outcome of the RTI movement.

REFERENCES

Alexander, P. (August, 2007). *Learning and teaching in postindustrial societies: New twist on an old plot.* Paper presented to the annual meeting of the American Psychological association, San Francisco.

Chittooran, M., & Tait, R. (2005). Understanding and implementing neuropsychologically-based written language interventions. In R. D'Amato, E. Fletcher-Janzen, & C. R. Reynolds (Eds.), *Handbook of school neuropsychology* (pp. 777–803). New York: Wiley.

Cozolino, L. (2002). *The neuroscience of psychotherapy: Building and rebuilding the human brain.* New York: Norton.

Fuchs, D., & Fuchs, L. S. (2006). *What the inclusion movement and responsiveness-to-intervention say about high-incidence disabilities.* Keynote for the Inaugural International Conference of the University of Hong Kong's Center for Advancement in Special Education. Hong Kong.

Fuchs, D., Fuchs, L., & Compton, D. (2004). Identifying reading disabilities by responsiveness-to-instruction: Specifying measures and criteria. *Learning Disability Quarterly, 27,* 216–227.

Fuchs, D., Mock, D., Morgan, P., & Young, C. (2003). Responsiveness to intervention: Definitions, evidence, and implications for the learning disabilities construct. *Learning Disabilities Research and Practice, 18*(3), 157–171.

Fuchs, D., & Young, C. (2006). On the irrelevance of intelligence in predicting responsiveness to reading instruction. *Exceptional Children, 73,* 8–30.

Galaburda, A. C., & Kemper, T. (1979). Cytoarchitectonic abnormalities in developmental dyslexia: A case study. *Annals of Neurology, 6,* 94–100.

Hartlage, L. C., & Reynolds, C. R (1981). Neuropsychological assessment and the individualization of instruction. In G. W. Hynd & J. Orbzut (Eds.),

Neuropsychological assessment and the school-age child: Issues and procedures. New York: Grune & Stratton.

Joseph, L. (2005). Understanding and implementing neuropsychologically-based literacy interventions. In R. D'Amato, E. Fletcher-Janzen, & C. R. Reynolds (Eds.), *Handbook of school neuropsychology* (pp. 738–757). New York: Wiley.

Lcrew, C. D. (2005). Understanding and implementing neuropsychological he-based arithmetic interventions. In R. D'Amato, E. Fletcher-Janzen, & C. R. Reynolds (Eds.), *Handbook of school neuropsychology* (pp. 758–776). New York: Wiley.

Nichols, R. C. (1978). Policy implications of the IQ controversy. In L. Schulman (Ed.), *Review of research in education, Vol. 6.* Itasca, IL: Peacock.

Niogi, S. N., & McCandliss, B. D. (2006). Left lateralized white matter microstructure accounts for individual differences in reading ability and disability. *Neuropsychologia, 44,* 2178–2188.

Posny, A. (March, 2007). *IDEA 2004—Top ten key issues that affect school psychologists.* Invited address to the annual convention of the National Association of School Psychologists, New York.

Reschly, D. (August, 2005). *RTI Paradigm Shift and the Future of SLD Diagnosis and Treatment.* Paper presented to the Annual Institute for Psychology in the Schools of the American Psychological Association, Washington, DC.

Reynolds, C. R. (August, 2007). *On the nexus between socio-emotional development and academic development.* Paper presented to the annual meeting of the American Psychological Association, San Francisco.

Reynolds, C. R. (August, 2005). *Considerations win RTI as a Method of Diagnosis of Learning Disabilities.* Paper presented to the Annual Institute for Psychology in the Schools of the American Psychological Association, Washington, DC.

Reynolds, C. R. (Ed.). (1994). *Cognitive assessment: An interdisciplinary perspective.* New York: Plenum.

Reynolds, C. R. (1988). Putting the individual into the aptitude-treatment interaction. *Exceptional Children, 54,* 324–331.

Reynolds, C. R. (1984). Critical measurement issues in assessment of learning disabilities. *Journal of Special Education, 18,* 451–476.

Reynolds, C. R., & French, C. (2005). The brain as a dynamic organ of information processing and learning. In R. D'Amato, E. Fletcher-Janzen, & C. R. Reynolds (Eds.), *Handbook of school neuropsychology* (pp. 86–119). New York: Wiley.

Reynolds, C. R., & Kamphaus, R. W. (2003). *Reynolds Intellectual Assessment Scales and Reynolds Intellectual Screening Test: Professional manual.* Lutz, FL: Psychological Assessment Resources.

Sattler, J. M. (2001). *Assessment of children: Cognitive applications.* San Diego: Jerome Sattler Publishing.

Semrud-Clikeman, M., Fine, J., & Harder, L. (2005). Providing neuropsychological services to students with learning disabilities. In R. D'Amato, E. Fletcher-Janzen, & C. R. Reynolds (Eds.), *Handbook of school neuropsychology* (pp. 403–424). New York: Wiley.

Shaywitz, S. E. (2005). Foreword. In R. D'Amato, E. Fletcher-Janzen, & C. R. Reynolds (Eds.), *Handbook of school neuropsychology* (pp. vii–viii). New York: Wiley.

Shaywitz, B. A., Shaywitz, S. E., Pugh, K. R., Mencl, W. E., Fulbright, R. K., Skud-larski, P., Constable, R. T., Marchione, K. E., Fletcher, J. M., Lyon, G. R., & Gore, J. C. (2002). Disruption of posterior brain systems for reading in children with developmental dyslexia. *Biological Psychiatry, 52,* 101–110.

Shinn, M. (August, 2005). *Who is LD? Theory, Research, and Practice.* Paper presented to the Annual Institute for Psychology in the Schools of the American Psychological Association, Washington, DC.

Siegel, L. S. (1989). IQ is irrelevant to the definition of learning disabilities. *Journal of Learning Disabilities, 22,* 469–478, 486.

3

Neuroscience and RTI: A Complementary Role

H. Lee Swanson

The purpose of this chapter is to highlight some of the applications of neurocognitive science to the field of learning disabilities (LDs). These applications are in the context of the current zeitgeist that emphasizes children's response to instruction (called *response to intervention* or RTI). One of the key contributions of neurocognitive science to the field of LD is to determine the underlying biological and cognitive structures that contribute to a student's overt performance. In contrast, the goal of RTI is to monitor the intensity of instruction and make systematic changes in the instructional context as a function of a student's overt performance. This is done by considering various tiers of instructional intensity. These two research approaches are complementary. RTI focuses on a systematic manipulation of the environmental context (i.e., instruction, classroom, school) to determine procedures that maximize learning, whereas neurocognitive science focuses on mapping the internal dynamics of learning. The unique application of cognitive neuroscience to the field of LD is (a) to explain *why* and predict *how* individual differences emerge in children at risk for LD after intense exposure to validated instructional procedures and (b) to document whether functional brain anatomy changes emerge as a function of intervention.

Before discussing some of the applications of neurocognitive science to the field of LD, however, three comments related to RTI and brain-based applications are necessary. First, RTI is an old paradigm. The concept of response to intervention as a means to further refine the definition of LD has been discussed since the inception of the field (see Haring & Bateman, 1977; Weiderholt, 1974, for a review). For example, the term itself, *learning disabilities,* originated to replace a focus on neurological mechanisms—such as minimal brain dysfunction (e.g., Clements, 1966) and thereby place an emphasis on *instruction*. In addition, several earlier writings made distinctions between children who fall by the way side because of poor instruction and those who are truly "learning disabled." For example, Haring and Bateman (1977) in a text entitled *Teaching the Learning Disabled Child* differentiated between "instruction disabled" and "learning disabled." As they stated, "many children who are labeled learning disabled are in truth instructionally disabled. That is, there are children who have no neurological disorder at all, but have had a series of unfortunate, unusually inadvertent, experiences in learning preacademic and academic tasks. . . . On the other hand, although a child may have no clinically observable signs of neurological disorders, he or she certainly may have some learning disabilities, that cannot be readily accounted for by poor instruction. These learning problems seem to persist in a very small number of children, even though their curriculum has been individualized and they have received systematic instruction" (p. 4). The authors further call for the use of precision teaching via continuous monitoring and recording of student performance on basic academic tasks. In fact, various forms of RTI as we see today, such as curriculum-based measurement and progress monitoring, can be traced to refinements or reformatting of precision-teaching procedures and the provision of instruction in various tiers or intensities reflects a reconfiguration of Deno's (1980) cascade model.

Second, RTI as an assessment approach to define LD has a weak experimental base. At the time of this writing, there have been no controlled studies randomly assigning children seriously at risk for LD to assessment and/or delivery models (e.g., tiered instruction versus special education [resource room placement]) that have measured outcomes on key variables (e.g., overidentification, stability of classification, academic and cognitive growth in response to treatment). The few studies that compare RTI with other assessment models (e.g., discrepancy-based or low-achievement-based models) involve post hoc assessments of children divided into overlapping and nonoverlapping clusters at posttest within the same sample. In addition, different states and school districts have variations in their interpretations on how RTI should be implemented thereby weakening any uniformity linking the science of instruction to assessing children at risk for LD.

Although there is enthusiasm for RTI among some practitioners (e.g., school psychologists) as a means to provide a contextual (or more ecologically valid) assessment of children at risk for LD when compared to other models (e.g., models based on inferences from behavioral data about internal processing), the use of RTI as a scientific means to identify children at risk for LD has several obstacles to overcome. The first obstacle is that, in contrast to standardized formats of testing and assessment, there are no standardized applications of evidence-based instruction. As will be discussed later, a mere call for evidence-based studies and/or progress monitoring does not yield uniformity in practice. A second obstacle is that teacher effects cannot always be controlled. The teacher variable plays a key role in mediating treatment outcomes for children. Further, this variance cannot be accounted for by merely increasing treatment fidelity. Procedures that control for treatment fidelity in applying evidence-based treatments account for a very small amount of variance in student outcomes (see Simmerman & Swanson, 2001, for discussion). Although the role of teacher effects can be controlled to some degree, there is no "expert teaching model" that has been operationalized and implemented for instructional delivery in evidence-based practices. Another obstacle is that, even under the best instructional conditions, individual differences in achievement in some cases will increase. There will be some instructional conditions that vastly improve achievement in both average achievers and children at risk for LD, but these robust instructional procedures will increase the performance gap between some children. Thus, significant performance differences will remain for some children with LD when compared to their counterparts even under the most intensive treatment conditions. Perhaps even more fundamental than these three major obstacles is the lack of consensus about what "nonresponsiveness" entails and how it should be uniformly measured.

Finally, neurocognitive science needs to be placed into perspective as it applies to the field of LD. Although correlational research between brain and behavior has a long history in the field of LD (e.g., studies by Orton, Benton, Reitan, Gaddes—see Hallahan & Cruickshank, 1973, for a review of this earlier research), there is a gap in the application of this research to instruction. Recent work with the advent of fMRI procedures and treatment outcomes is beginning to bridge this gap. However, the bridge between brain studies and education is not well developed (e.g., Bruer, 1997). Knowing precisely which brain centers are activated over time and how they are associated with instruction is rudimentary. Although brain studies linking neurological underpinnings to behavioral function are necessary to provide a theoretical context to understanding LD (this issue will be discussed later), altering instruction as a function of this knowledge base has not been clearly formulated.

I will now respond below to the questions proposed by the editors of this text. My major premise is that by combining efforts of RTI and neurocognitive science we will be in a better situation to have a science of LD.

WHAT DO YOU THINK NEUROSCIENCE HAS TO OFFER LAWS AND POLICIES ASSOCIATED WITH LEARNING DISABILITY DETERMINATION?

Laws need to be written in such a manner that they encourage research to seek the best procedures science has to offer in the identification, assessment, and remediation of LD. I view the current law (Individuals with Disabilities

Education Improvement Act [IDEIA], 2004, to be discussed in the following) with its allowance for alternative research-based procedures to determine a specific learning disability as having enough flexibility to allow such practices. Further, this law may serendipitously provide over the next few years a windfall for neurocognitive scientists to explore the bases of LD. This event will occur because of needs: (a) to provide a scientific explanation of why children fall behind in basic skills from their peers regardless of the treatment intensity (the search for why will be partly stimulated by parents and legislators who will hold teachers and schools legally accountable for children's performance gains) and (b) to validate subgroups of poor achievers who need to be separated into those who are casualties of instruction and those who truly suffer neurological constraints.

The issues I see related to policy and applications of neuroscience to defining LD are not the laws, but rather advocates of RTI overstating the research base. Before addressing these issues, I will briefly state a simple case for neurocognitive science as it applies to policy. Neuroscience offers to policy decisions on LD the potential for and the provision of explanations about why and how individual differences occur. Neurocognitive science has the potential to outline constraints in learning when individual differences cannot be explained as a function of best instructional practices. Not all children can meet educational benchmarks even when thoroughly enmeshed in the best that education has to offer. By ignoring the contributions of neuroscience to policy decisions, we place severe constraints on the science of LD. All indications are that scientific models of learning as expressed in the experimental literature (as well as in the field of LD) are employing both neural and behavioral aspects of learning. A causal review of the recent experimental research journals on cognition and learning (e.g., *Journal of Experimental Psychology, General*) show that both behavioral and brain-imaging methods are being advanced by researchers. Thus, research on the brains of children (those with and without LD) should not be trumped by research on interventions when it comes to policy decision. Both approaches are complementary and not competitive. A casual review of the literature shows that the link to neuropsychological data has been called for in previous definitions of LD and the field is historically based on the assumption that disabilities in such children are "intrinsic" and due to central nervous system dysfunction. Even if these assumptions are rejected (e.g., because the findings are inconclusive), neuroscience has clearly shown that behaviors that are behaviorally similar (such as in the areas of reading and math) may involve different neural mechanisms that have different causes and consequences for children. Valid categorizations of behaviors, according to neural function rather than the appearance of behavioral similarities, would enhance the validity of policies that include procedures to identify children with LD. Further, it is reasonable to assume that subgroups based on neurological function after intense instruction would better control for overidentification of children with LD.

Given these assumptions, why do some neuropsychologists feel they are out of the policy decision loop? It seems to me that neurocognitive science at the present time has failed to reach a consensus on the underpinnings of aptitude-achievement discrepancies, the role of aptitude (IQ) in classification criteria, and how psychometric measures (commonly used by neurocognitive scientists) significantly moderate the magnitude of treatment outcomes. With the Individuals with Disabilities Education Improvement Act (IDEIA, 2004) and the final regulations published August 14, 2006, the federal government recognized potential problems with the IQ-discrepancy method by formally stating that the IQ-achievement discrepancy method was not necessary for LD diagnosis. To facilitate identifying children with LD, three criteria were added to the law:

1. States are not required to use a severe discrepancy between intellectual ability and achievement.
2. The procedure must include a process wherein the children's response to scientifically based research interventions is considered in the assessment process.
3. States are permitted to use alternative research-based procedures to determine a specific learning disability.

Changes in the law were based on the assumption that IQ levels in children with low reading scores were irrelevant to a valid classification of LD. That is, children with low reading scores and low IQ scores are more behaviorally similar to children with high IQ and low reading scores, thus calling into question the validity of discrepancy scores for identification (e.g., Fletcher et al., 1992; Fletcher et al., 1994). IDEA 2004's support for an RTI alternative to the IQ-achievement discrepancy model for LD identification is interesting given its lack of strong empirical support as an identification model (Fuchs et al., 2003). Regardless, there are problems that will undermine some of the applications of RTI and that are highlighted in the following. These problems are related to the: (a) limitations of what we know from evidence-based instructional practices, (b) idea that IQ cannot be ignored in treatment outcomes, and (c) the fact that treatment outcomes are a product of how the sample is defined.

Limitations Related to Knowledge and Interpretation of Evidence-Based Educational Practices

A few years ago a major meta-analysis was funded by the U.S. Department of Education to synthesize all experimental intervention research conducted on children with LD over a 35-year period (see Swanson, Hoskyn, & Lee, 1999; as well as final report to Congress). Swanson and several colleagues (e.g.,

Swanson, 1999a, 2000b; Swanson & Deshler, 2003; Swanson & Hoskyn, 1998; Swanson & Sachse-Lee, 2000) synthesized articles, technical reports, and doctoral dissertations that reported on group-design and single-design studies published between the years of 1963 and 2000. Condensing over 3,000 effect sizes, they found a mean effect size (ES) of .79 for LD treatment versus LD control conditions for group-design studies (Swanson & Hoskyn, 1998) and 1.03 for single-subject-design studies (Swanson & Sachse-Lee, 2000). According to Cohen's (1988) classification system, the magnitude of the ES is small when the absolute value is at .20 or below, moderate when the ES is .60, and large when the ES is .80 or above. Thus, on the surface, the results are consistent with the notion that children with LD are highly responsive to intense instruction. However, when children with LD were compared to nondisabled children of the same grade or age who also were receiving the same best evidence intervention procedure, effect sizes (ES M = .97, SD = .52) were substantially in favor of nondisabled children (see Swanson et al., 1999, p. 162–169). More importantly, the mean ES difference increased in favor of children without LD (ES = 1.44; Swanson et al., p. 168) when psychometric scores related to IQ and reading were not included as part of sample reporting. Thus, the magnitude of RTI could not be adequately interpreted without recourse to psychometric measures. More importantly, effective instructional procedures did little to bridge the gap related to performance differences between children with and without LD with instruction treatments found to be highly effective in samples of children with and without LD.

There were two other important findings from this synthesis as applied to evidence-based instruction that place RTI into perspective. First, the analysis showed that combined direct and explicit strategy instruction (explicit practice, elaboration, strategy cuing) and small group interactive settings best predicted the size of treatment outcomes across various academic domains. The implication of this finding is that a combination of direct instruction and cognitive strategy instruction provided the best evidence-based instructional heuristic for improving academic performance (effect sizes > .80) in children with learning disabilities. However, these components accounted for less that 15% of the variance in predicting outcomes (Swanson, 1999a). This finding held when controls were made in the analysis for methodology, age, type of research design, and type of academic domain (e.g., reading, math, writing). Even the National Reading Panel's report (2000) that provided a definitive analysis of best practice in reading (teaching of phonics) accounts for approximately only 10% of the variance in reading treatment outcomes (Hammill & Swanson, 2006). Thus, a tremendous amount of variance is unaccounted for in studies considered the "best" of evidence-based practices.

Second, the results of "best evidence studies" cannot be taken at face value. In our syntheses of the literature, all studies had well-defined control groups and treatments and/or baseline conditions before their inclusion in the synthesis. We eliminated from the synthesis those studies of poor methodological quality (see Valentine & Cooper, 2005, for a rationale). Simmerman and Swanson (2001) analyzed these best evidence studies and found that slight variations in the internal and external validity significantly moderated the magnitude of treatment outcomes. Some violations that were significantly related to treatment outcomes included: teacher effects (studies that used the identical experimenter for treatment and control in administrating treatments yield smaller effect sizes than those studies that used different experimenters in administering treatments—this condition may be analogous to three-tiered instruction), reliance on *non* norm-referenced measures (studies that did not use standardized measures had much larger effect sizes than those that reported using standardized measures), and heterogeneous sampling (e.g., studies that included both elementary and secondary students yielded larger effect sizes than the other age-level conditions).

More importantly, studies that left out critical information commonly used in most neuropsychological test batteries (e.g., IQ and achievement scores) on individual differences data (or aggregated differences) greatly inflated treatment outcomes. For example, the underreporting of information related to ethnicity (studies that reported ethnicity yielded significantly smaller effect sizes than those that did not report ethnicity) and psychometric data (significantly larger effect sizes occurred when no psychometric information was reported when compared to the other conditions) positively inflated the magnitude of treatment outcomes. The magnitude of effect sizes was also influenced by whether studies relied on federal definitions (studies that did not report using the federal definition [PL-94-142] yielded the larger weighted effect score than those that did) or reported using multiple definitional criteria (studies that included multiple criteria in defining their sample yielded smaller effect sizes than those that did not report using multiple criteria) in selecting their sample.

In summary, our results indicated that "best evidence" studies are influenced by a host of environmental and individual differences variables that make a direct translation to assessing children at risk for LD based on an RTI-only model difficult. In addition, although RTI relies on evidence-based studies in the various tiers of instruction, especially in the area of reading, it is important to note that even under the most optimal instructional conditions (direction instruction) for teaching, reading less than 15% of the variance in outcomes is related to instruction (see Table 5, Swanson, 1999b).

Intelligence

The second issue I will raise is related to intelligence. Should IQ be maintained in current neuropsychological models of LD? Clearly, current legislation (IDEIA, 2004) is directly in response to using IQ as a measure of aptitude for determining LD. In the field of LD, intelligence has long been viewed as a measure of aptitude and is a critical construct in neuropsychological assessment (e.g., Riccio & Hynd, 2003). However, several authors have argued that variations in IQ tell us little about differences in processing when groups are defined at low levels of reading (e.g., Francis et al., 2005). Thus, by eliminating the discrepancy formula the concept of *potential*, as measured by IQ, has been removed from the definition. However, are variations in IQ and reading (former indicators of LD) really irrelevant? I will briefly review the literature on this issue because I believe some of the results have been over interpreted.

Three meta-analyses were done before the passing of IDEIA (2004; Fuchs et al., 2000; Stuebing et al., 2002; Hoskyn & Swanson, 2000). The contradictions in the three meta-analyses are reviewed in Stuebing et al. (2002). Stuebing et al. considered the Hoskyn and Swanson (2000) selection process of studies more conservative of the three, and therefore I want to highlight the findings related to the relevance of IQ. Hoskyn and Swanson (2000) analyzed only published literature comparing children who are poor readers but either had higher IQ scores than their reading scores or had IQ scores commiserate with their reading scores. The findings of the synthesis were consistent with previous studies outside the domain of reading that report on the weak discriminative power of discrepancy scores. Although the outcomes of Hoskyn and Swanson's synthesis generally supported current notions about comparable outcomes on various measures among the discrepancy and nondiscrepancy groups, verbal IQ significantly *moderated* effect sizes between the two groups. That is, although the degree of discrepancy between IQ and reading was irrelevant in predicting effect sizes, the magnitude of differences in performance (effect sizes) between the two groups were related to verbal IQ. They found that when the effect size differences between discrepancy (reading disabled group) and nondiscrepancy groups (low achievers in this case) on verbal IQ measures were greater than 1.00 (the mean verbal IQ of the reading disabled [RD] group was approximately 1.00 and the verbal IQ mean of the low achieving [LA] group was approximately 85) the approximate mean effect size on various cognitive measures was 0.29. In contrast, when the effect size for verbal IQ was less than 1.00 (the mean verbal IQ for the RD group was approximately 95 and the verbal IQ mean for the LA group were at approximately 90) estimates of effect size on various cognitive measures was close to 0 ($M = -0.06$). Thus, the further the RD group moved from IQs in the 80 range (the cut-off score used to select RD samples), the greater the chances their overall performance on cognitive measures would differ from the low achiever. In short, although the Hoskyn and Swanson's (2000) synthesis supports the notion that "differences in IQ and achievement" are unimportant in predictions of effect size differences on various cognitive variables, the magnitude of differences in verbal IQ between these two ability groups did significantly moderate general cognitive outcomes.

Interestingly, Stuebing et al. (2002) in their meta-analysis concluded that IQ was irrelevant to reading. However, as shown in their Table 6, IQ accounts for substantial amount of the explainable variance in reading (explainable variance ranges from approximately .47 to .58). This is certainly not a good argument to support the notion that IQ is completely irrelevant to reading level. Moreover, robust differences on measures between the two groups were found by Fuchs, Mathes, Fuchs, and Lipsey (2000). For example, Fuchs et al. (2000), comparing low achieving students with and without LD, found moderate effect sizes (ES = .61, see p. 94) in favor of low achievers without LD. My point in reviewing these major syntheses of the literature is to suggest that removing IQ as an aptitude measure in classifying children as LD, especially verbal IQ, from assessment procedures is not uniformly supported by the literature. Unfortunately, neuroscience has not played an active role in establishing the validity of IQ as a classification index. Perhaps more important to note is that if RTI is to be used for assessment purposes, rather than discrepancy models, one has to also rule out that IQ is irrelevant to treatment outcomes. This issue is discussed next.

Treatment Outcomes As a Function of Definition

Finally, one obvious test of using IQ as part of the identification criteria that has been overlooked is whether IQ is related to treatment outcomes. Although some studies have found very little relevance related to IQ levels within studies to treatment outcomes (e.g., Vellutino, Scanlon, & Lyon, 2000), the literature on the issue of whether IQ has relevance across an array of intervention studies has not been comprehensively studied. Responsiveness to instruction seems to be a missing test in the majority of studies comparing discrepancy and nondiscrepancy groups. However, does it matter for treatment outcomes whether samples with LD have high or low IQ scores, or have large or minimal discrepancies between IQ and reading, or if such children are merely defined by cut-off scores? Quite simply, do variations in how samples with LD are defined in terms of intelligence and reading have any relationship to treatment outcomes? This is not a trivial question because of current efforts to abandon the notion of a discrepancy between IQ and reading in defining LD. It would seem that efforts to completely disband IQ measures in assessing children's response to intervention would be premature if children high and low in IQ respond differently (quantitatively or qualitatively) as a function of treatment. We have argued that one means of evaluating whether aptitude variations in the LD sample interact with treatment is to compare the relationship between treatment outcomes with multivariate data that include different configurations of how samples with LD are defined. This can be accomplished by placing studies on the same metric (e.g., effect size) and comparing the magnitude of these outcomes as a function of variations in the sample definition (e.g., on measures of intelligence and reading). We have the most comprehensive data on this issue to date (Swanson et al., 1999). We show across the extant literature that significant LD definition–treatment interactions exist across evidence-based studies (see Swanson & Hoskyn, 1999, for review). We found that individual variations in IQ and reading level are important moderators of instructional outcomes in both group-design (Swanson & Hoskyn, 1998, 1999) and single-subject-design studies (Swanson & Sachse-Lee, 2000). We find in our meta-analysis of intervention studies that variations in standardized IQ and reading moderated the magnitude of treatment effects (Swanson & Hoskyn, 1998). The general pattern in our data is that studies that failed to report psychometric information on participants with LD yielded significantly higher effect sizes than those studies that reported psychometric information. Thus, poorly defined sample inflated treatment outcomes by introducing greater heterogeneity into the sample when compared to studies that selected samples based on psychometric criteria. Significant effects related to the magnitude of treatment outcomes were isolated to the severity of reading–intelligence interaction. The influence of IQ scores on the magnitude of the treatment outcomes became especially relevant when reading scores were below the 25th percentile. The effect sizes were moderate (0.52) when intelligence was above 90, but substantial (.95) when IQs were below 90. Thus, the implication of these findings is that variations in IQ and reading cannot be ignored when predicting treatment outcomes and therefore are a critical ingredient to the identification process.

Two other important findings emerge when we consider subsets of the Swanson and Hoskyn (1998) data set. First, we find that adolescent samples with discrepancies in intelligence and reading are more likely to yield lower effect sizes than those studies that report aggregated IQ and reading scores in the same low range (e.g., Swanson, 2001). This puts a new wrinkle on the literature that has called for the elimination of "discrepancy" criteria in classifying learning disabled students by suggesting that discrepancies may be important in predicting treatment outcomes. Second, we find that treatment measures related to reading recognition and comprehension vary as a function of IQ. Effect sizes for word-recognition studies are significantly related to samples defined by cut-off scores (IQ > 85 and reading < 25th percentile), whereas the magnitude of effect size for reading-comprehension studies were sensitive to discrepancies between IQ and reading when compared to competing definitional criteria.

Summary and Implications

The obvious implication is that IQ has relevance to any policy definitions of LD. Groups of students with LD who have aptitude profiles similar to generally poor achievers or slow learners (low IQ and low reading), produced higher effect sizes in treatment outcomes than those samples with a discrepancy between IQ and reading. Given that there has been very little research on why these discrepancies occur, it is important to recognize that some parts of the equation, such as IQ, may still have a role. RTI advocates make excellent points about our need to identify effective instructional programs in the classroom context in which we find children. However, a complete emphasis on the instructional context belittles the science we have. As I've stated sometime ago,

> I assume that even under the best contextual and instructional conditions, there will still be a subgroup of normal IQ children who are inferior to their normal counterparts on demanding cognitive tasks. This does not mean that such children's performance cannot be compensated for or improved upon, only that, currently, these children's performance deficiencies are not simply a product of inept teachers or curriculum. Granted, the residual differences in performance between LD and non-LD children may be altered because the task can be changed by social consensus (e.g., society can pick a task or activity in which individual differences are eliminated). I assume, however, that certain cognitive activities such as reading comprehension, computing story problems, written language, and so on, will remain because there is a contemporary cross-cultural "ring" and consistent, as well as historically based, social expectancy about them. (Swanson, 1988a, p. 297)

WHAT DO YOU THINK NEUROSCIENCE HAS TO OFFER THE ASSESSMENT AND IDENTIFICATION OF LEARNING DISABILITIES?

Neuroscience offers a conceptualization of behavioral outcomes. For example, consider the notion of *thinking*. Thinking is a covert process: Attending, encoding, retrieving, rehearsing, comprehending, planning, reasoning, and imagining are all invisible processes. If they weren't, the well-worn inquiry "What are you thinking about?" could retire from English discourse. What neurocognitive science has to offer to LD is three-fold. First, it establishes that there is biology of LD and that the problem is persistent. Second, it provides a measure of individual differences when behavioral outcomes are the same (this point was alluded to earlier but is illustrated differently in the following). And, finally, neurocognitive science contributes to a science of LD. I will review each of these points in order.

Biology

There is a biological bases to LD (see Shaywitz, Moody, & Shaywitz, 2006; Shaywitz & Shaywitz, 2003, 2005, for a review). For example, several studies (see Shaywitz & Shaywitz, 2003, for review) suggest that there are differences in the temporo-parieto-occipital brain regions between reading disabled and nonimpaired readers. The converging evidence using fMRI in adult dyslexic readers shows a failure in the left-hemisphere posterior brain system to function properly during reading. Some brain imaging studies also show differences in brain activation in frontal regions in dyslexic compared to nonimpaired readers. Most of this research has focused on the brain regions where previous research has implicated reading and language. The research shows clear activation patterns related to phonological analysis. For example, on nonword-rhyming tasks dyslexic readers experience a disruption of the posterior system that involves the posterior superior temporal gyrus (Wernicke's area, the angular gyrus, and the striate cortex.) The research demonstrates a persistent nature of a functional disruption in the left-hemispheric neural systems and indicates that the disorder is lifelong.

Although the majority of neurocognitive research focuses on reading disabilities, several studies characterize learning disabilities in reading by difficulties in segmentation, rapid and automatic recognition in decoding of single words, articulation, and anomia (see Shaywitz & Shaywitz, 2003, for a review). There is some consensus in this literature that a core problem of reading disabilities is difficulty in phonological processing. Neurobiological evidence for reading disabilities comes from postmortem, electrophysiological, family, and functional imaging (fMRI) studies. Evidence from this neurological data suggests the disruption of the neurological system for language in individuals with dyslexia. Brain-based research in dyslexia has focused on the planum temporale, gyral morphology of the perisylvian region, corpus colossum, as well as cortical abnormalities of the temporal-parietal region (e.g., Fine et al., 2007; see Miller, Sanchez, & Hynd, 2003, for review). Although at this point in time it is difficult to summarize this research, there is some consensus that the neural biological codes believed to underlie cognitive deficits in the reading disabled center on the left temporal-parietal region of the brain. Differences in the asymmetry of the planum temporale have consistently been found in association with reading disabilities. Specifically, symmetry of the planum temporale is due to a larger right plana. A reversal of normal pattern of left greater than right asymmetry has been found in individuals with developmental dyslexia (e.g., Riccio & Hynd, 2003). There is also a strong heritability component in the reading process, although there are many unknowns yet to be explored (e.g., Grigorenko, 2001).

Behavioral Similarities Involve Different Processes

Individual differences exist even when the psychometric score is the same. Neuroscience reveals the complexity of apparently simple events. For example, a simple task may not discriminate between LD and non-LD children's performance, yet it may be that mental processes used in such a task may be complex and the differences between ability groups subtle. To illustrate this point, consider an information-processing theory that views the human system as highly adaptive with individuals having at their disposal a large number of alternative means for achieving successful performance on any particular task (Newell & Simon, 1972). Now suppose that a task for children with and without LD is to remember a short list of visually presented nouns that are orthographically and phonemically distinct. Some of these children might activate centers of the brain related to primarily activating phonemic or semantic information, others might activate centers of the brain related to remembering the global shapes of the words and their referents, and still others might use a combination of strategies, yet the final levels of performance attained by these individuals might not differ. Thus, it may be possible to obtain similar levels of performance, for example on reading, math, and cognitive measures, from LD and other poor-reading children who have used different processing strategies, that is, subsets of mental resources that are quite distinct. The practical implication is that severe discrepancies may exist related to information processing in children with LD even when their performance is comparable to average achievers and/or poor achievers (e.g., LD children may use an inefficient processing route, but that route eventually leads them to a correct solution of a problem).

For example, comparable IQs between children with and without LD does not equate to the same processes. Swanson (1988b) found that children with LD did not rely on the same mental processes as nondisabled children on the subtests in the Wechsler although their overt performance was comparable to their normal achieving peers. He found that the two groups varied in the algorithms and heuristics used to solve the problems even though the task performance and the total number of actual mental processes reported were comparable. Further, my work on problem solving showed that children with LD use different routes or processes to problem solve, even though solution accuracy is comparable to CA-matched peers (Swanson, 1993). Swanson (1988b, 1993) found LD students successfully set up a series of subgoals for task solution. Further, their problem-solving performance was statistically comparable to their CA-matched peers on several fluid measures of intelligence (Picture Arrangement subtest on the WISC-R, Swanson, 1988b; Tower of Hanoi, Combinatorial, and Pendulum Task, Swanson, 1993). However, the studies also found that individuals with LD relied on different cognitive routes than skilled readers in problem solving. For example, on measures of fluid intelligence, problem solving was augmented by "emphasizing problem representation (defining the problem, identifying relevant information or facts given about the problem) rather than procedural knowledge or processes used to identify algorithms" (Swanson, 1993, p. 864). Thus, the important discrepancies in a child's intellectual functioning existed even when behavioral measures yield the same score as their counterparts.

In summary, neurocognitive science can show that traditional means of assessing some of the irregularities in LD children's performance fail to capture some truly underlying patterns of procesзing strengths and inefficiencies. Two learners earning the same test score may have very different information-processing strengths and weaknesses. Further, psychometric tests may not be able to separate children with RD from others with similar reading scores in terms of overt performance, yet actual processes used in such tasks may be complex and the differences between the ability groups subtle.

Theory

Some years ago I suggested procedures for validating a theory-based model of LD that includes both instructional outcomes and neurological correlates (Swanson, 1988c; see 1988a for reactions to this model). At that time understanding the links between theory and instructional practice in the field of LD was difficult because the data from basic research was meager. However, the research strategy outlined in Table 3.1 sketches a framework for validating a learning model of LD that integrates both instruction and neuroscience. I have updated some of these steps, but the model still provides for a clear integration of neurocognitive and instructional data.

The steps are outlined in Table 3.1. The model rested on the assumption that LD reflects a cognitive-processing limitation due to neurological inefficiencies (see Swanson, 1988c, for a more detailed discussion of the model). This series of steps had two functions: Identify those processing deficiencies that can be influenced by instruction (thus providing direction for instructional practice) and those that are not easily amendable to instruction and in need of compensation. Thus, the steps provide a cognitive-deficit explanation for LD and therefore a focus is placed on analyzing learning disabled children's performance in terms of human information processing. Specifically, an emphasis is placed on understanding the mental processes and knowledge structures that result in poor learning and subsequent performance. The revised strategy begins with a preliminary step (Step 1a) of studying children who have been provided intense instruction over an extended period of time (6 to 8 months) who fail to make adequate progress in an academic domain despite normal intelligence. The researcher next parsimoniously chooses constructs (Step 1b) that interlink with several cognitive processes and academic domains. At that time and even more recently working memory is an excellent candidate for this model (Swanson, 1999c; Swanson & Jerman, 2007; Swanson & Siegel, 2001) with additional applications to defining LD within English-language learning samples (e.g., Swanson, Sáez, & Gerber, 2006). Different components of WM have been related to the development of different regions of the brain. For example,

Table 3.1   Validating a Science-Based Model of Learning Disabilities

Step 1a. Select children who have average intelligence, score below the 25th percentile in reading and/or math, and been provided intense instruction but show limited growth in achievement.

Step 1b. Select a parsimonious domain embedded within a model of learning (e.g., Reading, Mathematics).

Step 2.   Select tasks that both represent the domain (e.g., working memory) and are sensitive to individual differences in learning (construct validity).

Step 3.   Determine the locus of ability group differences on those tasks.

Step 4.   Delineate the cognitive processes that underlie ability group performance.
  a. Relate process measures with ability differences in academic functioning.
  b. Determine if process measures account for the major variance in ability group academic performance.
  c. Determine which process measures best predict academic performance.
  d. Eliminate process measures that poorly correlate with academic performance.
  e. Demonstrate interaction between ability group and process manipulation.
  f. Partial out the effects of academic ability.
  g. Determine neurological correlates between children with and without LD.

Step 5.   Categorize processing difficulties.
  a. Parameter differences.
  b. Sequence differences.
  c. Route differences.
  d. Strategy differences.

Step 6.   Teach LD children to process as NLD children, thereby attempting to raise their performance to a level similar to their counterparts.
  a. If instruction fails to induce change, move to Step 7.
  b. If instruction induces change, determine if both ability groups used the same mechanism.
  c. Collect concurrent measures on classroom functioning.

Step 7.   Formulate a metatheory of learning disabilities by designating the parameters susceptible and not susceptible to instruction.
  a. If anomalous data occur, return to Step 1.
  b. If additional data confirm theory, broaden context (e.g., determine influence of noncognitive classroom variables on learning).

Adapted from Swanson (1988c).

STM (phonological loop) has been associated with the left temporal parietal region, whereas the executive system of WM is associated with the frontal lobes (Wagner & Smith, 2003; also see Kane, 2005, for a review). Thus, it seems reasonable from these studies that different processes as a function of disability may mediate the influence of WM on different intelligence and achievement measures. Evidence from fMRI studies suggests that development in fluid intelligence is related to the frontal lobe development (e.g., see Kane, 2005, for a review) and changes on crystallized intelligence measures, such as the area of reading, are related to the maturation of temporal and parietal sections of the brain (e.g., Paulesu et al., 1993).

Having selected a domain, such as working memory, the investigator next selects the tasks to be used in the study (Step 2). The tasks are chosen for their theoretical value as well as their ability to measure the construct under investigation (i.e., construct validity). The choice of task is based on an accumulation of basic research on learning and individual differences using such a task or measure. Once the tasks are selected, predefined ability groups are compared on these tasks using a conceptually sound research design (Step 3).

In Step 4, basic research efforts are made to establish the validity of underlying cognitive processes as an explanation of a learning disability. There are several parts to this step. For Part A, narrowly defined learning-disabled groups based on achievement (e.g., children with reading and/or math disabilities) are used to establish the relationship of each process to various academic measures (e.g., Swanson, Howard, & Sáez, 2006). In Part B, the processes are examined to determine the extent to which they account for the majority of variance between and within the academically defined ability groups. In Part C, the researcher attempts to isolate those mental processes that best predict classroom achievement. In Part D, the researcher attempts to determine which processing deficiencies are not related to task performance (divergent validity). The law of parsimony is invoked in that tasks (or processes) that have little predictive power are dropped from the subsequent analysis. In Part E, the researcher determines how the subgroups (e.g., defined as reading disabled and/or math disabled) respond to systematic interventions under experimental and control group conditions (e.g., Swanson, 2000a; Swanson & Sachse-Lee, 2001). The components of the experimental instruction are linked to (a) achievement outcome measures and (b) processing constructs (e.g., WM). If an interaction emerges, achievement and general intellectual ability are partialed out from the analyses (Part F). The partialling out of achievement and general aptitude allows one to better account for the variance in the processing measure. If the ability group intervention interaction remains, one is somewhat immune to challenges that achievement problems precipitated the processing disability. Finally, it is important that the cognitive- and academic-processing difficulties after and before intervention need to be tied to neurocognitive data. As stated several years ago, "a full account of the processing difficulty cannot be established unless verified by some independent index" (Swanson, 1988c, p. 199).

In Step 5, a more systematic attempt is made to categorize the underlying processing variables that discriminate between ability groups. Four categories are suggested. Parameter differences refer to those differences that exist in a stage of processing, such as phonological storage or executive processing (inhibition, updating). Sequence differences reflect the order in which various stages occur; for example, the child with LD might generate a hypothesis about using a strategy to learn new information, whereas a child without LD would wait until all the information is provided. Both individuals use all stages—it's simply that the order in which they occur varies. Route differences reflect qualitative differences in the stages actually used. The child with LD might use isolated components of that stage or completely skip a stage altogether, whereas the child without LD uses all components of the stage. Strategy differences refer to general control processing (e.g., rehearsal, elaboration) differences in how children encode and retrieve information.

Step 6 (as in Step 1a) is again linked to instruction. However, here the researcher makes a concerted effort to systematically compensate for or eliminate process differences between ability groups by directing instruction toward academic performance. Neurological indices (fMRI data) are gathered to determine if specific mental processes are influenced by such manipulations. If reliable ability group differences remain after instruction, then the processes unaffected by the instruction are assumed to account for the learning disability. This conclusion, of course, is contingent upon the fact that the instruction does affect the targeted learning processes and not incidental supporting processes. To determine if a failure to change performance in LD children results from a failure to change the target process, concurrent measures are taken during intervention to determine if the process under investigation is responsible for performance. Step 7 focuses on procedures for refining or rejecting the metatheory.

No doubt, these steps must be fleshed out with current syntheses on cognitive, neuropsychological, and intervention research on LD. The steps do illustrate, however, that neurocognitive science and instructional research can be critically linked to develop a comprehensive model of LD. Most research in LD begins and ends with instruction. It is doubtful, however, that instructional research can be matched to the characteristics of LD learners, or that researchers will be able to pinpoint the mediating processes that direct performance, without an understanding of the processes noted in a basic research program (Steps 1 through 5).

Summary

In summary, I would argue that biology is important to the diagnosis of LD because behavioral data leave a substantial amount of variance unaccounted for in treatment outcomes. Behavioral data can also fool us into thinking all children with LD approach learning in the same manner. Neuroscience can inform the public about why children with such low reading scores have higher intelligence than matched children with equally low reading scores. I would also argue that any advances in the field need an explicit model linking neurocognitive science and instruction. The aforementioned is one possible model.

HOW DO YOU RECONCILE RTI AS A MEANS OF DIAGNOSIS OF LD WITH KNOWLEDGE FROM THE CLINICAL NEUROSCIENCES?

A science of LD merges the data on the knowledge gained from RTI and clinical neurosciences. Thus, the field of LD will make little progress when fixated on such questions as "are learning disabilities more likely caused by instructional deficits than by basic cognitive deficits associated with neurological anomalies?" That is, even if environment plays the major role, some children with normal intelligences will never learn to read or compute well. Posing questions about the utility of RTI or cognitive neuroscience assessment as the sole or even the primary vehicle for determining a learning problem are not fruitful. Scientists who study children with LD should avoid software/hardware dualism distinctions. No serious scientist would argue that software operates independent of the existence of the hardware or that outcomes related to neuroscience can be separated from response to intervention. Education cannot be separated from the existence of the brain and visa versa. The knowledge that we would gain from RTI would have important implications for the neurocognitive psychologist in defining the environmental parameters of LD and a clear delineation of the neurological constraints that remain in children after instruction would have important implications for the assessment of LD from an RTI perspective. Clearly the link between the biology of learning and actual teaching of learning is emerging. However, the field will be stalled until both perspectives converge on a common theoretical model.

To advance the diagnosis of LD, I assume the following needs to occur in neuroscience (I already indicated the limitations of evidence-based instructional practices). I will list two limitations and two major contributions neuroscience can make toward diagnosis.

Limitations

First, the focus on neuroscience needs to be broadened. Often, the neurocognitive approach has been motivated by what has been called a *search for pathology*. That is, assessment determines the underlying cognitive and biological manifestations of a child's learning (e.g., reading) difficulties rather than terms of their poorly developed learning (reading) subskills. Typically, a child suspected as being at risk for LD is given an individually administered battery of tests that include intelligence, reading achievement, and various neuropsychological measures. Unfortunately, many of these tests are weakly linked to instruction. Information in terms of neural developmental anomalies will not inform the field unless they are placed in the context of their interactions with instructional outcomes.

Although I see the utility of psychometric assessment and even intelligence measures to aid in diagnosing learning problems, especially in terms of the high order cognitive activities such as reading comprehension or problem solving, neurocognitive assessments need to be tied into *repeated* behavioral observations related to instruction. For example, various neurocognitive measures need to be intertwined with progress-monitoring measures. It seems to me that neuroscience would benefit tremendously from RTI because RTI would serve as the initial period of the remedial intervention. That is, the first stage of diagnosis would be assessing outcomes related to treatment. Thus, neurocognitive data would not necessarily be used for classification but would provide guidance for purposes of initiating further remedial instruction. A child's additional response to intervention would be assessed and assessment of strengths and weaknesses related to the neurocognitive aspects could be crossvalidated with posttest scores.

Second, limitations of the database need to be clarified. In spite of significant progress in terms of our understanding some of the underlying biological causes of learning to read, for example, it is important to realize that there is no uniform consensus about the neurological causes of this specific learning disability. Although some models enjoy greater acceptance among different researchers, none have been able to provide a clear-cut, definitive, unequivocal set of diagnostic criteria that would pinpoint the ultimate neurobiological origin of a reading problem. As a consequence, the approach to diagnosing underlying causes of LD or reading disabilities varies as a function of the conceptual basis of the condition (e.g., this is usually manifested in the types of tasks selected for fMRI studies) and therefore there have been concerns about implementing a neurocognitive battery to determine a diagnosis of LD. The neurocognitive approach has not been fruitful in predicting student outcomes as a function of instructional conditions. Further, the literature on neurological subtypes and responsiveness to instruction lacks a consensus of data. For example, our synthesis of the literature found no subtypes meeting the selection criteria based on neurological data that interacted with treatment approach (e.g., Swanson et al., 1999). Thus, I think an understanding of the nature of LD, at least as it relates to diagnosis, is one that requires an understanding of the assumptions behind the limitations of what we know from evidence-based instruction and the limitations of what we know from neurocognitive science about LD.

Contributions

I think there are two immediate contributions of neurocognitive science to the diagnosis of LD. As I am a cognitive psychologist, I will focus mostly on the behavioral manifestations of cognition realizing that there are neurological correlates that can be attached to these assumptions.

One potential contribution of cognitive neuroscience is the delineation of how children with LD access information. *Accessibility* refers to the notion that information necessary for a task resides within the child because he or she has been taught that information. Several researchers (especially during the early 1990s) converged on the notion that children with LD have a difficult time accessing knowledge and it remains relatively inert unless they are actually provided key executive-processing and self-montoring strategies during instruction (see Swanson, 1990, pp. 26–27 for list of citations and overview of research findings; also see Rueda, Posner, & Rothbart, 2005, with applications to neurocognitive science). This research was abandoned during the 1990s up to the present because federal funding for LD was primarily directed to the basic reading process; however, the construct remains as foundational for experimental studies in learning, memory, and cognition. Although RTI would encourage children to use certain strategies on certain kinds of tasks, we do not have insight on how this occurs until we have some sense of how these children access information.

A second major contribution to our understanding of LD relates to how such children's knowledge representations are mentally or functionally organized. Thus, one contribution of neurocognitive science would be to begin mapping knowledge representations in an LD child's mind and how this representation compares to children who are generally poor readers or average readers. That is, how children organize information, how they understand information, and how they go beyond simple representation of simple facts to more complex systems and multiple relationships needs to be addressed with a sample of children with and without LD. Several studies show that often the child with LD has a general declarative knowledge about how to do the task, but why they fail to carry through procedurally is unclear (e.g., see Keeler & Swanson, 2001). Unfortunately, there is limited experimental work to explain why children who have been provided good instruction still are able to come up with average intelligence scores when their reading is at a dismal level.

WHAT ROLE DOES NEUROCOGNITIVE SCIENCE HAVE TO PLAY IN DESIGNING INTERVENTIONS IN THE CONTEXT OF RTI?

Several studies in the cognitive science literature have been directed to the psychology of instruction with application to LD (see Pellegrino & Goldman, 1990, for a comprehensive review). Robert Glaser (1976) indicated that a science of instruction must include: (a) an analysis of the components of performance, (b) a description of the initial state of the learners, (c) a description of conditions that foster the acquisition of skill or competence, and (d) an assessment of the effects of instructional implementation. RTI has made application to assessing the effects of instructional implementation, but places minimal emphasis on the first three aspects of the science of instructional design. Historically, neuropsychological assessment has shown application to the initial state of the learner, but has ignored parts a, c, and d.

Berninger and Richards' (2002) comprehensive review of brain research and literacy provides specific pedagogical principles derived from neurocognitive science (e.g., see pp. 320–321). Many of these principles come from studies of such concepts as executive functioning, automaticity, and developmental sequence. Some of these principles are:

1. teach components of an instructional system that are relevant to developmental stage,
2. overcome temporal capacity limitations of working memory,
3. provide sufficient practice in low level skills so that they become more automatic freeing resources for more complex activities,
4. integrate several codes of information so a child can form connections, and
5. provide activities in terms of executive functions that call for self-regulation and explicit strategies for self-regulation.

In addition to expanding the scientific bases of pedagogical principles to the instruction of children at risk for LD, I think that neurocognitive science can make several direct contributions to education if the following occurs.

First, establish clear analogs between classroom functioning and brain science. For example, if one is going to assess frontal lobe activity (via working memory and executive processing) then an analog needs to be found in the classroom. For example, one can assess a child's ability to follow a series of instructions, recite a poem, recall state capitals, and then relate those findings to neurocognitive data. Specifically, if difficulties are found in executive processing (working memory) on certain neurocognitive measures then these difficulties need to be linked to critical classroom activities, such as online reading comprehension (where one has to monitor different pieces of information, reactivate previous information, make inferences as they are reading, etc.). Clear analogs need to occur between the neurocognitive literature and what is actually being asked for in the academic context.

Second, establish *neurological records* of educational outcomes. Posner and Rothbart (2005, 2007a, 2007b) suggest that a central issue of relating neurocognitive science to education (more specifically, brain development to education) is whether classroom interventions can alter neural networks. Posner and Rothbart (2005) report that fMRI methods may provide a basis for understanding the differences in brains, both anatomically and functionally. Imaging shows that dyslexia involves an *underactivation* of two particular brain areas, the posterior phonological area and areas of the visual system. In normal reading, these two areas seem to work automatically because visual words are associated automatically with the appropriate sound. Interestingly, dyslexics show very little activation until after training. However, phonological training was found to induce activation of the phonological area (Simos et al., 2007; Shaywitz et al., 2004; also see review by Shaywitz & Shaywitz, 2003). Thus, educational treatment can influence the functional anatomy displayed by children after training. These findings suggest that combining both behavioral and neurocognitive methods can provide a circumspect view on treatment outcomes.

Finally, establish neurocognitive indices related to the cognitive load (processing demands) placed on children as a function of instruction. Neurocognitive science needs to explain a child's persistence, compensation, and adaptation to instruction (e.g., see Shaywitz et al., 2003, for application to adults with LD). For example, some children may have to activate all centers of the brain to achieve an academic goal (e.g., read a paragraph) and therefore heavy demands are placed upon information processes. In contrast, other children require very little activation because the difficulty level is perceived as rather automatic. These demands on brain processing in the former child require some modifications in instruction related to cognitive load. Thus, neurocognitive indices can provide for a crossvalidation between instruction demands and the cognitive load placed on the children.

SUMMARY

In summary, neurocognitive measures administered under experimental conditions serve as a complementary process to RTI. Although the RTI initiative has reminded us to shift some of our conceptualization of LD from test scores toward actual response to intervention as an important means of defining these children, a complementary approach is needed to explain why children with normal intelligence who receive intensive instruction fail to read, compute, and/or problem solve commensurate with their aptitude. Neurocognitive science can facilitate in better identifying those children who have true LD from those children who are instructional casualties. In contrast to the past tenuous links between a neurocognitive science of LD and educational intervention, current research is needed that integrates the findings of neurocognitive science with instructional remedial activities. Refinement in the categorization of children with LD should be directed toward integrating the effects of remediation with neurocognitive processing.

REFERENCES

Berninger, V., & Richards, T. L. (2002). *Brain literacy for educators and psychologists.* San Diego: Academic Press.

Bruer, J. T. (1997). Education and the brain: *Educational Researcher, 26,* 4–16.

Clements, S. D. (1966). Learning disabilities—Who? In Special Education: Strategies for educational progress-selected convention papers (44ᵗʰ Annual CEC Convention). Washington DC: Council for Exceptional Children.

Cohen, J. (1988). *Statistical power analysis for the behavioral sciences* (2ⁿᵈ ed.). Hillsdale, NJ: Erlbaum.

Deno, E. (1980). Special Education and developmental capital. *Exceptional Children, 37,* 229–237.

Fine, J. G., Semrud-Clikeman, M., Keith, T. Z., Stapleton, L. M., & Hynd, G. W. (2007). Reading and the corpus callosum: An MRI family study of volume and area. *Neuropsychology, 21,* 235–241.

Fletcher, J. M., Francis, D. J., Rourke, B. P., Shaywitz, S. E., & Shaywitz, B. A. (1992). The validity of discrepancy-based definitions of reading disabilities. *Journal of Learning Disabilities, 25,* 555–561.

Fletcher, J. M., Shaywitz, S. E., Shankweiler, D. P., Katz, L., Liberman, I. Y., Stuebing, K. K., Francis, D. J., Fowler, & Shaywitz, B. A. (1994). Cognitive profiles of reading disability: Comparisons of discrepancy and low achievement definitions. *Journal of Educational Psychology, 86,* 6–23.

Francis, D. J., Fletcher, J. M., Stuebing, K. K., Lyon, G. R., Shaywitz, B. A., & Shaywitz, S. E. (2005). Psychometric approaches to the identification of LD: IQ and achievement scores are not sufficient. *Journal of Learning Disabilities, 38*(2), 98–108.

Fuchs, D., Fuchs, L., Mathes, P. G., & Lipsey, M. (2000). Reading differences between low achieving students with and without learning disabilities. In R. Gersten, E. P. Schiller, & S. Vaughn (Eds.), *Contemporary special education research: Synthesis of knowledge base of critical issues.* Mahwah, NJ: Erlbaum.

Fuchs, D., Mock, D., Morgan, P., & Young, C. L. (2003). Responsiveness-to-intervention: Definitions, evidence, and implications for the learning disabilities construct. *Learning Disabilities Research & Practice, 18,* 157–171.

Glaser, R. (1976). Components of a psychology of instruction: Toward a science of design. *Review of Educational Research, 46,* 1–24.

Grigorenko, E. (2001). Developmental dyslexia: An update on genes, brains, and environments. *Journal of Child Psychology and Psychiatry, 42,* 91–125.

Hallahan, D. P., & Cruickshank, W. M. (1973). *Psychoeducational foundations of learning disabilities.* Englewood Cliffs, NJ: Prentice Hall.

Hammill, D. D., & Swanson, H. L. (2006). The national reading panel's meta-analysis of phonics instruction: Another point of view. *The Elementary School Journal, 107,* 17–26.

Haring, N. G., & Bateman, B. (1977). *Teaching the learning disabled child.* Englewood Cliffs, NJ: Prentice Hall.

Hoskyn, M., & Swanson, H. L. (2000). Cognitive processing of low achievers and children with reading disabilities: A selective meta-analytic review of the published literature. *School Psychology Review, 29,* 102–119.

Individuals with Disabilities Education Improvement Act of 2004 (IDEIA). PL 108-446, 20 U.S.C., 1400 et seq.

Kane, M. J. (2005). Full frontal fluidity? Looking in on the neuroimaging of reasoning and intelligence. In O. Wilhem & R.W. Engle (Eds.), *Handbook of understanding and measuring intelligence* (pp. 141–164). Thousand Oaks, CA: Sage.

Keeler, M. L., & Swanson, H. L. (2001). Does strategy knowledge influence working memory in children with mathematical disabilities? *Journal of Learning Disabilities, 34,* 418–434.
Miller, C. J., Sanchez, J., Hynd, G. W. (2003). Neurological correlates of reading
   disabilities. In H. L. Swanson, K. R. Harris, S. Graham (Eds.). *Handbook of learning disabilities* (pp. 242–255). New York: Guilford Press.
National Reading Panel. (2000). *Teaching children to read: An evidence-based assessment of the scientific research literature on reading and its implications for read-
   ing instruction. Summary report.* Washington, DC: National Institute of Child
   Health and Development.
Newell, A., & Simon, H. A. (1972). *Human problem solving.* Englewood Cliffs, NJ:
   Prentice Hall.
Paulesu, E., Demonet, J., Fazio, F., McCrory, E., Chanoine, V., Brunswick, N.,
   Cappa, S., Cossu, G., Habib, M., Frith, C., & Frith, U. (1993). Dyslexia, cultural
   diversity and biological unity. *Science, 291,* 2165–2167.
Pellegrino, J. W., & Goldman, S. R. (1990). Cognitive science perspectives on intel-
   ligence and learning disabilities. In H. L. Swanson & B. Keogh (Eds.), *Learning
   disabilities: Theoretical and research issues* (pp. 41–58). Hillsdale, NJ: Erlbaum.
Pellegrino, J. W., & Goldman, S. R. (1990). Cognitive science perspectives on intelligence and learning disabilities. In H. L. Swanson & B. Keogh (Eds.), *Learning
   disabilities: Theoretical and research issues* (pp. 41–58). Hillsdale, NJ: Erlbaum.
Posner, M. I., & Rothbart, M. K. (2007a). *Education, psychology, and the brain.*
   Washington, DC: American Psychological Association.
Posner, M. I., & Rothbart, M. K. (2007b). Research on attention networks as a
   model for the integration of psychological science. *Annual Review of Psychology,
   58,* 1–23.
Posner, M. I., & Rothbart, M. K. (2005). Influencing brain networks: Implications
   for education. *Trends in Cognitive Sciences, 9*(3), 99–103.
Riccio, C. A., & Hynd, G. W. (2003). Measurable biological substrates to verbal-
   performance differences in Wechsler scores. *School Psychology Quarterly, 15,*
   386–399.
Rueda, M. R., Posner, M. I., & Rothbart, M. K. (2005). The development of execu-
   tive attention: Contributions to the emergence of self-regulation. *Developmental
   Neuropsychology, 28,* 573–594.
Shaywitz, B. A., Shaywitz, S. E., Blachman, B. A., Pugh, K. R., Fulbright, R. K., &
   Skudlarski, P., et al. (2004). Development of left occipitotemporal systems for
   skilled reading in children after a phonologically-based intervention. *Biological
   Psychiatry, 55,* 926–933.
Shaywitz, S. E., Mody, M., & Shaywitz, B. A. (2006). Neural mechanisms in dys-
   lexia. *Current Directions in Psychological Science, 15,* 278–281.
Shaywitz, S. E., Shaywitz, B. A. (2003). Neurobiological indices of dyslexia. In
   H. L. Swanson, K. R. Harris, S. Graham (Eds.), *Handbook of learning disabilities*
   (pp. 514–531). New York: Guilford.
Shaywitz, S. E., & Shaywitz, B. A. (2005). Dyslexia (specific reading disability). *Bio-
   logical Psychiatry, 57,* 1301–1309.
Shaywitz, S. E., Shaywitz, B. A., Fulbright, R. K., Skudlarski, P., Mencl, W. E., &
   Constable, R. T., et al. (2003). Neural systems for compensation and persistence:

Young adult outcome of childhood reading disability. *Biological Psychiatry, 54,* 25–33.

Simmerman, S., & Swanson, H. L. (2001). Treatment outcomes for students with learning disabilities: How important are internal and external validity? *Journal of Learning Disabilities, 34,* 221–236.

Simos, P. G., Fletcher, J. M., Sarkari, S., Billingsley-Marshall, R., Denton, C. A., & Papanicolaou, A. C. (2007). Intensive instruction affects brain magnetic activity associated with oral word reading in children with persistent reading disabilities. *Journal of Learning Disabilities, 40,* 37–48.

Stuebing, K. K., Fletcher, J. M., LeDoux, J. M., Lyon, G. R., Shaywitz, S. E., & Shaywitz, B. A. (2002). Validity of IQ-discrepancy classifications of reading disabilities: A meta-analysis. *American Educational Research Journal, 39,* 469–518.

Swanson, H. L. (1988a). Comments, countercomments, and new thoughts. *Journal of Learning Disabilities, 21,* 289–298.

Swanson, H. L. (1988b). Learning disabled children's problem solving: Identifying mental processes underlying intelligent performance. *Intelligence, 12,* 261–278.

Swanson, H. L. (1988c). Toward a metatheory of learning disabilities. *Journal of Learning Disabilities, 21*(4), 196–209.

Swanson, H. L (1990). Intelligence and learning disabilities. In H. L. Swanson & B. Keogh (Eds.), *Learning disabilities: Theoretical and research issues* (pp. 23–39). Hillsdale, NJ: Erlbaum.

Swanson, H. L. (1993). An information processing analysis of learning disabled children's problem solving. *American Educational Research Journal, 30,* 861–893.

Swanson, H. L. (1999a). Instructional components that predict treatment outcomes for students with learning disabilities: Support for a combined strategy and direct instruction model. *Learning Disabilities Research & Practice, 14*(3), 129–140.

Swanson, H. L. (1999b). Reading research for students with LD: A meta-analysis in intervention outcomes. *Journal of Learning Disabilities, 32,* 504–532.

Swanson, H. L. (1999c). What develops in working memory? A life span perspective. *Developmental psychology, 35,* 986–1000.

Swanson, H. L. (2000a). Are working memory deficits in readers with learning disabilities hard to change? *Journal of Learning Disabilities, 33,* 551–566.

Swanson, H. L. (2000b). Searching for the best cognitive model for instructing students with learning disabilities: A component and composite analysis. *Educational and Child Psychology, 17,* 101–121.

Swanson, H. L. (2001). Research on interventions for adolescents with learning disabilities: A meta-analysis of outcomes related to higher-order processing. *The Elementary School Journal, 101,* 331–348.

Swanson, H. L., & Deshler, D. (2003). Instructing adolescents with learning disabilities: Converting a meta-analysis to practice. *Journal of Learning Disabilities, 36,* 124–135.

Swanson, H. L., & Hoskyn, M. (1998). Experimental intervention research on students with learning disabilities: A meta-analysis of treatment outcomes. *Review of Educational Research, 68,* 277–321.

Swanson, H. L., & Hoskyn, M. (1999). Definition × treatment interactions for students with learning disabilities. *School Psychology Review, 28,* 644–658.

Swanson, H. L., Hoskyn, M., & Lee, C. M. (1999). *Interventions for students with learning disabilities*. New York: Guilford.

Swanson, H. L., Howard, C. B., & Sáez, L. (2006). Do different components of working memory underlie different subgroups of reading disabilities? *Journal of Learning Disabilities, 39*, 252–269.

Swanson, H. L., & Jerman, O. (2007). The influence of working memory on reading growth in subgroups of children with reading disabilities. *Journal of Experimental Child Psychology, 96*, 249–283.

Swanson, H. L., & Sachse-Lee, C. (2001). A subgroup analysis of working memory in children with reading disabilities: Domain-general or domain-specific deficiency? *Journal of Learning Disabilities, 34*, 249–263.

Swanson, H. L., & Sachse-Lee, C. (2000). A meta-analysis of single-subject-design intervention research for students with LD. *Journal of Learning Disabilities, 33*, 114–136.

Swanson, H. L., Sáez, L., & Gerber, M. (2006). Growth in literacy and cognition in bilingual children at risk or not at risk for reading disabilities. *Journal of Educational Psychology, 98*, 247–264.

Swanson, H. L., & Siegel, L. (2001). Learning disabilities as a working memory deficit. *Issues in Education, 7*, 1–48.

Valentine, J. C., & Cooper, H. M. (2005). Can we measure the quality of causal research in education. In G. Phye, D. Robinson, & J. Levin (Eds.), *Empirical methods for evaluating interventions* (pp. 85–112). San Diego: Elsevier Academic Press.

Vellutino, F. R., Scanlon, D. M., & Lyon, G. R. (2000). Differentiating between difficult-to-remediate and readily remediated poor readers: More evidence against the IQ-achievement discrepancy. *Journal of Learning Disabilities, 33*, 192–199.

Wagner, T. D., & Smith, E. E. (2003). Neuroimaging study of working memory: A meta-analysis. *Cognitive, Affective, and Behavioral Neuroscience, 3*, 255–274.

Weiderholt, L. (1974). Historical perspective on the education of the learning disabled. In L. Mann & D. Sabatino (Eds.), *The second review of special education* (pp. 103–152). Austin: Pro-Ed.

4

The Education Empire Strikes Back: Will RTI Displace Neuropsychology and Neuroscience from the Realm of Learning Disabilities?

Merrill Hiscock and Marcel Kinsbourne

T hroughout the long and decidedly nonlinear history of the field of learning disabilities (LDs), the brain has experienced its share of ups and downs. Knowledge about the brain has been embraced at some times and eschewed at others, promoted by some specialists and rejected by others, and invoked in ways that range from reasonable to ridiculous. On the whole, the brain has fared well in recent decades. Beginning with an emphasis on selective perceptual or information-processing defects that were thought to underlie LD (e.g., Cruickshank et al., 1961; Frostig, Lefever, & Whittlesye, 1964), the field of LD quickly—and perhaps somewhat indiscriminately—incorporated concepts from neurology and the incipient specialty of neuropsychology. By the late 1970s William Cruickshank was forecasting a "springtime" for LD in which the mainstream would be informed by an interdisciplinary coalition of scientists that would include researchers from medicine, neuroscience, and related clinical specialties (Cruickshank, 1980).

Cruickshank's springtime arrived as predicted but it evidently has failed to progress smoothly into summer. The fact that this volume exists suggests that an unexpected and adverse climatological event occurred, or at least was perceived to have occurred. The abrupt reversal of perspective did not take place on the brain side of the LD-neuroscience coalition. Scores of cognitive neuroscientists have undertaken studies related to reading and calculation and to deficiencies in those skills. Moreover, cognitive neuroscience has grown rapidly during the American "decade of the brain" (the 1990s) and its potential usefulness has escalated as functional imaging techniques have become more refined and more readily available. From its vantage point, cognitive neuroscience is thriving.

The impasse that has overtaken the LD-neuroscience alliance can be attributed to two related conceptual changes that have taken place in the field of LD since the late 1970s and early 1980s (i.e., the beginning of Cruickshank's spring and the era that Hallahan and Mock [2003] call the "solidification period"). One is a sweeping emphasis on phonological processing as the key to reading disability, and the other is treating LD *symptoms* without knowing their underlying cause.

Before LD came to neuropsychological attention, it was regarded as essentially an educational or an emotional problem. After reading disability was subtyped into two neuropsychological syndromes (Kinsbourne & Warrington, 1963) it was regarded as heterogenous, and several further subtyping schemes were suggested. An individual child might have difficulty with reading or spelling or calculating, or with any combination of those basic skills. Moreover, in a child with a selective disability of reading, for example, the disability might be manifested in any number of ways. Some children with a reading disability seemed to decode words with difficulty whereas others decoded quite fluently but failed to extract much semantic information from their reading. Some children seemed to have a deficit in discriminating distinctive orthographic features whereas others were impaired in the serial ordering of stimuli. The heterogeneity of symptoms implied a heterogeneity of underlying neuropsychological causes, and they were analogized to well-known neuropsychological syndromes first described in adults. Consequently, the children were screened for the possible presence of concomitants of the core reading problem, such as a covert language delay or difficulty with sequencing or a tendency toward a visual or "right hemisphere" cognitive style, with tests adapted from tests designed for use with brain-injured individuals. Based on the outcome, the child was then fitted into a taxonomy based on (or influenced by) classical neuropsychological disease entities.

That neurologically influenced concept of heterogeneity in LD began to change with the accumulation of empirical and theoretical support for the idea that phonological processing deficits lie at the core of most instances of LD, and of reading disabilities (RDs) in particular (e.g., Bradley & Bryant, 1985; Wagner & Torgesen, 1987; Vellutino, 1979). If most cases of LD have a linguistic or metalinguistic cause, then it may not be necessary or desirable to assess the various cognitive, perceptual, and motor functions that are represented in a neuropsychological evaluation. The emphasis shifted from the individualized search for sometimes unusual patterns of neuropsychological deficit to the application of a standard and homogeneous approach to children with LDs. From here it is a logical next step to abandon psychoeducational assessment altogether in favor of direct diagnosis of deficient academic skills and an attempt to remediate those deficient skills (Fletcher, Morris, & Lyon, 2003; Gresham, 2002; Torgesen et al., 1999). This change of perspective did not arise at random. It coincided with, and perhaps was in response to, a great increase in the number of children who were labeled LD as the popularity of the term increased not only among teachers but also among parents, who preferred it to having their children called mentally retarded, idle, or emotionally disturbed. So children were called LD not only when they had a selective cognitive difficulty that expressed itself in a selective educational lag, but also when LD acted as an acceptable euphemism for more global difficulties. What they all had in common, nonetheless, was difficulty in learning to read, and teaching them more rigorously to read seemed to be the answer.

We interpret the six questions posed by the editors as derivatives of a more general question: What are the implications of the putative dissolution of the LD-neuroscience coalition? Consequently, our responses to the six questions will not be entirely independent of each other, but will reflect many of the same themes. These themes in turn reflect certain postulates about brain functioning, learning, and the relationship between brain functioning and learning. Before we address the six questions, we enumerate our postulates.

The first four postulates are truisms insofar as they either are supported by a substantial amount of evidence or are widely held by neuroscientists and "neurophilosophers" who write about brain and behavior.

1. *Materialism.* There is no place for mysticism when relating behavior to the brain. Cognition is a product of brain activity. Emotion depends on the brain and the autonomic nervous system. All explanatory roads lead ultimately to the brain.

2. *Levels of analysis.* To recognize that all behavior depends on brain activity does not invalidate behavioral variables or diminish the value of behavioral studies. In the realm of LDs, the variables of interest usually are behavioral variables (e.g., decoding speed, type of spelling errors).

3. *Reading is a learned skill.* Humans, in the course of brain maturation, attain the inherent biological capacity necessary for learning to read. Unlike spoken language, which is "picked up" from the social environment, reading must be specifically taught and learned. The same is true of writing, spelling, and calculating.

4. *Individual differences.* Sir Francis Galton (1870/1961) pointed out that all human abilities are distributed as a bell-shaped curve in the general (i.e., nonbrain-injured) population. We are aware of no exceptions to this

principle (except when measurement artifacts distort the distribution). Consequently, with respect to any ability, the general population will include individuals who are highly proficient and others who are markedly deficient. The labels we choose to apply to individuals with low ability (LD, mentally retarded, slow, clumsy, etc.) do not nullify Galton's principle.

Our answers to the six questions also are influenced by four additional postulates that are less likely to be accepted universally by neuroscientists.

1. *Neurological and neuropsychological tests do not provide the needed information.* In evaluating an individual with LD, the clinician ideally would test the functioning of those parts of the brain that subserve reading, spelling, and calculating. However, the neurological examination assesses functions that are performed lower in the neuraxis (e.g., simple sensory and motor functions), and neuropsychological tests assess a variety of cortical functions (e.g., verbal fluency and figural memory) that are of unknown relevance to the individual's academic disability. In short, the clinician assesses the functions of the nervous system that he or she knows how to assess rather than the functions that need to be assessed (Hiscock & Hiscock, 1991; Kinsbourne, 1973).

2. *There is a gap between neurological diagnosis and educational intervention.* Suppose clinicians were to become able to specify the brain basis of an individual's LD with pinpoint accuracy, for instance with the help of advanced functional imaging technologies. What happens then? Can this anatomical or physiological knowledge be translated into an educational prescription that would be more useful than a prescription formulated in the absence of such knowledge? We think not. An unbridgeable gap would remain between *diagnosis* and *treatment* (Mattis, 1981).

3. *Different stages of learning imply different problems.* Reading, spelling, and calculating are multifaceted skills. Different component skills develop at different rates. A particular component may become the primary source of difficulty at one stage of learning and then become less problematic with increased maturity and increased practice. It follows that a "one-size-fits-all" policy for intervention may not be appropriate. An intervention strategy that proves efficacious for the decoding of orthography, for instance, may fail egregiously when it is applied to the comprehension of text.

4. *The distinction between practice and research.* Interesting and theoretically important research questions may have little or no immediate relevance to educational practice. Conversely, educational policies and practices may be beneficial to children without being grounded in neuroscience. Neuroscience research on LDs can be justified quite apart from its actual or potential contribution to the remediation of LDs.

THE SIX QUESTIONS

Question 1. What do you think neuroscience has to offer laws and policies associated with learning disability determination?

One's answer to this question hinges on one's understanding of the inherent nature of LD. If the term is reified so as to represent a specific quasimedical disorder (e.g., a condition known as dyslexia) or a cluster of such disorders (e.g., Gerstmann syndrome), then neuroscientists might have a legitimate role in advising the officials who formulate laws and policies regarding LD. Neuroscience might possess information about the prevalence, etiology, symptomatology, or treatment of the disorder that would be unknown to educators or to researchers outside the field of neuroscience. For example, if the disorder were caused by a unique neurological abnormality that responds to biomedical therapies (drugs, depth electrodes, etc.), and if neuroscientists had developed an accurate test to identify children whose brain had that abnormality, policy makers should know about these discoveries and should understand their implications for educational policy.

Unfortunately, this scenario is science fiction rather than current reality. LD is an artifact, a hypothetical construct, a category created by humans within a particular educational, linguistic, and cultural context. Its definition has changed repeatedly across the past 100 years, and there is still disagreement, inconsistency, and confusion in defining and subdividing the disorder. Some children may have inherited a specific form of LD from one of their parents, but the problem that most children with LDs have is not acquired as part of a neurological syndrome. Many children have been taught inadequately, while others fall within the lower tail of the distribution for learning ability.

The cognitive and academic characteristics of children with LDs change as the proportion of identified children changes (Satz et al., 1978). If the bottom 5% of the distribution is labeled as LD, then the children so labeled will have one profile of ability and achievement. If the bottom 25% is labeled as LD, the cognitive and academic characteristics of children with LD will be quite different. Good laws and sensible policies regarding LD should reflect knowledge about ability distributions, societal resources, and statistical decision theory, as well as knowledge about treatment efficacy. These kinds of knowledge lie outside neuroscience.

Question 2. What do you think neuroscience has to offer the assessment and identification of learning disabilities?

Any contributions of neuroscience to the assessment and identification of LDs are general and indirect. Neuroscience provides a context into which LD can be placed, away from issues of emotional disorders, antiliterate attitudes, and environments nonconducive to learning. Studies of the normally developing brain have expanded understanding of synaptogenesis, maturational gradients, critical periods, lateralization of language, age-related changes in brain plasticity, and so on. Studies from clinical neuroscience (e.g., Towbin, 1978) have provided information about the etiology of prenatal and perinatal brain damage, differences in the consequences of early and late damage to the fetal brain, differences between damage to the child and adult brain, and so on. The well-intentioned LD specialist may be motivated to acquire broad knowledge of normal and abnormal brain development, but this knowledge does not lead to more competent assessments or more accurate identification of children with LD.

Consider a sports analogy. From physiological studies, movement scientists are learning more and more about the distinction between fast-twitch and slow-twitch skeletal muscles. Research indicates that humans show individual differences in the ratio of fast-twitch to slow-twitch muscles and there is some evidence that the ratio can be modified by intensive training (Andersen, Klitgaard, & Saltin, 1994). Is this information of interest to coaches? Presumably it is. Is this information *useful* to coaches? Probably not. Coaches have access to more relevant information (i.e., information about the athlete's actual performance). A stopwatch can provide the information needed to differentiate a sprinter from a 10,000-meter specialist, and the same stopwatch can tell the coach whether a particular training regime is more effective than an alternative regime. Track events are won or lost according to elapsed time, not the ratio of fast- and slow-twitch muscles.

This analogy reminds us that the ultimate criterion of athletic performance is behavioral, and our main point is that the ultimate criterion of academic performance is also behavioral. If we push the analogy a bit farther, however, we can argue that physiological information is potentially useful in the identification and treatment of LD in the future. We learn from the mass media that certain endurance athletes, such as the bicyclist Lance Armstrong, are endowed with extraordinary respiratory or cardiovascular capacities. Thus, there is justification for predicting unusual physical capability from physiological measures. Physiological data can also be used to quantify the effect of training. With further advancement in understanding the relation between training and performance, physiological measures can be used to optimize training programs and to predict an athlete's performance during competition (Taha & Thomas, 2003). Neurophysiological measures ultimately may play a similar role in (a) predicting individual differences in learning and (b) optimizing interventions. These possibilities will be discussed as part of our response to the third question.

Question 3. How will future developments in neuroscience affect how we classify and intervene with learning disabilities?

Event-related brain potentials (ERPs) in newborns and young children can be used to predict language proficiency and reading performance several years later (Espy et al., 2004; Guttorm et al., 2005). A recent magnetic source imaging (MSI) study indicates that intensive phonics and word-recognition training normalizes the pattern of brain activity in children with reading disabilities, but only if the children responded satisfactorily to the intervention (Simos et al., 2007). The practical implications of these studies are a matter of speculation at this time, but the studies do suggest that physiological characteristics might be useful in the future to identify children who are at high risk for LD and to help the clinician in designing programs for remediation. On the other hand, the best preschool predictors of reading in the first grade are simple measures of letter familiarity and phonological awareness (Adams, 1990; Byrne, Fielding-Barnsley, Ashley, & Larsen, 1997; Riley, 1996).

Physiological measures may prove to be as useful in the realm of education as in the realm of endurance sports. Nonetheless, in neither field can physiological measures displace behavioral measures. Much as the stopwatch remains the ultimate criterion of running performance, behavioral assessment remains the ultimate criterion of LD.

Question 4. How do you reconcile RTI as a means of diagnosis with knowledge from the clinical neurosciences?

This question is reminiscent of earlier arguments about the usefulness of cognitive science (or cognitive psychology) in the identification and treatment of LD. The method of cognitive psychology entails dissecting a complex process such as reading or writing into multiple sequential components. After a schematic diagram of the relevant system is constructed, it becomes possible in principle to specify the point at which functioning breaks down in the individual. Whereas this general approach has been widely accepted as a productive research strategy for decomposing skilled performance by normal adults (LaBerge & Samuels, 1974), it is more contentious when applied to children who are striving to learn the skills and especially to those who are falling behind. The difficulty seems to lie in the ease with which the cognitive science approach is subordinated to medical-model thinking. Deficient skill becomes a disorder (e.g., dyslexia) and an impaired component process becomes a cause. The clinician's job is to "diagnose" the disorder, to identify the specific "etiology" using psychoeducational tests, and then to prescribe appropriate "treatment" for the underlying deficit. Unfortunately, the literature on aptitude-by-treatment interactions (ATIs) in special education provides very little support for the idea of designing interventions to help children with specific profiles of strengths and weaknesses (Gresham, 2002).

One of the most compelling critiques of this rationale has been articulated by Brown and Campione (1986), who criticized the search for underlying deficits on two grounds. First, measurements of underlying deficits (e.g., in auditory short-term memory) vary across time and situations. The deficits may exist solely or primarily in the context of the problematic academic skill. Furthermore, interventions to ameliorate the underlying deficit, even if successful, seldom have an effect on the manifest problem. For example, even if the deficient auditory short-term memory could be improved by systematic training—which is unlikely—the improvement probably would have no effect on the child's progress in learning to read.

RTI answers Brown and Campione's (1986) criticisms by disregarding the putative perceptual and cognitive deficits that underlie LD. The disorder—irrespective of etiology—is no more than the symptom itself (e.g., difficulty in learning to read). The "diagnosis" can be made readily by teachers and special education personnel by means of achievement testing. The prescribed "treatment" addresses the academic problem rather than the perceptual or cognitive deficits presumed to underlie the problem. The academic problem is defined as a domain-specific failure to learn. Because any learning failure is necessarily also a teaching failure, the appropriate intervention is teaching that is individualized, both in its manner (how explicit) and in its pace (how fast, with how much rehearsal).

The need to reconcile RTI with the clinical neurosciences is no greater than the need to reconcile any behavioral intervention with underlying physiological processes. Another sports analogy may be helpful. Imagine that football strength coaches discover that an unorthodox regimen (e.g., two workouts per day for a week, followed by a week of rest) is especially effective for players who fail to increase strength and muscle mass sufficiently with conventional workout schedules. Imagine further that the efficacy of this unorthodox strength training is supported by research, but there is no physiological explanation for its effectiveness. Should strength coaches suspend their use of the regimen until the relevant physiological processes are understood? We would argue that they should not. A physiological explanation might be of interest to coaches and athletes, but the efficacy of the regimen is independent of the physiological explanation. Likewise, the efficacy of RTI is independent of the availability of a neurological explanation.

Question 5. What role does neuropsychology have to play in the diagnosis of LD?

For the majority of children with LD, RTI eliminates the need for neuropsychological evaluation. A child who is identified by school personnel as someone who is not progressing satisfactorily (e.g., in learning to read) is given intensive remedial instruction. If the instruction is effective, the problem has been resolved without any need for neuropsychological assessment. If the problem persists despite the remedial instruction, the school may refer the child for neuropsychological assessment with the expectation that the assessment will lead to a diagnosis and an alternative treatment plan, which could be educational (if the deficit is not rooted in phonological processing), biomedical, or both. RTI alters the sequence of events. The neuropsychologist plays the same role as in the past, but only if remedial instruction fails. From the neuropsychologist's perspective, children with learning problems would have been prescreened by first undergoing remedial instruction.

Assuming a significant success rate for the remedial instruction, and since after the neuropsychological evaluation the child still has to be taught, RTI is cost-effective. The frequency with which schools refer children for LD evaluations by neuropsychologists will decrease quite markedly. This is not to say that neuropsychologists will no longer be involved in LD evaluations. Despite RTI, some parents presumably will refer their children directly to a neuropsychologist for assessment. School districts will continue to refer LD children whose circumstances are atypical or complicated (e.g., children with multiple disabilities, possible psychiatric disorders, and known or suspected neurological abnormality). Neuropsychologists may be asked to help resolve disputes between parents and schools regarding the classification and treatment of children with LD. It is also likely that older children will require neuropsychological services.

If RTI is successful in addressing the needs of younger children with LD, it seems likely that the number of older children subsequently referred for neuropsychological evaluation will increase. The RTI model is most promising for dealing with problems, such as word decoding and automatization of math facts, that materialize in the first 3 or 4 years of elementary school. Mastery of these basic skills, of course, does not preclude deficits of comprehension and conceptualization at higher grade levels. These higher-level difficulties, which often reflect the cognitive limitations of the child rather than inadequate or inappropriate instruction, are less likely to be amenable to RTI. If RTI fails to be helpful in resolving these problems, many children in fourth grade and beyond will be candidates for neuropsychological assessment.

Question 6. What role does neuropsychology have to play in designing interventions in the context of RTI?

As noted previously, a successful RTI would obviate the need for neuropsychological assessment. The involvement of a clinical neuropsychologist might be beneficial if the intervention is ineffective for a particular child or if the child's LD is complicated by a treatable medical disorder such as Attention-Deficit/Hyperactivity Disorder (ADHD) or epilepsy. Thus, in some instances, the neuropsychologist may play an important role in designing or modifying interventions in the context of RTI.

Alternatively, the question may be construed not as a question about treating the individual child but about designing interventions for general implementation. This is a question about applied science, and we accordingly would emphasize the inclusiveness of science. Good ideas are good ideas, irrespective of their source. Remedial programs may come from sources outside education. There is no reason why neuropsychologists could not design an efficacious intervention in the context of RTI. However, the innovative method would still be educational, since no biomedical interventions have been reliably shown to be superior to individualized teaching in helping children to read, write, or calculate. There is no reason to assume that a successful intervention would have to be designed by neuropsychologists or even that its development would require neuropsychological input.

FINAL COMMENTS

Irrespective of the matter being discussed, we are often told that the devil is in the details. With regard to LD, the devil has resided for a long time in the details of the definition. Of all the changes that have occurred in the LD field, none is more striking or more important than the increasing inclusiveness of the LD label. To qualify for the label, a child no longer must have a selective and seemingly inexplicable impairment in the context of otherwise normal academic aptitude. Now, difficulty in learning to read may be the only attribute shared by children with the RD label. RTI's success encourages and justifies this inclusiveness. Nevertheless, children with selective impairments (specific learning disability, or SLD) still exist and will be seen by neuropsychologists if RTI programs fail to help them. This minority group within the LD population should also be examined intensively by cognitive neuroscientists because these children provide a unique perspective on brain-behavior relationships.

We now return to William Cruickshank's vision of springtime for LD, with its new embracement of multidisciplinary science. Has the advent of RTI blocked the progression of springtime into summer? On the contrary, support for the phonics instruction that underlies RTI comes from a huge corpus of multidisciplinary research into reading (Rayner et al., 2001). This collaborative science has shown conclusively that interventions are most effective when they address the deficient skill directly. The proximity-of-intervention principle probably will change the focus of neuroscience research into reading problems and their remediation, but it is difficult to see why it should pose a threat to the continuation of neuroscience's partnership with education.

REFERENCES

Adams, M. J. (1990). Beginning to read: Thinking and learning about print. Cambridge, MA: MIT Press.

Andersen, J. K., Klitgaard, H., & Saltin, B. (1994). Myosin heavy chain isoforms in single fibres from m. vastus lateralis of sprinters: Influence of training. Acta Physiologica Scandinavica, 151, 135–142.

Bradley, L., & Bryant, P. (1985). *Rhyme and reason in reading and spelling.* Ann Arbor: University of Michigan Press.

Brown, A. L., & Campione, J. C. (1986). Psychological theory and the study of learning disabilities. American Psychologist, 41, 1059–1068.

Byrne, B., Fielding-Barnsley, R., Ashley, L., & Larson, K. (1997). Assesssing the child's and the environment's contribution to reading acquisition: What we know and what we don't know. In B. Blachman (Ed.), *Foundations of reading acquisition and dyslexia* (pp. 265–285). Mahwah, NJ: Erlbaum.

Cruickshank, W. M. (1980). "When winter comes, can spring . . . ?" In W. M. Cruickshank (Ed.), Approaches to learning. Vol. 1: The best of ACLD (pp. 1–24). Syracuse, NY: Syracuse University Press.

Cruickshank, W. M., Bentzen, F. A., Ratzeburg, F., & Tannhauser, M. T. (1961). A teaching method of brain-injured and hyperactive children. Syracuse, NY: Syracuse University Press.

Espy, K. A., Molfese, D. L., Molfese, V. J., & Modglin, A. (2004). Development of auditory event-related potentials in young children and relations to word-level reading abilities at age 8 years. Annals of Dyslexia, 54, 9–38.

Fletcher, J. M., Morris, R. D., & Lyon, G. R. (2003). Classification and definition of learning disabilities: An integrative perspective. In H. L. Swanson, K. R. Harris, & S. Graham (Eds.), Handbook of learning disabilities (pp.30–56). New York: Guilford.

Frostig, M., Lefever, D. W., & Whittlesey, J. R. B. (1964). The Marianne Frostig Developmental Test of Visual Perception. Palo Alto, CA: Consulting Psychology Press.

Galton, F. (1961). Classification of men according to their natural gifts. In J. J. Jenkins & D. G. Paterson (Eds.), Studies in individual differences: The search for intelligence (pp. 1–16). New York: Appleton-Century-Crofts. (Original work published 1870).

Gresham, F. M. (2002). Responsiveness to intervention: An alternative approach to the identification of learning disabilities. In R. Bradley, L. Danielson, & D. P. Hallahan (Eds.), Identification of learning disabilities: Research to policy (pp. 467–519). Hillsdale, NJ: Erlbaum.

Guttorm, T. K., Leppänen, P. H. T., Poikkeus, A.-M., Eklund, K. M., Lyytinen, P., & Lyytinen, H. (2005). Brain event-related potentials (ERPs) measured at birth predict later language development in children with and without familial risk for dyslexia. Cortex, 41, 291–303.

Hallahan, D. P., & Mock, D. R. (2003). A brief history of the field of learning disabilities. In H. L. Swanson, K. R. Harris, & S. Graham (Eds.), Handbook of learning disabilities (pp.16–29). New York: Guilford.

Hiscock, M., & Hiscock, C. K. (1991). On the relevance of neuropsychological data to learning disabilities. In J. E. Obrzut & G. W. Hynd (Eds.), Neuropsychological foundations of learning disabilities (pp. 743–774). San Diego: Academic Press.

Kinsbourne, M. (1973). School problems. Pediatrics, 52, 697–610.

Kinsbourne, M., & Warrington, E. (1963). Developmental factors in reading and writing backwardness. *British Journal of Psychology, 54,* 145–156.

LaBerge, D., & Samuels, S. (1974). Toward a theory of automatic information processing. Cognitive Psychology, 6, 293–323.

Mattis, S. (1981). Dyslexia syndromes in children: Toward the development of syndrome-specific treatment programs. In F. J. Pirozzolo & M. C. Wittrock (Eds.), Neuropsychological and cognitive processes in reading (pp. 93–107). New York: Academic Press.

Rayner, K., Foorman, B. R., Perfetti, C. A., Pesetsky, D. D., & Seidenberg, M. S. (2001). How psychological science informs the teaching of reading. Psychological Science in the Public Interest, 2, 31–74.

Riley, J. L. (1996). The ability to label the letters of the alphabet at school entry: A discussion of its value. *Journal of Research in Reading, 19,* 87–101.

Satz, P., Taylor, H. G., Friel, J., & Fletcher, J. M. (1978). Some developmental and predictive precursors of reading disabilities: A six year follow-up. In A. L. Benton & D. Pearl (Eds.), Dyslexia: An appraisal of current knowledge (pp. 313–347). New York: Oxford University Press.

Simos, P. G., Fletcher, J. M., Sarkari, S., Billingsley, R. L., Denton, C., & Papanicolaou, A. C. (2007). Altering the brain circuits for reading through intervention: A magnetic source imaging study. Neuropsychology, 21, 485–496.

Taha, T., & Thomas, S. G. (2003). Systems modeling of the relationship between training and performance. *Sports Medicine, 33,* 1061–1073.

Torgesen, J. K., Wagner, R. K., Rashotte, C. A., Rose, E. Lindamood, P., Conway, J., & Garvan, C. (1999). Preventing reading failure in young children with phonological processing disabilities: Group and individual responses to instruction. Journal of Educational Psychology, 91, 579–593.

Towbin, A. (1978). Cerebral dysfunctions related to perinatal organic damage: Clinical-neuropathologic correlations. Journal of Abnormal Psychology, 87, 617–635.

Vellutino, F. R. (1979). Dyslexia: Theory and research. Cambridge, MA: MIT Press.

Wagner, R. K., & Torgesen, J. K. (1987). The nature of phonological processing and its causal role in the acquisition of reading skills. Psychological Bulletin, 101, 192–212.

5

Nature-Nurture Perspectives in Diagnosing and Treating Learning Disabilities: Response to Questions Begging Answers that See the Forest *and* the Trees

Virginia W. Berninger and James A. Holdnack

BIG PICTURE

We begin by explaining the big picture that informs the details in our following responses to the six questions posed by the editors of this volume. Contemporary American society is evolving in its attempts to deal with learning differences in otherwise normally developing students who struggle with reading, writing, math, and/or oral language. The initial approach was to qualify students for services by labeling those who were underachieving relative to their intellectual ability or grade as having a learning disability. This approach bypassed defining learning disability by qualifying students for special education services on the basis of exclusionary rather than inclusionary criteria: what a learning disability *is not* rather than what it *is*. The singular suffix on learning disability erroneously implied it was a homogeneous condition that one either had or did not have. Because the experts could not define what a learning disability is, states adopted different operational definitions for implementing the federal law. Thus, *whether* a student was qualified as having a learning disability depended to a large extent on the student's state

Acknowledgment: Grant No. HD25858 from the National Institute of Child Health and Human Development supported preparation of this manuscript.

of residence; in contrast, medical diagnoses are consistent across states. The number of other struggling students in the same school also influenced how many students could receive costly special education services.

The determination process has its basis in adult disability law that specifies the conditions under which an individual is entitled to social security benefits. The legal precedent established by the social security act likely influenced lawmakers in devising the IDEA laws. Adult disability laws clearly state that a medical condition must be present and the condition is severe, making the individual unable to work. Two independent criteria must be met: a diagnosis and low functioning. The law clearly indicates that either having a medical "condition" *or* being low functioning is not sufficient to receive the disability entitlement. In addition, the disability may not be caused by certain diagnoses such as alcoholism (e.g., exclusionary criteria).

Applying the model to schools, there has to be a diagnosis or disorder present and the disorder must be so severe that it interferes with the child's ability to learn. In the adult disability proceedings, the determination of a disorder is made not by the governing body but by a qualified medical practitioner while the determination of eligibility is made by the governing body (e.g., Social Security Administration). This approach clearly separates the concepts of diagnosis and disability; however, in schools the process of determining the diagnosis of a disorder is blurred with the disability determination. In schools the governing body makes both the diagnostic and disability determination, which often results, particularly for the category of specific learning disability, in the bypassing of the determination of a diagnostic condition and focuses on eligibility. Therefore, in many cases, qualifying for disability services becomes tantamount to having or not having the disorder. This becomes particularly confusing when children are "low functioning" but the presence of a disorder cannot be established. By legal standards, these children are not eligible for disability services; however, because they are low functioning they may be inappropriately assigned to a diagnostic category in order to receive services. Because of the blurring of the diagnostic and eligibility phases (i.e., both processes being made by the same governing body), children's diagnoses become based primarily on level of functioning rather than diagnosis. In order to break this cycle, it is incumbent on the individual clinician to separate out the diagnostic determination from the eligibility process.

The recent reauthorization of IDEA introduced flexibility—comprehensive assessment is required, but, the nature of the comprehensive assessment is not prescribed. Response to intervention (RTI) may be one part of that comprehensive assessment but may not be used alone. The former prescriptive, formulaic approach—give prescribed tests, enter scores in a table, and see if there is a discrepancy—leaves the thinking to the government and auditors. The new approach empowers the thinking professional who engages in reflective professional practice and, if necessary, thinks outside the box to help students who do not fit in the box to succeed in school.

Unfortunately, being empowered to think and practice one's profession in an evidence-based, flexible, accountable way is causing some practitioners to panic. What is at stake is not a simple choice between giving tests for diagnostic purposes and monitoring response to intervention. The gold standard in medical and psychological diagnosis has always been to combine test results and evaluation of any prior response to treatment in making a current diagnosis and monitoring response to any new treatment related to the new diagnosis. The confusion probably stems from (a) a lack of appreciation of the multiple assessment models on which top-notch professionals draw and apply as the case at hand warrants, and (b) a lack of understanding of the nature-nurture perspective.

Assessment Models

Three approaches to assessment are illustrated in Figure 5.1. The top figure illustrates comprehensive assessment that yields a profile highlighting strengths and weaknesses of the individual across multiple domains. The middle figure portrays an evidence-based constellation or pattern of behavioral expression that emerges from neurogenetic and neuropsychological research and is relevant for planning, conducting, and evaluating instruction. The bottom figure depicts a label qualifying a student for services without evaluating whether any evidence-based diagnoses of specific learning

• **Are students snow flakes?**
  Goal of assessment is to describe
  unique individual profile.

• **Are students constellations?**
  Goal of assessment is to describe
  patterns of phenotypes associated
  with specific disorders.

• **Are students categorical labels?**
  Goal of assessment is to qualify
  students for services.

Figure 5.1   Assessment Models

• Is student meeting daily, weekly, annual goals in
level or rate of growth within school year?

• Where is student in overall journey across school years to
becoming skilled in reading, writing, and math?

Figure 5.2   Progress Monitoring Models

disabilities apply. Figure 5.2 contrasts the two most important kinds of progress monitoring for response to intervention: Is the student meeting goals
or aims now *at target times within the school year* (top figure)? What kind
of developmental progress is the student making toward skilled reading,
writing, and math *across the school years* (bottom figure)? Figure 5.3 shows
the complexity that emerges when test results are interpreted and translated
into practice within a systems model that includes the individual student, the
class, and the family. Reference will be made to each of these models in filling
in the details for the big picture in the response to the six questions.

Nature-Nurture Perspective

The myth persists that biologically based variables are unchangeable. In
fact, the brain is an organ that not only mediates learning but also creates

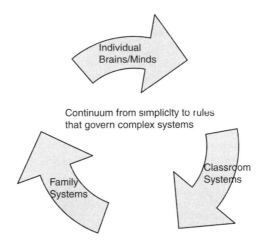

Figure 5.3   Assessment Models: Emergent Complexity

behavior and changes in behavior. Genetic variation can influence learning and behavior but, except for genetic-based diseases, does not determine behavior independent of environmental influences. Brain injury, depending on nature and degree, may alter normal nature-nurture interactions. However, in a biologically based disorder such as dyslexia, for which brain differences and genetic variations have been widely reported in the research literature (for review, see Berninger & Richards, 2002), many studies are pointing to plasticity of the brain in response to instruction, as illustrated in Figure 5.4; also see Posner and Rothbart (2007).

Additionally, a failure to appreciate the impact of environmental and socioeconomic factors may lead to inappropriate conclusions about children referred for special education services. For example, if a young examinee is raised primarily in a non-English speaking home, his or her performance on tests normed on children from primarily English speaking homes will have a direct impact on the interpretability of the test results for both linguistic and nonlinguistic skills, such as "executive functions," as well. A child reared in a home with minimal discipline or lenient attitudes to impulsive, aggressive, or even illegal behaviors may never have learned that one needs to control one's own behavior. The interpretation of the meaning of impaired functioning or low tests scores can only accurately reflect diagnosis and brain-behavior relationships when environmental, motivational, and linguistic background factors are accounted for in the interpretation (e.g., identifying Spanish speaking children as Intellectually Disabled based solely on test results normed on English speakers when the correct diagnosis is ESL).

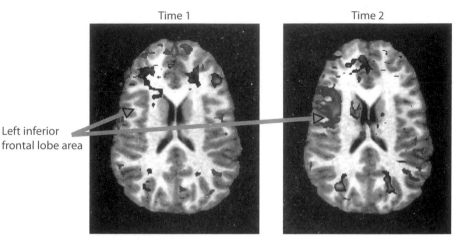

Pseudoword Reading Score: 23   33

Figure 5.4   fMRI Activation and Pseudoword Reading Score
Despite biological basis of dyslexia, specialized teaching can normalize functional brain activation. For example, brain activation normalized (see arrows) and word attack score improved following specialized treatment (see Richards et al., 2006a); also functional temporal connectivity from this left region to comparable brain region on right and middle frontal gyrus (working memory) normalized after specialized treatment (Richards and Berninger, 2007). Provided by Todd L. Richards, P.I., Learning Disability Center, University of Washington.

WHAT DO YOU THINK NEUROSCIENCE HAS TO OFFER LAWS AND POLICIES ASSOCIATED WITH LEARNING DISABILITY DETERMINATION?

Neuroscientists in collaboration with other disciplines have been unraveling the biological basis of many different kinds of educationally handicapping conditions, including but not restricted to learning disabilities and ranging from low incidence, severely handicapping to high incidence, moderately to mildly handicapping conditions. Learning disabilities are challenging to investigate scientifically because they are: (a) heterogeneous, (b) are not well defined, (c) exhibit high rates of comorbidities (e.g., Reading and Writing Disorders), and (d) are not well differentiated from other neurogenetic developmental disorders that exhibit similar behavioral expression but different etiologies. For example, different neurogenetic pathways (e.g., fragile X and dyslexia) can lead to the same measurable outcome (e.g., low reading achievement). Alternatively, similar behavioral expression may not be of neurogenetic origin—for example, children who struggle to learn to read because their first language is not the language of instruction or who lack oral and written language exposure and stimulation in the home.

Neuroscience, like any science, requires operational definitions of what is being studied so that others can replicate the studies and know to whom the results generalize. Many of the problems with the original federal special education legislation were related to defining learning disability on the basis of what learning disability is not rather than on what specific learning disabilities are. Because research is pointing to heterogeneity in genotypic basis of reading disability (e.g., Raskind et al., 2005), it is premature to enact laws and government policies that provide legal regulations for diagnosing and qualifying students as having a learning disability (a label model, bottom figure in Fig. 5.1) without evidence-based diagnoses with treatment relevance (middle figure in Fig. 5.1). When time permits, comprehensive assessment of the individual with results expressed as a profile with strengths and weaknesses highlighted (top figure in Fig. 5.1) may contribute to planning, conducting, and evaluating for differentiated instruction, whether or not a student qualifies for special education services (bottom figure Fig. 5.1). The recently revised flexible approach for thinking professionals will allow the various professions involved directly or indirectly in the education of students with specific learning disabilities to draw on current scientific knowledge as well as the art of implementing such knowledge into practice. Neuroscientific studies of learning disorders inform the clinician as to what brain-based cognitive processes are likely to be affected in specific disorders (e.g., phonology, orthography, morphology, and working memory for Reading Disorder), thus enabling the clinician to measure the appropriate skills necessary to make a diagnosis. Without the scientific literature to support the diagnosis, clinicians resort to a "shot-gun" approach to assessment, measuring all sorts of skills but not the ones critical to making the correct diagnosis.

Expert scientific-practitioner knowledge cannot be reduced to formulas that nonexperts can apply to achieve the same results. The route from neuroscientific knowledge to professional practice should not go directly to law and government but rather be mediated via the various professions involved in education. The recommended flow is summarized in this model:

Scientific Knowledge → Professions and Profession-Specific Practitioners → Legal Accountability

At the same time, accountability is important and lawyers may need to get involved if a reasonable amount of student progress is not made (Fig. 5.2), but reasonable progress may depend on knowledge of the typical developmental trajectories for specific kinds of learning disabilities. Also, affected individuals do have civil rights and the government should have policies to ensure these rights are not violated.

Federal laws and policies should require that multiple disciplines contribute their professional knowledge to the diagnosis and treatment of specific learning disabilities. The professions involved in diagnosis of students with specific learning disabilities include psychology, speech and language services, physical therapy, occupational therapy, and medicine. The professions involved in treatment of students with specific learning disabilities are general and special education teachers. Except for education, each of these professions has (a) required preservice course work on the brain and neuroscience and (b) recognized professional bodies that regulate the professional training, continuing education, and certification or licensure of its members. Implementation of evidence-based practices in general and special education for students with learning disabilities may benefit from (a) inclusion of course work on neuroscience in the education of teachers and (b) enhancing teaching as a profession.

In conclusion, as new, relevant, neuroscience research findings are reported, they should be added to the preservice and inservice curriculum of all the professions involved in education and translated by those professions into best practices for their professions. This knowledge is not directly translatable into legal or federal regulations and first requires translation into application by specific professions for specific diagnostic or treatment purposes. Not all reading, writing, and math problems are the same and evidence-based diagnosis and treatment requires professional judgment and expertise that cannot be captured in law in a way that generalizes to all accommodations the systems-level variables require to meet the needs of the individual (Fig. 5.3). Berninger (2006a) described a professional model that was in place before the federal regulations that had flexibility for differentiated instruction without an overbearing amount of paperwork and legal regulations. Nothing in federal or state law makes it illegal to implement professional practices that prevent severe learning disabilities through *proactive* assessment and treatment of reading, writing, and math problems.

Thus, in response to the first question posed by the editors, we raise three more questions. First, how can neuroscience research be translated into law if researchers cannot agree on how to define the specific kinds of learning disabilities that occur in the general population? Second, in an era when educators are expected to use evidence-based instructional practices, would it not make sense to also expect and allow use of evidence-based definitions for specific learning disabilities for diagnosis and treatment planning? Third, how can schools move beyond a purely labeling assessment approach for qualifying students for special education services (bottom of Fig. 5.1) to an evidence-based constellation approach to differential diagnosis and treatment planning (middle of Fig. 5.1) within a model of comprehensive assessment (top of Fig. 5.1)?

WHAT DO YOU THINK NEUROSCIENCE HAS TO OFFER THE ASSESSMENT AND IDENTIFICATION OF LEARNING DISABILITIES?

Findings of the University of Washington Multidisciplinary Learning Disabilities Center Research Program, which began in 1995 and combined brain imaging, family genetics (phenotyping and genotyping), and instructional treatment studies, are used as an example to illustrate how neuroscience can contribute to the diagnosis of specific learning disabilities. From this multidisciplinary approach grounded in neuroscience and molecular biology as well as behavioral expression of specific learning disabilities affecting acquisition of written language emerged evidence-based definitions for *dysgraphia* (impaired handwriting with or without impaired spelling), *dyslexia* (impaired word decoding and spelling), and *OWL LD* (impaired oral *and* written-language learning disability). None of these specific learning disabilities affecting written language is diagnosed on the basis of a single measure or single discrepancy; rather, each is based on a constellation or a set of phenotypic measures that include cognitive, linguistic, neuropsychological, and reading and writing measures. Common to all of these specific learning disabilities is impairment in one or more components of working memory (word-form storage, phonological and orthographic loops, and executive functions including inhibition and supervisory attention). Specific to each of them is impaired orthographic coding + or − grapho-motor planning (dysgraphia), orthographic and phonological coding + or − oral-motor planning (dyslexia), and orthographic, phonological, morphological/syntactic coding + or − oral-motor planning (OWL LD) (Berninger et al., 2008). The instructional studies identified, based on monitoring response to intervention, effective instructional treatments for dysgraphia and dyslexia (Berninger & Abbott, 2003). Without the assessment leading to the diagnosis, professionals do not know which writing and/or reading component to treat and how to develop specialized instruction that takes into account orthographic, phonological, morphological, syntactic, and grapho- or oral-motor planning problems.

The first clues about the common working-memory impairment came from the structural MRI studies showing children with dyslexia have anomalies in brain structures associated with phonological loop and executive functions (Eckert et al., 2003) and word-form storage (Eckert et al., 2005). Subsequent functional connectivity studies, which set seed points in the same regions of structural anomalies identified by Eckert et al. (2003), found impaired functional connectivity (temporal coordination) emanating from the same brain regions (Stanberry et al., 2006). Also, fMRI studies found anomalies in brain activation associated with tasks involving phonological, orthographic, and morphological word-form storage and processing

(Richards, Aylward, Berninger et al., 2006; Richards et al., 2005). Pheno-typing studies in the family genetics project confirmed that dyslexia was characterized by impaired phonological, orthographic, and morphological word forms, phonological loop, and executive functions (Berninger et al., 2001; Berninger et al., 2006). Links between some of these components and genotypes in our sample have now been identified (Berninger et al., 2008).

A complete program for diagnosing and treating these written-language disabilities, based on a conceptual model validated in this neuroscience, genetics, and instructional research, is available in Berninger (2007a, 2007c). A program for diagnosing and treating dyscalculia and identifying other kinds of problems in learning math concepts, which is based on research at the University of Washington and elsewhere, has also been developed (Berninger, 2007b, 2007c). For additional information on evidence-based differential diagnosis and treatment, see Berninger (2001, 2004, 2006a, in press), Berninger and O'Donnell (2004), and Berninger, Dunn, and Alper (2004).

HOW WILL FUTURE DEVELOPMENTS IN NEUROSCIENCE AFFECT HOW WE CLASSIFY AND INTERVENE WITH LEARNING DISABILITIES?

Neuroscience and genetics research findings are increasing rapidly. Parents are likely in the not-so-distant future to show up at Individual Education Plan (IEP) meetings with brain images and genotyping results attached to independent evaluations. Such assessment findings are most likely to influence educational practice in the long run if shown to have treatment validity. That is, when combined with progress monitoring of response to instruction, do more students improve in their reading, writing, and/or math skills after assessment and treatment procedures based on neuroscience research were introduced? Assessment and treatment approaches that have treatment validity are cost-effective in the long run for the student population in general. However, schools should also be mindful of the rare, unusual learning disabilities that may be more treatment resistant and more likely to lead to legal proceedings if not treated successfully. Thus, evaluation of treatment validity will need single-subject studies as well as meta-analyses of large-scale intervention studies. Moreover, systems-level variables (Fig. 5.3; e.g., relationship problems between student and teacher or student and peers or illness in the family) may interfere with response to evidence-based interventions.

The combined results of neuropsychological, academic, and psychological testing combined with imaging and genetics provide a stronger model for accurate diagnosis than any of the individual components in and of themselves. A child identified with reading problems without the genetic profile consistent with such a diagnosis forces the diagnostician to look further into the problem. Perhaps the issues are environmental or perhaps the child had a brain injury causing damage to areas inclusive of those related to reading but also incorporating other areas. These individual differences in the manifestation of the disorder should, at least in theory, lead one to proceed with a different course of intervention appropriate to the causal factors and profiles of cognitive strengths and weaknesses. If, in fact, genetic typing of individuals at risk for reading, writing, or language disorders becomes well established, then it would not be unexpected if large-scale screening and intervention programs were established based on these medical screening procedures. This approach to prevention would change the way that the school psychologist interacts with the system (e.g., assessing and intervening with much younger children) and views the families of children with genetic and nongenetic-based learning problems.

HOW DO YOU RECONCILE RTI AS A MEANS OF DIAGNOSIS OF LD WITH KNOWLEDGE FROM THE CLINICAL NEUROSCIENCES?

Measures that have been validated in research for defining the constellation of phenotypes (linked to genotypes) for specific learning disabilities are relevant to the diagnosis. Response to intervention (RTI) should not be used alone to diagnose learning disability (LD) for three reasons. First, even typically developing students show normal variation in response to the same instruction (Berninger & Abbott, 1992). Second, even at-risk readers and writers who improved in reading and writing showed normal variation in the set of measures of reading and writing and related skills on which they improved (Abbott et al., 1997). Third, failure to respond to instruction simply signals that another approach to instruction should be brainstormed, implemented, evaluated, and if necessary revised. These are the steps of problem-solving consultation. Evaluating response to instruction has been and always will be the gold standard for exemplary teaching. Master teachers assess prior knowledge before teaching (e.g., identifying instructional levels via criterion-referenced informal inventories), response during instruction (e.g., probes at end of lessons), or over time (e.g., class-wide end of a unit test in text books; school-wide CBM at beginning, middle, and end of school year; district-wide group-administered achievement or high-stakes tests given district-wide). The results of these measures of response to instruction should be used to evaluate individual student progress and school-wide local school curriculum. District-administered group tests such as high stakes can be used to evaluate district curriculum for the student body in general in the specific district (Fig. 5.2).

WHAT ROLE DOES NEUROPSYCHOLOGY HAVE TO PLAY IN THE DIAGNOSIS OF LD?

Neuropsychology plays an important role in Comprehensive Assessment (top figure in Fig. 5.1) and Constellations for Specific Learning Disabilities (middle figure in Fig. 5.1). For comprehensive assessment, we recommend obtaining assessment data for five domains of development in order to rule out other conditions that would make a diagnosis of specific learning disability inappropriate and possibly identify a more appropriate diagnosis (for further information, see Berninger, 2007c):

- Cognition and Memory
- Receptive and Expressive Language
- Fine and Gross Motor
- Attention and Executive Function
- Social and Emotional Function

Neuropsychology has generated many of the measures that have been validated for diagnosing specific learning disabilities involving written language. For example, rapid automatic naming (RAN), which assesses the phonological loop of working memory (Berninger, 2007c; Berninger et al., 2006), has been shown to identify a core impairment in dyslexia that is invisible without neuropsychological assessment—namely two classes of response across rows of RAN: (a) steady slow, and (b) slow and slower (Amtmann, Abbott, & Berninger, 2006). These classes of responding over time have treatment validity for predicting daily spelling during composing in response to a 4-month spelling intervention (Amtmann, Abbott, & Berninger, in press). Normally, naming speed increases with practice across rows, but affected individuals with impaired phonological loop in working memory have difficulty in sustaining effortful mental activity in working memory even when the stimuli are highly familiar. Holdnack developed a psychometric approach to assessing whether students with dyslexia show impairment in change in naming time over rows on RAN (see PAL II RW manual for administration and scoring, Berninger, 2007a). Other promising neuropsychological measures assess Executive Functions (e.g., Inhibition on Color Word-Form, Delis, Kaplan, & Kramer, 2001; see Berninger et al., 2006) and Rapid Automatic Switching (Berninger, 2007a), a measure of supervisory attention for switching mental set. RAS was the best predictor in theory-driven hierarchical linear regression of literacy outcomes in a longitudinal study of typically developing students and in a study of students with dyslexia (Altemeier, Abbott, & Berninger, 2007).

In addition to providing a brain-based model for diagnosing learning problems, neuropsychological assessment allows for a broader understanding of the child as a whole rather than confined to the disability. For example, a child diagnosed with a learning disorder may experience concomitant difficulties with social interactions. Without assessing the nature of the social impairments more thoroughly one might assume a causal link between the poor learning skills and the impaired social relations. In actuality, the social problems may be caused by a different set of cognitive variables such as inability to recognize emotions, or poor theory of mind skills, or inhibitory control problems. The child's poor behavioral regulation may be interfering with the ability to actively participate in the intervention designed for the disability and these problems need to be targeted as part of the overall intervention. Assessment of comorbid diagnoses and behavioral issues enables the clinician to more accurately identify the primary diagnosis and how comorbid diagnoses and cognitive limitations manifest as behavioral and learning impediments in addition to the core diagnosis.

WHAT ROLE DOES NEUROPSYCHOLOGY HAVE TO PLAY IN DESIGNING INTERVENTIONS IN THE CONTEXT OF RTI?

Neonatal assessment of some developmental disorders like PKU and deafness are now routinely assessed at birth so that if a newborn is affected treatment can begin immediately; as a result the incidence of Mental Retardation related to PKU and language-comprehension problems related to deafness has been reduced. Likewise, universal screening of students for those at risk for writing, reading, oral language, and math disabilities followed by evidence-based assessments could greatly reduce the incidence and severity of academic learning problems (Berninger, 2006b). In designing these interventions for the lowest achievers across many classrooms in many schools and several school districts, we turned to neuropsychology for conceptualizing the nature of the initial interventions that brought half the children up to or above grade level in one school year in reading (Berninger, Abbott, et al., 2000) and spelling (Berninger et al., 1998), and the subsequent interventions the following school year that brought the other half up to grade level in reading (Berninger et al., 2002) and spelling (Berninger, Vaughan et al., 2000). For both reading and spelling the gains were maintained at the beginning and end of the second school year. These interventions taught all levels of language close in time (subword, word, and text) to overcome working-memory constraints; in addition, teachers modeled cross word-form mapping and its transfer to decoding or spelling words and taught executive function strategies for independent, self-regulated reading or writing (Berninger et al., 2008).

Brain activation normalized in response to specialized instruction for students with dyslexia in the summer following grades 4, 5, or 6 (Berninger et al., 2007) in the left inferior frontal gyrus (see Fig. 5.4, which has been adapted to show brain activation on the left side of the image in contrast to the convention of showing it on the right). However, not only the region of interest showed normalization of activation following specialized instruction, but other changes in temporal coordination—that is, functional connectivity—of relevant neural networks occurred as well (Richards & Berninger, 2007). A study combining brain imaging (Richards et al., in press) and treatment (Berninger et al., 2007, Study 2) showed the benefit of engaging hands in improving phonological awareness of spoken words and phonological decoding of written words. Hand activity presumably influenced postcentral gyrus activation, which in turn had an effect on the nearby supramarginal gyrus that is known to be involved in phonological processing. Although neuroscience does not translate directly from brain scan to lesson plan, it does inform and validate instructional research for improving the reading and writing skills of students with specific learning disabilities.

REFERENCES

Abbott, S., Reed, L., Abbott, R., & Berninger, V. (1997). Year-long balanced reading/writing tutorial: A design experiment used for dynamic assessment. *Learning Disability Quarterly, 20,* 249–263.

Altemeier, L., Abbott, R., & Berninger, V. (2007). Contribution of executive functions to reading and writing in typical literacy development and dyslexia. *Journal of Clinical and Experimental Neuropsychology.*

Amtmann, D., Abbott, R., & Berninger, V. (2006). Mixture growth models for RAN and RAS row by row: Insight into the reading system at work over time. *Reading and Writing. An Interdisciplinary Journal.* Published Springer online: 28 November 2006.

Amtmann, D., Abbott, R., & Berninger, V. (in press). Identifying and predicting classes of response to explicit, phonological spelling instruction during independent composing. *Journal of Learning Disabilities.*

Berninger, V. (2001). Understanding the lexia in dyslexia. *Annals of Dyslexia, 51,* 23–48. Reprinted in Hebrew, 2002.

Berninger, V. (2004). Understanding the graphia in dysgraphia. In D. Dewey & D. Tupper (Eds.), *Developmental motor disorders: A neuropsychological perspective* (pp. 328–350). New York: Guilford.

Berninger, V. (2006a). A developmental approach to learning disabilities. In I. Siegel & A. Renninger (Eds.), *Handbook of child psychology. Vol. IV: Child psychology and practice* (pp. 420–452). New York: Wiley.

Berninger, V. (2006b). Research-supported ideas for implementing reauthorized IDEA with intelligent and professional psychological services. *Psychology in the Schools, 43,* 781–797.

Berninger, V. (in press). Defining and differentiating dyslexia, dysgraphia, and language learning disability within a working memory model. In E. Silliman &

M. Mody (Eds.), *Language impairment and reading disability-interactions among brain, behavior, and experience.* New York: Guilford.

Berninger, V. (2007a). *PAL II Diagnostic Test for Reading and Writing* (2nd ed.). *PAL II RW.* San Antonio, TX: The Psychological Corporation.

Berninger, V. (2007b). *PAL II Diagnostic Test for Math. PAL II M.* San Antonio, TX: The Psychological Corporation.

Berninger, V. (2007c). *PAL II User's Guide* (CD). San Antonio, TX: The Psychological Corporation.

Berninger, V., & Abbott, R. (1992). Unit of analysis and constructive processes of the learner: Key concepts for educational neuropsychology. *Educational Psychologist, 27,* 223–242.

Berninger, V., Abbott, R., Brooksher, R., Lemos, Z., Ogier, S., Zook, D., et al. (2000). A connectionist approach to making the predictability of English orthography explicit to at-risk beginning readers: Evidence for alternative, effective strategies. *Developmental Neuropsychology, 17,* 241–271.

Berninger, V., Abbott, R., Thomson, J., & Raskind, W. (2001). Language phenotype for reading and writing disability: A family approach. *Scientific Studies in Reading, 5,* 59–105.

Berninger, V., Abbott, R., Thomson, J., Wagner, R., Swanson, H. L., Wijsman, E., et al. (2006). Modeling developmental phonological core deficits within a working-memory architecture in children and adults with developmental dyslexia. *Scientific Studies in Reading, 10,* 165–198.

Berninger, V., Abbott, R., Vermeulen, K., Ogier, S., Brooksher, R., Zook, D., et al. (2002). Comparison of faster and slower responders to early intervention in reading: Differentiating features of their language profiles. *Learning Disability Quarterly, 25,* 59–76.

Berninger, V., & Abbott, S. (2003). *PAL Research-Supported Reading and Writing Lessons.* San Antonio, TX: The Psychological Corporation.

Berninger, V., Dunn, A., & Alper, T. (2004). Integrated models for branching assessment, instructional assessment, and profile assessment. In A. Prifitera, D. Saklofske, L. Weiss, & E. Rolfhus (Eds.), *WISC-IV Clinical use and interpretation* (pp. 151–185). San Diego: Academic Press.

Berninger, V., & O'Donnell, L. (2004). Research-supported differential diagnosis of specific learning disabilities. In A. Prifitera, D. Saklofske, L. Weiss, & E. Rolfhus (Eds.), *WISC-IV Clinical use and interpretation* (pp. 189–233). San Diego: Academic Press.

Berninger, V., Raskind, W., Richards, T., Abbott, R., & Stock, P. (in press). A multidisciplinary approach to understanding developmental dyslexia within working-memory architecture: Genotypes, phenotypes, brain, and instruction. *Developmental Neuropsychology.*

Berninger, V., & Richards, T. (2002). *Brain literacy for educators and psychologists.* New York: Academic Press.

Berninger, V., Vaughan, K., Abbott, R., Brooks, A., Abbott, S., Reed, E., et al. (1998). Early intervention for spelling problems: Teaching spelling units of varying size within a multiple connections framework. *Journal of Educational Psychology, 90,* 587–605.

Berninger, V., Vaughan, K., Abbott, R., Brooks, A., Begay, K., Curtin, G., et al. (2000). Language-based spelling instruction: Teaching children to make multiple connections between spoken and written words. *Learning Disability Quarterly, 23,* 117–135.

Berninger, V., Winn, W., Stock, P., Abbott, R., Eschen, K., Lin, C., et al. (2007). Tier 3 specialized writing instruction for students with dyslexia. *Reading and Writing: An Interdisciplinary Journal.* Printed Springer online: May 15, 2007.

Delis, D. C., Kaplan, E., & Kramer, J. H. (2001). *The Delis-Kaplan executive function system: Examiner's manual.* San Antonio: The Psychological Corporation.

Eckert, M., Leonard, C., Richards, T., Aylward, E., Thomson, J., & Berninger, V. (2003). Anatomical correlates of dyslexia: Frontal and cerebellar findings. *Brain, 126* (no. 2), 482–494.

Eckert, M., Leonard, C., Wilke, M., Eckert, M., Richards, T., Richards, A., & Berninger, V. (2005). Anatomical signature of dyslexia in children: Unique information from manual-based and voxel-based morphometry brain measures. *Cortex, 41,* 304–315.

Posner, M., & Rothbart, M. K. (2007). *Educating the human brain.* Washington DC: American Psychological Association.

Raskind, W., Igo, R., Chapman, N., Berninger, V., Thomson, J., Matsushita, M., et al. (2005). A genome scan in multigenerational families with dyslexia: Identification of a novel locus on chromosome 2q that contributes to phonological decoding efficiency. *Molecular Psychiatry, 10*(7): 699–711.

Richards, T., Aylward, E., Berninger, V., Field, K., Parsons, A., Richards, A., et al. (2006). Individual fMRI activation in orthographic mapping and morpheme mapping after orthographic or morphological spelling treatment in child dyslexics. *Journal of Neurolinguistics, 19,* 56–86.

Richards, T., Aylward E., Raskind, W., Abbott, R., Field, K., Parsons, A., et al. (2006). Converging evidence for triple word form theory in children with dyslexia. *Developmental Neuropsychology, 30,* 547–589.

Richards, T., & Berninger, V. (2007). Abnormal fMRI connectivity in children with dyslexia during a phoneme task: Before but not after treatment. *Journal of Neurolinguistics.* Posted online Springer.

Richards, T., Berninger, V., Nagy, W., Parsons, A., Field, K., & Richards, A. (2005). Brain activation during language task contrasts in children with and without dyslexia: Inferring mapping processes and assessing response to spelling instruction. *Educational and Child Psychology, 22*(2), 62–80.

Richards, T., Berninger, V., Winn, W., Stock, S., Wagner, R., Muse, A., et al. (2007, November). fMRI activation in children with dyslexia during pseudoword aural repeat and visual decode: Before and after instruction. *Neuropsychology.*

Stanberry L., Richards, T., Berninger, V., Nandy, R., Aylward, E., Maravilla, K., et al. (2006). Low frequency signal changes reflect differences in functional connectivity between good readers and dyslexics during continuous phoneme mapping. *Magnetic Resonance Imaging, 24,* 217–229.

6

Compatibility of Neuropsychology and RTI in the Diagnosis and Assessment of Learning Disabilities

Cynthia A. Riccio

There is considerable debate regarding the current movement to use Response to Intervention (RTI) as a means of defining learning disabilities and reducing rates of special education placement (Fuchs & Deshler, 2007; Fuchs et al., 2003; Gresham, 2006). Within the context of this debate, the use of formal assessment procedures, including the use of intelligence tests and standardized achievement tests consistent with the ability-achievement discrepancy model, is often viewed as the antithesis of RTI. Rather than an either–or discussion, four specific issues related to RTI and formal assessment as conceptualized from the perspective of neuropsychology will be addressed herein. Initially, the similarities and ways in which neuropsychology—including what is known about learning disabilities from the perspective of neuroscience, based on the premise that learning disabilities are due to dysfunction of the central nervous system (Hammill et al., 1981)—and the use of RTI as a means of diagnosis are presented. With this as a foundation, the second section addresses the ways in which neuropsychology and neuroscience can improve upon RTI in the identification and assessment process for learning disabilities. This is then expanded in the section on the role of neuropsychology in the diagnosis of learning disabilities. Finally, the fourth section addresses the role of neuropsychology in the design of interventions.

HOW DO YOU RECONCILE RTI AS A MEANS OF DIAGNOSIS OF LD WITH KNOWLEDGE FROM THE CLINICAL NEUROSCIENCES?

The lack of response to intervention (or resistance to intervention) as an indicator that the individual has a disability is borne out by the evidence of a very similar phenotype of children with reading disabilities and adults with reading disabilities (Flowers, Wood, & Naylor, 1991; Galaburda, 2005; Pennington, 1995; Shaywitz et al., 2003). In particular, one characteristic of both children and adults with reading disabilities is their difficulty in decoding and subsequently slower reading rate (Cardoso-Martins & Pennington, 2004; Gross-Glenn et al., 1991; Snowling, 2000); these differences persist despite interventions and despite the use of compensatory approaches. Clearly, of the individual subskills required in reading, phonological awareness, rapid naming of letters, and oral language capabilities are implicated in success in learning to read (Snow, Burns, & Griffin, 1998), or, conversely, in difficulty learning to read (Vellutino et al., 2004).

So how does this compare with a neuropsychological approach? The neuropsychological approach to assessment and case conceptualization incorporates information from various behavioral domains believed to be related to functional neurological systems, including those responsible for reading, math, written, and oral expression (Luria, 1980). The discussion here will focus on reading as that is where most of the research has occurred, but similar arguments would apply for other academic areas. Research consistently indicates patterns of structural anomalies and functional differences in children and adults with dyslexia. For example, both adults and children with dyslexia have consistently been found to have smaller regions in language areas (left planum, bilateral insular regions, and right anterior region) (Foster et al., 2002; Hugdahl et al., 2003; Paul et al., 2006; Pugh et al., 2000; Shaywitz et al., 2003). The variations in processes and structures best support a conceptualization of reading as involving a widely distributed functional system, with any impairment or developmental deficit in the system resulting in distinct patterns of reading failure (Shaywitz & Shaywitz, 1999, 2005). It is fairly well acknowledged that this functional system subserves not only reading, but a variety of component subskills (e.g., Shaywitz & Shaywitz, 1999, 2005; Simos et al., 2005).

One of the major premises of RTI is that, for some children who have difficulty with the approach being used classwide (Tier 1), all that is needed is a more intensive intervention (Tier 2) using a supplemental, evidence-based intervention. The identification of a learning disability occurs only for those children who do not benefit from the more intensive intervention(s) (Fuchs & Deshler, 2007). A good deal of the RTI research to date focuses on early reading and the development of phonological decoding or ability to identify rhyme in beginning readers. This is consistent with research that adults with dyslexia showed the greatest differences as compared to good readers on activities that involved sounding out the words (converting letters to speech sounds, phonological tasks) rather than making visual matches (Shaywitz et al., 1998).

The use of RTI as a means of identifying learning disabilities implies that failure to attain specific academic skills when provided with high-quality, evidence-based instruction in an intensive manner is sufficient evidence to indicate that a disability exists. This premise presumes some plasticity of the brain and that attaining skills has an effect on brain function (Richards et al., 2006); this potential for acquisition of reading skills to have an effect on structure and function (i.e., areas of the brain activated) has been documented. For example, functional magnetic resonance imaging (fMRI) of children and adults engaged in reading tasks show developmental shifts in regions of the brain activated (Simos et al., 2007). These changes are believed to be associated with increased reading ability and automaticity (Poldrack et al., 1999; Turkeltaub et al., 2003), or developmental maturity of specific brain structures (Chugani, 1999). Moreover, successful reading interventions in children at risk of reading disability (what would be considered Tier 2 under RTI) have been found to result in increased response in left-hemisphere posterior regions on reading tasks (Richards et al., 2006; Simos et al., 2002; Temple et al., 2000). This reflects a more "normalized" pattern of activation. Additional studies also indicate the potential for remediation programs to affect patterns of brain function (Simos et al., 2007). Unfortunately, because multiple interventions are occurring simultaneously, which interventions have this effect for which children is not yet known and more focused research is needed in this area. Two areas often targeted at Tier 2 involve phonological processing and rhyme detection.

Neurobiology of Phonological Processing

Developmentally, the initial step in learning to read is recognition of words based on visual features or context; the child then begins to use a few prominent letters as phonetic cues (Turkeltaub et al., 2005). This progresses to full understanding of mapping of print to sound and decoding of words letter by letter. As vocabulary and automaticity improve, letter sequences are identified as wholes and new words are read by analogy to those previously learned. It has been posited that there are two possible reading routes. The phonological decoding route is predominantly associated with words that are infrequent, new, and spelled according to phonetic rules, while the direct retrieval route is associated with reading of words that are short, frequent, and irregular. In typical or normal readers, both of these routes are simultaneously activated.

Turkeltaub and colleagues (2003) found that phonological awareness, phonetic retrieval, and phonological working memory mapped onto different cortical areas, and that three major areas of the brain (left superior temporal cortex, left inferior frontal gyrus, left ventral extrastriate cortex) were involved in learning to read. Using fMRI, brain correlates to reading words and pseudowords supported the dual-route model of reading acquisition with pseudowords requiring longer processing times than real words (Heim et al., 2005). With serial word reading and both positron emission tomography (PET) and regional cerebral blood flow (rCBF), indications are that adults with dyslexia with deficits in word recognition evidence less activation in the right posterior cortex as compared to normals (Hynd et al., 1987). When those deficits were in phonological processing, there was less activation bilaterally, suggesting that both hemispheres are involved in reading (Hynd et al., 1987). Other studies further support the importance of phonological processing and differences in brain activation in those with dyslexia as compared to nondisabled readers (Shaywitz & Shaywitz, 2006).

Neuroscience of Rhyme Detection

A second area often associated with early reading problems and potentially targeted with Tier 2 interventions is related to ability to detect rhyme (Cao et al., 2006; Rumsey et al., 1992; Savage & Frederickson, 2006). On tasks of rhyme detection, results implicated the tempoparietal regions, such that nondisabled readers demonstrated activation in the left parietal region near the angular gyrus, the left middle temporal region (e.g., Wernicke's area), in the left posterior frontal region, the right middle temporal, and the right parietal area. In contrast, adults with dyslexia failed to activate the left temporoparietal region on the rhyming task; this was associated with decreased performance on the rhyming task as well. Additional neurological correlates to rhyme detection have also been identified (Cao et al., 2006; Khateb et al., 2007). The extent to which interventions targeting early reading or rhyme detection impact on these patterns of brain activation is not known at this time.

Progress Monitoring in RTI

A major contribution of RTI as a process in the identification of learning disabilities is the frequent monitoring of performance to determine growth or change in targeted behaviors (Fuchs & Deshler, 2007). Neuropsychological assessment with children, like RTI, is concerned with documenting changes in behavior and development (Hynd & Willis, 1988). In conjunction with RTI, change is monitored via benchmarks or cut-scores in specific subskills; benchmarks in RTI often emphasize fluency (i.e., the speed and accuracy with which the student can complete a specific task) such as reading a passage, reading a word list, or completing math computations (Ardoin et al., 2004; Hintze & Christ, 2004). Specific measures have been developed for this purpose (Good, Simmons, & Kame'enui, 2001), or curriculum-based measures may be implemented. Speed of processing has been found to differentiate fluent and nonfluent readers (Powell et al., 2007; Semrud-Clikeman, Guy, & Griffin, 2000). The use of a fluency-based measure as part of the assessment process also is important from a neuropsychological perspective in that slow processing or difficulty retrieving information rapidly may be one effect of some neurological disorders, including problems with executive function (Blair & Razza, 2007; Gaskins, Satlow, & Pressley, 2007). Further, this slow rate of processing or decreased level of automaticity likely has cumulative effects on the educational process, not only in the area being assessed by RTI, but across areas and skills.

WHAT DO YOU THINK NEUROSCIENCE HAS TO OFFER TO THE ASSESSMENT AND IDENTIFICATION OF LEARNING DISABILITIES?

When conceptualized as multitiered intervention, RTI provides important information on how the student responds (or does not respond) to specific interventions. As such, RTI is a valid component in the assessment and identification of learning disabilities; it places an emphasis on academic instruction and specific academic objectives, rather than on perceptual processes or the cause of the difficulties observed. This is not an entirely new concept, with an emphasis on specific academic skills in the discussion of learning disabilities being advocated for more than 25 years (Hutton, Dubes, & Muir, 1992). At the same time, neuropsychological techniques have been used in the assessment of children for special education (Gersten, Clarke, & Mazzocco, 2007; Semrud-Clikeman, 2005) and have resulted in improved understanding of learning disabilities (Gersten et al., 2007; Riccio & Hynd, 1996), as well as other disorders. Moreover, there is evidence to suggest that cognitive ability is relevant to the diagnosis of learning disabilities and that environmental and psychosocial factors may be more salient for those children with lower abilities (Wadsworth et al., 2000). The arguments for the incorporation of neuropsychological methods in the assessment process focus on the desire to integrate cognitive and behavioral data, thus increasing the ability to deal with the multidimensionality of individuals (Riccio & Reynolds, 1998), and creating a unified or holistic picture of the student's functioning.

With recognition that severe reading disabilities may be attributable to deficient neurological processes (Paul et al., 2006; Shaywitz et al., 2003, 1998; Simos et al., 2005)—as well as recognition that normal reading development involves a dual-route, sequential, bottom-up process (Frith, 1985)—the importance of focusing on more than a single skill or approach is apparent. In effect, normal reading requires a combination of logographic (simultaneous) and phonologic (sequential) processing (Van Orden, 1987; Van Orden & Kloos, 2005); excessive dependence (or instructional emphasis) on one of these processes could lead to the individual continuing to use strategies specific to one route exclusively, impeding the normal development of reading (Aaron, 1989). Alternatively, it has been suggested that a more balanced perspective would stress the interactive role of the phonologic, logographic, and orthographic systems (Adams, 1990; Spear-Swerling & Sternberg, 1994). This perspective highlights the interaction of visual, semantic, syntactic, and pragmatic aspects of the reading process rather than focusing on the lower levels of phonologic and logographic processing. Consistent with this perspective, neuropsychological assessment examines individual performance across a range of functional domains including linguistic, perceptual, sensori-motor, attention, memory and learning, executive control/planning, speed of processing, and emotional functioning (Riccio & Reynolds, 1998; Silver et al., 2006). In addition to language processing as a critical component in learning disabilities, working memory and executive function emerge as contributing to difficulties in skill acquisition (Gazzinga, Ivry, & Mangun, 2002; McLean & Hitch, 1999; Semrud-Clikeman et al., 2000; Teeter & Semrud-Clikeman, 1997).

Neuroscience, and particularly neuropsychology, look beyond the failure to attain the specific academic skill in question to the underlying brain-behavior relation that contributes to this failure, and may indicate increased likelihood of failure in attaining other academic, functional, social, or behavioral skills (Riccio, Hynd, & Cohen, 1993; Riccio & Reynolds, 1998). Neuropsychological assessment can be a valuable approach for determining not only deficits, but also individual strengths or intact cognitive functions. Provision of a more holistic assessment can provide information that highlights individual strengths, as well as deficits, as they relate to educational, adaptive, and emotional functioning. A more unified picture of the individual should increase the predictive value of the assessment as it relates to achievement as well as realistic life planning (Riccio et al., 1993; Silver et al., 2006; Teeter & Semrud-Clikeman, 1997). Although there is a presumption with RTI that early intervention will decrease the likelihood of later academic difficulties, there is no attempt to predict or avert difficulties in attaining later skills other than by ensuring that immediately targeted skills are attained.

WHAT ROLE DOES NEUROPSYCHOLOGY HAVE TO PLAY IN THE DIAGNOSIS OF LD?

Fletcher and colleagues (2007) proposed a comprehensive model that includes the consideration of both RTI and neurobiological factors. The first level is conceptualized as the primary manifestation of difficulty as evidenced in the specific skill deficits as might be seen in the acquisition of early reading skills; this presumably occurs in Tier 1. With RTI, this would then generate a Tier 2 intervention in hopes that the student will respond to the intervention (Fuchs & Deshler, 2007). Within the Fletcher et al. model, the secondary level is comprised of child characteristics. These are described as those core cognitive processes that directly impact on academic skills (e.g., phonological processing, memory, automaticity), rather than the academic skills themselves. Related to these processes, in the third level of analysis, the focus is on environmental factors and neurobiological factors. Instructional techniques (including Tier 1 and Tier 2 approaches) would be included in the environmental factors along with psychosocial factors, and presumably factors related to academic ecology. The role of neuropsychology is most evident in the inclusion of core cognitive processes and neurobiological factors in the model. Neurobiological factors include both genetic factors, as well as brain structure and function, and recognize the underlying neurological basis of learning disabilities. This model further provides an interactive framework to represent the various sources of variability that lead to academic outcomes associated with learning disabilities.

Reliance on RTI alone cannot address all the components of this model— RTI only provides information on progress monitoring of a specific skill or subskill as a result of a particular intervention without consideration for the psychosocial factors (e.g., motivation, anxiety), the academic environment beyond the instructional method, or the range of functions that could be impacting on skill acquisition. In addition to incorporating measures of cognitive ability, the range of diagnostic techniques available with neuropsychological assessment extends the range of behaviors or skills that can be sampled using standardized techniques. Comprehensive evaluation that takes into consideration not only individual skills and abilities, core cognitive processes, and neurobiological considerations, but also health, family, and educational context, is critical when making decisions relating to diagnosis, as well as to how and where a given student will be educated (Wodrich, Spencer, & Daley, 2006). How a child responds to specific instructional methods is one piece of information used in case conceptualization from a neuropsychological perspective. Taken together (results of neuropsychological evaluation and student responsiveness to intervention), the resulting conceptualization can meet the requirements of Fletcher and colleagues (2007) that the identification of learning disability must reflect the historical construct of *unexpected underachievement* and not solely be based on the presence of academic deficits.

Historically, one of the standards used to determine if a method or approach to identifying a particular clinical group was sufficient was the ability of that method or approach to differentiate between clinical groups, or between the clinical group in question and a control group. Given the multiple possible explanations for difficulty in learning, as well as the high frequency of disorders that co-occur with learning disabilities, it is imperative to consider all aspects of child functioning when developing a remediation plan (Semrud-Clikeman, 2005). Clearly, one major component of methods used to assess and diagnose learning disabilities, if there is to be a reliable differentiation between learning disability and Mental Retardation, is some consideration of cognitive ability (Wodrich et al., 2006). While arguments can be made that there is no need to differentiate between children who fall in what has traditionally been referred to as the *slow learner* category and children with learning disabilities as both groups evidence similar difficulties and require similar interventions (Stanovich, 1988), there is no empirical evidence to support similar needs, course, or prognosis for these two groups of children with multiple potential problems (Wodrich et al., 2006).

Differential diagnosis of learning disabilities relative to normal controls, as well as other clinical groups, has been conducted (Braze et al., 2007; Bruno et al., 2007; Willcutt et al., 2005). Comparative study of clinical groups with Attention-Deficit/Hyperactivity Disorder (ADHD) and reading disability, for example, indicate that verbal fluency did not differentiate the groups; further, a profile of rapid-naming deficits in conjunction with impaired working memory was indicated for children with co-occurring ADHD and reading disability (Bental & Tirosh, 2007). Rapid naming and fluency are often both used in the benchmarking process of RTI (Good et al., 2001; Speece & Case, 2001); as such, inability to demonstrate "response to intervention" may be indicative of some factor or disability other than specific learning disability. It is particularly important to obtain sufficient information, above and beyond a lack of academic progress over time or RTI, that the cause of that lack of progress is not Mental Retardation (Wodrich et al., 2006) or other circumstance, including Limited English Proficiency (LEP) or status as an English Language Learner (ELL). These differentiations need to be valid and reliable, and not the result of clinical judgment.

WHAT ROLE DOES NEUROPSYCHOLOGY HAVE IN THE DESIGN OF INTERVENTIONS IN THE CONTEXT OF RTI?

In the past 20 years, increased attention has been focused on the need for assessment to inform the intervention-planning process. Assessment data should be linked to the design of intervention programs (Riccio et al., 1993; Riccio & Reynolds, 1998). The decision or design of intervention programs should not be limited to the assignment of a label (or not); Silver et al. (2006) asserted that neuropsychological evaluation answers not only "what" is going on academically or behaviorally, but also the "why" or causal features. RTI presumes the knowing of "why" based on "what" without any additional assessment. Treatment or intervention design from a neuropsychological perspective frequently goes beyond the labeling or placement process to include the identification of specific management or rehabilitation techniques, speech-language interventions, medical management approaches, vocationally related goals, and environmental modifications or physical aspects that need to be addressed (Silver et al., 2006). The neuropsychological perspective leads to better understanding of underlying causes of learning and behavior problems that in turn results in an increased ability to develop appropriate interventions or circumvent future problems. Within the field of neuropsychology, there has been an increase in the activities related to neuropsychological rehabilitation that are multidimensional in nature (Eslinger & Oliveri, 2002).

Neuropsychological models of intervention suggest that treatment for children with specific learning disabilities needs to be comprised of methods that capitalize on the individual child's strengths (intact functions) in conjunction with compensatory strategies (Riccio & Reynolds, 1998). By capitalizing on the child's intact functions or preferred processing or learning style, alternative approaches to instruction can be determined that may result in optimal functioning. The neuropsychological paradigm thus offers an alternative approach to identifying the intervention to be used based on the strengths and weaknesses of the individual child (Riccio & Reynolds, 1998). Again, using the realm of reading and the reading process as subserved by a widely distributed functional system, it is important not only to recognize that there is some deviation or dysfunction in the system, but to identify the parameters of the dysfunction. Furthermore, it is important to determine the best times developmentally for specific remediation programs (Semrud-Clikeman, 2005).

Rehabilitation approaches generally either target underlying impairments as in deficit models or use intact processes or external means to address those functional areas affected (Glisky & Glisky, 2002). From a deficit approach, restoration and optimization approaches target the deficit or underlying impairment for remediation; to some extent this would include many Tier 2 interventions. For example, if phonological decoding deficits are the target, the intervention might include repetition and drill specific to this skill area. The premise of repeated drill and practice to restore or develop an ability is not based on a theoretical premise. From a neuropsychological perspective, it is based on the assumption that repeated stimulation of neuronal connections through drill and practice may potentially result in establishing alternate neuronal pathways or regeneration of damaged structures or pathways. The need to focus on strengths or intact processes comes in part from evidence that previous attempts to address deficits (i.e., the deficit approach) within special education have met with less than optimistic results based on treatment validity studies (Kavale, 1990; Kavale & Forness, 1987). As related to the educational context, the objectives of cognitive approaches involve restoration, or development of, specific skills and abilities, or compensatory training with the ultimate goal of optimizing adjustment and outcome (Eslinger & Oliveri, 2002).

The exclusive emphasis on the underlying impairment ignores those intact functions of the individual; the individual may have strong language skills (suggesting a whole language approach to reading) or strong visual memory (suggesting a sight-word approach as an alternative). Finally, as suggested by the aptitude by treatment interaction studies, there is no evidence that any progress made through the drill and practice generalizes beyond the training situation. A second approach focuses on optimizing the remaining function in the area of the deficit. Although there is a continued goal of restoring or developing that functional ability to the extent feasible, there is more of a focus on refining how the functional capacities that remain can be used (Anderson, 2002). Instead of drill and practice, the emphasis is on alternative instructional approaches, or, as task complexity increases, strategy instruction and metacognitive training. These methods may be most appropriate for individuals with mild to moderate impairments who have sufficient intact abilities to master the strategies or can benefit from alternative approaches.

In contrast to deficit models, compensatory models focus not on the underlying impairment, but on the functional deficits that result from the impairment and how to compensate for the impairment to improve everyday living (Glisky & Glisky, 2002). Compensation approaches identify methods to bypass deficit skills through the use of intact functions or external aids or substitute methods of reaching the same goal (Anderson, 2002). Compensation approaches may include strategy instruction that incorporates intact functions, or in the use of supplemental aids (e.g., texts on audiotape). Approaches that use external aids may be better suited for individuals with severe impairment (i.e., less intact functions). All too often, proponents of one approach to intervention do not consider the potential for additive effects of multiple methods in the intervention process (Freund & Baltes, 1998). Intervention activities need to be designed in a way that assists the individual in moving from a more dependent, externally monitored or supported state, to a more independent, internally supported, and self-regulated state. The selection of specific intervention strategies should be based on the individual's level of environmental dependency, the constellation of preserved and impaired functions, and his or her level of awareness (Mateer, 1999). This combination requires more information than that an individual did not respond to a given intervention.

To develop appropriate interventions, evaluation needs to include assessment of the contexts in which the child currently functions, as well as the increasing demands of the academic context, present and future (Lee & Riccio, 2005). Given the evaluation data on the child, various contexts, and current as well as anticipated future circumstances, specific goals are formulated. For each goal, an adequate approach to intervention is selected and implemented with data kept on performance (i.e., outcome-based measures) to monitor the ongoing effects of the treatment. Generalization strategies also should be developed and implemented from the onset of treatment. Finally, there should be an evaluation of the efficacy of the intervention and determination made about the impact of functioning in natural contexts (Mateer, 1999; Sohlberg & Mateer, 1989). This is not unlike the process of RTI or the process of developing an individualized educational plan; however, the choice of Tier 2 interventions is made with additional information, and the goals and alternative for intervention are expanded beyond the immediate academic or curricular demands.

Research efforts related to evidence-based interventions for use at Tier 2 should include identification of those characteristics that help to predict the success of a specific treatment for a specific individual (i.e., based on cognitive characteristics, behavioral variables, psychopathology, demographic variables, etiology, severity) as well as the deficits (functional and attentional) that are to be targeted. There is a need to look at the extent of generalization and transfer of training of the method over the long term as well as short term.

DISCUSSION

There is little disagreement that intervention procedures may be beneficial to children struggling in the acquisition of a specific skill. The disagreement is in whether a child's response to that intervention is sufficient or necessary for identification or diagnosis of a learning disability (or some other disorder). In effect, there could be multiple reasons why an individual makes progress or fails to make progress, including the choice of the intervention, developmental readiness of the child, or ancillary activities that the child is engaged in. Comprehensive evaluation of children struggling academically has the potential to inform the choice of intervention and to identify both deficit and intact processes. To some extent, with increased technology in neuroscience, not only is it possible to gain a better understanding of the brain-behavior relations required for skill performance, but there is evidence of alteration to structures activated in task performance as a result of intervention and increased skill mastery (Simos et al., 2005). The problem with reliance on RTI arises, however, in that the failure to respond or lack of progress despite intervention does not add to what is known about the nature of the impairment (Wodrich et al., 2006). Comparative study of clinical groups with ADHD and reading disability, for example, indicates that verbal fluency did not differentiate the groups (Bental & Tirosh, 2007). There is a critical need for additional research to determine the contribution of knowledge about core cognitive processes and their relation to effective teaching and learning (Caffrey & Fuchs, 2007). Moreover, the problem may not be with the skill acquisition per se (and therefore amenable to intensive intervention for that skill), but may represent a more permeating aspect of the child (e.g., sluggish tempo) that warrants a more global intervention or basic accommodations that could easily be made in general education (e.g., extended time).

Finally, to rely solely on RTI presumes that there are effective academic interventions, with adequate empirical support, for the full range of skills to be mastered across the curriculum, at all grade levels (Wodrich et al., 2006), and that this approach can be applied regardless of the age of the child. The research evidence to support RTI across age ranges and curricular demands is insufficient at this time (Fuchs & Deshler, 2007). While there are some promising practices that may help students who are struggling in specific areas, there is some indication that even with these programs students who are struggling do not close the gap with their classmates—obviously if programs were identified that would close these gaps, these would be implemented. The argument that special education does not work as evidenced by the fact that the students identified continue to fall behind their same-class peers also demonstrates the lack of knowledge in the area of best or evidence-based interventions. In fact, few promising programs have been identified, predominantly within the reading area; even these may not be equally as matched to each student's needs (Wodrich et al., 2006).

REFERENCES

Aaron, P. G. (1989). *Dylsexia and hyperlexia*. Boston: Klüwer.

Adams, M. J. (1990). *Beginning to read: Thinking and learning about print*. Cambridge, MA: MIT Press.

Anderson, S. W. (2002). Visuospatial impairments. In P. J. Eslinger (Ed.), *Neuropsychological interventions: Clinical research and practice* (pp. 163–181). New York: Guilford.

Ardoin, S. P., Witt, J. C., Suldo, S. M., Connell, J. E., Koenig, J. L., Resetar, J. L., et al. (2004). Examining the incremental benefits of administering a maze and three version one curriculum-based measurement reading probe when conducting universal screening. *School Psychology Review, 33*, 218–233.

Bental, B., & Tirosh, E. (2007). The relationship between attention, executive functions and reading domain abilities in attention deficit hyperactivity disorder and reading disorder: A comparative study. *Journal of Child Psychology and Psychiatry, 48*, 455–463.

Blair, C., & Razza, R. P. (2007). Relating effortful control, executive function, and false belief understanding to emerging math and literacy ability in kindergarten. *Child Development, 78*, 647–663.

Braze, D., Tabor, W., Shankweiler, D. P., & Mencl, W. E. (2007). Speaking up for vocabulary: Reading skill differences in young adults. *Journal of Learning Disabilities, 40,* 226–243.

Bruno, J. L., Manis, F. R., Keating, P., Sperling, A. J., Nakamoto, J., & Seidenberg, M. S. (2007). Auditory word identification in dyslexic and normally achieving readers. *Journal of Experimental Child Psychology, 97,* 183–204.

Caffrey, E., & Fuchs, D. (2007). Differences in performance between students with learning disabilities and mild mental retardation: Implications for categorical instruction. *Learning Disabilities Research & Practice, 22,* 118–127.

Cao, F., Bitan, T., Chou, T., Burman, D. D., & Booth, J. R. (2006). Deficient orthographic and phonological representations in children with dyslexia revealed by brain activation patterns. *Journal of Child Psychology and Psychiatry, 47,* 1041–1050.

Cardoso-Martins, C., & Pennington, B. F. (2004). The relationship between phoneme awareness and rapid serial naming skills and literacy acquisition: The role of developmental period and reading ability. *Scientific Studies of Reading, 8,* 27–52.

Chugani, H. T. (1999). PET scanning studies of human brain development and plasticity. *Developmental Neuropsychology, 16,* 379–381.

Eslinger, P. J., & Oliveri, M. V. (2002). Approaching interventions clinically and scientifically. In P. J. Eslinger (Ed.), *Neuropsychological interventions: Clinical research and practice* (pp. 3–15). New York: Guilford.

Fletcher, J. M., Lyon, G. R., Fuchs, L. S., & Barnes, M. A. (2007). *Learning disabilities: From identification to intervention.* New York: Guilford.

Flowers, D. L., Wood, F. B., & Naylor, C. E. (1991). Regional cerebral blood flow correlates of language processes in reading disability. *Archives of Neurology, 48,* 637–643.

Foster, L. M., Hynd, G. W., Morgan, A. E., & Hugdahl, K. (2002). Planum temporale asymmetry and ear advantage in dichotic listening in developmental dyslexia and attention-deficit/hyperactivity disorder (ADHD). *Journal of the International Neuropsychological Society, 8,* 22–36.

Freund, A. M., & Baltes, P. B. (1998). Selection, optimization, and compensation as strategies of life management: Correlations with subjective indicators of successful aging. *Psychology and Aging, 13,* 531–543.

Fuchs, D., & Deshler, D. D. (2007). What we need to know about responsiveness to intervention (and shouldn't be afraid to ask). *Learning Disabilities Research & Practice, 22,* 129–136.

Fuchs, D., Mock, D., Morgan, P., & Young, C. (2003). Responsiveness to intervention: Definitions, evidence, and implications for the learning disabilities construct. *Learning Disabilities Research & Practice, 18,* 157–171.

Galaburda, A. M. (2005). Neurology of learning disabilities: What will the future bring? The answer comes from the successes of the recent past. *Learning Disability Quarterly, 28,* 107–109.

Gaskins, I. W., Satlow, E., & Pressley, M. (2007). Executive control of reading comprehension in the elementary school. In L. Meltzer (Ed.), *Executive function in education: From theory to practice* (pp. 194–215). New York: Guilford.

Gazzinga, M. S., Ivry, R. B., & Mangun, G. R. (2002). *Cognitive neuroscience*. New York: W. W. Norton.

Gersten, R., Clarke, B., & Mazzocco, M. M. M. (2007). Historical and contemporary perspectives on mathematical learning disabilities. In D. B. Berch & M. M. M. Mazzocco (Eds.), *Why is math so hard for some children? The nature and origins of mathematical learning difficulties and disabilities* (pp. 7–27). BaltimoreBrookes.

Glisky, E. L., & Glisky, M. L. (2002). Learning and memory impairments. In P. J. Eslinger (Ed.), *Neuropsychological interventions: Clinical research and practice* (pp. 137–162). New York: Guilford.

Good, R. H., Simmons, D. C., & Kame'enui, E. J. (2001). The importance and decision-making utility of a continuum of fluency-based indicators of foundational reading skills for third-grade high-stakes outcomes. *Scientific Studies of Reading, 5,* 257–288.

Gresham, F. M. (2006). Response to Intervention. In G. G. Bear & K. M. Minke (Eds.), *Children's needs III: Development, prevention, and intervention* (pp. 525–540). Washington, DC: National Association of School Psychologists.

Gross-Glenn, K., Duara, R., Barker, W. W., Loewenstein, D., Chang, J. Y., & Yoshii, F. (1991). Positron emission tomographic studies during serial word-reading by normal and dyslexic adults. *Journal of Clinical and Experimental Neuropsychology, 13,* 531–544.

Hammill, D. D., Leigh, J. E., McNutt, G., & Larsen, S. C. (1981). A new definition of learning disabilities. *Learning Disability Quarterly, 4,* 336–342.

Heim, S., Alter, K., Ischebeck, A. K., Amunts, K., Eickhoff, S. B., Mohlberg, H., et al. (2005). The role of the left Brodmann's areas 44 and 45 in reading words and pseudowords. *Cognitive Brain Research,* 982–993.

Hintze, J. M., & Christ, T. J. (2004). An examination of variabilitiy as a function of passage variance in CBM progress monitoring. *School Psychology Review, 33,* 204–217.

Hugdahl, K., Heiervang, E., Ersland, L., Lundervold, A., Steinmetz, H., & Smievoll, A. I. (2003). Significant relation between MR measures of planum temporale area and dichotic processing of syllables in dyslexic children. *Neuropsychologia, 41,* 666–675.

Hutton, J. B., Dubes, R., & Muir, S. (1992). Assessment practices of school psychologists: Ten years later. *School Psychology Review, 21,* 271–284.

Hynd, G. W., Hynd, C. R., Sullivan, H. G., & Kingsbury, T. B. (1987). Regional cerebral blood flow (rCBF) in developmental dyslexia: Activation during reading in a surface and deep dyslexic. *Journal of Learning Disabilities, 20,* 294–300.

Kavale, K. A. (1990). Effectiveness of special education. In T. B. Gutkin & C. R. Reynolds (Eds.), *The handbook of school psychology* (2nd ed., pp. 868–898). New York: Wiley.

Kavale, K. A., & Forness, S. R. (1987). A matter of substance over style: A quantitative synthesis assessing the efficacy of modality testing and teaching. *Exceptional Children, 54,* 228–239.

Khateb, A., Pegna, A. J., Landis, T., Michel, C. M., Brunet, D., Seghier, M. L., et al. (2007). Rhyme processing in the brain: An ERP mapping study. *International Journal of Psychophysiology, 63,* 240–250.

Lee, D., & Riccio, C. A. (2005). Cognitive retraining. In R. C. D'Amato & C. R. Reynolds (Eds.), *Handbook of school neuropsychology* (pp. 701–720). New York: Wiley.

Mateer, C. A. (1999). The rehabilitation of executive disorders. In D. T. Stuss, G. Winocur, & I. H. Robertson (Eds.), *Cognitive rehabilitation* (pp. 314–322). Cambridge, UK: Cambridge University Press.

McLean, J. F., & Hitch, G. J. (1999). Working memory impairments in children with specific arithmetic learning difficulties. *Journal of Experimental Child Psychology. Special Issue: The development of mathematical cognition: Arithmetic, 74*(3), 240–260.

Paul, I., Bott, C., Heim, S., Eulitz, C., & Elbert, T. (2006). Reduced hemispheric asymmetry of the auditory N260m in dyslexia. *Neuropsychologia, 44,* 785–794.

Pennington, B. F. (1995). Genetics of learning disabilities. *Journal of Child Neurology, 10*(Suppl 1), S69–S77.

Poldrack, R. A., Selco, S. L., Field, J. E., & Cohen, N. J. (1999). The relationship between skill learning and repetition priming: Experimental and computational analyses. *Journal of Experimental Psychology: Learning, Memory, and Cognition, 25*(1), 208-235.

Powell, D., Stainthorp, R., Stuart, M., Garwood, H., & Quinlan, P. (2007). An experimental comparison between rival theories of rapid automatized naming performance and its relationship to reading. *Journal of Experimental Child Psychology, 98,* 46-68.

Pugh, K. R., Menel, W. E., Jenner, A. R., Katz, L., Frost, S. J., Lee, J. R., et al. (2000). Functional neuroimaging studies of reading and reading disability (developmental dyslexia). *Mental Retardation and Developmental Disabilities Research Reviews, 6,* 207–213.

Riccio, C. A., & Hynd, G. W. (1996). Neuroanatomical and neurophysiological aspects of dyslexia. *Topics in Language Disorders, 16*(2), 1–13.

Riccio, C. A., Hynd, G. W., & Cohen, M. J. (1993). Neuropsychology in the Schools: Does it belong? *School Psychology International, 14,* 291–315.

Riccio, C. A., & Reynolds, C. R. (1998). Neuropsychological assessment of children. In C. R. Reynolds (Ed.), *Comprehensive clinical psychology* (Vol. 4, pp. 267–301). Oxford: Elsevier.

Richards, T. L., Aylward, E. H., Berninger, V. W., Field, K. M., Grimme, A. C., Richards, A. L., et al. (2006). Individual fMRI activation in orthographic mapping and morpheme mapping after orthographic or morphological spelling treatment in child dyslexics. *Journal of Neurolinguistics, 19,* 56–86.

Rumsey, J. M., Anderson, P., Aquino, T., King, A. C., Hamburger, S. D., Pikus, A., et al. (1992). Failure to activate the left temporoparietal cortex in dyslexia. *Archives of Neurology, 49,* 527–534.

Savage, R. S., & Frederickson, N. (2006). Beyond phonology: What else is needed to describe the problems of below-average readers and spellers? *Journal of Learning Disabilities, 39,* 339–413.

Semrud-Clikeman, M. (2005). Neuropsychological aspects for evaluating learning disabilities. *Journal of Learning Disabilities, 38,* 563–568.

Semrud-Clikeman, M., Guy, K. A., & Griffin, J. D. (2000). Rapid automatized naming in children with reading disabilities and attention deficit hyperactivity disorder. *Brain and Language, 74,* 70–83.

Shaywitz, S. E., & Shaywitz, B. A. (1999). Cognitive and neurobiologic influences in reading and in dyslexia. *Developmental Neuropsychology, 16,* 383–384.

Shaywitz, S. E., & Shaywitz, B. A. (2005). Dyslexia (Specific Reading Disability). *Biological Psychiatry, 57,* 1301–1309.

Shaywitz, S. E., & Shaywitz, B. A. (2006). Dyslexia. In M. D'Esposito (Ed.), *Functional MRI: Applications in clinical neurology and psychiatry* (pp. 61–79). Boca Raton, FL: Informa Healthcare.

Shaywitz, S. E., Shaywitz, B. A., Fullbright, R. K., Skudlarski, P., Mencl, W. E., Constable, R. T., et al. (2003). Neural systems for compensation and persistence: Young adult outcome of childhood reading disability. *Biological Psychiatry, 54,* 25–33.

Shaywitz, S. E., Shaywitz, B. A., Pugh, K. R., Fulbright, R. K., Constable, R. T., Mencl, W. E., et al. (1998). Functional disruption in the organization of the brain for reading in dyslexia. *Proceedings of the National Academy of Sciences of the United States of America, 95,* 2636–2641.

Silver, C. H., Blackburn, L. B., Arffa, S., Barth, J. T., Bush, S. S., & Koffler, S. P. (2006). The importance of neuropsychological assessment for the evaluation of childhood learning disorders: NAN policy and planning committee. *Archives of Clinical Neuropsychology, 21,* 741–744.

Simos, P. G., Fletcher, J. M., Bergman, E., Breier, J. I., Foorman, B. R., Castillo, E. M., et al. (2002). Dyslexia-specific brain activation profile becomes normal following successful remedial training. *Neurology, 58,* 1202–1213.

Simos, P. G., Fletcher, J. M., Sarkari, S., Billingsley, R. L., Denton, C., & Papanicolaou, A. C. (2007). Altering the brain circuits for reading through intervention: A magnetic source imaging study. *Neuropsychology, 21,* 485–496.

Simos, P. G., Fletcher, J. M., Sarkari, S., Billingsley, R. L., Francis, D. J., & Castillo, E. M. (2005). Early development of neurophysiological processes involved in normal reading and reading disability: A magnetic source imaging study. *Neuropsychology, 19,* 787–798.

Snow, C., Burns, M. S., & Griffin, P. (1998). *Preventing reading difficulties in young children.* Washington, DC: National Academy Press.

Snowling, M. J. (2000). *Dyslexia* (2nd ed.). Malden, MA: Blackwell.

Sohlberg, M. M., & Mateer, C. A. (1989). *Introduction to cognitive rehabilitation.* New York: Guilford.

Spear-Swerling, L., & Sternberg, R. J. (1994). The road not taken: An integrative theoretical model of reading disability. *Journal of Learning Disabilities, 27,* 91–103, 122.

Speece, D. L., & Case, L. P. (2001). Clasification in context: An alternative approach to identifying early reading disability. *Journal of Educational Psychology, 93,* 735–749.

Stanovich, K. E. (1988). Explaining the differences between the dyslexic and the garden-variety poor reader: The phonological-core variable-difference model. *Journal of Learning Disabilities, 21,* 590–604, 612.

Teeter, P. A., & Semrud-Clikeman, M. (1997). *Child neuropsychological assessment and intervention*. Boston: Allyn & Bacon.

Temple, E., Poldrack, R. A., Protopapas, A., Nagarajan, S., Salz, T., Tallal, P., et al. (2000). Disruption of the neural response to rapid acoustic stimuli in dyslexia: Evidence from functional MRI. *Proceedings of the National Academy of Sciences of the United States of America, 97*(25), 1307–1312.

Turkeltaub, P. E., Gareau, L., Flowers, D. L., Zeffiro, T. A., & Eden, G. F. (2003). Development of neural mechanisms for reading. *Nature Neuroscience, 6*, 767–773.

Turkeltaub, P. E., Weisberg, J., Flowers, D. L., Basu, D., & Eden, G. F. (2005). The neurobiological basis of reading: A special case of skill acquisition. In H. W. Catts & A. G. Kamhi (Eds.), *The connections between language and reading disabilities* (pp. 103–129). Mahwah, NJ: Lawrence Erlbaum.

Van Orden, G. C. (1987). A ROWS is a ROSE: Spelling, sound, and reading. *Memory & Cognition, 15*, 181–198.

Van Orden, G. C., & Kloos, H. (2005). The question of phonology and reading. In M. J. Snowling & C. Hulme (Eds.), *The science of reading: A handbook* (pp. 61–78). Malden, MA: Blackwell.

Vellutino, F. R., Fletcher, J. M., Scanlon, D. M., & Snowling, M. J. (2004). Specific reading disability (dyslexia): What have we learned in the past four decades? *Journal of Child Psychology and Psychiatry, 45*, 2–40.

Wadsworth, S. J., Olson, R. K., Pennington, B. F., & DeFries, J. C. (2000). Differential genetic etiology of reading disability as a function of IQ. *Journal of Learning Disabilities, 33*, 192–199.

Willcutt, E. G., Pennington, B. F., Olson, R. K., Chhabildas, N., & Hulslander, J. (2005). Neuropsychological analyses of comorbidity between reading disability and attention deficit hyperactivity disorder: In search of the common deficit. *Developmental Neuropsychology, 27*, 35–78.

Wodrich, D. L., Spencer, M. L. S., & Daley, K. B. (2006). Combining RTI and psychoeducational assessment: What we must assume to do otherwise. *Psychology in the Schools, 43*, 797–806.

7

Assessment Versus Testing and Its Importance in Learning Disability Diagnosis

Julie A. Suhr, Ph.D.

A s a professor and scientist-practitioner, I strive to keep myself and my graduate students up to date on the science underlying, and policies affecting, assessment of neuropsychological disorders, including learning disability (LD). Therefore, when I was invited to contribute to this volume, my initial positive response was primarily related to a need to conduct my yearly update of LD lecture notes and clinical assessment procedures—why not write a chapter about it along the way? However, while immersing myself in the latest LD research, I found I was drawn back to longstanding issues in the understanding of what assessment and diagnosis entail and their critical role in the current controversies surrounding LD diagnosis. My answers to the questions we were posed are thus based on my understanding of both current and classical neuroscience, neuropsychology, and other psychological assessment research, as well as my experience of the application of this research in practice.

WHAT DO YOU THINK NEUROSCIENCE HAS TO OFFER THE ASSESSMENT AND IDENTIFICATION OF LD?

In my opinion, neuroscience has already contributed significantly to the understanding of the neurological basis of reading and reading disabilities (RDs) and consequently its assessment. I remember learning in

I thank my colleagues Heather Alvarez, Laura Fox, Julie Owens, and Eric Zimak for their helpful comments on drafts of this chapter.

graduate school about focal reading- and writing-based deficits consequent to acquired brain lesions (e.g., Aaron, Baxter, & Lucenti, 1980; Coslett, Gonzalez Rothi, & Heilman, 1985; Funnell, 1983; McCarthy & Warrington, 1986; Saffran & Marin, 1977) and wondering why these neuropsychological findings were not informing the clinical and research literature in developmental RD. Further exploration of the neuropsychological literature on RD only puzzled me further about this issue. By the mid-1980s there was strong neuropsychological evidence for a focal information-processing deficit underlying much of RD—an impairment in phonological processing (e.g., Boder, 1973; Brying & Pulliainen, 1984; Denckla, Rudel, & Broman, 1981; Hulme & Snowing, 1988; Mattis, French, & Rapin, 1975; Patterson, 1981; Snowling, 1980; Stanovich, 1988)—yet both my personal experience with school systems at the time and published RD research suggested these findings were not translating into either assessment- or intervention-based educational practice (e.g., Christensen, 1992; Dorman, 1985; Hynd & Hynd, 1984).

Since that time, with the proliferation of neuroscience research methods (especially functional neuroimaging), evidence for specific neuronal pathways involved in both the normal reading process and in *well-defined* cases of RD has been demonstrated (e.g., Georgiewa et al., 1999; Gross-Glenn et al., 1991; Pugh et al., 2000; Rumsey et al., 1992, 1997; Simos et al., 2000), supporting an important assumption made in varying definitions of LD—the presence of focal CNS dysfunction. Further neuropsychological assessment and intervention studies have supported the usefulness of phonological decoding assessment in the identification of RD and the effectiveness of phonological intervention in its treatment (see National Institute of Child Health and Human Development, 2000, for a review). More interestingly, recent neuroscience work has demonstrated normalization of brain-activation patterns in individuals with RD following predominantly phonologically focused reading intervention (Shaywitz, Lyon, & Shaywitz, 2006; Simos et al., 2006).

It has taken years to develop this supportive literature, and I feel one of the major hindrances to finding consistencies across both assessment- and intervention-based research studies has been the "garbage in/garbage out" phenomenon. Because existing studies sometimes included participants who were poorly or inconsistently diagnosed with RD, it is not surprising that research results have not been consistent. This is likely a major reason for the lack of progress in research in mathematics- or writing-based academic impairments. However, despite the consistent evidence for the role of phonological decoding in normal reading and RD, this knowledge has still not been fully integrated into standard educational practice.

HOW DO YOU RECONCILE RESPONSE TO INTERVENTION (RTI) AS A MEANS OF DIAGNOSIS OF LD WITH KNOWLEDGE FROM THE CLINICAL NEUROSCIENCES?

RTI appears, at least in part, to be a response to perceived inadequacies in current LD diagnosis, as well as an attempt to provide earlier intervention for children who are struggling academically. I agree completely with the goal of providing early intervention and believe that RTI shows promise as a process for *selecting* those who receive specialized/intensive academic interventions. This, however, does not equate to evidence for RTI as a *diagnostic* procedure. I believe many of the perceived inadequacies with LD diagnosis stem from a lack of understanding and application of proper assessment methods, a point I shall address in great detail in my response to the next question. Furthermore, perceived weaknesses in one diagnostic method should not be interpreted as evidence in support of a proposed alternative (but not validated) method. I have additional concerns about RTI that are important to consider when contemplating its potential use for LD diagnosis in the educational system, and these I will discuss forthwith.

Intervention Is not Standardized

RTI is based on the premise that all students are receiving the same empirically supported instructional methods, and, thus, if a specific child is not responsive to instruction, he or she can be identified quickly and provided with more intensive and individualized instruction. Given the neuroscience literature previously reviewed, one would imagine that standard reading instruction, including training in phonological decoding, is provided consistently in today's classrooms. However, data suggest that there is no standardized method of instruction in contemporary classrooms, much less standardized interventional teaching in response to a child who falls behind (Lyon et al., 2001; National Research Center on Learning Disabilities, 2005). I see this regularly when I obtain school histories from individuals I am evaluating. It is still common to hear from students that only whole-word reading methods were used in their schools or that they never received formal instruction in grammar or learned only "creative" spelling. Further, many university students I re-evaluate who were diagnosed with LD as children report receiving only accommodation for their LD but no actual intervention (often confirmed when detailed school records are reviewed and parents are interviewed). Shaywitz and colleagues have referred to such individuals as "instructional casualties" (Shaywitz et al., 2006, p. 623). This is strong evidence for the lack of trickle down of neuroscience, neuropsychological, and educational research to current educational practice.

Assessment Methods Are *not* Independent of Intervention Methods

Let's assume for the moment that the interventional/teaching method is in fact standardized and empirically supported. How would one then assess whether a given child has been responsive to the intervention? Appropriate assessment methods should be *independent of the intervention*. Many models of RTI suggest that weekly curriculum-based measurement data would both serve as the objective measure of RTI success and failure and be diagnostic of LD. But data are not independent of the teaching method itself, creating circularity in the intervention for and diagnosis of the disorder. This is a basic research methodological issue that is not addressed in most RTI models (although see Fletcher et al., 2005, for suggestions on serial independent assessment of achievement skills as a component of RTI).

Lack of Responsiveness to Treatment Does *not* Identify the Underlying Problem

Now let's assume that not only is the interventional method standardized, but independent assessment of the intervention suggests the child is not responsive to treatment. RTI still does not answer the question of *why* an individual is having difficulties, information that could help guide what the next "individualized" interventional step should be. For example, does the lack of progress in reading reflect more generalized cognitive impairment? Research suggests this is an important distinction to make in considering prognosis and intervention in RD (Shaywitz et al., 2006). Does the individual show focal cognitive deficits such as phonological processing impairments, attention/information processing deficits, visuoperceptual impairments, memory difficulties, or executive dysfunction, which may be contributing to the lack of responsiveness to the instructional method? Is there a psychological, neurodevelopmental, or medical condition contributing to the academic difficulties? How can one provide more intense and individualized academic intervention as the next step of RTI without knowing what the underlying reason for the lack of responsiveness to standard instruction might be?

Some RTI models do suggest a "comprehensive" evaluation if a child fails to respond to the first steps in an RTI model. However, the definition of *comprehensive* evaluation in such models demonstrates a lack of understanding of what a comprehensive assessment should entail. For example, Fuchs (2007) describes an RTI process in which a child who fails both general instruction and more intense (Tier 2) instruction would receive a "comprehensive" evaluation, which is exemplified by two subtests of an abbreviated scale of intelligence and an adaptive behavior rating form. This is certainly not comprehensive assessment and is not even comprehensive testing. My response to the following question will further outline what psychologists and neuropsychologists mean by assessment and why neuropsychological assessment has the potential to add much to the diagnosis of LD beyond the simplistic notion of ability/achievement testing.

Early Identification Matters

There is no question that there is a need for early identification of impairment in order to provide appropriate academic intervention as early as possible in a child's education. I agree that descriptions of procedures utilized in the past for identification of children with LD (ability/achievement discrepancy) have resulted in delays to treatment (the "wait to fail" model) that should be avoided in order to prevent "instructional casualties." But, as I will argue in the following, use of mere ability/achievement discrepancy (which is *not* equivalent to diagnosis), and misuse/misunderstanding of that discrepancy, is the major contributor to delayed identification and thus delayed receipt of appropriate intervention. Let me illustrate this point using an unidentified case example (note the client is a prototypic case representing many individuals referred to me and my colleagues in our training clinic).

> Child A is a 9-year-old fourth grader who has struggled with reading since he first entered school; school records show that every one of his teachers expressed concern and requested that he be evaluated for possible RD, and he was unable to pass yearly reading proficiency tests. In the third grade he was evaluated by his school psychologist, who indicated that his reading achievement composite score did not fall 2 grade levels below his current grade, and that his reading achievement composite score was not significantly discrepant from his overall intelligence. Because of this he was not diagnosed with RD and was denied services. Unsatisfied with this response, his parents referred him for a second evaluation. A comprehensive neuropsychological evaluation showed significant scatter within the indices comprising his overall intellectual score, with borderline to low average auditory working memory and processing speed, but average to high average verbal comprehension and perceptual reasoning skills. In addition, his performance on subtests of reading achievement showed that, although his reading composite fell in the average range, there was significant scatter in his reading skills—with performance in the borderline range on sight-word reading and phonological decoding tasks, as well as spelling—but performance in the high average range for his age on contextual reading comprehension. Additional neuropsychological tests confirmed that Child A had auditory working memory weaknesses (but normal spatial working memory skills) and significant problems with speeded reading and naming tasks, as well as performance in the impaired range on additional measures of phonological decoding. Thus, Child A showed evidence of focal cognitive impairment that was impairing his real-world reading skills, although he did not show an ability/achievement discrepancy using composite scores.

We diagnosed him with RD and his parents sought out independent reading tutoring focused on his phonological processing problems after his school did not accept the diagnosis given in the second-opinion evaluation.

When kids are not responsive to standard education, they should be identified early and intervention should happen early. RTI is, at least in part, a reaction to the lack of early identification that can arise from poor understanding of and application of a definition of LD based solely on ability/achievement discrepancy testing. Of note, Child A would likely have been denied services based on an "achievement" only definition if the tester used only the composite reading achievement score. It is unclear whether the "assessment" component of RTI is anything beyond "poor achievement" as a diagnostic criterion for LD and thus also may lead to delayed intervention, although RTI proposals do suggest assessing for evidence of poor achievement (lack of progress) in a shorter period of time than is typical in current achievement testing.

WHAT ROLE DOES NEUROPSYCHOLOGY HAVE TO PLAY IN THE DIAGNOSIS OF LD?

My opinion, based on years of clinical and research experience, is that one of the strongest roles for neuropsychology is its focus on comprehensive and integrative assessment. As mentioned previously, much of the movement toward RTI and other alternative LD diagnostic methods has been as a response to criticism over the use of ability/achievement discrepancy in *testing* as a diagnostic method. But *assessment* is *not* the same thing as *testing* (Matarazzo, 1990) and a good assessor would not use an ability/achievement test discrepancy alone to diagnose LD.

The strength of neuropsychological assessment is its *integration* of neuroscientific knowledge (understanding of brain structure and function) with knowledge of psychometrics and psychological assessment issues. In addition to neuroscience training, individuals who assess and diagnose brain-based conditions should also receive extensive didactic and practical training on the measurement and assessment of behavior, including psychometric issues in test development, administration, and interpretation. Furthermore, they should also receive extensive didactic and practical training in understanding nonneurological factors that can affect test behavior and thus test performance (i.e., presence of psychopathology, personality characteristics, social/cognitive or health/medical factors). This extensive and integrated psychological assessment training is well beyond simply learning to administer tests in a standardized fashion and following the manual to score them and look for statistical discrepancies. It requires that information gathered through behavioral observation, collateral report, school records, medical and neurological records, and administration of standardized tests be integrated and applied, based on psychological and neuropsychological science, to the test patterns seen in a given evaluation. Concretely, it requires more than a quarter- or semester-long course focused on administration and scoring of intellectual and achievement tests.

With regard to diagnosis of LD, I agree with many clinicians, researchers, and educators that simply using a *test* discrepancy between intellect and achievement to diagnose someone with an LD will do more harm than good. As noted previously, I believe there is the same risk for harm using an achievement-only definition of LD, which is a potential implication of RTI and other proposed alternative diagnostic methods. A well-trained and competent *assessor* would consider and interpret all the test data in the context of a comprehensive assessment of the individual before interpreting a simple ability/achievement discrepancy (or achievement test results) as a valid indicator of LD. Thus, application of this *one* aspect of diagnosis by psychological and educational professionals who have learned to administer and score *tests*, but who don't understand important *assessment* issues that would influence test selection, test interpretation, and final diagnostic impressions, is the problem—not the diagnostic heuristic itself.

Perhaps some clinical examples will help illustrate this point. As noted for the previous case, these are fictionalized prototypic cases, both to protect the identities of the individuals being assessed, but also because these are very common issues arising from testing results (I will not call them assessments) from school psychologists, rehabilitation psychologists, counseling psychologists, clinical psychologists, and neuropsychological colleagues.

Taking into Account Low Levels of Intellect

Ms. B was referred for formal assessment of her RD after being diagnosed by her vocational counselor, who completed paperwork to request that Ms. B be able to take the GED with extended time limits to accommodate her reading difficulties. Because the diagnosis was based on Ms. B's performance on a computerized reading "screener," the diagnosis was not accepted by the GED committee. Ms. B completed less than 6 years of formal schooling and reported that she cannot read; she has struggled with all aspects of her vocational training. Formal assessment, including testing and review of her school records, showed a history of special education placement since first grade, general intellect in the mildly mentally retarded range, and academic achievement skills commensurate with her general intellect and her years of formal education.

Not all "poor readers" are equal in terms of their other cognitive skills or even in terms of their reading strengths/weaknesses (hence the "garbage in/garbage out" problem in research on "poor readers"). Poor readers with intellectual skills in the borderline to developmentally disabled range or with other cognitive weaknesses (for example, poor memory) differ from individuals with nonreading cognitive strengths but who cannot read in terms of their ability to benefit from reading intervention, because there are other cognitive issues to take into account for their interventional needs. In addition, they differ in terms of their ability to attain a GED or benefit from standard job-training methods without other nonreading accommodations, because additional cognitive issues also affect their abilities. While it is certainly possible for individuals with low levels of intellect to have RD or other LD, a full understanding of the impact of the reading problem on their real-world (academic and nonacademic) functioning requires a full assessment of their nonreading cognitive abilities.

Taking into Account High Levels of Intellect

Teen C, a 16-year-old high school sophomore, was referred for a second-opinion evaluation by his school, who did not agree with the RD diagnosis given in a prior assessment. By his parents' report, Teen C is bright and does well in school, but does "poorly" on timed standardized tests. Review of his academic records showed that Teen C passed all proficiency testing throughout his schooling and received A and B grades without exception and without accommodation. Formal test results from prior testing showed that Teen C has both verbal and nonverbal intellectual strengths (very superior range), with mathematics achievement scores in the high average range relative to same-age peers and reading skills varying from average to high average, depending on the reading skill assessed. The prior report included computerized printouts calculating all possible achievement/intellect discrepancy scores, which suggested significant and relatively rare test discrepancies between Teen C's intellect and some isolated aspects of reading; the conclusion of the prior report was RD.

A common complaint, and one I agree with, is the diagnosis of LD in an individual of superior intellect with "average" academic scores simply on the basis of an achievement/intellect discrepancy, particularly when there is no evidence of actual academic impairment in his or her educational history. It is important to note in this context that the presence of real-world impairment is also a central core to most diagnoses of LD. Furthermore, understanding psychometric issues, such as regression to the mean or raw score distribution and how this can affect standard scores on tests, can be crucial to considering a "discrepancy" in someone who attains very superior intellectual ability scores and "only" high average academic achievement scores—high average may well be the highest score attainable on a particular achievement test. While using conormed tests that use predictive equations to determine the statistical and clinical significance of ability/achievement discrepancies addresses some of these concerns, they still must be considered when interpreting an individual's test performance.

Taking into Account Patterns of Performance on "Intelligence" Tests

Ms. D, a college freshman, was referred by her French instructor for evaluation of possible RD after she failed the introductory level French course for a third time. Ms. D was evaluated for possible RD in her freshman year of high school but was told that the "difference" in her intelligence and achievement was not significant and therefore she did not meet diagnostic criteria for RD. Review of her academic records showed a pattern of below average performance in reading- and writing- (especially spelling) related coursework and proficiency test scores (which led to her prior evaluation). Prior testing showed a pattern of very superior nonverbal reasoning skills, high average visuomotor processing speed skills, but low average auditory working memory and verbal reasoning skills, which were highly discrepant from her nonverbal abilities. Despite this scatter, her well below average reading achievement scores (particularly on tests of phonological processing) were compared to her overall IQ, which was in the low average to average range.

I have seen a number of second-opinion referrals from individuals with Ms. D's presentation. Often the pattern of intellectual strengths/weaknesses seen in a traditional IQ test is consistent with the Matthew effect (Stanovich, 1988), in which adults with RD score lower on measures of crystallized verbal intellect (vocabulary, verbal comprehension, fund of information) due to years of poor verbal achievement in school secondary to their RD. Thus comparing their overall intelligence with their reading achievement is an invalid discrepancy comparison, because their RD affected both their "crystallized" intellectual skills and their achievement test scores through their educational history. There is also evidence to suggest that RD and other LDs are associated with neuropsychological weaknesses that will manifest themselves in clinically meaningful scatter among subtests or indices on intellectual/ability instruments. For example, individuals with LD often have significantly lower performance on Processing Speed and Working Memory indices relative to Verbal Comprehension and Perceptual Organizational indices on the Wechsler instruments (Psychological Corporation, 1997), making a full-scale IQ score difficult to interpret in such cases.

A good assessor starts with what he or she knows about the person, looks at the intellectual score profile and interprets it based on its psychometric properties, together with what is known about the person *and* about known patterns of intellectual test performance in the disorder in question, and then decides in a hypothesis-driven fashion what makes most sense for this person, in terms of providing an estimate of their general intellectual skills, to compare to other test results (including achievement tests and other neuropsychological tests). These decisions are not "one size fits all," but must be supported by the preponderance of data obtained about the person and the scientific data about the disorder.

Taking into Account Other Factors that May Explain Test Performance

Mr. E., a senior elementary education major, was referred for math disability assessment after failing the math portion of the Praxis exam. Review of Mr. E's educational history showed that Mr. E performed adequately in mathematics courses and on mathematics proficiency tests through his elementary and middle school years, but then took the minimum math required to graduate from his high school and to complete his elementary education major. Mr. E reported that he "hates" math; in formal assessment, Mr. E put forth good effort on all tasks except math ones. For example, as soon as he was informed that the next task involved math, he fidgeted and breathed more heavily. He often discontinued math items well before time limits were up and to most math questions he simply replied "I don't know how to do that" or "I never learned how to do that." His math scores, while below expectations for his same-age peers or his years of college education, were relatively consistent with the level of formal mathematics education he had received.

Ms. F was referred for LD evaluation after she failed her freshman composition class. She reported that she did not know the rules of grammar and was a horrible speller; her instructor wondered whether she had a "writing disability." Review of her academic records, including proficiency testing and course grades, revealed no academic weaknesses, but Ms. F reported that she had never written a research paper before coming to college and that her school emphasized "creative" writing and did not grade for grammar or spelling. During formal assessment, Ms. F's effort on writing tasks seemed diminished (for example, she spent very little time writing sentences, paragraphs, or a sample essay, and did not take advantage of scratch paper given to her for writing rough drafts or outlines ahead of time). Test scores indicated performance well below expectations on writing achievement relative to her intellect and relative to reading and mathematics skills, all of which were in the average to high average range. When asked about her approach to writing in college, she reported that she usually began writing papers the evening before they were due.

Do these students have LD? Based on discrepancy between intellect and achievement on testing and evidence of current real-world "impairment," some testers would likely diagnose them as having LD. However, an important exclusionary criterion in most definitions of LD is lack of prior opportunity to learn the material. In Mr. E's case, the opportunity might have been there, but not taken; in Ms. F's case the opportunity may have appeared to be there, but in reality was not. Just looking at a transcript to see what courses a student completed in school may not be enough to address the issue of prior exposure to academic material—a comprehensive and detailed interview is a necessary component of a good assessment before one can reach a conclusion about the meaning of the test data.

Both cases also illustrate the importance of observing behavior during evaluation and considering other psychological contributions to test scores. For example, both cases raise the possibility that the students were not putting forth full effort when completing tasks that they felt tapped their weaknesses. Poor effort could be related to negative expectations for one's own test performance when facing what is perceived to be a difficult task, anxiety when completing tests, depression leading to a learned helplessness approach when facing one's weakness, or outright malingering of impairment; whatever the etiology, poor effort can lead to invalid test scores that underestimate an individual's actual cognitive abilities. There are data to suggest that individuals concerned that they have a LD can exaggerate or fabricate cognitive impairment in order to receive special accommodations, with some studies finding rates of failure on effort tests in adults referred for LD testing similar to that seen among personal injury litigants (Alfano & Boone, 2007). Unfortunately, malingering/poor effort is not restricted to adults; studies show children can and do malinger cognitive impairment (Constantinou & McCaffrey, 2003; Donders, 2005; Lu & Boone, 2002). Diagnosis of malingering is another diagnostic conundrum and there is not sufficient space to discuss it here; nevertheless, considering factors such as anxiety, negative expectations, depression, and diminished effort is key for proper interpretation of cognitive test results.

These cases illustrate how testing does not equal assessment and reiterate that blind application of test discrepancies not only does not consider other important diagnostic criteria for LD, but is not appropriate assessment and diagnosis. The issues I raise are relevant not only to "in the trenches" professionals who are conducting LD assessments, but also to those who are working to redefine the criteria for diagnosis of LD. For example, I believe the "knee jerk" reaction of eliminating "IQ testing" as part of the LD diagnosis reflects, at least in part, a lack of understanding of the complexity of interpreting performance on an intellectual battery, interpreting an IQ/achievement discrepancy, and integrating such a discrepancy with other test scores and a client's history and behavioral presentation into a full assessment. Thus, criticism of the discrepancy model is often criticism of its poor application by someone with less than adequate assessment training and experience, and application of an LD model defined only by poor achievement would result in the same problems.

WHAT ROLE DOES NEUROPSYCHOLOGY PLAY IN DESIGNING INTERVENTIONS IN THE CONTEXT OF RTI?

Neuropsychological Assessment Is an Important Step in an RTI Model

As reviewed previously, the first steps of RTI are primarily intervention based and show promise for the goal of early intervention, provided that empirically supported general instructional methods are in fact consistently provided by teachers. Since I am being asked my opinion, I will suggest my own "steps" to assessment and intervention.

Step 1: Children who are not responsive to standardized and empirically supported instruction in the general classroom, as assessed by serial academic achievement testing *independent of the direct teaching methods,* would qualify for more specialized and empirically supported intervention (for example, in RD, perhaps a more intensive phonological decoding intervention). However, their performance on achievement tests would *not be viewed as equivalent to diagnosis.* To quote RTI advocates Lyon and colleagues (2001), a "label is not necessary for implementation of prevention programs, and the costs of delaying intervention are too great to wait" (p. 277). Unfortunately, barriers presented by current IDEA regulatory laws make it difficult for children to receive intervention without a diagnosis, an issue I hope some of my colleagues will address by suggesting ways in which we can change these policies. In any event, the consistent provision of empirically supported instructional methods to all children would likely lead to a significant decrease in the number of students who show poor academic progress and thus might be in need of comprehensive assessment that I will suggest in Step 2. Further, serial independent achievement testing throughout the school year would not only lead to early identification of poor responders but also provide initial clues to the nature of the underlying information-processing impairment that may be contributing to the student's lack of response to instruction and that could guide the next step of intervention.

Step 2: If a student continues to show poor progress (again using independent serial academic achievement testing), he or she should then be referred for a comprehensive neuropsychological assessment to determine whether there is evidence for any specific or general information-processing impairments or other noncognitive impairments that may be contributing to the lack of academic progress. Such assessment should be carried out by someone with appropriate assessment training and experience and *not* merely be based on overall ability/achievement test scores. The goal of assessment should primarily be identification of individual difference variables and/or impairments that suggest the need for alterations to standard instructional methods, provision of additional empirically supported instructional methods, or accommodation for underlying deficits that will allow learning to take place and to be demonstrated; additionally, it may or may not involve diagnosis of psychological, medical/neurological, or neurodevelopmental conditions, including LD.

Research

The methods previously outlined would also assist in minimizing the "garbage in/garbage out" problem previously identified as a hindrance to LD research. At the point of referral for comprehensive assessment, individuals who have clearly demonstrated lack of progress using already accepted teaching methods could be clearly identified, eliminating some of the exclusionary criteria in current LD definitions and thus minimizing heterogeneity of presentation among those who participate in research. Comprehensive assessment and intervention research would then help to identify individual difference factors that may be consistently related to lack of academic progress and that could be used in prospective intervention designs as potential predictors of successful interventional techniques (as is true in the case of phonological processing assessment in the earliest phases of education).

Evaluation As Intervention

Let me make one final point about the role of good assessment in children and adults with LD. A consistent theme that arises in interviews and in feedback sessions during evaluations of students for LD, no matter the age of the students, is that their failure in school has led them to "feel dumb" and respond with poor self-esteem, depressive symptoms, a dislike of school, and a learned-helplessness approach to learning. Identification of their overall pattern of cognitive strengths and weaknesses is in itself therapeutic, especially when coupled with exploration of their feelings about their particular information-processing weakness, the implications of those weaknesses for their educational and career goals, their attitudes toward academic intervention versus accommodation, and their psychological reactions to their educational failures. Such a model of assessment feedback is consistent with the philosophy of good assessment as its own intervention (Armengol et al., 2001; Finn & Tonsager, 1992; Lewak & Hogan, 2003) and in my clinical experience has been crucial to the academic and psychological health of those whom I have assessed.

REFERENCES

Aaron, P. G., Baxter, C. F., & Lucenti, J. (1980). Developmental dyslexia and acquired dyslexia: Two sides of the same coin? *Brain and Language, 11,* 1–11.

Alfano, K., & Boone, K. B. (2007). The use of effort tests in the context of actual versus feigned attention-deficit/hyperactivity disorder and learning disability. In K. B. Boone (Ed.), *Assessment of feigned cognitive impairment: A neuropsychological perspective* (pp. 366–383). New York: Guilford.

Armengol, C. G., Moes, E. J., Penney, D. L., & Sapienza, M. M. (2001). Writing client-centered recommendations. In C. G. Aemengol, E. Kaplan, & E. J. Moes (Eds.), *The consumer-oriented neuropsychological report* (pp. 141–160). Lutz, FL: Psychological Assessment Resources.

Boder, E. (1973). Developmental dyslexia: A diagnostic approach based on three atypical reading-spelling patterns. *Developmental Medicine and Child Neurology, 15,* 663–687.

Byring, R., & Pulliainen, V. (1984). Neurological and neuropsychological deficiencies in a group of older adolescents with dyslexia. *Developmental Medicine and Child Neurology, 26,* 765–773.

Christensen, C. A. (1992). Discrepancy definitions of reading disability: Has the quest led us astray? A response to Stanovich. *Reading Research Quarterly, 27,* 276–278.

Constantinou, M., & McCaffrey, R. J. (2002). Using the TOMM for evaluating children's effort to perform optimally on neuropsychological measures. *Child Neuropsychology, 9,* 81–90.

Coslett, H. B., Gonzalez Rothi, L. J., & Heilman, K. M. (1985). Reading: Dissociation of the lexical and phonologic mechanisms. *Brain and Language, 24,* 20–35.

Denckla, M. B., Rudel, R. G., & Broman, M. (1981). Tests that discriminate between dyslexic and other learning-disabled boys. *Brain and Language, 13,* 118–129.

Donders, J. (2005). Performance on the Test of Memory Malingering in a mixed pediatric sample. *Child Neuropsychology, 11,* 221–227.

Dorman, C. (1985). Defining and diagnosing dyslexia: Are we putting the cart before the horse? *Reading Research Quarterly, 20,* 505–508.

Finn, S. E., & Tonsager, M. E. (1992). Therapeutic effects of providing MMPI-@ test feedback to college students awaiting therapy. *Psychological Assessment, 9,* 374–385.

Fletcher, J. M., Francis, D. J., Morris, R. D., & Lyon, G. R. (2005). Evidence-based assessment of learning disabilities in children and adolescents. *Journal of Clinical Child and Adolescent Psychology, 34,* 506–522.

Fuchs, L. S. (2007). *NRCLD update on responsiveness to intervention: Research to practice.* Retrieved August 1, 2007 from http://www.nrcld.org.

Funnell, E. (1983). Phonological processes in reading: New evidence from acquired dyslexia. *British Journal of Psychology, 74,* 159–180.

Georgiewa, P., Rzanny, R., Hopf, J. M., Knab, R., Glauche, V., Kaiser, W. A., & Blanz, B. (1999). fMRI during word processing in dyslexic and normal reading children. *Neuroreport, 10,* 3459–3465.

Gross-Glenn, K., Duara, R., Barker, W. W., Loewenstein, D., Chang, J. Y., Yoshii, F., Apicella, A. M., Pascal, W., Boothe, T., & Sevush, S. (1991). Position emission tomographic studies during serial word-reading by normal and dyslexic adults. *Journal of Clinical and Experimental Neuropsychology, 13,* 531–544.

Hulme, C., & Snowling, M. (1988). The classification of children with reading difficulties. *Developmental Medicine and Child Neurology, 20,* 398–402.

Hynd, G. W., & Hynd, C. R. (1984). Dyslexia: Neuroanatomical/neurolinguistic perspectives. *Reading Research Quarterly, 19,* 482–498.

Lewak, R., & Hogan, L. (2003). Applying assessment information. In L. E. Beutler & G. Groth-Marnat (Eds.), *Integrative assessment of adult personality* (2nd ed). New York: Guilford.

Lu, P. H., & Boone, K. B. (2002). Suspect cognitive symptoms in a 9-year-old child: malingering by proxy? *The Clinical Neuropsychologist, 16,* 90–96.

Lyon, G. R., Fletcher, J. M., Shaywitz, S. E., Shaywitz, B. A., Torgesen, J. K., Wood, F. B., Schulte, A., & Olson, R. (2001). Rethinking learning disabilities. In C. E. Finn, Jr., A. J. Rotherham, & C. R. Hokanson, Jr. (Eds.). *Rethinking special education for a new century.* Thomas B. Fordham Foundation.

Matarazzo, J. D. (1990). Psychological assessment versus psychological testing: Validation from Binet to the school, clinic, and courtroom. *American Psychologist, 45,* 999–1017.

Mattis, S., French, J. H., & Rapin, I. (1975). Dyslexia in children and young adults: Three independent neurological syndromes. *Developmental Medicine and Child Neurology, 17,* 150–163.

McCarthy, R. A. & Warrington, E. K. (1986). Phonological reading: Phenomena and paradoxes. *Cortex, 22,* 359–380.

National Institute of Child Health and Human Development (2000). The report of the National Reading Panel: An evidence-based assessment of the scientific research literature on reading and its implications for reading instruction. Bethesda, MD.

National Research Center on Learning Disabilities (2005). *Executive summary of the NRCDLD topical form applying responsiveness to intervention to specific learning disability determination decisions.* Retrieved August 1, 2007, from http://www.nrcld.org.

Patterson, K. E. (1981). Neuropsychological approaches to the study of reading. *British Journal of Psychology, 72,* 151–174.

Psychological Corporation (1997). *WAIS-III WMS III Technical Manual.* San Antonio, TX: Author.

Pugh, K. R., Mencl, W. E., Jenner, A. R., Katz, L., Frost, S. J., Lee J. R., Shaywitz, S. E., & Shaywitz, B. A. (2000). Functional neuroimaging studies of reading and reading disability (developmental dyslexia). *Mental Retardation and Developmental Disabilities Research Reviews, 6,* 207–213.

Rumsey, J. M., Andreason, P., Zametkin, A. J., Aquino, T., King, A. C., Hamburger, S. D., Pikus, A., Rapoport, J. L., & Cohen, R. M. (1992). Failure to activate the left temporoparietal cortex in dyslexia. An oxygen 15 positron emission tomographic study. *Archives of Neurology, 49,* 527–534.

Rumsey, J. M., Nace, K., Donohue, B., Wise, D., Maisog, J. M., & Andreason, P. (1997). A positron emission tomographic study of impaired word recognition and phonological processing in dyslexic men. *Archives of Neurology, 54,* 562–573.

Saffran, E. M., & Marin, O. S. (1977). Reading without phonology: Evidence from aphasia. *Quarterly Journal of Experimental Psychology, 29,* 515–525.

Shaywitz, B. A., Lyon, G.R., & Shaywitz, S. E. (2006). The role of functional magnetic resonance imaging in understanding reading and dyslexia. *Developmental Neuropsychology, 30,* 613–632.

Simos, P. G., Breier, J. I., Fletcher, J. M., Berman, E., & Papanicolaou, A. C. (2000). Cerebral mechanisms involved in word reading in dyslexic children: A magnetic source imaging approach. *Cerebral Cortex, 10,* 809–816.

Simos, P. G., Fletcher, J. M., Denton, C., Sarkari, S., Billingsley-Marshall, R., & Papanicolaou, A. C. (2006). Magnetic source imaging studies of dyslexia interventions. *Developmental Neuropsychology, 30,* 591–611.

Snowling, M. J. (1980). The development of grapheme-phoneme correspondence in normal and dyslexic readers. *Journal of Experimental Child Psychology, 29,* 294–305.

Stanovich, K. E. (1988). Explaining the differences between the dyslexic and the garden-variety poor reader: The phonological-core variable-difference model. *Journal of Learning Disabilities, 21,* 590–604.

8

Comprehensive Assessment Must Play a Role in RTI

Steven J. Hughes

HOW DO YOU RECONCILE RTI AS A MEANS OF DIAGNOSIS OF LD WITH KNOWLEDGE FROM THE CLINICAL NEUROSCIENCES?

Developed in response to the 2004 revision to IDEA, response to intervention (RTI) describes a set of procedures in which established *best practices* in teaching are applied, student progress is closely monitored, and research-proven interventions are provided to those who fail to demonstrate adequate progress. RTI aims to rapidly identify those who are failing to meet expectations in the regular classroom setting, and provide supplemental instruction to ensure they "catch up" before falling too far behind. Those who consistently fail to respond graduate to more intensive interventions.

RTI is implemented in a layered, or *tiered* manner, with regular education and careful progress monitoring at the bottom, and progression through two or three higher tiers of increasingly intensive evaluation and education support for those who fail to learn. Only at the highest tier is designation of a learning disability (LD) and special education placement considered (National Center for Learning Disabilities, 2006).

A typical three-tier RTI implementation is described In *A Parent's Guide to Response-to-Intervention* (National Center for Learning Disabilities, 2006). In Tier 1, students in regular education settings are identified as "at risk" through use of universal screening measures, and those who are flagged receive supplemental instruction (small-group based) in the classroom, with close monitoring of their academic progress. Those who fail to show improvement are moved to more intensive services in Tier 2. These services are also provided in small groups in the regular education setting as a supplement to general instruction. Those failing to show progress during Tier 2 move on to Tier 3, where they may undergo further assessment and will receive *individualized, intensive interventions* to address identified weaknesses. Tier 3 allows for determination of eligibility to receive special education services under the Individuals with Disabilities Education Act (IDEA), utilizing the information obtained while the student passed through Tiers 1 and 2 to help make this determination (National Center for Learning Disabilities, 2006).

While descriptions of Tier 3 generally include *comprehensive evaluation*, the degree of evaluation at this stage varies across models, which is a key issue. Some models propose only limited academic and intellectual testing, or even expressly omit comprehensive assessment, and rely on the intervention process as a kind of diagnostic tool (Cortiella, 2006). Other models do call for a comprehensive evaluation to be conducted by a multidisciplinary team (National Center for Learning Disabilities, 2006; National Joint Committee on Learning Disabilities, 2005).

The degree to which comprehensive evaluation plays a role in RTI remains unresolved among those engaged in the debate. However, while RTI does not prohibit comprehensive evaluations, this now-common procedure will almost certainly become less common as RTI models that de-emphasize comprehensive assessment come into practice. This is of concern to school psychologists and neuropsychologists (including the author), who clearly see a role for broad assessment in understanding the educational needs of children who fail to respond to Tier 1 and Tier 2 interventions (Semrud-Clikeman, 2005; National Association of School Psychologists, 2007).

Many weaknesses have been identified in the ability/achievement discrepancy model, which prior to the 2004 reauthorization of IDEA was the manner in which LD was defined. These include: (a) the expense of the necessary educational testing; (b) problems distinguishing disability from low achievement (or inadequate instruction); (c) overidentification of children from disadvantaged backgrounds as learning disabled (*false positives*); (d) the requirement for teacher referral; (e) failure to identify some students with actual needs (*false negatives*); (f) denial of needed intervention for children who (often through expensive and/or Herculean efforts from families) fail to demonstrate the required *severe discrepancy between achievement and intellectual ability*, but have histories of academic struggle; (g) the stigmatizing effects for children of being labeled as *learning disabled;* and (h) inability to differentiate LD from underachievement (Fuchs et al., 2003; Vaughn & Fuchs, 2003; Fletcher et al., 2004; Hale et al., 2006).

As a way of addressing learning issues, RTI represents an appealing shift from a "'test and treat' model to a 'treat and test' model" (p. 309, Fletcher, Coulter, Reschly, & Vaughn, 2004). RTI promises a number of other benefits, including: (a) earlier identification of students having problems; (b) reduced numbers of children requiring special education; (c) fewer minority children identified as LD; (d) information that is *maximally relevant* for educators; (e) increased accountability for student outcomes; (f) separation of students with true learning disabilities from those who show weak performance due to inadequate instruction; (g) reduction in numbers of children requiring special education; and (h) provision of services simply on the basis of need (National Joint Committee on Learning Disabilities, 2005; Fuchs et al., 2003). Perhaps the most appealing aspect of RTI is that "*the focus shifts from eligibility to concerns about providing effective instruction*" (emphasis in original; Fletcher et al., 2004, p. 311), something that parents, teachers, and everyone else with an interest in education certainly favor.

No single formulation of RTI has been universally accepted, and advocates remain divided about how such a system should be implemented. Models differ in the number of tiers, the degree to which individualized evaluation is incorporated, and the form of intervention that should be provided at different tiers (Hale et al., 2006). Nevertheless, all RTI models advocate for *core concepts*, which are inarguably beneficial. As Hale et al. (2006) note, "use of research-based instruction, regular student progress monitoring, single-subject experimental designs, and empirical decision making should be required of all schools" (p. 753).

A Parent's Guide to Response-to-Intervention provides two examples of the manner in which RTI might function. In one vignette, "Paul" is identified as being at risk for reading failure in Tier 1 due to performance falling below the cut score on a universal screening measure. He and his peers undergo 5 weeks of progress monitoring, and Paul is found to have low performance on a word-fluency task. With the consent of his parents, he is advanced to Tier 2 of the school's RTI program. Here, he receives small-group, preventive tutoring with two of his peers. Progress monitoring continues and, at the end of 8 weeks under Tier 2 intervention, he shows progress beyond expectations and is returned to Tier 1 (regular education) with continued monitoring to ensure that his progress continues normally.

In a case such as this, RTI seems perfectly suitable as a method to guide children to prereferral intervention. Paul does not have an LD; like many first graders, he has been slow to develop early reading skills, and the method through which his problem was addressed should—with or without RTI—be routine in any school.

A Parent's Guide to Response-to-Intervention also tells the story of "Susan." Like Paul, she is identified as "at-risk" for reading problems at the start of the school year. At the end of 5 weeks, she is found to be non-responsive to Tier 1 education and is advanced to Tier 2 for more intensive reading instruction. Preventive tutoring is unsuccessful; Susan fails to respond to Tier 2 intervention and is moved to Tier 3. Permission from her parents is obtained "to conduct an abbreviated evaluation in order to gather additional information," rule out Mental Retardation (with an IQ test) and assess her language functioning (National Center for Learning Disabilities, 2005, p. 8). This information, combined with classroom observation, parent interview, and data gathered during monitoring of Susan's progress in Tier 1 and 2, is used to determine that Susan has a learning disability. No additional diagnostic testing is done. An IEP is written, and Susan receives special education in Tier 3 in the form of one-to-one intervention from a special education teacher. She also receives supplemental programming by spending 30 minutes, four times per week, working with a computer program designed to improve reading skills. "[This] additional help increased Susan's reading rate of growth to a rate that would make up for her earlier lack of progress" (p. 8).

Paul's story illustrates how RTI can be effective in addressing a delay in reading development through a prereferral intervention. The procedures of Tier 1 and Tier 2 are structured and standardized, and there is a clearly identified "way forward" for him and peers with similar issues in reading acquisition.

In contrast, Susan's case illustrates how RTI—as described—is an inadequate method for diagnosing LD. Through her lack of progress in Tiers 1 and 2, we know that Susan is having significant difficulty learning to read. Through the limited testing done in Tier 3 (the RTI model implemented in her school apparently does not specify routine comprehensive assessment in Tier 3), we also know that she is not mentally retarded.

We do not know anything about the underlying nature of Susan's reading disability. Does she have a primary problem with phonemic awareness? What about fluency? What about listening comprehension? How do auditory attention, working memory, and auditory processing impact her learning? What about her mood? If more was known about these issues, would we be better able to address her learning problem?

We also don't know about other factors that may be affecting learning. For example, 20 to 50% of children diagnosed with a reading LD also meet diagnostic criteria for Attention-Deficit/Hyperactivity Disorder (ADHD; Gilger, Pennington, & DeFries, 1992; Semrud-Clikeman et al., 1992; Wilcutt & Pennington, 2000). As a girl, Susan is unlikely to have shown visible signs of ADHD (hyperactivity) during classroom observation. What about objective assessment of her attention skills (Greenberg & Waldman, 1993)? Without any of this information, the chances that Susan's reading intervention will be anything more than a "one-size-fits-all" approach are essentially nil, and it is difficult to imagine how her "Individualized Educational Plan" could in any way be "individualized." It is possible to know so much more about her that the approach to RTI described in this vignette fails to provide.

The goal of a comprehensive evaluation is to provide a model or diagnosis that: (a) accurately characterizes an individual's functioning; (b) facilitates thinking about the individual; (c) explains his or her current difficulties;

(d) guides effective intervention; and (e) provides a basis for expectations of growth or change with intervention over time. RTI models that omit comprehensive evaluation provide almost none of this information. Further, they appear to hold the assumption that academic failure has a unitary cause with a clear intervention. This ignores decades of research on the underlying neuropsychological components of learning disorders.

While RTI does offer a framework for early identification and intervention in young children struggling with (primarily) reading problems, it does not provide an acceptable framework for diagnosis of LD. This weakness is now well recognized (Vaughn & Fuchs, 2003; Hale et al., 2004; Semrud-Clikeman, 2005; Silver et al., 2006; Reynolds, 2005; National Association of School Psychologists, 2007). Diagnosis through treatment failure tells us little about the nature of an underlying cause of failure (which could be from a multitude of causes) and can lead to inappropriate or unhelpful interventions.

While this critique has focused on the lack of adequate assessment in some RTI models, other fundamental concerns are also present. According to Fuchs, Mock, Morgan, and Young (2003), shifts from the discrepancy model has been not in the direction of a well-validated substitute.

One key issue is the lack of basic research addressing methods of screening. Semrud-Clikeman (2005) commented on the vagueness with which this component of RTI is characterized, ". . . this difficulty is reminiscent of the original definition of a learning disability that required a 'significant discrepancy' but did not define what 'significant' entailed" (p. 244). Common methodology used to monitor the effectiveness of interventions (analysis of change scores) may be fatally flawed (Prieler & Raven, 2002), and Fuchs, Fuchs, and Compton (2004) report that different screening methods identify different sets of children. Which children actually have a problem? What is the best method of screening? What are the valid criteria? How do we accurately monitor change?

Reynolds (2005) offers additional criticisms. These include the observations that: RTI is *at its root* an example of a severe discrepancy analysis that assumes everyone is equivalent in ability or aptitude; RTI creates ability tracking by overidentifying as LD those with IQs less than 90; RTI ignores children with high ability; RTI "ignores the processing disorder component of the definition of learning disability"; RTI "diagnoses by treatment failure" (which medicine has shown us is a weak approach); and RTI supports a "one-size-fits-all" method of intervention that "ignores over 100 years or research on individual differences" (p. 2).

Recent RTI models have begun to recognize the need for comprehensive assessment. Integrating the best of the old and the new, Hale et al. (2006) propose a model that formally integrates comprehensive evaluation into a three-tiered RTI model. In this approach, the standardized RTI approach is to be implemented at Tier 1, an *individualized problem-solving approach* model is applied at Tier 2, and comprehensive assessment occurs as part of Tier 3. Hale and colleagues report that their model is similar to that recommended by Fuchs et al. (2003), Semrud-Clikeman (2005), and the National Association of School Psychologists (2005). This model appears to be gaining support (and is the approach advocated by this author).

Whether or not an integrated model is broadly accepted, still other issues remain at the level of intervention. RTI assumes that appropriate interventions have been developed, can be selected through RTI, and are readily at hand. This is simply not true. Intervention studies have predominantly addressed basic reading problems in early grades, but do not adequately address higher-level reading ability or other content areas (National Joint Committee on Learning Disabilities, 2005). Indeed, even as the *Parent's Guide to Response-to-Intervention* informs us that RTI calls for "curriculum and educational interventions that are research based and have been proven to be effective for most students" (p. 2), we find that the specific computer software selected by her special education teacher to "enhance Susan's special education program" (and with which she is to spend 2 hours each week) was reported by the U.S. Department of Education's Institute of Education Sciences to produce "no discernible effects" (p. 1) in either fluency or reading comprehension (Institute of Education Sciences, 2007). As Vaughn and Fuchs (2003) state, "validated intervention methods for testing responsiveness to instruction require further attention" (p. 142).

Overall, RTI is a potential advance in that its principles clearly encourage *best practices* in elementary education and provide a good supportive framework for prereferral intervention (primarily for reading). It is equally clear that RTI models that do not integrate comprehensive assessment are inadequate for diagnosis and management of significant LD.

For RTI to be effective, significant amounts of research must be directed toward fundamental issues associated with the methodology of identification and intervention. For it to be truly helpful to children with learning disabilities, it should resemble that proposed by Fuchs et al. (2003), Semrud-Clikeman (2005), the National Association of School Psychologists (2007), and Hale et al. (2006).

WHAT ROLE DOES NEUROPSYCHOLOGY HAVE TO PLAY IN THE DIAGNOSIS OF LEARNING DISABILITIES?

Neuropsychology is a discipline that has as its goal the characterization of an individual's cognitive functioning in terms of known neuroanatomical behavioral relationships (Lezak, 1995). While there is overlap in the training, knowledge, and practice of neuropsychologists and clinical psychologists (Baron, 2004), neuropsychologists are unique in their extensive training and focus on the neurological foundations of behavior and learning, and in the breadth and specialization of the tools commonly used in neuropsychological assessment. There is some overlap with the profession of school psychology, and a recent innovation in the field has been the hybrid training of *school neuropsychologists* (D'Amato, Fletcher-Janzen, & Reynolds, 2005), who combine training in school psychology with specialization in pediatric neuropsychology.

Much of the work done by neuropsychologists who specialize in pediatric work occurs in hospitals or other medical settings. This work has the goal of helping medical professionals and caregivers understand the cognitive and developmental effects of diseases, injuries, or other conditions that impact brain functioning (Baron, Fennell, & Voeller, 1995). These conditions vary widely and can include: epilepsy (Gunduz, Demirbilek, & Korkmaz, 1999; Baker, 2001), genetic disorders (Pizzamiglio, Piccardi, & Guariglia, 2003; Moore et al., 2004; de Vries & Hunt, 2006; Plotts & Livermore, 2007), diabetes (McCarthy et al., 2002; Jameson, 2006), spina bifida (Dennis et al., 2006), metachromatic leukodystrophy (Shapiro, Lipton, & Krivit, 1992; Weber Byars et al., 2001; Bjoraker, Delaney et al., 2006), late effects of treatment for diseases such as cancer (Mulhern, Fairclough, & Ochs, 1991; Spencer, 2006; West, 2006), as well as a range of other medical conditions. Neuropsychologists in medical settings also play an important role in consulting with educators about the educational potential and needs of their patients.

While assessment of medically involved individuals is challenging and rewarding, most pediatric neuropsychologists also see many children who are referred for evaluation of learning and attention problems. Yeates, Ris, and Taylor (1995) recorded the primary diagnoses received by a total of 472 children who had been referred to the pediatric neuropsychology clinics of three hospitals. Their survey showed that the most common diagnosis rendered in this sample was that of a learning disability (followed by traumatic brain injury and ADHD). For all of their expertise in diseases, injuries, and congenital malformations, most pediatric neuropsychologists spend a considerable amount of time identifying the bases of school problems in nonclinical populations. The number of referrals for evaluations of this nature suggests that parents, teachers, and other referral sources in the community appreciate this approach to LD diagnosis.

As defined in *Diagnostic and Statistical Manual for Mental Disorders—Fourth Edition* (DSM-IV; American Psychiatric Association, 1994), a *learning disability* is present when performance on a standardized measure that assesses academic achievement falls "substantially below that expected given the person's chronological age, measured intelligence and age-appropriate education" (p. 50). This definition reflects the discrepancy model of LD originally specified in 1975 with the passage of PL 94-142. The 2004 amendments to the law (the Individuals with Disabilities Educational Improvement Act) provided for alternatives to this model, which led to the development of

RTI-based models to diagnose LD, some of which incorporate comprehensive assessment in making such a diagnosis (Hale et al., 2006).

Bernstein (2006) notes that a diagnosis is specific to the nosological scheme in which it is defined, and the "rules of evidence" that apply in that scheme. The discrepancy component of the "discrepancy model" framework can be satisfied on the basis of relatively limited testing (comparing performance on IQ and achievement tests). It is also possible in the RTI framework to render an LD diagnosis on the basis of academic failure at multiple stages of intervention, making use of little or no testing. Neither method requires a neuropsychological evaluation.

However, as Semrud-Clikeman (2005) notes, these approaches to diagnosis are quite narrow, and provide no information about possible strategies for remediation (or about the presence of other conditions that may affect learning). They fail to consider "the neuropsychological functions underlying the ability to read, speak, comprehend, write and do mathematics well" (p. 243).

In providing both a diagnosis and an examination of critical underlying cognitive functions, neuropsychological assessment provides abundant information about strategies for remediation. Mather and Gregg (2006) describe a diagnostic process that illustrates this approach. Their method makes "an initial domain-specific classification in reading, writing, or math" and then "[identifies] the deficient cognitive and linguistic processes that underlie the disorder" (p. 103). This model consists of the following steps:

1. Observe a limitation in one or more of the following areas of achievement: reading (basic skills, fluency, or comprehension); written language (basic skills, fluency, or expression); or mathematics (basic skills, fluency, or application). Rule out alternative explanations for the limitation (e.g., Mental Retardation, lack of opportunity).
2. Document the limitation using multiple sources of data (e.g., standardized or curriculum-based measurements using multiple test formats; response to intervention; teacher, student, and parent reports; class work samples; and educational history).
3. Identify the specific cognitive and/or linguistic correlates that appear to be related to the identified area of underachievement relative difficulty. Rule out alternative explanations for the cognitive or linguistic difficulties. (p. 103)

This approach ensures accurate detection of LD, rules out (or in) additional sources of impairment, and provides a direction for remediation. Additional review of the broader social context and history of the child, and consultation with educators and other important figures in the child's life, allows the neuropsychologist to (as Bernstein states), address the broader goal of promoting optimal development for the child (2006).

Broad-scope neuropsychological assessment is not necessary to formulate a diagnosis. It is, however, immensely helpful in promoting optimal progress of children with LD.

It is both professionally and personally rewarding when, after their child has undergone a neuropsychological evaluation, a mother or father declares that they now—*finally*—understand their child and can now find a way forward. No other discipline or diagnostic approach facilitates such understanding, and this probably accounts for the broad interest that has been shown in this approach to LD diagnosis.

WHAT DO YOU THINK NEUROSCIENCE HAS TO OFFER THE ASSESSMENT AND IDENTIFICATION OF LEARNING DISABILITIES?

Modern tools of neuroscience research have provided us with the ability to observe and measure previously hidden processes that underlie learning and cognition. The use of technologies such as positron emission tomography, magnetic resonance imaging, magnetoencephalography, and diffusion tensor imaging have made it possible to measure the morphology and activity of the brains of normal learners, and compare it with that of individuals diagnosed with LDs. This work has revealed differences in patterns of activation between the brains of normal and affected individuals with dyslexia (Shaywitz, Lyon, & Shaywitz, 2006; Fine et al., 2007; Simos, Fletcher et al., 2006), dyscalculia (Kucian et al., 2006), and differences in activation and morphology in the brains of individuals with disorders that impact learning, such as ADHD (Filipek et al., 1997; Shaywitz, Fletcher & Shaywitz, 1995).

Differences between normal and LD-diagnosed children have also been observed in EEG spectra, and in event-related potentials (Lubar et al., 1985; Spironelli et al., 2006; Burgio-Murphy et al., 2007; Arns et al., 2007). In addition, genetic linkage analysis has identified specific gene sequences that are associated with reading disabilities (Francks, MacPhie, & Monaco, 2002; Francks et al., 2004).

Brain-imaging studies have shown changes in activity associated with mastery of complex cognitive tasks (Haier, 1992; Haier, 1999), and with remediation of learning problems (Simos, Fletcher, Sarkari, Billingsley, Denton, & Papanicolaou, 2007; Simos, Fletcher, Sarkari, Billingsley-Marshall, Denton, & Papanicolaou, 2007). All of this work has led to rapid gains in knowledge of the neurological foundations of learning disorders, and will almost certainly lead to improvements in their identification and treatment.

The knowledge gained through neuroscience research encourages what Denckla (1996) has described as an "inside-to-outside" approach to diagnosis. In this approach, deficits in higher-order skills (such as reading) are "viewed as outcomes arising within a context of other associated but more fundamental deficits" (p. 115). These fundamental deficits themselves are the specific targets of assessment. Our awareness and knowledge of these fundamental processes has improved dramatically as neuroscience technology has evolved, and it is likely that the development and use of future assessment tools will be guided by their relationship to anatomical (Shaywitz, Lyon, & Shaywitz, 2006) or biological activity (Llorente et al., 2006) revealed through neuroscience research. Increased granularity of the tools utilized in clinical assessment will lead to routine measurement of increasingly narrow aspects of cognition and, ultimately, the characterization of narrower subtypes of LD.

Advances in our knowledge of the neuroanatomical and physiological foundations of higher-order cognitive functions are occurring faster than diagnostic criteria can accommodate this knowledge. As Denckla (1996) writes,

> . . . neuropsychologists and cognitive neuroscientists . . . broaden the concept of LD to include several discrepancy profiles, in which a cognitive strength (or set of strengths) gives evidence of normal aptitude (perhaps on only one scale, either verbal or performance, of the conventional IQ test) although some specific oral language, visuospatial, or social-emotional aspect of cognitive is prominently impaired. The diagnosis of LD as stated in DSM-IV, however, is more closely allied to the aptitude-achievement discrepancy model adhered to by the education establishment. Cognitive neuroscience is thus out of line with the definitions of LD currently important in clinical as well as educational classifications. (p. 115)

As neuroscience continues to advance, it is possible that clinicians will reference LD subtypes that are not yet formally recognized (much as subtypes of ADHD with specific impairment of function in the anterior or posterior attention systems can be identified; Dennis, 2006).

The schism described by Denckla will not soon be resolved. The gap between current diagnostic criteria and the state of knowledge regarding the cognitive disorders they attempt to describe will only increase with time. Adoption of RTI-based models of LD diagnosis that fail to incorporate broad assessment will only increase the gap between knowledge and practice.

WHAT ROLE DOES NEUROPSYCHOLOGY HAVE TO PLAY IN DESIGNING INTERVENTIONS IN THE CONTEXT OF RTI?

Neuropsychology has the potential to play a critical role in helping to diagnosis and guide intervention if it is incorporated into the model of RTI that is implemented in a given school building or district.

Diagnosis of LD based solely on a child's failure to respond to intervention is a bad idea for reasons previously described by the current author, and likely articulated by others throughout this book. Models that incorporate comprehensive assessment of this nature (Semrud-Clikeman, 2005; Hale et al., 2006) describe a method that facilitates relatively efficient identification and support of individuals requiring remedial support in reading development, and provides those who do not respond to mild or moderate efforts at intervention a thorough evaluation that should lead to an individualized intervention tailored to address the underlying source(s) of their learning disability.

To illustrate, we can return to the example of Susan, whose course through a three-tier RTI model is described in *A Parent's Guide to Response-to-Intervention* (National Center for Learning Disabilities, 2006). Recall that, based on her failure to develop reading skills in Tiers 1 and 2 of her school's RTI model, she was advanced to Tier 3, where, through consideration of her prior academic failure, classroom observation, a parent interview, and results from IQ and language testing, she was determined to be suffering from a learning disability.

The RTI approach to diagnosis described provides little or no information regarding the fundamental deficits (Denckla, 1996) that underlie her learning problems, and certainly does not adequately address possible co-occurring disorders that affected her ability to learn. No information is available to guide the design of her intervention, and Susan will be provided with a reading intervention that may or may not adequately meet her needs.

If Susan's school implemented a model of RTI that incorporated comprehensive assessment in Tier 3, it would be possible to provide a clear summary of her cognitive status, areas of specific impairment, and recommendation of specific interventions. Such an evaluation would include a summary of findings that might look something like this:

> Susan is a girl of average intellectual ability who shows signs of a significant learning disability in the area of reading associated with poor phonemic awareness, below-average listening comprehension, and mildly weak auditory attention. Her learning difficulties are exacerbated by the presence of Attention-Deficit/Hyperactivity Disorder, Predominantly Inattentive Type. Intensive intervention should be directed at improving her phonological awareness, with additional work directed at strengthening her auditory comprehension skills. Susan will benefit from classroom accommodations that make it easier for her to watch and listen to her teacher, and her caregivers might consider referral for consideration of medical treatment of her attention problem. Her mood is a possible contributing factor to her poor academic progress, as she is beginning to express doubt over her worthiness and is reporting somatic symptoms that appear to be associated with her own concerns about her learning.

Such a characterization sums up relevant information about her cognitive status, areas of concern, and co-occurring disorders. It represents the kind of information that is routinely assembled in a neuropsychological evaluation. RTI models that fail to consider the availability of such information ignore years of research on learning and the brain and will not adequately serve the needs of the children they aim to serve.

REFERENCES

American Psychiatric Association. (1994). *Diagnostic and Statistical Manual of Mental Disorders, Fourth Edition.* Washington, DC: American Psychiatric Association.

Arns, M., Peters, S., Breteler, R., & Verhoeven, L. (2007). Different brain activation patterns in dyslexic children: Evidence from EEG power and coherence patterns for the double-deficit theory of dyslexia. *Journal of Integrative Neuroscience, 6*(1), 175–190.

Baker, G. A. (2001). Psychological and neuropsychological assessment before and after surgery for epilepsy: Implications for the management of learning-disabled people. *Epilepsia, 42*(Supp 11), 41–43.

Baron, I. S. (1994). *Neuropsychological evaluation of the child.* New York: Oxford University Press.

Baron, I. S., Fennel, E. B., & Voeller, K. K. (1995). *Pediatric neuropsychology in the medical setting.* New York: Oxford University Press.

Bernstein, J. (February, 2006). From field and lab to clinic and life. Using the 'evidence base' in pediatric practice. Continuing Education Workshop, International Neuropsychological Society meeting, Boston, MA.

Bjoraker, K. J., Delaney, K., Peters, C., Krivit, W., Shaprio, E. G. (2006). Long-term outcomes of adaptive functions for children with mucopolysaccharidosis I (Hurler Syndrome) treated with hematopoietic stem cell transplantation. *Journal of Developmental & Behavioral Pediatrics, 27*(4), 290–296.

Burgio-Murphy, A., Klorman, R., Shaywitz, S. E., Fletcher, J. M., Marchione, K. E., Holahan, J., et al. (2007). Error-related event-related potentials in children with attention-deficit hyperactivity disorder, oppositional defiant disorder, reading disorder, and math disorder. *Biological Psychology, 75*(1), 75–86.

Cortiella, C. (2006). Response-to-Intervention—An emerging method for LD identification. Retrieved on August 11th, 2007 from http://www.schwablearning .org/articles.aspx?r=840.

D'Amato, R. C., Fletcher-Janzen, E., Reynolds, C. R. (Eds.). (2005). *Handbook of school neuropsychology.* New York: Wiley.

de Vries, P. J., & Hunt, A. (2006). The importance of comprehensive assessment for cognitive and behavioral problems in tuberous sclerosis complex. *Epilepsy & Behavior, 9*(2), 373.

Denckla, M. B. (1996). Biological correlates of learning and attention: What is relevant to learning disability and attention-deficit hyperactivity disorder? *Journal of Developmental & Behavioral Pediatrics, 17*(2), 114–119.

Dennis, M. (2006). Attention in individuals with spina bifida: Assets and deficits. Retrieved on September 10th, 2007 from http://sbaa.omnibooksonline.com/ 2006/data/papers/016.pdf.

Dennis, M., Landry, S., Barnes, M., & Fletcher, J. (2006). A model of neurocognitive function in spina bifida over the lifespan. *Journal of the International Neuropsychological Society,12,* 285–296.

Filipek, P. A., Semrud-Clikeman, M., Steingard, R. J., & Renshaw, P. F. (1997). Volumetric MRI analysis comparing subjects having attention-deficit hyperactivity disorder with normal controls. *Neurology, 48*(3, Pt 2), 589–601.

Fine, J. G., Semrud-Clikeman, M., Keith, T. Z., Stapleton, L. M., & Hynd, G. W. (2007). Reading and the corpus callosum: An MRI family study of volume and area. *Neuropsychology, 21*(2), 235–241.

Fletcher, J., Coulter, W., Reschley, D., & Vaughn, S. (2004). Alternative approaches to the definition and identification of learning disabilities: Some questions and answers. *Annals of Dyslexia, 54*(2), 304–331.

Francks, C., MacPhie, I. L., & Monaco, A. P. (2002). The genetic basis of dyslexia. *Lancet Neurology, 1*(8), 483–490.

Francks, C., Paracchini, S., Smith, S. D., Richardson, A. J., Scerri, T. S., Cardon, L. R., et al. (2004). A 77-kilobase region of chromosome 6p22.2 is associated with dyslexia in families from the United Kingdom and from the United States. *American Journal of Human Genetics, 75*(6), 1046–1058.

Fuchs, D., Fuchs, L., & Compton, D. (2004) Identifying reading disabilities by responsiveness-to-instruction: Specifying measures and criteria. *Learning Disability Quarterly, 27,* 216–227.

Fuchs, D., Mock, D., Morgan, P., & Young, C. (2003). Responsiveness to Intervention: Definitions, evidence and implications for the learning disabilities construct. *Learning Disabilities Research & Practice, 18,* 157–171.

Gilger, J. W., Pennington, B. F., & DeFries, J. C. (1992). A twin study of the etiology of comorbidity: Attention deficit-hyperactivity disorder and dyslexia. *Journal of the American Academy of Child and Adolescent Psychiatry, 31,* 343–348.

Greenberg, L. M., & Waldman, I. D. (1993). Developmental normative data on the test of variables of attention (T.O.V.A.). *Journal of Child Psychology & Psychiatry & Allied Disciplines, 34*(6), 1019–1030.

Gunduz, E., Demirbilek, V., & Korkmaz, B. (1999). Benign rolandic epilepsy: Neuropsycholgical findings. *Seizure, 8*(4), 246–249.

Haier, R. J. (1999). PET studies of learning and individual differences. In J. L. McClelland & R. S. Siegler (Eds.), *Mechanisms of cognitive development: Behavioral and neural perspectives.* New Jersey: Erlbaum. 2001.

Haier, R. J., Siegel, B. V., McLachlan, A., Soderling, E., Lottenberg, S., & Buchsbaum, M. S. (1992). Regional glucose metabolic changes after learning a complex visuospatial/motor task: a positron emission tomographic study. *Brain Research, 570*(1–2), 134–143.

Hale, J., Kaufman, A., Naglieri, J., & Kavale, K. (2006). Implementation of IDEA: Integrating response to intervention and cognitive assessment methods. *Psychology in the Schools, 43*(7), 753–770.

Individuals with Disabilities Education Improvement Act of 2004, PL 108-446 Section 614.

Institute of Education Sciences (2007). What works Clearinghouse: Read Naturally. Retrieved September 3, 2007 from http://ies.ed.gov/ncee/wwc/reports/beginning_reading/read_naturally/index.asp.

Jameson, P. (2006). Diabetes, cognitive function and school performance. *School Nurse News,* (May), 34–36.

Kucian, K., Loenneker, T., Dietrich, T., Dosch, M., Martin, E., & von Aster, M. (2006). Impaired neural networks for approximate calculation in dyscalculic children: A functional MRI study. *Behavioral & Brain Functions* [Electronic Resource]: *BBF, 2,* 31.

Lezak, M. D. (1995). *Neuropsychological assessment* (3rd ed.). New York: Oxford University Press.

Llorente, A. M., Voigt, R. G., Jensen, C. L., Berretta, M. C., Fraley, J. K., & Heird, W. C. (2006). Performance on a visual sustained attention and discrimination task is associated with urinary excretion of norepinephrine metabolite in children with attention deficit/hyperactivity disorder (AD/HD). *Clinical Neuropsychologist, 20*(1), 133–144.

Lubar, J. F., Bianchini, K. J., Calhoun, W. H., Lambert, E. W., Brody, Z. H., & Shabsin, H. S. (1985). Spectral analysis of EEG differences between children with and without learning disabilities. *Journal of Learning Disabilities, 18*(7), 403–408.

Mather, N., & Gregg, N. (2006). Specific learning disabilities: Clarifying, not eliminating, a construct. *Professional Psychology: Research and Practice, 37*(1), 99–106.

McCarthy, A., Lindgren, S., Mengeling, M., Tsalikian, E., & Engvall, J. (2002). Effects of diabetes on learning in children. *Pediatrics, 109*(1), e9.

Moore, C. J., Daly, E. M., Schmitz, N., Tassone, F., Tysoe, C., Hagerman, R. J., et al. (2004). A neuropsychological investigation of male premutation carriers of fragile X syndrome. *Neuropsychologia, 42*(14), 1934–1947.

Mulhern, R., Fairclough, D., & Ochs, J. (1991). A prospective comparison of neuropsychologic performance of children surviving leukemia who received 18-Gy, 24-Gy, or no cranial irradiation. *Journal of Clinical Oncology, 9,* 1348–1356.

National Association of School Psychologists. (2007). NASP position statement on identification of students with specific learning disabilities. Retrieved August 17, 2007 from http://www.nasponline.org/about_nasp/positionpapers/SLDPosition_2007.pdf.

National Center for Learning Disabilities. (2006). *Parent Advocacy Brief: A Parent's Guide to Response-to-Intervention.* Retrieved July 15, 2007 from http://www.ncld.org/images/stories/downloads/parent_center/rti_final.pdf.

National Joint Committee on Learning Disabilities. (2005). *Responsiveness to intervention and learning disabilities.* Retrieved on July 15, 2007 from www.ldonline.org/?module=uploads& func=download&fileId=461.

Pizzamiglio, M. R., Piccardi, L., & Guariglia, C. (2003). Asymmetries in neuropsychological profile in cri-du-chat syndrome. *Cognitive Processing, 4*(Suppl), 20.

Plotts, C. A., & Livermore, C. L. (2007). Russell-silver syndrome and nonverbal learning disability: A case study. *Applied Neuropsychology, 14*(2), 124–134.

Prieler, J., & Raven, J. (2002). *The measurement of change in groups and individuals, with particular reference to the value of gain scores: A new IRT-based methodology for the assessment of treatment effects and utilizing gain scores.* Retrieved July 25, 2007 from http://home.earthlink.net/~rkmck/vault/priravf/prirav.pdf.

Reynolds, C. (August, 2005). Considerations in RTI as a method of diagnosis of learning disabilities. Paper presented to the Annual Institute for Psychology in the Schools of the American Psychological Association, Washington, DC.

Semrud-Clikeman, M. (2005). Neuropsychological aspects for evaluating learning disabilities. *Communication Disorders Quarterly, 26*(4), 242–247.

Semrud-Clikeman, M., Biederman, J., Sprich-Buckminster, S., Krifcher Lehman, B., Faraone, S., & Norman, D. (1992). Comorbidity between ADDH and learning disability: A review and report in a clinically referred sample. *Journal of the American Academy of Child and Adolescent Psychiatry, 31*, 439–448.

Shaywitz, B. A., Lyon, G. R., & Shaywitz, S. E. (2006). The role of functional magnetic resonance imaging in understanding reading and dyslexia. *Developmental Neuropsychology, 30*(1), 613–632.

Simos, P. G., Fletcher, J. M., Sarkari, S., Billingsley, R. L., Denton, C., & Papanicolaou, A. C. (2007). Altering the brain circuits for reading through intervention: A magnetic source imaging study. *Neuropsychology, 21*(4), 485–496.

Simos, P. G., Fletcher, J. M., Denton, C., Sarkari, S., Billingsley-Marshall, R., & Papanicolaou, A. C. (2006). Magnetic source imaging studies of dyslexia interventions. *Developmental Neuropsychology, 30*(1), 591–611.

Simos, P. G., Fletcher, J. M., Sarkari, S., Billingsley-Marshall, R., Denton, C. A., & Papanicolaou, A. C. (2007). Intensive instruction affects brain magnetic activity associated with oral word reading in children with persistent reading disabilities. *Journal of Learning Disabilities, 40*(1), 37–48.

Spironelli, C., Penolazzi, B., Vio, C., & Angrilli, A. (2006). Inverted EEG theta lateralization in dyslexic children during phonological processing. *Neuropsychologia, 44*(14), 2814–2821.

Shapiro, E. G., Lipton, M. E., & Krivit, W. (1992). White matter dysfunction and its neuropsychological correlates: A longitudinal study of a case of metachromatic leukodystrophy treated with bone marrow transplant. *Journal of Clinical and Experimental Neuropsychology, 14*(4), 610–624.

Shaywitz, B. A., Fletcher, J. M., & Shaywitz, S. E. (1995). Defining and classifying learning disabilities and attention-deficit/hyperactivity disorder. *Journal of Child Neurology, 10*, S50–S57.

Silver, S., Blackburn, L., Arffa, S., Barth, J., Bush, S., Kifler, S., Pliskin, N., Reynolds, C., Ruff, R., Troster, A., Moster, R., & Eliott, R. (2006). The importance of neuropsychological assessment for the evaluation of childhood learning disorders: NAN policy and planning committee. *Archives of Clinical Neuropsychology 21*, 741–744.

Spencer, J. (2006). The role of cognitive remediation in childhood cancer survivors experiencing neurocognitive late effects. *Journal of Pediatric Oncology Nursing, 23*(6), 321–325.

Vaughn, S., & Fuchs, L. (2003) Redefining learning disabilities as inadequate response to instruction: The promise and potential problems. *Learning Disabilities Research and Practice, 18*(3), 137–146.

Weber Byars, A. M., McKellop, M., Gyato, K., Sullivan, T., & Franz, D. N. (2001). Metachromitic leukodystrophy and nonverbal learning disability: Neuropsychological and neuroradiological findings in heterozygous carriers. *Child Neuropsychology, 7*(1), 54–58.

West, R. L. (2006). Review of survivors of childhood and adolescent cancer: A multidisciplinary approach, second edition. *Journal of the American Academy of Child & Adolescent Psychiatry, 45*(11), 1387–1388.

Willcutt, E. G., & Pennington, B. F. (2000). Comorbidity of reading disability and attention-deficit/hyperactivity disorder: Differences by gender and subtype. *Journal of Learning Disabilities, 33,* 179–191.

Yeates, K. O., Ris, M. D., & Taylor, H. G. (1995). Hospital referral patterns in pediatric neuropsychology. *Child Neuropsychology, 1*(1), 56–62.

9

The Need to Integrate Cognitive Neuroscience and Neuropsychology into a RTI Model

Daniel C. Miller

WHAT DO YOU THINK NEUROSCIENCE HAS TO OFFER LAWS AND POLICIES ASSOCIATED WITH LEARNING DISABILITIES?

The term *learning disabilities* gained widespread use with its inclusion in P.L. 94-142 in 1975. The National Joint Committee for Learning Disabilities (NJCLD) is an interorganizational group that meets twice a year to facilitate communication between the groups on best practices related to specific learning disabilities (SLDs) and to provide guidance to public policy makers. In 1981, the NJCLD proposed a long-standing definition of learning disabilities suggesting "these disorders are intrinsic to the individual and presume to be due to central nervous system dysfunction" (Hammill et al., 1981, p. 340). In 2002, the Office of Special Education Programs within the U.S. Department of Education sponsored a Learning Disabilities Roundtable discussion that issued a final report entitled *Specific Learning Disabilities: Finding Common Ground* (Learning Disabilities Roundtable, 2002). There were several key portions in the consensus statements that are important to review:

- The concept of *Specific Learning Disabilities* (SLDs) is valid and supported by strong converging evidence.
- Specific learning disabilities are neurologically based and intrinsic to the individual [and the statutory definition of SLD should be maintained in IDEA reauthorization].

- Individuals with SLD show intraindividual differences in skills and abilities.
- The ability-achievement discrepancy formula should not be used for determining eligibility.
- Decisions regarding eligibility for special education services must draw from information collected from a comprehensive evaluation using multiple methods and sources in gathering relevant information.

The 2002 Learning Disabilities Roundtable consensus report was not without critics. In the 2003 report for the National Center for Learning Disabilities, *And Miles to Go. . . .: State SLD Requirements and Authoritative Recommendations,* Reschly, Hosp, and Schmied (2003) expressed concerns about the Roundtable report and provided some survey data about SLD identification practices across states. Reschly et al. (2003) reported that:

> The LD Roundtable participants did not recommend changes in the IDEA definition of SLD, although the National Joint Committee on Learning Disabilities (NJCLD) formulated an SLD definition in 1988 that did not mention psychological process disorders (Hammill, 1990). It is likely that this was not a mere oversight, but more likely a conscious effort to focus on the most pressing issues, elimination of the ability-achievement discrepancy and development of a reasonable set of alternative procedures. (p. 7)

Despite years of empirical evidence, which proves that learning disabilities are a result of neuropsychological deficits, some educational policy makers remain unconvinced. After passage of P.L. 94-142 in the 1970s, researchers began to investigate the neurobiological bases of learning disabilities and behavioral disorders (Obrzut & Hynd, 1996a, 1996b). The past 30 years have yielded substantial evidence for the biological bases of behavior. There is strong neurobiological evidence for Attention-Deficit/Hyperactivity Disorder (see Pliszka, 2003 for a review), reading disorders (see Feifer & DeFina, 2000; Feifer & Della Toffalo, 2007; Fischer, Immordino-Yang, & Waber, 2007; Hale & Fiorello, 2004, for reviews), written language disorders (see Feifer & DeFina, 2002; Hale & Fiorello, 2004, for reviews), mathematics disorders (see Fiefer & DeFina, 2005; Hale & Fiorello, 2004, for reviews), and pervasive developmental disorders (see Bauman & Kemper, 2005, for a review).

Researchers who have established, and practitioners who have applied, the biological bases of behavior have become increasingly concerned about the strong behavioral orientation of federal legislation. Neuroscientists must educate legislators about what has been learned about brain-behavior relationships during the 1990's *decade of the brain* and work to translate research into educational practice. In the inaugural journal of a new organization called the International Mind, Brain, and Education Society, the editors stated:

The discovery of powerful brain-imaging tools; the remarkable, burgeoning discoveries that are transforming genetics; and the growing power of methods for assessing cognition, emotion, and learning make possible an alliance that can illuminate human leaning and development. (Stern, 2005, as referenced in Fisher et al., 2007, p. 1.)

Neuroscientists, cognitive psychologists, and school neuropsychologists must continue to advocate for the maintenance of the SLD definition in the federal law that recognizes the biological bases of the SLD. There is a contingency of professionals who would like to have SLD redefined and exclude the notion that SLDs are neurologically based.

WHAT DO YOU THINK NEUROSCIENCE HAS TO OFFER THE ASSESSMENT AND IDENTIFICATION OF LEARNING DISABILITIES?

In the early years of neuropsychology (1940–1950s), the emphasis was on using single behavioral measures to detect brain damage (Hartlage, Asken, & Hornsby, 1987; Rourke, 1982). This *single-test approach* stage was followed by the *test battery/lesion specification* stage from the 1950s to 1980s (Rourke, 1982). The test battery/lesion specification stage emphasized using a battery of tests to predict brain dysfunction. Rourke (1982) termed the next stage in clinical neuropsychology the *functional profile stage* that started in the 1970s. The functional profile stage deemphasized the localization of brain lesions and emphasized the identification of what brain functions were impaired and spared. With the advent of neuroimaging techniques (e.g., CAT scans) in the 1970s, neuropsychologists were not needed to hypothesize the location of structural deficits.

Miller (2007) labeled the current stage of the neuropsychology field (1990s to the present) as the *integrative and predictive stage*. The integrative and predictive stage emphasizes the multidisciplinary synthesis of brain research. Research from many brain-related disciplines, such as neuroimaging, neurochemistry, electrophysiology, test theory, statistical modeling, genetics, and so on, are all converging to provide a better understanding of brain-behavior relationships. As an example, the Test of Memory and Learning (TOMAL: Reynolds & Bigler, 1994) was one of the first neuropsychological measures to use neuroimaging techniques for construct validation. In the future, neuroimaging techniques such as functional magnetic imaging (fMRI) will be increasingly used to validate the neuropsychological constructs that report to measure the basic psychological processes required in a SLD evaluation.

Anatomical magnetic resonance imaging (aMRI) is being used more frequently to study neuroanatomical differences between children with specific learning disabilities and matched controls. The results have been mixed, but this may be due to the methodological differences used across studies (Fletcher et al., 2007). aMRI imaging will continue to be used with children because it is safe and noninvasive. As methodological issues are resolved the aMRI result will provide direct evidence of neuroanatomical differences in children with developmental disorders.

Neuroimaging techniques will be increasingly used to evaluate the efficacy of educational interventions (see Fletcher et al., 2007, for a review). For example, Shaywitz (2003) used functional imaging techniques to evaluate the effects of specific reading interventions. She documented "inefficient" cognitive processing prior to an intervention and "efficient" cognitive processing after an intervention. Using fMRI techniques to validate the efficacy of educational interventions is very exciting and has the potential to revolutionize educational practice.

Many children with SLDs are placed on a wide assortment of medications designed to improve aspects of learning or help regulate behavior. Neuroscience is helping drug companies develop smarter drugs that will target selective neural pathways. These "smart drugs" are not decades away, but years away. As researchers learn more about the neurochemistry of the brain, medications will improve to help children with known learning and behavioral difficulties (Miller, 2007).

In addition, researchers have been investigating the genetic bases to common learning disabilities such as reading disorders. Reading problems have a tendency to run in families. Grigorenko (2007) provided a comprehensive review of the influences of genetics on developmental dyslexia. Genetic factors do not account for all of the reading difficulty outcomes. With the completion of the Human Genome Project and the continued research in identifying genes that influence behavior, we are one step closer to understanding the genetic predisposition for certain disorders such as specific learning disabilities. In the not-too-distant future, educators will be presented with neuroimaging data and genetic reports that provide baseline information about a child's inefficient cognitive processing or a genetic predisposition for a particular disability. Armed with this sophisticated information, educators will be able to target interventions designed to prevent or minimize specific learning disabilities.

HOW DO YOU RECONCILE RTI AS A MEANS OF DIAGNOSIS OF LD WITH KNOWLEDGE FROM THE CLINICAL NEUROSCIENCES?

The widespread use of the discrepancy model approach in the identification of learning disabilities created many problems for the school psychology profession and for education in general. Research showed that the use of discrepancy models overidentified children from minority groups, was too costly, did not differentiate with sufficient validity between underachievers and children with SLD, and did not address the underlying processing disorders inherent in children with learning disabilities (Learning Disabilities Roundtable, 2002; Report of the President's Commission on Excellence in Special Education, 2002). In 2002, the Learning Disabilities Roundtable group suggested that a response-to-intervention approach could be used as an alternative to special education identification rather than the discrepancy model.

Many school psychologist practitioners have tried for years to shed the traditional discrepancy and the "refer, test, and, place" assessment models in favor of a more consultative role. Given the ever-growing shortage of school psychologist practitioners (Miller & Palomares, 2000), it makes sense that not all children with educational concerns can be individually administered a comprehensive assessment. However, change from the "bottom-up" remained elusive for many school psychologists for decades as the educational system would not allow for modification in service delivery. As a result of the 2004 federal changes to IDEA, educational administrators have been returning from their professional conferences with a mandate that school psychologists have to change to a more consultative role. This "top-down" push to change the delivery of school psychological services is finally allowing many school psychologists to assume the roles and functions they have wanted to assume for decades. This alteration in public policy at the federal level and the resulting willingness of educational administrators to allow school psychologists to change their roles and functions will be the most important legacy of the RTI approach.

It is important to remember that RTI is just a process of systematically applying evidence-based interventions with the primary goal of preventing academic problems. The school psychology and educational professions have advocated many of the RTI components for decades. For example, the value of prereferral interventions and a general problem-solving approach has consistently been touted as best practice by the school psychology professional organizations. Another key component of RTI that has been around a long time is the emphasis on the prescriptive linkage between assessment and intervention. What makes RTI new is not necessarily the ideas contained within, but how these educational practices have been packaged.

Unfortunately, the implementation of RTI has created a schism within the profession. Groups within school psychology are interpreting the RTI approach radically different. One group equates the RTI approach with a strict curriculum-based approach to assessment and intervention while another group asserts that there is still a need for a comprehensive evaluation of a child's basic psychological processes prior to SLD diagnosis (Hale et al., 2006). The CBM advocates assert that educators, including school psychologists, should only be concerned with dependent variables, such as reading level. They also assert that the major thrust of education should be to seek agreement as to what constitutes measurable outcomes of the dependent measures.

The cognitive-processing advocates assert that there are many independent variables that mediate and influence dependent variables such as reading achievement. Mediating variables can include a child's socioeconomic status, cognitive strengths and weakness, physiological status (e.g., health and well being), emotional status, and quality of instruction. Differences emerge between these two groups when it comes to the identification of SLD. The CBM advocates contend that failure to respond to systematically applied and monitored interventions could lead to a SLD classification, whereas the cognitive-processing advocates contend that deficits in basic psychological processes are the cause of underachievement and must be assessed comprehensively (Hale et al., 2006). Specific to the identification of SLD, Hale et al. (2006) have argued that the RTI model ignores the underlying definition of SLD, which specifies that a child must have a disorder in one or more of the basic psychological processes. Hale and Fiorello (2004) and Fletcher-Janzen (2005) point out that the only way to adhere to the SLD definition and document processing deficits is to administer cognitive and neuropsychological measures.

Equating RTI with CBM will not address the issue of why the child is not learning. The National Association of School Psychologists (NASP) has adopted a balanced position paper on the best practices of SLD identification that recognized the need for comprehensive individualized assessment in addition to progress monitoring (NASP, 2007). Many states are adopting RTI as a model of identification for special education. States should be cautioned not to implement rules of SLD identification that exclude the assessment of the underlying deficits in basic brain functions.

The overreliance on discrepancy models for the identification of SLD was a disservice to the profession of school psychology. Calculating a numerical discrepancy became too easy in the identification of SLD. Many assessment specialists have lost sight of the importance of evaluating the cognitive-processing deficits that help explain the learning deficits, which remains central to the definition of SLD. When deficits in basic cognitive processing are identified and are linked to the current learning difficulty, it makes targeting evidence-based interventions easier and increases the likelihood of the effectives of the intervention(s). We need to put our understanding of brain functions (cognitive psychology and cognitive neuroscience) back into the professional practices of SLD identification and in guiding our educational interventions.

WHAT ROLE DOES NEUROPSYCHOLOGY HAVE TO PLAY IN THE DIAGNOSIS OF LD?

Many of the newer cognitive measures have incorporated measures of neuropsychological processes in their batteries (e.g., Mirsky's [1996] model of attention within the WJ-III-COG; working memory and processing speed with the WISC-IV: Wechsler, 2003; Lurian theory within the Cognitive Assessment System: Naglieri & Das, 1997; and the K-ABC-2: Kaufman & Kaufman, 2005). At a minimum, assessment specialists must be better informed about neuropsychological theory in order to interpret the major tests that are in use today (Miller, 2007). Measures of cognitive abilities and academic achievement are typically included in a traditional psychoeducational assessment. In a psychoeducational assessment, there may or may not be adequate information about processing deficits depending upon which cognitive abilities test is selected. For some undertrained assessment personnel, there may be a temptation to say a child does not have any memory problems when an average score is achieved on the WISC-IV Working Memory Index. However, working memory is only a subcomponent of memory and learning (Miller, 2007), and if memory deficits are part of the referral question a more comprehensive memory assessment should be conducted using a comprehensive test of memory and learning (e.g., Wide Range Assessment of Memory and Learning: Sheslow & Adams, 2003).

Since the advent of the integrative and predictive stage of neuropsychology starting in the 1990s and continuing to the present, school psychologists and school neuropsychologists have been granted access to an increasing number of tests specifically designed for children, and instruments that are psychometrically sound and based on neuropsychological theory (see Miller, 2007, for a review). A wide variety of neuropsychological tests are contained in batteries (e.g., Delis-Kaplan Executive Functions System: Delis, Kaplan, & Kramer, 2001; NEPSY-2: Korkman, Kirk, & Kemp, 2007; WISC-IV Integrated: Wechsler et al., 2004) or specialized tests of specific cognitive processes (e.g., Dean-Woodcock Sensory-Motor Battery: Dean & Woodcock, 2003; WRAML-2: Sheslow & Adams, 2003). What these neuropsychological measures add to the understanding of SLD is a clear assessment of the underlying disorders in one or more of the basic psychological processes.

If neuropsychological assessment is going to be used as part of a comprehensive SLD assessment, it is suggested that practitioners be familiar with the Cognitive Hypothesis Testing (CHT) model proposed by Hale and Fiorello (2004) and the school neuropsychological conceptual model proposed by this author (Miller, 2007). An assessment model will provide a systematic framework for evaluating a child suspected of having a SLD. In addition, practitioners should be familiar with the literature on the neuropsychological correlates to common developmental disabilities, such as word recognition, writing, mathematical calculations, and so on. The known neuropsychological correlates to a suspected disorder will help the practitioner to generate hypotheses about the child's cognitive strengths and weaknesses and verify those hypotheses with a carefully planned assessment.

WHAT ROLE DOES NEUROPSYCHOLOGY HAVE TO PLAY IN DESIGNING INTERVENTIONS IN THE CONTEXT OF RTI?

It could be argued that the RTI model may still be a wait-to-fail model (Miller, 2007). For example, many public schools have limited financial resources and frequently purchase only one district-wide curriculum for a subject such as reading. The problem is that one size does not fit all when it comes to teaching reading to children. Many school districts have purchased reading curriculums that focus almost exclusively on developing phonetics. Teaching phonics in isolation may not be associated with improvement in reading fluency (Posner & Rothbart, 2007). Too often, educators try offering a greater frequency of the same intervention when it does not seem to be working. However, offering more of the same intervention does not work if the intervention does not address the underlying cause for the reading problem in the first place (Miller, 2007). For example, if the child is *dysphonetic*, a subtype of dyslexia, a child will have difficulty learning to read using a phonemic approach. How long would a school district have to intervene in the Tier 2 portion of the RTI model before the child would be comprehensively assessed? If the child was assessed when problems became apparent and identified as *dysphonetic*, intervention could be provided earlier and targeted to the specific type of reading disability.

It is imperative that assessments inform interventions. Neuropsychological assessments can generate an individualized profile of a child's strengths and weaknesses and relate the data to known neuropsychological correlates of common developmental disorders. Most importantly, neuropsychological assessments can help identify subtypes of reading, writing, and math disorders, and then evidence-based interventions can be selected that have been shown to be effective with these particular subtypes (see Feifer & DeFina, 2000, 2002, 2005; and Feifer & Della Toffalo, 2007, for intervention reviews).

Identifying evidence-based interventions is a current challenge in education. Many of the intervention techniques that educators have used for years have good face validity but are lacking in scientific validation. Questions still arise as to what constitutes an evidence-based intervention. If an intervention has been shown to be effective on a sample of 50 children in Minnesota, does that make it evidence based? If the same effectiveness of an intervention is replicated in multiple samples, does that warrant an evidence-based label? Several task forces across professional organizations are working to establish guidelines on what constitutes an evidence-based intervention. Neuropsychological assessment data will help guide interventions, but practitioners need to treat each child as a single-subject design (Hale & Fiorello, 2004). The literature on evidence-based practice can serve as a starting point for intervention ideas, but the individual differences of the child will need to be considered in evaluating the efficacy of the intervention.

REFERENCES

Bauman, M. L., & Kemper, T. L. (Eds.). (2005). *The neurobiology of autism*. Baltimore: Johns Hopkins University Press.

Dean, R. S., & Woodcock, R. W. (2003). *Dean-Woodcock Neuropsychological Battery*. Itasca, IL: Riverside Publishing.

Delis, D., Kaplan, E., & Kramer, J. H. (2001). *Delis-Kaplan Executive Function System Examiner's Manual*. San Antonio, TX: The Psychological Corporation.

Feifer, S. G., & DeFina, P. A. (2000). *The neuropsychology of reading disorders: Diagnosis and intervention*. Middletown, MD: School Neuropsych Press.

Feifer, S. G., & DeFina, P. A. (2002). *The neuropsychology of written language disorders: Diagnosis and intervention*. Middletown, MD: School Neuropsych Press.

Feifer, S. G., & DeFina, P. A. (2005). *The neuropsychology of mathematics disorders: Diagnosis and intervention*. Middletown, MD: School Neuropsych Press.

Feifer, S. G., & Della Toffalo, D. A. (2007). *Integrating RTI with cognitive neuroscience: A scientific approach to reading*. Middletown, MD: School Neuropsych Press.

Fischer, K. W., Daniel, D. B., Immordino, M. H., Stern, E., Battro, A., & Koizumi, H. (2007). Why mind, brain, and education? Why now? *Mind, Brain, and Education, 1*, 1–2.

Fletcher, J. M., Lyon, G. R., Fuchs, L. S., & Barnes, M. A. (2007). *Learning disabilities from identification to intervention*. New York: Guilford.

Fletcher-Janzen, E. (2005). The school neuropsychological examination. In D. C. D'Amato, E. Fletcher-Janzen, & C. R. Reynolds. (Eds.), *Handbook of school neuropsychology*. Hoboken, NJ: Wiley.

Grigorenko, E. L. (2007). Triangulating developmental dyslexia: Behavior, brain, and genes. In D. Coch, G. Dawson, & K. W. Fischer. *Human behavior, learning, and the developing brain: Atypical development* (pp. 117–144). New York: Guilford.

Hale, J. B., & Fiorello, C. A. (2004). *School neuropsychology: A practitioner's handbook*. New York: Guilford.

Hale, J. B., Kaufman, A., Naglieri, J. A., & Kavale, K. A. (2006). Implementation of IDEA: Integrating response to intervention and cognitive assessment methods. *Psychology in the Schools, 43*, 753–770.

Hammill, D. D. (1990). On defining learning disabilities: An emerging consensus. *Journal of Learning Disabilities, 23*, 74–84.

Hammill, D. D., Leigh, J. E., McNutt, G., & Larsen, S. C. (1981). A new definition of learning disabilities. *Learning Disabilities Quarterly, 4*, 336–342.

Hartlage, L. C., Asken, M. J., & Hornsby, J. L. (Eds.). (1987). *Essentials of neuropsychological assessment*. New York: Springer.

Kaufman, A. S., & Kaufman, N. L. (2005). *Kaufman Test of Educational Achievement – Second Edition*. Circle Pines, MN: American Guidance Service Publishing.

Korkman, M., Kirk, U., & Kemp, S. (2007). *NEPSY-II: A developmental neuro-psychological assessment*. San Antonio, TX: The Psychological Corporation.

Learning Disabilities Roundtable. (2002). *Specific learning disabilities: Finding common ground*. Washington, DC: U.S. Department of Education. Division of Research to Practice. Office of Special Education Program.

Miller, D. C. (2007). *Essentials of school neuropsychological assessment*. New York: Wiley.

Miller, D. C., & Palomares, R. (2000, March). Growth in school psychology: A necessary blueprint. *Communique', 28*(6), 1, 6–7.

Mirsky, A. F. (1996). Disorders of attention: A neuropsychological perspective. In G. R. Lyon & N. A. Krasnegor (Eds.), *Attention, memory and executive function*. (pp. 71–95). Baltimore: Brookes.

Naglieri, J., & Das, J. P. (1997). *Das-Naglieri Cognitive Assessment System*. Itasca, IL: Riverside Publishing Company.

NASP Position Statement on Identification of Students with Specific Learning Disabilities. (July, 2007). Bethesda, MD: National Association of School Psychologists.

Obrzut, J. E., & Hynd, G. W. (1986a). *Child neuropsychology. Volume 1: Theory and research*. San Diego: Academic Press.

Obrzut, J. E., & Hynd, G. W. (1986b). *Child neuropsychology. Volume 2: Clinical practice*. San Diego: Academic Press.

Pliszka, S. R. (2003). *Neuroscience for the mental health clinician*. New York: Guilford.

Posner, M. I., & Rothbart, M. K. (2007). *Educating the human brain*. Washington, DC: American Psychological Association.

Report of the President's Commission on Excellence in Special Education. (2002). *A new era: Revitalizing special education for children and their families*. Washington, DC: U.S. Department of Education, Author.

Reschly, D. J., Hosp, J. L., & Schmied, C. M. (2003). *And miles to go . . . : State SLD requirements and authoritative recommendations*. Report to the National Research Center on Learning Disabilities.

Reynolds, C. R., & Bigler, E. D. (1994). *Test of Memory and Learning: Examiner's manual*. Austin, TX: PRO-ED.

Rourke, B. P. (1982). Central processing deficits in children: Toward a developmental neuropsychological model. *Journal of Clinical Neuropsychology, 4*, 1–18.

Shaywitz, S. (2003). *Overcoming dyslexia: A new and complete science-based program for reading problems at any level*. New York: Alfred A. Knopf.

Sheslow, D., & Adams, W. (2003). *Wide range assessment of memory and learning – Second edition*. Wilmington, DE: Wide Range, Inc.

Stern, E. (2005). Pedagogy meets neuroscience. *Science, 310,* 745.

Wechsler, D. (2003). *Wechsler Intelligence Scale for Children – Fourth Edition*. San Antonio, TX: Harcourt Assessment, Inc.

Wechsler, D., Kaplan, E., Fein, D., Morris, E., Kramer, J. H., Maerlender, A., & Delis, D. C. (2004). *The Wechsler Intelligence Scale for Children – Fourth Edition. Integrated Technical and Interpretative Manual*. San Antonio, TX: Harcourt Assessment, Inc.

10

Neuropsychological Assessment and RTI in the Assessment of Learning Disabilities: Are They Mutually Exclusive?

David Breiger and Lawrence V. Majovski

WHAT DO YOU THINK NEUROSCIENCE HAS TO OFFER THE ASSESSMENT AND IDENTIFICATION OF LEARNING DISABILITIES?

There has been tremendous growth in our knowledge of learning disabilities (LDs) over the past several decades. The most detailed information has been accumulated from studies of children and adults who have significant difficulty acquiring reading skills, primarily single-word decoding, but that also includes reading fluency and reading comprehension (Vellutino et al., 2004). Significant advances in understanding reading disabilities have occurred in both basic neuroscience/neuropsychology as well as applied neuroscience/ neuropsychology. In particular, reading disabilities are now thought to be best described as a dimensional disorder (i.e., occur upon a continuum; Shaywitz, Gruen, & Shaywitz, 2007; Francis et al., 2005; Jensen & Breiger, 2005). Much is now known regarding the epidemiology, underlying etiologies, and neurocognitive and neurobiological processes of reading disorders. The information derived from neuroscience approaches to learning disabilities has had significant influence on current practices in the assessment and identification of learning disabilities within research, clinical, and school settings. Much less is known regarding learning disabilities that involve arithmetic and written language. However, reading is intimately involved in the learning and mastery of other academic endeavors. Gains in our knowledge of reading will surely influence and improve our ability to understand learning disabilities and other areas. Due to the maturity of the area of neuroscience of reading disabilities the rest of this review will focus upon learning disabilities in the area of reading.

Reading disability is the most common form of LD, accounting for 50 to 80% of all diagnosed learning disorders with a prevalence rate as high as 17 to 20%, and with similar rates between boys and girls (Jensen & Breiger, 2005). Longitudinal studies that have obtained a representative sample of all young children entering school have found that reading disability does not represent a delay and persists through school years and into adulthood (Shaywitz et al., 2007). It is also interesting that recent research has begun to question a previously held notion that dyslexia only occurs in individuals who speak alphabetic languages, and not in individuals who speak logographic languages such as Chinese (Jensen & Breiger, 2005).

Nearly 75% of children classified as reading disabled in the third grade continue to demonstrate significant reading problems in the ninth grade. Specifically, adults who were identified as having a reading disability as children often continue to demonstrate difficulties with decoding unfamiliar words, spelling, and fluency. Reading can continue to be quite frustrating for these adolescents and adults whose comprehension often depends upon a laborious, time-consuming process of relatively slowed word retrieval. This is especially true for those bright individuals whose academic or vocational ambitions require a considerable amount of reading.

Many children with RD exhibit a reluctance to attend school, moodiness, self-derogatory comments about their ability, and disruptive behavior due to boredom, frustration, and/or shame. School dropout rates for children and adolescents with LD are estimated to be as high as nearly 40%, resulting in major problems with employment as adults. Other profound lifelong psychosocial correlates of dyslexia include self-perceptions of lower intellectual ability, more generalized psychological distress, and less social mobility.

Information regarding the most accurate prevalence of learning disorders that includes rates for different ages and sexes is necessary in order to evaluate the accuracy and sensitivity of assessment schemes. For example, school districts can use this type of information in order to better evaluate the accuracy of their identification efforts of learning disabled students.

Etiologies/Pathogenesis

Reading disability has been shown to be both familial and heritable with a nearly 80% concordance rate reported in monozygotic (MZ) twins in comparison to less than 50% concordance rate in dizygotic (DZ) twins and other siblings (Pennington, 1999). Furthermore, if one family member is affected, the rates for other members are much higher than that in the general population. For example, the rates of reading problems in children of dyslexic parents have been found to be as high as 30 to 60%. Parents of children with RD are also more likely to have reading problems (25 to 60%), with a higher risk for fathers (46%) compared to mothers (33%) (Jensen & Breiger, 2005). Finally, linkage studies suggest a major role for chromosomes 6 (Shaywitz, Gruen, & Shaywitz, 2007). The data from genetic linkage studies support the view that reading disabilities are the result of complex etiology that includes both genetic and environmental factors. This research highlights the importance of early screening and identification of children at increased risk for the development of learning disabilities based upon family history and also the possible late identification of parents with learning disabilities who may have not been earlier detected. In addition, by studying the pattern of development of individuals at increased risk for learning disabilities, differences in the pattern of presentation as well as response to intervention may be revealed. Assessment tools that have been found to be sensitive to the early identification of at-risk populations have improved the assessment and identification of all disabled learners (Vellutino et al., 2004).

Neurocognitive Processes

The development of proficient reading skills is critical for success in academic settings as well as many life activities. The neural substrate for reading has been studied over the last 15 years using functional brain imaging techniques. These studies have used both control subjects as well as children with dyslexia. Behavioral research has indicated that phonological skills processing is for the development of proficient single-word reading (Vellutino et al., 2004).

Neurobiology/Brain Changes in Reading

Functional neuroimaging has been used over the past 15 years in attempts to identify brain systems involved in reading proficiency. These studies have used both control subjects as well as children with dyslexia. Investigations using reading and phonological based assessments have indicated involvement of neural systems both anterior (inferior frontal gyrus) and posterior (middle temporal gyrus) (Shaywitz, Lyon, & Shaywitz, 2006). A portion of the posterior reading system (occipital temporal area) has been shown to be critical for the development of skilled reading and appears important for quick recognition of the printed word. Brain activation in this region increases as reading skill increases. These studies provide information that may be used in the future to develop heuristics that combine functional imaging with other assessment tools to identify children who may not respond to typical interventions/curriculums. For example, in a study of a group of learning-disabled children and non-LD children investigating brainstem timing, cortical processing of stimulus differences, and literary skills, it was shown that there may be a potential biological marker regarding brainstem timing in relation to cortical processing in the group of children with LDs (Banai et al., 2005). In one study of lateralization and auditory semantic processing in young children the results indicated that one cortically activated region (i.e., left fusiform gyrus) was observed to be associated in semantic processing concerning the task's accuracy, showing strong left-lateralized pattern of activation, a process consistent with patterns of early word recognition and language development (Balsamo, Xu, & Gaillard, 2006).

The most important results to date have come from recent studies investigating brain-activation patterns in children with dyslexia who have engaged in phonological-based reading interventions. These studies have demonstrated that intensive evidence-based reading intervention results in improvements in reading accuracy, fluency, and significant and long-lasting changes in brain organization (Temple et. al., 2003; Simos et al., 2005). The changes in brain activation over time resemble those of typical readers. The results of these studies have important implications for the use of evidence-based interventions with young children who are experiencing difficulty in acquiring reading skills (Aylward et al., 2003; Simos et al., 2005).

The result of ongoing research and neuroscience of learning disabilities provides critical information necessary for the accurate assessment and identification of learning disabilities. As outlined previously, an impressive body of evidence has been accumulated regarding epidemiology, underlying etiologies, and neurocognitive and neurobiological processes of learning disabilities. In addition, evidence has been accumulating regarding brain changes in response to evidence-based interventions as well as possible subgroup by intervention interactions. The identification of children with learning disabilities in both clinical practice and school settings will continue to improve from the information derived from neuroscience evaluations of learning disabilities. These studies from neuroscience support the view that the neural systems are plastic and respond to intervention positively. Current and future research will include studies that will better define group by intervention interactions, which will allow for more efficient and effective intervention efforts.

HOW WILL FUTURE DEVELOPMENTS IN NEUROSCIENCE AFFECT HOW WE CLASSIFY AND INTERVENE WITH LEARNING DISABILITIES?

Advances in the past decade in neurosciences, and especially neuroimaging technologies, have facilitated our understanding of brain and behavior functions in humans, and in children in particular. In similar development within the field of neuropsychology over the past 3 decades, clinical neuropsychologists have broadened their role to include more refined assessment of the cognitive aspects of a child's performance and abilities; behavioral deficits in a wide-ranging spectrum of disorders; and neuroimaging tools that have provided an experimental as well as clinical database contributing to our current understanding of brain development in healthy, normal children versus brain disordered individuals.

Neuropsychological and neurological literature regarding research findings that have added newer research findings have added considerable neuroscientific knowledge and a better understanding of many brain disorders. They have also showed that even mild neurological impairments in a young child may affect cognitive processing, verbal comprehension skills, motor skills, and LDs (Olsen et al., 1998; Stiles et al., 2005; Taylor et al., 2004; Allin et al., 2006).

In a 5-year, NIH-funded, multicenter project on "normal, healthy brain development (birth through 18 years)" findings released in July 2006 (www .nih.gov), researchers stated that this is the first and largest systematic clinical study regarding the neurobiology and brain development in healthy children. This database will serve as a clinical benchmark by which healthy, normal brain development can be measured and matched with behavior, cognitive processes, and neuroanatomy, from birth through adolescence.

This neuroscientific clinical database will also provide insights into what goes wrong in early development. Whatever the cause of a neurological disorder, poor communication between neurons is almost always one of the results. When considering that there are an estimated 100 billion neurons developing at the rate of 250,000 cells per minute with each having dozens of dendrites, the connections that form can number anywhere from 60,000 to 100,000 connections *per neuron*. Cognitive functioning occurs when billions of brain cells communicate with each other at the same time; and when they do not communicate properly, the result is cognitive problems that may occur and affect how a child acquires skills, learning, and memory (i.e., higher cortical functioning).

The NIH brain project includes six centers in the United States, 385 males and females selected from 35,000 families screened in order to address racial, ethnic, and socioeconomic demographics, as well as selecting a mix for right- versus left-handers. Exclusion criteria was applied to account for illnesses, genetic predisposition, teratogenicity factors, drug/toxicity, all of which can affect the developing brain. Neuroimaging tools involved three techniques: magnetic resonance imaging (MRI) which can detect gray matter changes (nerve cells); diffusion tensor imaging to monitor white matter (i.e., axons; connecting nerve fibers); and magnetic resonance spectroscopy (MRS), which avoids radiation as in positron emission tomography (PET), but labels a wide variety of brain molecules involved in mapping physiological and metabolic activity onto images versus just showing anatomy and movement as MRI and CT brain scans do. The MRS technology essentially is mapping a molecular fingerprint onto structure.

An array of neuropsychological tests have been given in order to assess cognitive and intellectual functioning in the children in the NIH project at the appropriate levels, with the aim toward matching changes in brain anatomy to psychological abilities so that these children can be followed, longitudinally, over the course of their development and into adolescence. This becomes important because, not only is every newborn brain different from another, but the variables that can occur within each child also differ as to changes as well (Majovski & Breiger, 2007). The contribution of the NIH brain project with potential findings from research and how it will impact future developments in the areas of clinical neuropsychology and education suggests that the clinical child neuropsychologist will be able to understand and better classify problems that interrupt healthy brain-behavior functioning as well as in cases of severe, mild, and subtle but complex disorders (e.g., autism, Asperger's syndrome, ADHD, ADHD plus epilepsy, nonverbal learning disorders [NVLDs], Landau-Kleffner syndrome, very premature term and very low birth weight babies, hypoxic-ischemic encephalopathy due to perinatal asphyxia). Educators who serve children with LD, SLD, or developmental lags should be able to match alterations in an individual child's brain map with more complete, reliable, and accurate information in formulating strategies, interventions, or programs that will foster progress for a child's learning. By incorporating information to be gathered from the NIH project regarding healthy brain development and the mechanisms involved in psychological processes, newer technologies will allow for better descriptions, classification, and perhaps more tailored interventions for LD children. Without incorporating these developments and newer neuroscientific-based information, educational, diagnostic, remedial, and therapeutic efforts will only be partially effective for LD children.

One recent neuroimaging technology that has shown promise in studying neurological disorders and neuropsychological functions involves near infrared spectroscopy (fNIRS). This methodology offers a noninvasive, portable, low-cost, indirect, as well as direct means of monitoring brain activity (Zabel & Chute, 2002). This methodology is a wireless, portable means and ecologically valid, which can monitor cortical activity extending beyond the confines of a laboratory setting or a magnetic bore tube. Zabel and Chute (2002) have discussed the educational and neuroimaging applications of fNIRS in regards to real-time monitoring of cognitive functions for both research and clinical studies. Studies with children ages 1.5 years old in pediatric settings have been conducted. This technology, although still in its infancy, requires more refinement and validation efforts with other neurotechnologies but holds the future potential for describing in greater detail brain-behavior relationships in brain disorders and can be integrated with neuropsychological testing as well.

Several neurotechnological methods have been used for studying children's brains and neuropsychological functioning (i.e., MRI, MRS, fMRI, MEG/EEG, MSI, PET; Majovski & Breiger, 2007). To highlight some of the technology's applications for studying brain activity in children, the following studies will be cited for illustrative purposes as to technology's impact on clinical neuroscience and cognitive functions measurements. In a recent study using MRI technology (Sowell et al., 2004) involving 45 children between the ages of 5 and 11 years old, scanned twice with MRI 2 years apart, developmental changes were observed for the first time regarding brain size, thickness of gray matter, and structure-function relationships recorded within the same subject, longitudinally, during the progression of cognitive development.

A study using magnetic encephalography (MEG) and magnetic source imaging (MSI), functional imaging tools that have demonstrated capability of directly observing electrophysiological activity of neurons and localizing corresponding neuromagnetic field sources onto MR high-resolution images, have advanced our understanding of the spatiotemporal relationship complexities in both normal and brain-disorder functioning—and development in young children's brains. These two methodologies have been used in studying children with epileptic foci and also are useful in complementing EEG recordings and neuropsychological testing (Chuang et al., 2006).

Language development including lateralization and auditory semantic processing in young children has made use of functional magnetic resonance imaging (fMRI). Normal, healthy developing children ages 5 to 10 years old were studied using blood oxygen-dependent (BOLD) fMRI while engaging in an auditory semantic decision-making task of varying difficulty. The findings of a study (Balsamo et al., 2006) suggested that auditory semantic processing in young children may recruit cortical regions associated with word reading in adults before initiating a semantic category decision. An area of recent neuroscientific research interest involves left fusiform gyrus, which was observed to be associated with semantic processing concerning the task's accuracy. The authors assert that they have made observations showing strong left-lateralization pattern of activation, a finding consistent with patterns of early word recognition and language development in children.

Research studies regarding reading disorders and developmental dyslexia have shown disrupted function in brain regions associated with phonological processing (Temple et al., 2003). The previously cited authors reported in their study that neural deficits in children with dyslexia showed improvements with behavioral mediation demonstrated by evidence obtained from fMRI technology. A recent study of brainstem timing and language-based LDs (Banai et al., 2005) was conducted on a group of children with and without LD, which investigated brain timing and cortical processing of stimulus differences in literary skills. They reported that there may be a potential biological marker regarding brainstem timing in relation to cortical processing.

The previously mentioned neuroimaging technology and methods regarding brain-behavior functioning, and in particular language and reading, have proven to be useful tools when investigating cognitive processes with children utilizing electromagnetic correlates and changes in brain physiology and metabolism. Regarding the understanding of neural correlates relating to language and reading, current research and future developments in our neuroscientific understanding will continue to expand, impacting the role and services of a clinical neuropsychologist as well as educators when addressing issues of diagnosis and interventions with LD and strategies that will improve the academic outcome for individual LD children.

Sigmund Freud, early on in his career in the late 1800s as a histopathologist who studied under Brücke and Charcot, conceived what he called his *project* for scientific psychology, attempting to link an understanding of the mind to an understanding of the brain and its functions. He abandoned his effort because he realized that too little evidence was then available and the experimental technology was limited to a microscope when examining static versus dynamic neurological processes. Although he had no idea regarding the future neuroimaging discoveries and technology, in his 1900 work, *Interpretation of Dreams*, he postulated that the answers to understanding the mind and how it works would lie in physics and chemistry. Over the last 3 decades, neuroscience and neuroimaging methodologies have integrated findings regarding psychopharmacology, brain imaging, and cognitive neuroscience, which has led to Freud's postulate proving to be accurate in being able to map brain function onto structure—a neurobiological mosaic portraying the mind of the adult and, via the NIH brain project, the child's brain.

Until recently, very little was known about how normal human brains change as they develop due to limitations in older invasive techniques used with studying severely neurologically impaired children. Today, using MRS, quantification is a "holy grail" of molecular imaging (i.e., mapping physiology and metabolic brain activity onto anatomical images). Freud's prediction has come true. Past and current molecular imaging advances are a promise of things to come in neurotechnology that will further revolutionize detection, diagnosis, and treatment management for children as well as adults.

One of the most recent discoveries in neuroscience and the first ever recorded in history involves direct visualization of a memory. A team of neuroscientists led by Gary Lynch at the University of California at Irvine reported in August of 2007 to have captured for the first time ever images of the changes in brain cell connections following a common form of learning. Lynch and his colleagues at UC Irvine conducted laborious and carefully executed experiments that led to long-term potentiation (LTP) markers appearing during learning associated with expanded synaptic activity in the hippocampi (the structures involved with memory storage). Because the size of the synapse relates to its effectiveness in transmitting chemical messages between nerve cells, the UC Irvine team's findings indicate that learning improves communication between particular brain cells.

The significance of the reported experimental findings by Lynch and colleagues applies to memory and learning in the following manner: It opens up the way for one of the great subjects of neuroscience—mapping the distribution of memory across the brain's regions and actually visualizing it occurring! Lynch, in a UC Irvine interview that took place in August of 2007, stated that this is the first time that anyone has seen the physical substrate, the "face" of a newly encoded memory regarding synaptic changes responsible for LTP (a physiological-chemical effect).

Freud's prediction regarding the answers to understanding the mind (i.e., that it resided in the ultimate understanding through physics and chemistry) has come true based on current insights from neuroimaging technology methods that directly can study brain-behavior functioning. Another neuroscientist, Donald Hebb (1949), postulated in his writing, *The Organization of Behavior: A Neuropsychological Theory*, that the engram he proposed was the means by which neural cell assemblies laid down memory. Lynch and his UC Irvine colleagues, through a series of extensive experiments, demonstrated synaptic changes responsible for long-term potentiation, a physiological effect of a newly encoded memory captured on first-time-ever images regarding changes in a brain cell's connections following a learning paradigm (i.e., an engram). The relevance of these discoveries sheds insight on the recent neuroscientific developments and its impact on understanding of the cleft that separates neurons and underconnectivity between brain regions, which is at the heart of the neurological disorders—the synapse. Regionally different synapse dysfunction implies you are going to have differences between different brain regions. This is one of the most significant developments in psychological neuroscience that will potentially direct scientists and clinicians toward gaining newer and more accurate insights into studying memory, learning, and applications for learning disorders and disabilities in children.

HOW DO YOU RECONCILE RTI AS A MEANS OF DIAGNOSIS OF LEARNING DISABILITIES WITH KNOWLEDGE FROM THE CLINICAL NEUROSCIENCES?

The recent neuroscientific accumulated evidence shows that the neural substrates for language including speech and reading are already well-lateralized and brain-region specific in the child's first decade (Balsamo et al., 2002; Ahmad et al., 2003). A current picture is emerging of language consolidation and reading from longitudinal fMRI studies of normal language development conducted over the past 5 years in children ages 5 to 7. Young readers activate the left inferior temporo-occipital region, left fusiform gyrus, middle temporal, frontal gyri, and the supplementary motor areas during reading (Gaillard et al., 2003; Yuan et al., 2006). These neuroscientific findings provide support for viewing childhood language development as a process involving maturation and progressive organization of active interbrain region interactions. This conceptual neuroscience-based view in early brain development holds for multiple neuropsychological areas as well (Majovski & Breiger, 2007).

In 2004, Congress reauthorized the Individuals with Disabilities Education Improvement Act (IDIEA). It was stated that a learning disorder identified as an academic deficit is defined as a *disorder* in "one or more of the basic psychological processes" (e.g., memory, attention, information processing, self-regulation). A specific learning disability (SLD) is a developmental disorder that adversely impacts performances in one or more academic areas. A child who has an LD, however, does not necessarily have deficits in all areas of cognitive functioning. In order to determine which area or deficits are present, a comprehensive psychological or neuropsychological assessment is essential when making an evaluation and addressing exclusionary factors in a child's history since an LD or SLD is unwarranted if some or any of these apply: fatigue; ethnolinguistic/cultural differences; limited language ability; economic impoverishment; emotional/mental disturbance; developmental lag due to illness or disease; ineffective instruction early on; and poor motivation. In order to rule these factors out, a comprehensive neuropsychological assessment first starts with a thorough history and interview with parent(s)/caregiver(s), collecting as much information as is available to determine what factors in the child's development might be of clinical importance, which raises questions and directs the examiner's hypothesis-testing for conducting a comprehensive neuropsychological evaluation (Baron, 2004).

Response-to-intervention (RTI) has been described as a method of diagnosis of LDs (Fuchs et al., 2003). Two major groups have been advocating for either a RTI approach for SLD identification or a methodology that includes a comprehensive evaluation for SLD identification and intervention. Others have proposed a multitiered approach to serving children with LDs (Hale et al., 2006).

RTI as an approach to providing intervention to a child with SLD can be highly valuable and can advance the improvement of instructional practice overall. As a method of diagnosis of an individual child, it is flawed. RTI is an approach to intervention and remediation that promotes a one-size-fits-all perspective. RTI ignores the processing component regarding the definition of an LD and it is based on a model for diagnosis by treatment failure and ignores the likelihood of problems due to other factors, for example emotional/psychiatric, ADHD, nonverbal learning disability, seizures, TBI, and other neurologic-based disorders. It does not incorporate past and recent research on individual differences, rehabilitation strategies, and especially memory and learning from cognitive and clinical neuroscience research, especially over the past 10 years. RTI bypasses the comprehensive assessment approach (i.e., neuropsychological evaluation) and can lead to misdiagnosis and potentially a flawed intervention approach.

Accurate diagnosis and comprehensive information about a child's brain-related strengths and weaknesses is essential to identify potential sources of problems and providing suggestions and input for recommendations. The primary value in conducting a comprehensive neuropsychological evaluation is to determine a child's strengths and weaknesses that are present at a given age to provide accurate and reliable information to address, in some cases, why an intervention has or has not been successful and to prevent misdiagnoses based on assessment of brain-related factors (e.g., a child's memory, problem-solving, mode of efficiently acquiring and retaining information), all of which may be useful to educators, multidisciplinary team members, and parents.

Schools do not typically provide neuropsychological comprehensive evaluations as part of their multidisciplinary team assessments due to the nature and scope of training and knowledge base, legal/organizational constraints, or lack of neuropsychological and clinical neuroscience knowledge. In order to conduct a comprehensive analysis of brain-behavior functioning and address consequences of neurological, medical, and behavioral conditions, which a teacher or an MDT team typicallly does not do, members need to know *how* to provide for the child's instructional program and specific educational strategies. A comprehensive neuropsychological evaluation can provide specific information to assist teachers in designing programs or strategies tailored to the child's ability profile.

The previous approach when conducting a comprehensive neuropsychological evaluation to address a wide range of brain-behavior functions, skills, and emotional/psychological functioning can offer a more all-inclusive means of diagnosis and identification of learning problems with knowledge based on current clinical neuroscientific research on healthy, normal brain development. In addressing the issue of whether a child's LD or SLD is related to poor, ineffective instruction delivery versus other important factors a child may be experiencing, knowing not only *what* are the child's abilities versus weaknesses, but *how* the child's cognitive processing skills manifest themselves across brain-behavior domains at different age levels, allowing more complete information in order to go about addressing a child's learning needs more effectively.

Without current updated knowledge about healthy brain-behavior development and functions from clinical neuroscience and neuroimaging technological advances in the area of pediatric and child domains, educators may not be able to say that they have accurate and complete information available from such body of knowledge regarding the nature of a child's brain functioning, and a child's presumed LD. Lacking in such knowledge would leave educators without having complete knowledge in going about setting goals and making plans for instruction or modifications as to what would be most effective for a child since no two brains are alike. Hale et al. (2006) have asserted that RTI and cognitive assessment methods should be weighed as to their merits and limitations and incorporate the best of both perspectives melded in a balanced practice model that "maximizes SLD diagnostic accuracy and optimizes educational outcomes for this heterogenous and enigmatic population" (p. 753). It has been asserted by both educators and psychologists that both approaches are valuable, each having its own role in identifying, using research-based instruction, N = 1 designs in empirical decision making in designing interventions for children with LDs. Common sense would indicate that RTI and neuropsychological evaluations can both serve to inform and support the other if wisely applied for a child's academic needs. What recent clinical neuroscience research and clinical neuropsychology bring to this issue in addressing the value of diagnosing LDs and SLD can be summed up as follows: Having more complete knowledge and information about *what* the child's abilities are and *how* they manifest themselves across brain-behavior areas at different stages in maturation allows for using neuropsychological information and testing data to be integrated regarding *how* the brain is functioning and observing a child's performance, thus making it useful and necessary not only for diagnosis but aiding in designing or reevaluating effectiveness of intervention versus accepting a common educational approach that may not be effective for an individual LD or SLD child.

WHAT ROLE DOES NEUROPSYCHOLOGY HAVE TO PLAY IN THE DIAGNOSIS OF LEARNING DISORDERS?

The specialty of neuropsychology and in particular child neuropsychology (also referred to as *developmental neuropsychology* or *pediatric neuropsychology*) is composed of individuals who are interested in better understanding brain-behavior relationships. Significant advances over the last 30 years in our knowledge base of children's neuropsychological development have occurred through clinical practice and research. Of particular importance has been the broadening of interest from studying clinical populations to an increased emphasis on better understanding typical brain development and behavior. The area of diagnosis, assessment, and intervention in learning disabilities has been a major topic of interest for child neuropsychology.

Neuropsychological research has demonstrated and provided information for the support of the construct of learning disabilities, as well as the existence of different subgroups of learners (Vellutino et al., 2004). Researchers have reported that justification (for diagnosing a learning disability) that relies on single measure or single observation is questionable (Francis et al., 2005). They argue that there is a need for a fully articulated model that takes into consideration the multiple classes of influence on development of academic skills.

Neuropsychological assessment is focused upon understanding the entire child, by assessing factors influencing behavior, which includes biological influences, neuropsychological functioning, psychological functioning, and social influences (e.g., family, school, community). In addition, neuropsychological assessments frequently obtain information regarding a child's functioning in multiple environments including microenvironments, such as an individual classroom. The results of neuropsychological assessment potentially provide valuable information that can be used to identify the presence of learning disabilities and develop intervention recommendations. Information from a neuropsychological assessment can be used to support the development of a well-articulated model of the child's development of academic skills. There are a number of excellent discussions of child neuropsychology that provide considerable support for the role of neuropsychology in understanding and evaluating learning disorders and that also provide well-articulated models detailing areas of the evaluation and their relationship to function (e.g., Rourke, Van Der Vlugt, & Rourke, 2002; Baron, 2004; Yeates, Ris, & Taylor, 2000).

The referral to a neuropsychologist is typically made in order to obtain information that is not known regarding a child's functioning. Referrals for children suspected of having a learning disability are one of the most common reasons for referral to a neuropsychologist. The neuropsychological assessment will involve evaluation of functioning in a number of areas that have been shown to be related to competency in academic, community, and social settings. The areas evaluated typically include cognitive abilities, executive functioning, language skills, visual-spatial, visual-perceptual, visual-motor, learning and memory (recall), academic functioning, and social functioning. Evaluating for the possibility of other conditions that may be related to problems learning in school is critical to understanding a child who is experiencing difficulty acquiring academic skills. A large number of other conditions have also been found to be associated with learning difficulties. For example, co-occurring disorders such as language disorders, dysgraphia, and ADHD may also interfere with learning. A large number of disorders/conditions have been found to be associated with learning difficulties. The following is not an exhaustive list but is representative for conditions that have been studied: autism spectrum disorders, Tourette's, neurofibromatosis, leukemia, brain tumors, epilepsy, prematurity, sickle cell disease, diabetes, turner syndrome, human immunodeficiency virus, and psychiatric disorders. Clinical applications of child neuropsychology include providing assessment, treatment, management, and habilitation/rehabilitation of children with neurological conditions, neurodevelopmental conditions, psychiatric, psychological, medical conditions/diseases, and developmental differences.

In general, the child referred for a neuropsychological evaluation has had a history of difficulties acquiring academic skills, which may be quite lengthy and may include receiving some intervention provided at school or privately. Interventions can significantly vary in terms of a large range of features: amount of time, content of intervention, appropriateness of intervention to child's needs, and systematic nature of intervention. In addition, the initial quality of instruction can also significantly vary. This type of information is important to consider as it provides a valuable context when evaluating a child's performance on measures of academic achievement. It is this degree of variability that much of the debate regarding RTI misses. Without evidence of empirically supported systematic initial teaching, frequent probes to assess amount and rate of learning, information regarding child's responses to instruction, it seems quite challenging to develop an appropriate intervention using only curricular probes. The RTI approach would appear to be most useful early on in a child's academic career when academic content is limited (e.g., beginning readers). However, for most children currently experiencing academic difficulties, the assumptions made for RTI are not currently met (Wodrich, Spencer, & Daley, 2006).

Neuropsychology provides heuristics to aid in understanding the relationship between the demands made by the immediate environment and an individual's behavior. For example, difficulty with rapid recall of overlearned material could be used to predict that certain aspects of arithmetic would be more challenging or that the student would require preparation prior to being called on in class. In addition, a neuropsychological assessment can aid families and educators to better understand the child and may include testable predictions that could be used in developing a curriculum. Information from the neuropsychological assessment will often include information related to the child's functioning outside of school. It is clear there is a bidirectional, frequently transactional relationship between behavior and performance in school and at home. Recommendations can be made to facilitate learning both at school and at home. For example, interventions regarding optimal learning strategies, behavior management, and organizational skills development at home could be suggested. Teaching or interventions implemented at home or in the community could enhance the response to an RTI program or actually enable it to be successful. For example, organizational skills training could provide the needed skills for improving written expression.

Thoughtful discussions have been recently published regarding RTI approaches, so a detailed review will not be made here. Interested readers can find thoughtful discussions of RTI, which include strengths and weaknesses, in the two-part special issue of *Psychology in the Schools,* volume 43 (7,8), 2006. Willis and Dumont, (2006) provide a useful frame from which to understand the relationship between RTI and what they call *cognitive assessment* and could be more broadly called *neuropsychological assessment.* They conclude that the two approaches are complementary and that each is beneficial depending upon the individual child. RTI approaches can be viewed as preliminary approaches to assess a child's mastery of specified curriculum, which can be more efficient that more comprehensive evaluations. In particular, RTI approaches will be best when children are beginning to learn a single, well-defined curriculum (e.g., single-word reading, addition/subtraction) and have not experienced an extended period of failure. As the task becomes more complicated and multifaceted, it appears that the RTI approach will be less useful and lead to extended periods of failure if no other evaluation data is collected.

Neuropsychology as a field and neuropsychological assessment in particular can provide information that can help "narrow the focus" of interventions. The following two examples illustrate this point. An individual who has been found to have significant visual-spatial difficulties that impacts his or her scanning, written work, and aligning numbers when completing an arithmetic problem would benefit from visual supports, initially, during reading intervention or math intervention rather than experiencing failure for some period of time before these weaknesses are uncovered. Research in children with hydroencephalus and those who suffered a traumatic brain injury has uncovered important differences in the underlying causes of their poor performance on measures of reading comprehension. While both groups perform poorly on measures of reading comprehension, the group with hydroencephalus frequently have difficulties with semantic-pragmatic functions and word knowledge, while the children with traumatic brain injury frequently experience difficulty with reading fluency. This suggests that providing the same intervention based upon curriculum-based assessment of level of reading comprehension to both groups would likely be inappropriate for at least one. While this example includes individuals who have known medical conditions it does highlight the importance of understanding expected patterns of performance in certain subgroups, as well as collecting information regarding the processes that influence an individual's success on a given task. Neuropsychological assessments provide important additional information that are relevant to academic success—these include various aspects of attention, impulsivity, executive functions, and psychosocial functioning. Assessments of curricular progress are helpful. The evaluation of students with complex problems are occasions when neuropsychology can add additional information that will be beneficial in understanding the child's strengths and weaknesses and aid in the development of appropriate interventions.

Another important area neuropsychology has to play in the diagnosis of learning disorders has to do with increasing understanding of "nonresponders" of RTI. Neuropsychological research has provided valuable information in terms of areas to be evaluated, significance of patterns, and levels of performance, documenting the existence of subtypes of learning disabled individuals and describing the relationship between neuropsychological results and intervention (Rourke et al., 2002).

RTI can provide information regarding what a child is learning and how well, but not why an intervention was ineffective (Mather & Kaufman, 2006). Neuropsychology can aid in answering the question of what then can lead to a focus on how to adapt and modify or change the intervention to make it more successful. There are a variety of reasons why a student may not respond to an intervention, which is not apparent from his or her lack of success.

Response intervention as an approach is not able to discriminate between different types of learners and it naturally then follows that it is not useful in the classification of disabled learners (Hale et al., 2006). An RTI approach has been discussed by many as a prereferral model, and, due to its narrow focus, would seem to be useful at the very beginning level of instruction and activities such as beginning reading. However, even with beginning readers there may be a number of areas of difficulty outside of phonological skills that will interfere with reading acquisition. There is a significant risk that a reliance on only curricular probes for modifying interventions in children with several problem areas will lead to slow and uneven progress. Response intervention in these situations will be an inefficient exercise in developing interventions (Willis and Dumont, 2006). These are the situations where information from a neuropsychological assessment can be very valuable and provide information that is not apparent from a child's failure to progress. The combination of RTI approaches with focused neuropsychological evaluations when warranted is recommended rather than an exclusive reliance on either valuable approach.

REFERENCES

Ahmad, B. S., Balsamo, L. M., Sachs, B. C., Xu, B., & Gaillard, W. D. (2003). Auditory comprehension of language in young children. *Neurology, 60,* 1598–1605.

Allin, M., Rooney, M., Griffiths, T., Cuddy, M., Wyatt, J., Rifkin, L., & Murray, R. (2006). Neurological abnormalities in young adults born preterm. *Journal of Neurology, Neurosurgery and Psychology, 77,* 495–499.

Aylward, E. H., Richards, T. L., Berninger, V. W., Nagy, W. E., Field, K. M., Grimme, A. C., Richards, A. L., Thomson, J. B., & Cramer, S. C. (2003). Instructional treatment associated with changes in brain activation in children with dyslexia. *Neurology, 61*(2), 212–219.

Balsamo, L. M., Xu, B. & Gaillard, W. D. (2006). Language Literalization and the role of fusiform gyrus in semantic processing in young children. *Neuroimage, 31*(3), 1306–1315.

Balsamo, L. M., Xu, B., Grandin, C. B., Petrella, J. R., Branieki, S. H., & Elliot, T. K. (2002). A functional magnetic resonance imaging study of left hemisphere language dominance in children. *Archives of Neurology, 59,* 1168–1174.

Banai, K., Nicol, T., Zecker, S., & Kraus, N. (2005). Brainstem timing: Implications for cortical processing and literacy. *Journal of Neuroscience, 25*(43), 9850–9857.

Baron, I. S. (2004). *Neuropsychological evaluation of the child.* New York: Oxford University Press.

Chuang, N. A., Otsubo, H., Pang, E. W., & Chuang, S. H. (2006). Pediatric magnetoencephalography (MEG) and magnetic source imaging (MSI). *Neuroimaging Clinics of North America, 16*(1), 193–210.

Francis, D., Fletcher, J., Stuebing, K., Lyon, G., Shaywitz, B., & Shaywitz, S. (2005). Psychometric approaches to the identification of LD: IQ and achievement scores are not sufficient. *Journal of Learning Disabilities, 38*(2), 98–108.

Freud, S. (1900). *The interpretation of dreams.* Vol. I. New York: Basic Books (Ernest Jones; 1955 edition).

Fuchs, D., Mock, D., Morgan, P., & Young, C. (2003). Responsiveness to intervention: Definition, evidence and implications for learning disabilities. *Learning Disabilities Research and Practice, 18,* 157–171.

Gaillard, W. D., Balsamo, M. A., Ibrahim, B. A., Sachs, B. C., & Xu, B. (2003). fMRI identifies regional specialization of neural networks for reading in young children. *Neurology, 60,* 94–100.

Hale, J. B., Kaufman, A., Naglieri, J. A., & Kavale, K. A. (2006). Implementation of IDEA: Integrating responses to intervention and cognitive assessment methods. *Psychology in the Schools, 43,* 753–770.

Hebb, D. O. (1949). *The organization of behavior: A neuropsychological theory.* New York: Wiley.

Jensen, J., & Breiger, D. (2005). Learning disorders. In K. Cheng & K. M. Myers (Eds.), *Child and adolescent psychiatry: The essentials* (pp 281–298). Baltimore: Lippincott, Williams & Wilkens.

Majovski, L.V., & Breiger, D. (2007). Development of higher brain functions: Birth through adolescence. In C. R. Reynolds & E. Fletcher-Janzen (Eds.), *Handbook of clinical child neuropsychology* (3rd ed.) New York: Press (in press).

Mather, N., & Kaufman, N. (2006). Introduction to the special issue, part two: it's about the what, the how well, and the why. *Psychology in the Schools, 43*(8), 829–834.

Olsen, P., Vainionpaa, L., Paakko, E., Korkman, M., Pyhtinen, J., & Jarvelin, M.R. (1998). Psychological findings in children related to neurologic status and magnetic resonance imaging. *Pediatrics, 102,* 329–336.

Pennington, B. F. (1999). Toward an integrated understanding of dyslexia: Genetic, neurological, and cognitive mechanisms. *Developmental Psychopathology, 11,* 629–654.

Rourke, B., Van Der Vlugt, H., & Rourke, S. (2002). Practice of child-clinical neuropsychology: An introduction. Swets & Zeitlinger: The Netherlands.

Shaywitz, S., Gruen, J., & Shaywitz, B. (2007). Management of dyslexia, its rationale, an underlying neurobiology. *Pediatric Clinics of North America, 54,* 609–623.

Shaywitz, B. A., Lyon, G. R., & Shaywitz, S. E. (2006). The role of functional magnetic resonance imaging in understanding reading and dyslexia. *Developmental Neuropsychology, 30*(1), 613–632.

Simos, P., Fletcher, J., Sarki, S., Billingsley, R., Francis, D., Castillo, E., Pataraia, E., Denton, C., & Papanicolaou (2005). Early development of neurophysiological processes involved in normal reading and reading disability: A magnetic source imaging study. *Neuropsychology, 19*(6), 787–798.

Sowell, E. R., Thompson, P. M., Leonard, C. M., Welcome, S. E., Kan, E. R., & Toga, A. W. (2004). Longitudinal mapping of cortical thickness and brain growth in normal children. *Journal of Neuroscience, 24,* (38), 8223–8231.

Stiles, J., Reilly, J., Paul, B., & Moses, P. (2005). Cognitive development following early brain injury: Evidence for neural adaptation. *Trends in Cognitive Sciences, 9,* 136–143.

Taylor, H. G., Minich, N., Bangert, B., Filipek, P. A., & Hack, M. (2004). Long-term neuropsychological outcomes of very low birth weight: Associations with early risks for periventricular brain insults. *Journal of the International Neuropsychological Society, 10,* 987–1004.

Temple, E., Deutsch, G. K., Poldrack, R. A., Miller, S. L., Tallal, P., Merzenich, M. M., & Gabrielli, J. E. (2003). Neural deficits in children with dyslexia ameliorated by behavioral remediation: Evidence from functional MRI. *Proceedings of the National Academy of Sciences of the United States of America, 100*(5), 2860–2865.

Vellutino, F., Fletcher, J., Snowling, M., & Scanlon, D. (2004). Specific reading disability (dyslexia): What have we learned in the past four decades? *Journal of Child Psychology and Psychiatry, 45, 1,* 2–40.

Willis, J., & Dumont, R. (2006). And never the twain shall meet: Can response to intervention in cognitive assessment be reconciled? *Psychology in the Schools, 43*(8), 901–908.

Wodrich, D., Spencer, M., & Daley, K. (2006). Combining RTI and psychoeducational assessment: What must we assume to do otherwise. *Psychology in the Schools, 43*(8), 797–806.

Yeates, K., Ris, D., & Taylor, G. (Eds.). (2000). Pediatric neuropsychology: research theory and practice. New York: Guilford.

Yuan, W., Szaflarski, J. P., Schmithorst, V. J., Schapiro, M., Byars, A. W., Strawsburg, R. H., & Holland, S. K. (2006). fMRI shows atypical language lateralization in pediatric epilepsy patients. *Epilepsia, 47,* 593–600.

Zabel, T. A., & Chute, D. L. (2002). Educational neuroimaging: A proposed neuropsychological application of near-infrared spectroscopy (nIRS). *Journal of Head Trauma Rehabilitation, 17*(5), 477–488.

11

Learning Disabilities: Complementary Views from Neuroscience, Neuropsychology, and Public Health

Ronald T. Brown, Brian P. Daly, and Gerry A. Stefanatos

WHAT DO YOU THINK NEUROSCIENCE HAS TO OFFER IN THE ASSESSMENT AND IDENTIFICATION OF LEARNING DISABILITIES?

Over the past 2 decades, substantial gains have been made in our understanding of the cognitive basis, etiology, and underlying pathophysiology of developmental learning disabilities. These advances have benefited in no small measure from the integration of ideas, concepts, and technical breakthroughs from the neurosciences, particularly, but not exclusively, in the area of functional neuroimaging. Hemodynamically based functional neuroimaging procedures such as functional magnetic resonance imaging (fMRI) and positron emission tomography (PET) permit the measurement of regional alterations in cerebral blood flow and oxygen utilization that occur secondary to changes in neural activity. These procedures can be used to localize the cortical networks activated during cognitive operations such as reading with millimeter-level spatial resolution (Rumsey et al., 1999; Shaywitz & Shaywitz, 2005). Electromagnetically based methods such as electroencephalography (EEG) and event-related potentials (ERPs) provide more direct measures of neural activity, but these have traditionally had poor spatial resolution. However, newer adaptations of these techniques, such as low resolution electromagnetic tomographic analysis (LORETA) (Gamma et al.,

2004; Moisecu-Yiflach & Pratt, 2005) or magnetoencephalography (MEG) (Simos et al., 2007), can disclose the temporal dynamics of activated cortical networks on a millisecond-level time scale and with reasonable spatial localization of underlying sources. Together, these complementary functional neuroimaging procedures provide extraordinary new windows with which to view the neuroanatomical and neurophysiological correlates of specific kinds of learning disabilities.

In recent years, such techniques have successfully characterized the function, localization, and distribution of at least three left-hemisphere based neural networks that are involved in different aspects of reading (Dehaene et al., 2005; Price & Michelli, 2005). These findings have informed cognitive models of the disorder, which serve as invaluable frames of reference for understanding the breakdown of function that occurs in children with specific learning disabilities. For over 100 years, there has been debate as to where in the complex processing stream, from the perception of letters to lexical access, the reading process is most susceptible to failure in children with learning disabilities. Neuroimaging studies have provided confirmatory evidence that deficiencies in some children can occur early in auditory (Temple et al., 2000) or visual (Eden et al., 1996) processing, and have substantiated a long-standing, if sometimes controversial, view that deficits in phonology are the most robust specific deficits associated with the disorder.

These studies also offer another vantage point from which to view developmental variations in the neural dysfunction associated with learning disabilities. While differences in activation between good and impaired readers may be evident at all ages, there appears to be some resolution of abnormalities in anterior regions of the brain (inferior frontal gyrus) with age so that differences in older children may be limited to the two posterior networks involved in reading: the occipital-temporal system and the parietal-temporal system (Shaywitz et al., 2004).

These procedures also shed important light on the effects of behavioral interventions in both typically developing and reading-disabled children (Temple et al., 2000; Shaywitz et al., 2004). Treatment studies using functional neuroimaging indices as outcome measures, for example, have provided encouraging data to suggest that the neural systems subserving the ability to read demonstrate substantial experience-dependent plasticity. Appropriate and effective intervention can result in significant changes, even normalization of neurophysiological function (Simos et al., 2007).

The capacity of functional neuroimaging techniques to index differences in brain function between groups of neurotypical and learning-disabled children has been critically important from a theoretical standpoint. Information gleaned with these procedures has served to verify and in some cases extend neuropsychological models of learning disabilities. The more precise conceptualizations of learning disabilities derivative of this work have in turn suggested merit of assessing particular domains of neurocognitive function. This may ultimately result in more streamlined and accurate methods to assess and identify learning disabilities.

However, the functional neuroimaging data collected to date mark only a preliminary and rudimentary step toward possibly incorporating neuro-imaging methods in the assessment and identification of learning disabilities. Much work is required to validate these observations and systematize procedures before these techniques can be incorporated as measures to aid diagnosis or guide treatment planning. To allow meaningful interpretation of neuroimaging data at the level of the individual, substantial technical and conceptual challenges must first be addressed. This may be particularly true of techniques such as fMRI and SPECT, which do not provide a direct measure of brain activity, but instead represent indirect measures of brain activation that depend on the coupling between neural activity, metabolic utilization, and cerebral blood flow. This coupling is incompletely under-stood, and may be affected by age, disease, and medications. In addition, by virtue of how hemodynamic measures are derived with these techniques, they provide only relative estimates of neural activity referenced to baselines that may vary over time, both within and between sessions. This issue also complicates the comparison of data obtained at different sites or using different instrumentation.

Even when site and instrumentation remain constant, hemodynamic neu-roimaging procedures often show considerable interindividual variability so that individual activation patterns may deviate substantially from mean activations observed for group data. Moreover, procedures for identifying statistically significant activations (often compared to rest) within a group or between groups vary and can entail procedures and transformations that are different from those used to identify and localize significant activations for individual data. In addition, neuromaturational and neuroanatomical differences between the brains of children with learning disabilities and neuro-typical controls can sometimes confound or complicate the interpretation of differences in functional activations.

Finally, task variables can cause significant differences in brain activations. For example, children with developmental dyslexia demonstrate reduced activation of the angular gyrus during reading and phonological tasks (Pugh et al., 2000), and the extent of decreased perfusion appears to be associated with the severity of dyslexia (Rumsey et al., 1999). However, in some con-texts, the extent or magnitude of activation can increase with difficulty level or decrease with practice. Equating or controlling for such factors across children of different ages and levels of function may be quite challenging. In addition, movement artifacts can have devastating effects on fMRI and it is not uncommon to have to discard data due to such artifacts. As a conse-quence, one must be wary that such factors may result in sampling bias.

In summary, recent advances in neuroimaging have served to extend and refine cognitive models of learning disabilities. They have added valuable information to help define the natural history of the disorder, the levels at which processing deficiencies may emerge, the neuroplastic changes that can occur in the normal course of development, and the response to treatment. However, these contributions are based on group studies comparing children with learning disabilities and controls. Irrespective of procedural variability and flaws inherent in the experimental design of some of the studies, there are fundamental technical and conceptual problems that limit conclusions based on analysis of data at the individual level.

To date, neuroimaging studies have often been limited to small samples of children, frequently identified on the basis of somewhat crude behavioral distinctions and without regard to considerations such as etiologic heterogeneity or the existence and type of comorbid conditions. Without more careful experimental design and sufficiently uniform or homogeneous groups, it may not be possible to precisely delineate robust associations between specific neurologic signatures and particular processing abnormalities. If these associations could be reliably disclosed, this may open up the possibility of utilizing neuroimaging data to guide treatment planning with particular rationally based and targeted therapeutic interventions.

HOW WILL FUTURE DEVELOPMENTS IN NEUROSCIENCE AFFECT HOW WE CLASSIFY AND INTERVENE WITH LEARNING DISABILITIES?

Over the past several years, there have been significant developments in the neurosciences. In fact, the past 3 decades have been referred to as the *age of the brain,* during which there have been greater advances in understanding the role and the influence of neurotransmitters, hormones, structural brain differences, and genetic influences in the brains of children with learning disabilities relative to their normally developing peers. In particular, with the advancement of neuroradiological and electrophysiological assessment techniques, there has been a more complete understanding of the central nervous system and its role in cognitive processing in general, and in learning disorders specifically. It is our position specifically that greater advancements in research in understanding the neurotransmitters, neuroradiological techniques, genetics, pharmacogenetics, and neuropharmacology will undoubtedly influence the classification of children and adolescents with learning disabilities, the clinical identification of these children, and intervention approaches designed to remediate these learning impairments. We now turn our discussion to the role of these various influences in the identification and intervention efforts for learning disabilities.

Neuroimaging Studies

The role of the central nervous system has long been implicated in abnormalities and developmental delays in brain functioning and more specifically in learning disorders (for review see, Provencal & Bigler, 2005). The majority of magnetic resonance imaging (MRI) studies have focused on dyslexia given that this is the most pervasive learning disability found among children and adults (Provencal & Bigler, 2005). The rationale is that since typical reading requires the interaction of both nonlanguage-based (e.g., visual perception, memory) and language-based processing, then impairment in any underlying brain function may give rise to specific impairments in reading skills. Various regions of the brain have been implicated in specific learning disabilities. MRI has been used to evaluate brain structures in adults and children with specific learning disabilities where children with reading disabilities as well as those with language impairments have been found to have abnormal asymmetries in the temporo-parieto-occipital region of the left hemisphere (Collins & Rourke, 2003; Frank & Pavlakis, 2001; Vellutino, Fletcher, Snowling, & Scanlon, 2004). Differences in morphology between those with reading disabilities and normally developing individuals also have been found in the temporal lobe, planum temporale, and corpus collosum, with many investigations reporting aberrant asymmetry or differences in size of these various structures within these regions. There also are compelling data to suggest specific morphometric findings in the planum temporale, which is implicated in language processing and auditory comprehension (Hynd & Semrud-Clikeman, 1989; Morgan & Hynd, 1998). Finally, functional imaging studies also have implicated the left-hemisphere regions of the brain that is posited to be associated with information processing for children and adolescents with dyslexia (Breier et al., 2003; Shaywitz et al., 2002). These data are consistent with those of Shaywitz and Shaywitz (2003), implicating three neural systems in reading including the anterior system in the left inferior frontal region, and two posterior systems—the parietal temporal system and an occipital temporal system.

While some inconsistencies across neuroimaging studies have been revealed, there are very compelling data from both structural and functional magnetic resonance imaging to suggest that reading disabilities do involve structural impairments in the brain. In fact, some investigators have suggested that such impairments have their origins in embryological development (for review see, Castellanos, 1996). There is no doubt that advances in neuroimaging technology will continue to unfold over the next decade and will identify additional structural differences in the brains of children with learning disorders. Moreover, advances in the development of functional magnetic resonance imaging that includes a greater sensitivity for localization of activity have spawned a corpus of research into the possible impairments of the brain regions in children and adults with learning disabilities. While the use of neuroimaging techniques is not yet part of the standard clinical assessment battery in the identification of individuals with learning disabilities, these techniques are nonetheless important as they allow for the demonstration of the construct validity of learning disabilities as well as the validity of the role of brain abnormalities in the cognitive and behavioral impairments that has been so consistently demonstrated for these children and adolescents.

Genetic Contributions

In recent years, there has been considerable research conducted to identify specific genetic contributions to learning disabilities. It is well recognized that there are high rates of learning disabilities within families of children with learning disabilities. More recent research has underscored the evidence of the familial nature of learning disabilities. Molecular genetic studies and research investigating twins and adopted children suggest that genes predispose individuals to learning disabilities. Heredity has been implicated for the majority of learning disabilities, with up to 40% of relatives of children with learning disabilities evidencing similar problems. Faraone, Biederman, and Lehman (1993) also have found that the risk for learning disabilities is highest among relatives of probands with a comorbid diagnosis of learning disabilities and Attention-Deficit/Hyperactivity Disorder. Further, for twins with reading disabilities, heredity has accounted for 25 to 50% of the variance in the heredity of the learning disability (DeFries & Fulker, 1988). More compelling is the research that has linked specific genetic markers for specific reading and spelling disabilities on chromosome 15 and chromosome 6 (DeFries & Decker, 1982; Grigorenko et al., 1987; Smith, Kimberling, Pennington, & Lubs, 1983).

While neurological and genetic factors are likely the primary determinants of learning disabilities, we must be cautious in interpreting these data as no studies to date have demonstrated causality. In addition, many of the monozygotic twin studies may in fact be affected by rater bias. Specifically, since caregivers may perceive monozygotic twins as being more alike than dizygotic twins, they may also rate their symptoms of learning disabilities similarly whereby other parents may even exaggerate differences in learning between dizygotic twins (Barkley, 2006). Finally, it has been suggested that environmental factors including toxins, maternal substance use during pregnancy including alcohol (Shaywitz, Cohen, & Shaywitz, 1980), and low socioeconomic status may also predispose a child to the learning disability phenotype (Wadsworth et al., 1992). Whether genetic factors are necessary for this exposure still remains unclear. As Goldstein and Kennemer (2006) have astutely observed, children who inherit genes for dyslexia can range in exhibiting a phenotype from no apparent disability to severe impairments, with profiles of impairment varying across family members.

While there is not necessarily a clear genotype for learning disabilities and the specific genetic mechanism of the disorder is unknown at this point in time, it is clear that learning disability is a disorder that does occur in families. More importantly to intervention efforts with these children and adolescents, there is emerging research related to pharmacogenetics whereby specific subtypes of children with specific genetic predispositions have been demonstrated to respond positively to specific pharmacotherapies and adversely to others. Consequently, the interface of genetics and learning disabilities is a field that is very ripe for future investigation.

Neurotransmitters and Neuropharmacology

Particularly with the advances in neuropharmacology, the notion of neurotransmitter dysfunction has been posited as being etiologic in learning disabilities. As Shaywitz and Shaywitz (1994) have observed, there is compelling evidence to suggest that learning and memory occur at the level of the synapse, and this may be partly mediated by the neurotransmitters, including dopamine. While response to medication certainly cannot be used to support the notion of a biological or chemical abnormality among children and adolescents with learning disabilities, there has been some compelling literature to suggest decreased brain dopamine among children with ADHD (for review see, Pliszka, McCracken, & Mass, 1996), although evidence from other studies do not entirely support this notion (Halperin et al., 1997). While evidence in human studies is not entirely conclusive at this time, there are some compelling animal models to support the dopamine hypothesis for attentional problems, which are certainly pervasive among children and adolescents with learning disabilities. Thus, while the data are not yet definitive with regard to specific neurotransmitters that are implicated in children with learning disorders, selective deficiencies in the availability of both dopamine and norepinephrine have been posited.

Summary and Conclusions

There are compelling data from the neuroimaging literature to suggest a significant role in brain morphology and genetics for individuals with learning disabilities. There is evidence to suggest significant asymmetries in both the right and left hemispheres as well as smaller sizes in the anatomical structures of specific regions in the brains of children and adolescents with learning disabilities relative to their typically developing peers. Moreover, functional imaging clearly suggests differences in brain activity across these various structures. Further, family studies clearly suggest a markedly elevated risk of learning disabilities among biological relatives of learning disabled individuals, with parental learning disability being particularly contributory to offspring. Specific genes have been implicated for individuals with learning disabilities, although this research is still in its infancy. While no single neurotransmitter has been established in being etiologic among individuals with learning disabilities, clearly the role of dopamine at the level of the synapse is fairly compelling for both memory and attentional deficits.

While no single biological marker has been implicated among individuals with learning disabilities, there is evidence from genetics, neuroimaging studies, and studies of the neurotransmitters to suggest that this disorder is firmly routed in biology. This literature, although largely in its infancy, awaits significant developments over the next several years. The data to date are especially compelling and lend external evidence to the validity of the disorder. While neuroradiographic and genetic studies are not yet the standard in the assessment of individuals with learning disabilities, there is convincing evidence to attest to the fact that various brain morphologies and genetic markers serve as specific biological markers for individuals with learning disabilities. Moreover, these markers also hold particular promise for the early identification of learning disabilities so that remediation may begin either in infancy or during early childhood. These data are exciting and they clearly have significant implications for the identification and treatment of learning disabilities.

The identification of specific morphometric findings related to the brains of children and adolescents with learning disabilities lend specificity to the development of treatment programs for individuals with the disorder. First, as noted previously, the early identification of specific biological markers associated with learning disabilities may allow for early identification and remediation of these learning impairments during early childhood and even preschool. We know from other developmental disabilities, including autism and Mental Retardation, that early intervention is critical for enhancing the delays among children in the areas of language and motor development. In addition, the knowledge of specific risk factors for learning disabilities including a remarkable family history also allows for early identification so that remediation may occur early so as to prevent ongoing disability, ensuing failure, and the associated psychosocial adjustment difficulties that often accompany the failure of children at school, including demoralization and depression. Morphometric findings also may allow intervention techniques that are specifically linked to various intervention approaches including remediation of attentional problems that may be associated with asymmetries in the frontal lobes, memory impairments that may be related to a smaller hippocampus, and motor impairments that may be linked to a functionally impaired cerebellum. In addition, specific genetics markers that are associated with learning disabilities may also lead to both early intervention efforts as well as the identification of approaches that have been demonstrated to be efficacious among family members or other individuals with similar genetic profiles. Finally, significant advances have been made in the field of pharmacogenetics in which specific pharmacologic agents have been demonstrated to be efficacious for individuals with specific genotypes. Coupled with our advances in understanding the neurotransmitters and their role in memory and attention, it is likely that important developments will occur in the area of specific neuropharmacological approaches for various types of learning disabilities. Of course, these approaches loom on the empirical horizon, although they remain promising in the identification, classification, and intervention for individuals with learning disabilities.

WHAT ROLE DOES NEUROPSYCHOLOGY HAVE TO PLAY IN THE DIAGNOSIS OF LD?

Accurate identification and diagnosis of learning disabilities are frequently considered challenging endeavors due to differences in etiology, variability in individual performance, and factors associated with the person–environment interaction as these relate to learning difficulties. Although challenging, the accurate diagnosis of the underlying source of learning disability is necessary for proper treatment. The neuropsychology model, through its focus on brain-behavior relationships, is considered a comprehensive perspective that may aid in the precise detection of dysfunction in underlying cognitive processes. As such, neuropsychology is able to play an important role in the diagnosis of learning disabilities.

Etiology

The etiology of learning disabilities is considered multifactorial, resulting from compromised brain structure or function and genetic influences (American Academy of Pediatrics, 1998). There is growing consensus that all learning disabilities are the result of underlying central nervous system dysfunction (Learning Disabilities Roundtable, 2004), with evidence indicating that dysfunction of pre- and/or postnatal neurodevelopmental processes is the primary contributing factor for learning disabilities (Emerson et al., 2000). For example, the left perisylvan region of the brain subserves neurolinguistic function and disorders of this region have been implicated in dyslexia. In addition, dyscalculia is believed to result from dysfunction in the posterior right hemisphere, while compromised function in the hippocampal area of both hemispheres is related to disorders of memory. Given that neuropsychology focuses on the specific brain abnormalities and the functional consequences of those abnormalities, it has been argued that the neuropsychology perspective is more comprehensive and thus preferable to the traditional IQ-achievement discrepancy model when evaluating, diagnosing, and intervening on behalf of students with learning disabilities (D'Amato et al., 2005).

Although the traditional IQ-achievement discrepancy model may accurately identify learning problems for some children, compromised academic skill development in other children may necessitate a neuropsychological evaluation as these assessments are considered more sensitive at diagnosing subtle brain dysfunction of a developmental nature (Silver et al., 2006). Similarly, for children who have medical diseases or disorders that compromise their academic progress, neuropsychological evaluations may prove especially valuable in both discerning a child's brain-related strengths and weaknesses and clarifying which cognitive abilities are impaired or preserved in children with brain injury or illness.

Individual Differences

Research has consistently demonstrated that significant variability is present in learning styles and potential for individual children and adolescents with suspected learning disabilities. For example, multiple areas of cognitive functioning, beyond intelligence and academic skills, are recognized as contributing to the complete learning profile of a child, including attention, memory, auditory and visual processing, language, and processing speed, to name just a few. Two individuals with learning disabilities are never exactly alike, so knowing that an individual has a learning disability relates incomplete information about that person. A particular strength of the neuropsychology model is that it provides a comprehensive approach to diagnosing learning disabilities in that it allows for the assessment of a wide range of abilities beyond intellectual functioning and academic achievement (Black & Stefanatos, 2000). For example, the neuropsychological model assesses specific cognitive abilities such as reasoning, attention, language, memory, visual, sensory-perceptual, motor, and motivation, as well as broad functions, including general intellectual functioning, academic achievement, and emotional and behavioral functioning. This comprehensive approach is particularly important given that patterns of performance on intelligence tests have failed to demonstrate reliability for the diagnosis of learning disabilities in individual children (D'Angiulli & Siegel, 2003). Thus, neuropsychology offers the opportunity to differentiate neuropsychological underpinnings of learning disability from typical individual differences in learning potential.

The neuropsychological model seeks to understand how students learn and process information (D'Amato et al., 2005) and utilizes a strength-based approach when evaluating and diagnosing students with possible learning disabilities (D'Amato et al., 2005). Thus, one of the goals of the neuro-psychological model is to identify areas of strength and weakness within the child, thus providing a more complete and accurate assessment of the child's skills and coping strategies that may guide targeted interventions. Therefore, the field of neuropsychology—with its focus on the functions of the nervous system and brain and their impact on cognitive functions such as language, memory, and perception—is well-positioned to offer insights into the diagnosis of learning disabilities. Indeed, research on the utility and sensitivity of the neuropsychological assessment approach in the diagnosis of learning disability reveals a high rate of accuracy in distinguishing children with valid learning disabilities as compared to their nondisabled peers (Kilpatrick & Lewandowski, 1996).

Person–Environment Interaction

The neuropsychology model offers an ecological perspective in the diagnosis of learning disability because it incorporates an assessment of the interaction between both person (e.g., social and emotional factors) and environmental variables (e.g., cultural differences, insufficient/inappropriate instruction) (D'Amato et al., 2005). Specifically, neurospychology is concerned not only with brain-based functions, but also with how the environment may promote or interfere with a student's learning. In this manner, the neuro-psychology perspective attends to the relevance of primary physical-sensory problems (e.g., visual or hearing problems, physical handicap), psychological adjustment symptoms (e.g., depression, anxiety), and societal factors (e.g., environmental, ethnic differences, economic disadvantage) and assesses the combined impact of these sources on student learning. When assessment of individual strengths and weakness are combined with an examination of environmental and psychological variables, appropriate interventions may be developed as opposed to categorical and/or selective placements (D'Amato et al., 2005).

Given that learning disabilities are comorbid with other psychiatric disorders such as ADHD, anxiety, and depression (Martínez & Semrud-Clikeman, 2004), the neuropsychology perspective may prove especially valuable in discriminating between neurological and psychiatric disorders. Accurate differential diagnosis is important because other disorders and syndromes may interfere with the acquisition and use of skills, such as listening, speaking, reading, writing, and mathematical abilities (National Joint Committee on Learning Disabilities, 1994). A final advantage of the neuropsychology perspective is that it espouses a developmental approach. This approach is critical for monitoring progress or deterioration over time in an individual's cognitive capacity and academic skill development (Black & Stefanatos, 2000), and for measuring differences in severity and settings.

Summary and Conclusions

Following the reauthorization of IDEA in 2004, alternative methods for assessing possible learning disabilities have diverged from the traditional IQ-achievement discrepancy model to curriculum-based assessment (CBA) or response-to-intervention (RTI). Nonetheless, because the etiology of learning disabilities is multifactorial, and the learning profiles of children are both unique and variable, identifying learning disabilities remains a challenging endeavor. For example, some children may experience learning challenges as a result of a neurologically related disability while other children struggle to learn due to a slow acquisition rate of learning material (Merz, Buller, & Launey, 1990). Further, factors inherent in the individual (compromised listening ability) or in the environment (poverty or a chaotic home environment) may contribute to the student's learning problems. Thus, given that learning skills are likely affected by multiple factors, neuropsychology may be applied as a diagnostic method to aid in the detection of both subtle and pronounced forms of learning disabilities. The comprehensiveness of the neuropsychology perspective allows professionals and parents to understand more about children's personalities, intellectual abilities, and strengths and weaknesses in learning, thereby resulting in an accurate diagnosis that may inform and guide successful interventions and program/treatment planning based on the individuals' unique educational needs.

WHAT ROLE DOES NEUROPSYCHOLOGY HAVE TO PLAY IN DESIGNING INTERVENTIONS IN THE CONTEXT OF RTI?

Neuropsychology and its role in the development of interventions for RTI may best be understood within the context of a public health model. There is a high incidence and prevalence of learning disabilities in the United States. The majority of these learning disabilities have their etiology attributable to a broad spectrum of issues associated with the central nervous system. On an increasing basis, children's learning disabilities have been attributable to specific medical risk factors including prematurity, traumatic brain injury, as well as the result of sequelae due to early exposure to environmental toxins such as the teratogenic effects of alcohol exposure during the prenatal period or lead exposure during early childhood, both critical periods for the development of the central nervous system. Learning disabilities limit vocational choices, represent a specific risk factor for juvenile delinquency, and clearly diminish quality of life both for children and adolescents as well as their adult counterparts. Hence, the diagnosis and management of learning disabilities represent a national public health concern in our society.

Silver et al. (2006) have argued that the purpose of a neuropsychological evaluation is to identify the pattern of brain-related strengths and weaknesses in understanding both the nature and etiology of the impairments associated with the learning disability. As D'Amato, Rothlisberg, and Work (1998) have emphasized, the "cornerstone of any evaluation" (p. 463) must be the provision of an efficacious intervention. Silver et al. (2006) observe that a neuropsychological approach to assessment should first formulate a specific diagnosis and subsequently provide recommendations for intervention. An understanding of typical developmental processes and cognition, typical and abnormal brain functioning, and the specific patterns underlying the cognitive performance associated with various learning disabilities including dyslexia and dyscalculia as well as nonverbal learning disabilities are believed to have their etiologies in neurodevelopmental impairments (Zeffiro & Eden, 2000).

We argue here that interventions for children with learning disabilities should follow a public health model that considers three levels of intervention including primary, secondary, and tertiary intervention approaches. We also suggest that intervention approaches must be understood in the context of processing deficits that have been the foundation of the literature pertaining to learning disabilities for nearly one-half of a century.

Primary Prevention

Primary prevention efforts include those interventions that prevent the occurrence of a learning disability or associated disorders. Primary prevention programs for learning disabilities are most appropriately implemented during preschool or early childhood after known risk factors are identified that are apt to predispose a child to a learning disability. The child would not yet have identifiable problems but may be at risk for specific learning disabilities due to a high-risk pregnancy or an environment characterized by potential for exposure to toxins. Thus, for example, a child who is born prematurely with a very low birth weight is designated to be at marked risk for a learning disability. A primary prevention program would provide specialized intervention services for this child who does not yet have a diagnosable learning disability yet who is believed to be at marked risk for developing such a disorder. The intervention would most appropriately be administered during early childhood for the purpose of mitigating the traditional processing deficits associated with prematurity during early elementary school (e.g., language, reading problems) despite the fact that a child may not meet specific criteria for a diagnosable disorder.

Secondary Prevention

Secondary prevention efforts refer to those interventions designed to prevent exacerbations of specific neurocognitive problems that are identified during the early years of elementary school yet have not emerged into identifiable academic achievement problems. Using our case for a child who has been born premature with a low birth weight, an example of a secondary prevention effort would be the use of a developmental first-grade classroom for the same child due to the fact that she evidences some specific delays in the area of language, yet does not meet criteria for a specific learning disability. Thus, the secondary intervention or a developmental classroom may be employed for the presence of cognitive impairments and their subsequent remediation and hence the prevention of a specific learning disability during the primary grades.

Tertiary Intervention

Finally, the use of tertiary intervention efforts include the traditional approaches used for managing specific learning impairments including special education services for children and adolescents with readily identifiable learning disabilities. The majority of efforts aimed at prevention services in this country have been at the level of tertiary prevention efforts whereby a child may be diagnosed with a specific learning disability such as a reading disability with eventual placement in a special education program. Until recently, the primary use of tertiary prevention efforts has characterized the health care system in the United States because of its emphasis on treatment efforts for various diseases including cardiovascular disease and cancer. However, with the rising cost of health care in this country, greater efforts have been placed on both primary and secondary prevention efforts with the purpose of diminishing those risk factors associated with cancer and heart disease including programs related to smoking prevention, an example of primary prevention, and smoking cessation, an example of a secondary prevention approach, rather than simply the last stage efforts of treating lung cancer, an example of a tertiary prevention approach.

NEUROPSYCHOLOGICAL APPROACHES AND A PUBLIC HEALTH MODEL

We argue that a processing approach to the identification of specific neurocognitive impairments is essential for prescriptive approaches to be employed in the context of evidence-based RTI approaches. Johnson, Mellard, and Byrd (2005) have observed that children with learning disabilities differ from their counterparts with low academic achievement due to disorders associated with neuropsychological processes. In essence, that which represents the hallmark of a learning disability is "the emphasis on deficits or disorders in psychological processes" (p. 571). Based on this notion, any intervention approach must therefore emphasize the complex nature of the learning disability with specific attention to processing skills. Neuropsychological approaches also offer the hope that we may be able to identify children at risk for learning disabilities at an earlier age and thus enable us to diminish some of the social and emotional difficulties that may be comorbid with these learning disabilities.

The literature pertaining to neuropsychological impairments among children with learning disabilities is compelling and clearly has had a formidable research foundation for the past 4 decades. In general the extant literature has suggested that various areas of brain functioning including cognitive skills of attention, executive functioning, memory, language, visuospatial abilities, sensory-perceptual functioning, and fine motor skills offer assistance in comprehending both the nature of the learning disability as well as the origin of the disability so as not only to formulate a diagnosis but more importantly to develop intervention programs that are evidenced based. Without the focus on such processing deficits, intervention programs are not likely to be efficacious. For example, deficits in attention and executive functioning have been employed to describe a group of children with ADHD (American Psychiatric Association, 2000; Barkley, 2006). The identification of these core deficits is important in constructing and specifically tailoring remedial approaches for these children. Without the specific focus on attention within the learning setting, such programs are not likely to be effective. It is clear that learning disabilities represent a heterogeneous diagnostic category and the careful and judicious use of neuropsychological assessments allows for greater homogeneity of various subtypes of learning disabilities so that more focused interventions may ensue.

It is likely that the hallmark of any successful intervention program would be an amelioration of specific processing deficits that previously characterized the learning disability. While intervention programs also may be successful if they simply enable children to employ compensatory strategies in managing specific cognitive deficits, the importance of understanding the neuropsychological impairments underlying any disorder is necessary in designing and developing effective intervention programs. Consequently, the incorporation of remedial approaches designed to manage the specific deficits associated with any learning disability should be the focus of a successful intervention program. Thus, the successful ingredients of any intervention program must rely on careful neuropsychological assessment of specific processes underlying the learning disability.

Primary Prevention

Neuropsychological approaches can prove especially valuable in identifying preschoolers who may be at risk for learning disabilities so that early intervention efforts might take place. For example, the presence of a receptive language delay among young preschoolers may be identified by a routine neuropsychological screening examination. Due to the fact that delays in expressive or receptive language development may place children at risk for learning disabilities, particularly in the area of reading, a primary prevention program such as a Head Start preschool program focusing on the development of receptive language skills would provide significant specificity to such a primary prevention program. Thus, the intervention program may be tailor-made due to the initial identification of the neurocognitive deficit that is believed to be etiologic in the learning disability.

Secondary Prevention

The identification of processing deficits by means of a thorough neuropsychological assessment will allow for the identification of specific cognitive impairments that ultimately may result in the design of a secondary prevention program employed for the purpose of preventing a later learning disability that may have its origins in these specific processing deficits. Thus, when attention problems, working memory, and executive function processing problems are identified early and remediation takes place prior to the primary grades, the intervention may include the remediation of the attention problems, working memory, as well as other skills that encourage from the child careful planning and problem-solving skills. By having a working knowledge of the essential deficits characteristic of the child's diagnostic profile, an intervention may be composed that includes the essential ingredients associated with the child's processing deficits. This allows for a more delineated remediation of the difficulty and hopefully prevention of the learning disability may be the result.

Tertiary Prevention

There is a voluminous literature attesting to the role of neuropsychological processing deficits among individuals with learning disabilities (for review see Johnson et al., 2005; Kavale, 2005; Silver et al., 2006). The tailoring of specific programs for children with learning disabilities that include the basic ingredients designed to target such processing deficits is of paramount importance in designing effective and evidenced-based intervention programs. The end result hopefully is the custom design of a program to match the deficits of a particular child with a learning disability.

SUMMARY AND CONCLUSIONS

Over the past several years, there has been a corpus of literature to suggest that learning disabilities are frequently associated with disorders of the central nervous system and specifically the brain. In fact, the more sophisticated that the literature has become in the neurosciences, specifically in the area of genetics, brain morphology, and brain functioning, the more compelling the data in suggesting clear differences between children and adolescents with learning disabilities and their normally developing peers with regard to these aforementioned variables. Genetic testing and neuroimaging at this time would be precluded in the routine assessment of children suspected with learning disabilities due to both ethical issues and the cost-prohibitive nature of these invasive procedures. However, the use of neuropsychological approaches in the identification of specific processing problems that allow us to tailor remedial approaches for the underlying deficit of the central nervous system has withstood the scrutiny of many years of sound empirical investigation. The approach is not invasive and is cost effective and ultimately will assure the efficacy of our interventions. Given that children's education and quality of life are at stake, this does not seem to be such a bad deal.

REFERENCES

American Academy of Pediatrics (AAP), Committee on Children with Disabilities, American Academy of Ophthalmology (AAO), and the American Association for Pediatric Ophthalmology and Strabismus (AAPOS). (1998). Learning disabilities, dyslexia, and vision: A subject review. *Pediatrics, 102,* 1217–1219.

American Psychiatric Association. (2000). *Diagnostic and statistical manual of mental disorders—text revision (DSM-IV-TR).* (4th ed.) Washington, DC: American Psychiatric Association.

Barkley, R. (2006). *Attention-Deficit Hyperactivity Disorder: A handbook for diagnosis and treatment* (3rd ed.). New York: Guilford.

Barkley, R. A. (2006). *Attention deficit hyperactivity disorder: A Handbook diagnosis and treatment.* New York: Guilford.

Black, L. M., & Stefanatos, G. (2000). Neuropsychological assessment of developmental and learning disorders. *Clinical Practice Guidelines.* Bethesda, Maryland: ICDL Press.

Breier, J. I., Simos, P. G., Fletcher, J. M., Castillo, E. M., Zhang, W., & Papanicolaou, A. C. (2003). Abnormal activation of temporoparietal areas in children with dyslexia during speech processing. *Neuropsychology, 17,* 610–621.

Castellanos, F. X., Giedd, J. N., Marsh, W. L., Hamburger, S. D., Vaituzis, A. C., & Dickstein, D. P. (2003). Quantitative brain magnetic resonance imaging in attention-deficit/hyperactivity disorder. *Archives of General Psychiatry, 53,* 607–616.

Collins, D. W., & Rourke, B. P. (2003). Learning-disabled brains: A review of the literature. *Journal of Clinical and Experimental Neuropsychology, 25,* 1011–1034.

D'Amato, R. C., Crepeau-Hobson, F. C., Huang, L. V., & Geil, M. (2005). Ecological neuropsychology: An alternative to the deficit model for conceptualizing and serving students with Learning Disabilities. *Neuropsychology Review, 15,* 97–103.

D'Amato, R. C., Rothlisberg, B. A., & Work, P. H. L. (1998). Neuropsychological assessment for intervention. In C.R. Reynolds & T. B. Gutkin (Eds.), *The handbook of school psychology* (3rd ed., pp. 452–475). New York: Wiley.

D'Angiulli, A., & Siegel, L. S. (2003). Cognitive functioning as measured by the WISC-R: Do children with learning disabilities have distinctive patterns of performance? *Journal of Learning Disabilities, 36,* 48–58.

DeFries, J. C., & Fulker, D. W. (1988). Multiple regression analysis of twin data: aetiology of deviant scores versus individual differences. *Acta Geneticae Eneticae Medicae Et Gemellologiae, 37,* 205–216.

DeFries, J. C., & Decker, S. N. (1982). Genetic aspects of reading disability: A family study. In R. N. Malatesha & P. G. Aaron (Eds.), *Neuropsychology of developmental dyslexia and acquired alexia: Varieties and treatments* (pp. 255–279). New York: Academic Press.

Dehaene, S., Cohen, L., Sigman, M., & Vinckler, F. (2005). The neural code written for written words: A proposal. *Trends in Cognitive Sciences, 9,* 335–341.

Eden, G. F., VanMeter, J. W., Rumsey, J. M., Maisog, J. M., Woods, R. P., & Zeffiro, T. A. (1996). Abnormal processing of visual motion in dyslexia revealed by functional brain imaging. *Nature, 382,* 66–89.

Emerson, E., Hatton, C., Bromley, J., & Caine, A. (Eds.). (1998). *Clinical psychology and people with intellectual disabilities.* Chichester: Wiley.

Faraone, S. V., Biederman, J., Lehman, B. K., Keenan, K., Norman, D., Seidman, L. J., et al. (1993). Evidence for the independent familial transmission of attention deficit hyperactivity disorder and learning disabilities: results from a family genetic study. *American Journal of Psychiatry, 150,* 891–895.

Frank, Y. & Pavlakis, S. G. (2001). Brain imaging in neurobehavioural disorders. *Pediatric Neurology, 25,* 278–287.

Gamma, A., Lehmann, D., Frei, E., Iwata, K., Pascual-Marqui, R. D., & Vollenweider, F. X. (2004). Comparison of Simultaneously Recorded [H$_2$ ^{15}O]-PET and LORETA During Cognitive and Pharmacological Activation. *Human Brain Mapping, 22,* 83–96.

Goldstein, S., & Kennemer, K. (2006). Learning disabilities. In S. Goldstein & C. R. Reynolds (Eds.), *Handbook of neurodevelopmental and genetic disorders in adults.* New York: Guilford.

Grigorenko, E. L., Wood, F. B., Meyer, M. S., Hart, L. A., Speed, W. C., Shuster, A., et al. (1997). Susceptibility loci for distinct components of developmental dyslexia on chromosomes 6 and 15. *American Journal of Human Genetics, 60,* 27–39.

Halperin, J. M., Newcorn, J. H., Kopstein, I., McKay, K. E., Schwartz, S. T., Siever, L. J., & Sharma, V. (1997). Serotonin, aggression, and parental psychopathology in children with attention-deficit hyperactivity disorder. *American Academy of Child and Adolescent Psychiatry, 36,* 1391–1398.

Hynd, G. W., & Semrud-Clikeman, M. (1989). Dyslexia and brain morphology. *Psychological Bulletin, 106,* 447–482.

Johnson, E., Mellard, D. F., & Byrd, S. E. (2005). Alternative models of learning disabilities identification: Considerations and initial conclusions. *Journal of Learning Disabilities, 38,* 569–572.

Kavale, K. A. (2005). Identifying specific learning disability: Is responsiveness to intervention the answer? *Journal of Learning Disabilities, 38,* 553–562.

Kilpatrick, D. A., & Lewandowski, L. J. (1996). Validity of screening tests for learning disabilities: A comparison of three measures. *Journal of Psychoeducational Assessment, 14,* 41–53.

Learning Disabilities Roundtable (2004). *Comments and recommendations on regulatory issues under the individuals with disabilities education improvement act of 2004: Public Law 108-446*. U.S. Department of Education, Office of Special Education Programs: Washington, DC (released February, 2005).

Martínez, R. S., & Semrud-Clikeman, M. (2004). Psychosocial functioning of young adolescents with multiple versus single learning disabilities. *Journal of Learning Disabilities, 37,* 411–420.

Merz Sr., W. R., Buller, M., & Launey, M. (1990). Neuropsychological assessment in schools. *Practical Assessment, Research & Evaluation, 2*(4). Retrieved August 20, 2007 from http://PAREonline.net/getvn.asp?v=2&n=4.

Moisecu-Yiflach, T., & Pratt, H. (2005). Auditory event related potentials and source current density estimation in phonologic/auditory dyslexics. *Clinical Neurophysiology, 116,* 2632–2647.

Morgan, A. E., & Hynd, G. W. (1998). Dyslexia, neurolinguistic ability, and anatomical variation of the planum temporale. *Neuropsychology Review, 8,* 79–93.

National Joint Committee on Learning Disabilities (1994). *Secondary to postsecondary education transition planning for students with disabilities*. National Joint Committee on Learning Disabilities.

Pliszka, S. R., McCracken, J. T., & Mass, J. W. (1996). Catecholamines in ADHD: current perspectives. *Journal of the American Academy of Child and Adolescent Psychiatry, 35,* 264–272.

Price, C., & Michelli, A. (2005). Reading and reading disturbance. *Current Opinion in Neurobiology, 15,* 231–238.

Provencal, S., & Bigler, E. D. (2005). Behavioral neuroimaging: What is it and what does it tell us? In D'Amato, R. C., Fletcher-Janzen, E., & Reynolds, C. R. (Eds.), *The handbook of school neuropsychology* (pp. 327–361). Hoboken, NJ: Wiley.

Pugh, K. R., Mencl, W. E., Shaywitz, B. A., Shaywitz, S. E., Fulbright, R. K., Constable, R. T., et al. (2000). The angular gyrus in developmental dyslexia: task-specific differences in functional connectivity within posterior cortex. *Psychological Science, 11,* 51–56.

Rumsey, J. M., Horwitz, B., Donahue, B. C., Nace, K. L., Maisog, J. M., & Andreason, P. (1999). A functional lesion in developmental dyslexia: left angular gyral blood flow predicts severity. *Brain & Language, 70,* 187–204.

Shaywitz, B., & Shaywitz, S. (2005). Dyslexia (Specific Reading Disability). *Biological Psychiatry, 57,* 1301–1309.

Shaywitz, B., Shaywitz, S., Blachman, B., Pugh, K., Fulbright R., Scudlarski, P., et al. (2004). Development of left occipital temporal systems for skilled reading in children after a logically based intervention. *Biological Psychiatry, 55,* 926–933.

Shaywitz, B. A., Shaywitz, S. E., Pugh, K. R., Mencl, W. E., Fulbright, R. K., Skudlarski, P., et al. (2002). Disruption of posterior brain systems for reading in children with developmental dyslexia. *Biological Psychiatry, 52,* 101–110.

Shaywitz, S. E., & Shaywitz, B. A. (2003). The science of reading and dyslexia. *Journal of the American Association for Pediatric Ophthalmology and Strabismus, 7,* 158–166.

Shaywitz, S. E., Cohen, D. J., & Shaywitz, B. A. (1980). Behavior and learning difficulties in children of normal intelligence born to alcoholic mothers. *Journal of Pediatrics, 96,* 978–982.

Silver, C. H., Blackburn, L. B., Arffa, A., Barth, J. T., Bush, S. S., et al. (2006). The importance of neuropsychological assessment for the evaluation of childhood learning disorders. NAN policy and planning committee. *Archives of Clinical Neuropsychology, 21,* 741–744.

Simos, P. G., Fletcher, J. M., Sarkan, S., Billingsley, R. L., Denton, C., & Papanicalaou, A. C. (2007). Altering the brain circuits for reading through intervention: A magnetic source imaging study. *Neuropsychology, 21,* 485–496.

Smith, S. D., Kimberling, W. J., Pennington, B. F., & Lubs, H. A. (1983). Specific reading disability: Identification of an inherited form through linkage analysis. *Science, 219,* 1345–1347.

Temple, E., Poldrack, R. A., Protopapas, A., Nagarajan, S., Salz, T., Tallal, P., et al. (2000). Disruption of the neural response to rapid acoustic stimuli in dyslexia: evidence from functional MRI. *Proceedings of the National Academy of Sciences (USA), 97,* 13907–13912.

Vellutino, F. V., Fletcher, J. M., Snowling, M. J., & Scanlon, D. M. (2004). Specific reading disability (dyslexia): what we have learned in the past four decades. *Journal of Child Psychology and Psychiatry, 45,* 2–40.

Wadsworth, S., DeFries, J., Stevenson, J., Gilger, J., & Pennington, B. (1992). Gender ratios among reading-disabled children and their siblings as a function of parental impairment. *Journal of Child Psychiatry, 33,* 1229–1239.

Zeffiro, T. J., & Eden, G. (2000). The neural basis of developmental dyslexia. *Annals of Dyslexia, 50,* 1–30.

12

Integrating Science and Practice in Education

Richard Boada, Margaret Riddle, and Bruce F. Pennington

WHAT DO YOU THINK NEUROSCIENCE HAS TO OFFER LAWS AND POLICIES ASSOCIATED WITH LEARNING DISABILITY DETERMINATION?

Our broad perspective is that there needs to be a closer alignment between science and practice in the fields of both special and regular education. There is a curious dualism in both educational and health insurance policy when it comes to learning disorders. Health insurance companies refuse to fund diagnosis and treatment for dyslexia, autism, and other learning disorders because they are "educational disorders." A school sometimes eschews diagnostic labels like dyslexia and even autism because they are based on the "medical model," even while they accept diagnoses like Traumatic Brain Injury (TBI). Of course, for the neuropsychologist, TBI, dyslexia, and autism are all brain disorders and their effective diagnosis and treatment requires the best that neuroscience can provide.

So, if we accept the premise that there needs to be a closer alignment between science and practice in education, then it is an inevitable conclusion that neuroscience is relevant for laws and policies associated with learning disability determination.

Because of the emergence of evidence-based practice (EBP) in several healthcare fields (Spring, 2007), including medicine and clinical psychology, it will be easier to bring EBP to the treatment of learning disorders by all

Some information in this chapter also appears in: Pennington, B.F. (in press). *Diagnosing Learning Disorders* (2nd ed.). New York: Guilford.

professionals. In what follows, we recommend changes in training and policy to accomplish this goal.

Training

In the fields of medicine and clinical psychology, future practitioners are being trained in the research skills necessary to evaluate new assessments and therapies. But the scientist-practitioner model has had much less impact in the fields of education, speech language pathology (Koenig & Gunter, 2005), and occupational therapy, with the result that these fields are more susceptible to fad diagnoses and treatments.

A stronger emphasis on scientific training in both initial graduate education and continuing education could eventually address this problem. The accrediting bodies in these fields should require higher standards for scientific training in graduate and continuing education in these fields. This recommendation is particularly important for those in leadership positions in these fields. Decisions about educational and therapeutic intervention programs in schools and clinics should be made by policy makers with the relevant scientific training, sometimes in consultation with outside experts.

An FDA for Behavioral Assessments and Treatments?

Public money for education and healthcare funds much of the clinical work that is done with children with learning disorders. For many of these disorders, scarce public money does not begin to meet all the real clinical needs these children have. What is disturbing is that some of this scarce public money is wasted on controversial therapies. If there were greater accountability for how existing resources are spent, these public dollars could be used more effectively.

So it seems reasonable to demand greater accountability for public money spent on educational and clinical interventions for children with learning disorders. One way to accomplish this would be to set up a national agency that would evaluate behavioral assessments and treatments. A new medical treatment must be carefully evaluated by the Food and Drug Administration (FDA) before it is deemed safe and effective for clinical application. Health insurers, both private and public (e.g., Medicare, Medicaid, CHPS), do not ordinarily reimburse for treatments that have not been approved by the FDA. More generally, health insurers have rigorous and specific standards for what constitutes "reasonable and customary care" for various medical illnesses. Recently, Medicare and Medicaid have gone a step further and based reimbursement levels on performance, including whether doctors and hospitals are actually implementing proven therapies (like administration of the pneumonia vaccine for hospitalized older patients).

There is nothing approaching this level of accountability in the diagnosis, treatment, and education of children with learning disorders. This was possibly justifiable in the past, when there was much less research on these topics, but it is not justifiable today. But, if a national agency or some other clearing-house were established to set science-based standards for the diagnosis, treatment, and education of children with learning disorders, then there would be much clearer guidance for how public dollars should be spent.

Integrating the Systems that Serve Children with Learning Disorders

Learning disorders pose a considerable public health burden because they are prevalent and chronic disorders. But public health policy for dealing with them is uneven and at times poorly integrated. There ought to be a seamless integration of the efforts of healthcare providers and educators to promote early identification and empirically validated treatment of learning disorders. Achieving this goal will require the previously discussed changes in training of professionals, and the regulation of behavioral assessments and treatments just discussed. It will also require implementation of better early screening for these disorders and better early intervention. Given the current educational and healthcare systems in the United States, these kinds of changes in public health policy sound hopelessly unrealistic and perhaps expensively unattainable. But such practices are already in place in other developed countries.

Moreover, one of the lessons of other changes in public health policy, such as early screening for PKU, putting fluoride in the drinking water, or vaccinating children for polio, is that they not only greatly reduce human suffering, they also save enormous amounts of money.

Health economists evaluate the impact of various disorders by estimating their *burden*—how much they reduce productivity of affected individuals. The burden to society in terms of lost productivity is a function of the prevalence, severity, and chronicity of the disorder. Based on their prevalence, severity, chronicity, and cost of care, it is clear that learning disorders pose a considerable burden. For instance, epidemiologists have estimated the lifetime costs to society for a person with autism to be 4 million in 1998 dollars (Newschaffer & Curran, 2003). Even with a very conservative estimate of the prevalence of autism (say 1 per 1,000), there would be around 300,000 affected individuals in the United States, with a total lifetime cost of over a trillion dollars. Improvements in public health and educational policy could reduce this burden and be cost-effective. What would these improvements look like?

Currently, the frontline for identifying learning disorders are primary care pediatricians and the school systems. Schools have procedures in place (i.e.,

Child Find) for the early identification of more severe learning disorders, such as Mental Retardation, cerebral palsy, speech and language problems, and autism, but not for dyslexia or Attention-Deficit/Hyperactivity Disorder (ADHD). Primary care pediatricians also screen for these and other disorders (e.g., cerebral palsy, hearing loss, vision impairment), but they are often not extensively trained about developmental disabilities or learning disabilities. So one recommendation would be to increase the training of pediatricians in these areas. Another would be for schools to implement early screening for all learning disorders.

WHAT DO YOU THINK NEUROSCIENCE HAS TO OFFER THE ASSESSMENT AND IDENTIFICATION OF LEARNING DISABILITIES?

Our answer to this question has been mostly covered by our answer to Question 1: There needs to be a closer alignment between science and practice in the fields of special and regular education, and the main relevant scientific field is neuroscience, especially developmental cognitive neuroscience. Because of basic scientific progress over the last few decades, a diagnostic construct like dyslexia has gone from being something whose very existence was questioned to an accepted scientific construct that has been validated at multiple levels of analysis: genetic etiology, developmental neurobiology, brain imaging, neuropsychology, and response to treatment. Just as we use the best available science to guide the identification and monitoring of children with diabetes, the same should be true for children with dyslexia and other learning disabilities. A diagnostic construct like dyslexia is now much more than a purely behaviorally defined disorder. Rather, it is becoming an increasingly refined theoretical construct that links etiology to brain mechanisms to cognitive processes and explains why a child reads poorly.

WHAT IS THE ROLE OF NEUROPSYCHOLOGY IN THE DIAGNOSIS OF LEARNING DISABILITIES?

The term *specific learning disability* (SLD) has been generally understood to refer to difficulty acquiring academic skills involving dysfunction of one or more neuropsychological systems that affect the acquisition of academic skills. These processing weaknesses are thought to have a circumscribed impact, affecting achievement in some areas, but not in others. Further, as the term has been traditionally understood, these difficulties are thought to be fundamentally intrinsic to the child. Thus, as currently stated in the federal definition, a specific learning disability is characterized by a "disorder in one or more of the basic psychological processes" affecting learning. Furthermore, it should "not include learning problems that are primarily the result of visual, hearing, or motor disabilities, of mental retardation, of emotional disturbance, or of environmental, cultural, or economic disadvantage" (Federal Register/Vol 71.No. 156/ August 14, 2006/Rules and Regulations 46757). It is important to note, however, that this has not been generally understood to mean that the environment has no role. Rather, it is currently generally accepted that genetic and environmental factors interact to produce the difficulties, but that a specific learning disability is not primarily the result of an environmental cause. Thus, children with SLD show what has often been described as *unexpected underachievement.*

Given the federal SLD definition, neuropsychology, as the branch of psychology that seeks to understand how the structure and function of the brain relate to psychological processing, learning, and behavior, would seem to be the field that is uniquely suited to help identify children with SLD. Specifically, neuropsychological assessment is able to conceptualize the disruptions in cognitive and psychological processes that are mediating the child's low achievement.

The general conceptualization of learning disabilities described previously has been embodied in federal legislation dating from 1975, when the federal government first mandated that all children were entitled to a free appropriate public education (Education for All Handicapped Children Act; P.L. 94-142). Subsequent to the passage of P.L. 94-142, the U.S. Office of Education issued regulations pertaining to the identification of children with learning disabilities. These specified that a child could be found to have an SLD if the child had a "severe discrepancy between achievement and intellectual ability in one or more of the following areas: oral expression, listening comprehension, written expression, basic reading skill, reading comprehension, mathematics calculation or mathematics reasoning" (USOE, 1977). This method seemed a logical way to identify children who were experiencing the unexpected underachievement in a specific area that was inherent in the definition. Most states adopted some form of discrepancy criterion that fundamentally required that a child show a significant discrepancy between IQ and academic skill achievement in a particular area.

Over time, considerable dissatisfaction developed with this method of identification. Arguments against it have been advanced from many perspectives, statistical and otherwise. Major concerns included that this method of identification resulted in delayed diagnosis. Proponents of change argued that children had to "wait to fail" since it was difficult to obtain a sufficient discrepancy until a few years into school. Important research (see Lyon et al., 2001) demonstrated that early intervention for children having trouble learning to read was far more powerful than later intervention, fueling the demand for early identification and intervention. Neuropsychologists studying reading difficulties also were having significant success in understanding the underlying processing difficulties related to reading disability.

Studies appeared that showed that there were not differences in terms of the underlying difficulties with phonological processing between children with IQ-discrepant versus non-IQ–discrepant reading difficulties (Hoskyn & Swanson, 2000; Steubing et al., 2002). Additionally, the claim was made that, in regard to progress in learning basic early reading skills, these two groups of children performed similarly. The argument has thus advanced that testing of IQ was not necessary for the identification of SLD. Rather, what was essential was to identify those children who were lagging in terms of their skill acquisition.

It was in this environment that the 2004 IDEA was drafted. While there was no change in terms of the basic definition of SLD in this law, required use of a *severe discrepancy* between intellectual ability and achievement for identifying such children was specifically prohibited. The law also *permitted* the use of response to intervention as a means of identifying children with SLD. It further permitted the use of "other alternative research-based procedures" for determining whether a child has an SLD.

These changes in the operationalization of the SLD definition also required states and local districts to provide specific guidelines to special educators regarding procedures required to identify children with SLD. Proposals include that the child "shows academic skill deficits" and "insufficient progress in response to scientific research-based intervention," and that these two factors be sufficient for the identification of children as learning disabled (e.g., Colorado Rules for the Administration of the Exceptional Children's Educational Act—ECEA Rules 7/12/07).

The switch to this problem-solving RTI model for identification of SLD, however, has led to proposals for the elimination of assessment procedures to identify and understand the cognitive processes that may be mediating poor achievement, even though the latter is still an important component of the SLD definition. Indeed, as specifically stated in proposed procedures for Colorado, "The Department [of Education] does not believe that an assessment of psychological or cognitive processing should be required in determining whether a child has an SLD." Further, "an assessment of intra-individual differences in cognitive functions does not contribute to identification and intervention decisions for children suspected of having an SLD" (Courage to Risk presentation by Myers & Bieber, 1/19/2007).

If these proposals are adopted in Colorado there would indeed be little role for neuropsychology in the identification of SLD, despite its apparent relevance, given the federal statutory definition of SLD and the advances to the understanding of factors leading to reading disability. Rather, children would be identified as learning disabled on the basis of their academic skill deficits and their response to evidenced-based instruction. These methods of identification would seem to result in the term SLD specifying simply a group of low-achieving children, who were not responding well to good instruction. This group of children would almost inevitably be far more heterogeneous in terms of the underlying causes of their underachievement than those now identified as having SLD. Those identified would certainly include some children whose primary difficulties were attentional or emotional, motivational, or environmental, including instructional; these subgroups may very well account for a significant number of children.

While the goal of providing all children with evidence-based instruction is laudable, from a practical point of view, that goal would seem nearly impossible to achieve in the near future across all grades and academic areas specified as relevant to specific learning disabilities. For many of these seven categories at various grade levels there certainly are not such programs. Further, even if there were, the task of ensuring reliable administration of best-practices instruction by teachers would require a massive teacher training effort and constant monitoring.

In addition to introducing an increased level of heterogeneity into children classified as learning disabled, many children with above average cognitive ability who are now considered to have SLD would not be identified under proposed new criteria because their "average" range achievement would not bring them to clinical attention. They would likely be excluded from services and accommodations, despite the fact that their relative deficit in a particular academic domain could cause psychological distress as well as unexpected underachievement. Children so excluded and their advocates could readily point to current research that makes it clear that children across the range of IQ can be affected by similar processing difficulties that slow the rate at which a child learns to read. Because the federal definition continues to define SLD as a disorder of psychological processes that affect learning, strong logic would support their argument against exclusion from accommodation and services.

In addition to practical concerns, from a conceptual and scientific point of view, operationalizing what constitutes having a specific learning disability to simply low achievement and failure to respond to good instruction at a time when there is a rapidly increasing knowledge base about the component processes that underlie disorders of learning would seem to be a giant step backward. Rather, the goal should be to bring scientific knowledge in the realms of neuroscience and neuropsychology and the best clinical practices into educational practice.

All children need to be taught to read, but some children move through the process with far greater efficiency than others. Assuming that general reading instruction in classrooms is adequate, then variability across children is likely to be due to how the educational context interacts with the cognitive resources that the child brings to bear on the task of reading. When introducing an intervention to children who are failing despite general classroom instruction, educators will likely want to address more proximal causes of the reading difficulty. Delineating which components are relevant to developing reading competency and outlining the profile of strengths and weaknesses in these components for a particular child will help educators select an appropriately focused remediation approach. For example, a child lagging behind in literacy in third grade may do so for a variety of reasons: (a) he or she may lack adequate phonological awareness skills that allow for the application of sound-letter correspondence rules when decoding unfamiliar words; (b) reading fluency may be the bottleneck, despite adequate accuracy of decoding; (c) the child may struggle with orthographically irregular words rather than those that follow conventional phonological rules; or (d) the child may have a broader language disorder, characterized by poor semantic and phonological memory ability, which, in turn, affects the linguistic processing of connected text and reading comprehension in general.

There may also be comorbid factors that affect this child's progress in reading. He or she may have an attentional disorder, which influences the types of errors made when reading connected text, as well as the motivation to engage in reading practice. Alternatively, the child may have additional deficits in fluid reasoning and psychomotor processing speed, which can have an impact on the degree to which he or she may spontaneously generalize rules and patterns from one context to another and how much phonological and linguistic information can be integrated before it is lost to short-term memory decay (e.g., delay is the enemy of working memory). In all these cases, understanding the broader cognitive and psychological profile of the child will lead to a more accurate set of diagnoses and a more refined selection of intervention strategies.

Particularly when one moves to categories of academic weakness other than in basic reading skills, such as reading comprehension, written expression, or mathematical problem solving, the importance of comprehensive testing within a neuropsychological framework becomes very apparent. Reading comprehension is a useful example to consider, since it is a specific area of underachievement that often brings a child to attention in school and is one, like many others, in which the overt problem can have different underlying causes. While deficits in the area of reading comprehension can be related to poor basic word-decoding skill or impaired fluency, it may also arise as an area of concern in children who are fluent readers. The underlying etiology of the comprehension problem in the latter case may in fact be a general language impairment, lower cognitive ability, or an attentional disorder. These domains would be difficult to elucidate without formal testing.

The same kinds of examples could be provided for children whose troubles are noted to be in the areas of listening comprehension, written expression, or mathematical problem solving. Success in these and many other academic areas depends on the interaction of a complex set of skills and abilities, disruptions in any one or more of which can produce "academic deficits" or failure to respond to intervention. Informal methods, such as classroom observation, work product review, checklists, and brief screening measures, especially when conducted by professionals whose primary expertise is not in clinical neuropsychology or school psychology, are unlikely to result in clear diagnostic conceptualizations, which are important for guiding intervention efforts.

Our argument is that the discipline of neuropsychology—which brings both validated and reliable methods of data collection, looks at different component skills and underlying neuropsychological processes, and does so in a conceptual framework in which to understand such data—should continue to have a central role in identifying children who have SLD. With differential diagnosis being a critical step in selecting appropriate treatments, not only do children with different neurodevelopmental learning difficulties (e.g., dyslexia, nonverbal learning disability, language impairment, mathematical disorder, low IQ) need to be differentiated, but also children with medical conditions who have concomitant learning difficulties (e.g., neurofibromatosis, epilepsy, head injury, ADHD). Such procedures are likely to be most successful in reaching the goals espoused by many of linking educational practice with current scientific knowledge. Such an alignment would seem to offer the best hope of providing all children with optimal educational opportunity.

WHAT ROLE DOES NEUROPSYCHOLOGY HAVE TO PLAY IN DESIGNING INTERVENTIONS IN THE CONTEXT OF RTI?

Neuropsychology has an important role in designing and implementing interventions for learning disabilities in the context of RTI. As the study of brain-behavior relationships, clinical neuropsychology and developmental cognitive neuroscience have made significant contributions to the understanding of learning disabilities, and in particular, dyslexia, over the past 2 decades. Although not an exhaustive list, what follows are four important ways in which neuropsychology applies to the designing and implementation of interventions in the context of RTI.

First, most scientists and teachers would agree that the first step in solving a problem is to define it and understand its nature. Without clarity in this regard, remediation approaches run the risk of being inefficient at best, or completely ill-conceived at worst. Cognitive scientists have been approaching the problem of definition from two perspectives: How does the skill in question develop over time under normal circumstances, and what are the factors and contexts that hinder or interrupt this normal developmental progression? The learning domain that has received the most attention and for which there is a more mature cognitive model is reading. Numerous research studies have focused on the role of phonological processing, rapid automatized naming, semantic and oral language skills, orthographic coding, as well as basic auditory and visual perception skills, in order to predict reading outcome. More recently, multiple deficit models of reading have also highlighted the role of nonverbal IQ as an additional contributor of unique explanatory variance. What has also become clear is that children will vary in the extent to which they have deficits in these cognitive components; few, if any, are now considered to be necessary and sufficient causes of reading disability. Therefore, the full range of cognitive factors must be assessed in order to understand the specific set of deficits that are affecting reading for any one particular child. The process by which this is accomplished is via use of a validated and reliable battery of cognitive and neuropsychological tests, the utility of which has been addressed in the answer to the previous question.

A second important role of neuropsychology is to help select the active ingredients that should be a part of the intervention. Research on empirically validated treatments has shown that only some aspects of a therapeutic program may be beneficial. For example, when using psychotherapy to treat mood disorder, the level of therapeutic alliance between therapist and client as well as the client's level of engagement are both predictive of outcome.

Neuropsychology can guide the development of appropriate and efficacious treatment programs by identifying the potential factors that underlie the problem, as well as describing the mutability of such underlying cognitive processes in the face of focused practice or other specific intervention. For example, psychomotor processing speed, fluid reasoning, and verbal working memory capacity are known to be relatively stable constructs that do not lend themselves as readily to direct manipulation. Of course, these skills increase along a developmental trajectory, but it is not an easy task to improve skills in these areas beyond the improvements that come with development. Other aspects of cognition and language are more malleable, such as vocabulary and syntactic development and phonological awareness. If all of these components are known predictors of reading outcome, then a treatment approach that focuses on those aspects that are susceptible to change will likely lead to more efficient gains in reading.

Treatment-outcome studies informed by neuropsychological and cognitive theory follow rigorous methodology that allows inferences to be made regarding the effectiveness of an intervention. Not only should active ingredients be chosen judiciously based on the best working cognitive model of the skill in question, but the efficacy of the intervention needs to be measured. In an era of limited resources, it is imperative that we find out which interventions and delivery methods are best for which types of students. One important distinction mentioned previously is the ability to show that a therapeutic intervention actually yields gains above and beyond what would be expected from usual practices and development alone. Second, it would be beneficial to streamline the intervention by distilling the active therapeutic ingredients and provide more of these during the day and week. We also need to understand the intensity and frequency levels for the intervention that will maximize outcome. Lastly, there is the issue of distinguishing improvement in children whose skills have been measured at the lower end of an ability continuum from statistical regression to the mean. Regression-based change formulas have been used in neuropsychology to help identify meaningful change in test-retest situations with patients whose medical conditions and treatments predict change in skills over time.

We should not assume that the interventions currently being applied are the best for all children, as their distinct learning profiles might predict inter-active effects. Different service delivery models may also be selected depending on the particular combination of strengths and weaknesses shown by subgroups of children with "learning disabilities." For example, a child with weaknesses in reading and language processes may benefit from an intensive language classroom where various important components (e.g., vocabulary acquisition, syntactic development, phonological processing) are all targets of intervention simultaneously. In the case where a child has a more specific weakness, such as only in reading fluency, a more targeted approach to intervention may be sufficient, and, in fact, beneficial, as the student could benefit from continued participation with peers in the rest of the academic curriculum.

A third important role of neuropsychology in the design and implementation of intervention is in guiding the decision of who will receive such intervention. Significant strides have been made recently in identifying factors at younger ages (before formal instruction of reading commences) that are predictive of reading outcome in later elementary school. Combining such factors as family history risk, early speech and language development, print exposure in the home, and early letter and sound knowledge skills has been found to correctly classify over 90% of children in terms of reading outcome at age 8. If such factors could be screened in preschool, then targeted intervention could start earlier, possibly even reducing the risk for a full-blown manifestation of a specific learning disability such as dyslexia.

Judicious application of neuropsychological assessment tools can also ensure that we are not missing children who seem to be performing at grade level in some aspects of reading (e.g., single-word decoding), but who really are floundering in the higher grades due to problems with reading fluency, integration of information from written text, or expository writing. Developmental neuropsychology research has identified which tasks are the most sensitive and reliable for measuring constructs at different ages. For example, we use rhyme judgment and syllabic segmentation tasks to test phonological awareness at age 4, but tasks such as pig-latin and phoneme reversal to measure the same construct at age 9. Similarly, reading fluency using paragraph level text is the gold standard test for children in third grade and beyond, but timed single-word and pseudoword decoding might be more appropriate in the early elementary school grades. Children with "grade level" performance on some discrete measures may in fact be very discrepant on other more integrative tasks relative to their peers and to skills in other domains. These children would also benefit from intervention.

The fourth area where neuropsychology can inform the treatment process is in helping educators select when focused interventions should end. What is an appropriate set of goals and expectations for a particular child? This can often be a very difficult question to resolve, given that there are often different sets of expectations from caregivers and teachers; nevertheless, it should be addressed in the context of intervention planning. In the context of RTI, children who are not performing at grade level in a given academic domain would qualify for more focused intervention. The expectation is that this child will improve functioning in that area so that he or she is no longer lagging behind age- or grade-level expectations. This presumes that the intervention will be able to increase the rate of growth in the weak area such that it "catches up" to the growth rate seen in other domains. The latter, of course, depends not only on the efficacy of the intervention, but also on the reaction range of the skill that is being modified, and on general constraints to learning efficiency that a child may exhibit more globally. If the rate of growth is increased such that a child who was previously below the 2nd percentile in reading is now functioning at the 25th percentile, and this is commensurate with his or her skills in other academic, linguistic, and cognitive domains, one option may be to withdraw focused intervention and see if the child can maintain this growth rate in the regular educational environment. The problem is that a child functioning at the 25th percentile may still be "below grade level." This is inevitable if we assume that academic skills are normally distributed and "grade level" is set at or near the 50th percentile. But is it justifiable to expect a child to develop a learning trajectory in reading, for example, that is significantly higher than the rest of his or her academic abilities? Understanding a child's neuropsychological profile across interrelated domains of cognitive, linguistic, and academic functioning can help educators with this type of decision.

REFERENCES

Hoskyn, M., & Swanson, H. L. (2000). Cognitive processing of low achievers and children with reading disabilities: A selective meta-analytic review of the published literature. *School Psychology Review, 29,* 102–119.

Koenig, M., & Gunter, C. (2005). Fads in speech-language pathology. In J. W. Jacobson, R. M. Foxx, & J. A. Mulick (Eds.), *Controversial therapies for developmental disorders* (pp. 215–234). Mahwah, NJ: Erlbaum.

Lyon, G. R., Fletcher, J. M., Shaywitz, S. E., Shaywitz, B. A., Torgesen, J. K., Wood, F. B., Schulte, A., & Olson, R. (2001). In C. E. Finn, A. J. Rotherham, & C. R. Hokanson (Eds.), *Rethinking Special Education for a New Century* (pp. 259–287). Washington, DC: Progressive Policy Institute and Thomas B. Fordham Foundation.

Newschaffer, C. J., & Curran, L. K. (2003). Autism: an emerging public health problem. *Public Health Report, 118*(5), 393–399.

Spring, B. (2007). Evidence-based practice in clinical psychology: What it is, why it matters; what you need to know. *Journal of Clinical Psychology, 63*(7), 611–631.

Steubing, K. K., Fletcher, J. M., LeDoux, J. M., Lyon, G. R., Shaywitz, S. E., & Shaywitz, B. A. (2002). Validity of IQ discrepancy classification of reading disabilities: A meta-analysis. *American Educational Research Journal, 39,* 469–518.

U. S. Office of Education (1977). Assistance to states for education of handicapped children: Procedures for evaluating specific learning disabilities. *Federal Register, 42*(250), 65082–65085.

13

Perspectives on RTI from Neuropsychology

Scott L. Decker, Jessica A. Carboni, and Kimberly B. Oliver

WHAT DO YOU THINK NEUROSCIENCE HAS TO OFFER THE ASSESSMENT AND IDENTIFICATION OF LEARNING DISABILITIES?

Since the mid 1970s learning disabilities (LDs) have been recognized as a disability category under federal law. In 1999 there were approximately 3 million students served under the category of *learning disabled* (U.S. Department of Education, 2001, as cited by Reid & Lienemann, 2006), and that number continues to grow. Today, students with LDs constitute the largest group of students with special needs within the United States (Reid & Lienemann, 2006).

Traditionally, a discrepancy formula has been utilized to determine the existence of a disability. However, the reauthorization of the Individuals with Disabilities Education Act (IDEA) in 2004 has brought about a paradigm shift in the way students are deemed eligible for special education services. A 20 point discrepancy between ability and achievement scores is no longer required within the schools. This opens the door for a Response-to-Intervention (RTI) model. In basic terms, RTI can be defined as a change in a student's performance as a result of early intervention strategies.

RTI relies on the utilization of evidence-based intervention (EBI) techniques, which are becoming standard within the field of school psychology. Evidence-based techniques are important tenets in both RTI and cognitive neuropsychology. According to Feifer (in press) the effect of the compilation of science and evidence-based instruction as a foundation for current practices creates new avenues for the study of brain-based relationships as a force in unifying education with science.

Utilizing the RTI approach, a student is found eligible for special education if that student fails to respond to well-implemented, research-based interventions. Therefore, if a student fails to respond to an intervention one may assume that a disability exists; however, it cannot be proven. Schmitt and Wodrich (in press) argue that neuropsychological tools are essential at this point. Neuroscience can provide an important foundational understanding for learning disabilities because a learning disability is an interaction between an environment that demands academic skills, and a child with a weakness in a processing skill required by the academic environment. Of course, if children did not have to attend school, a learning disability would be of little consequence. Additionally, such disabilities are not resolved through simple environmental changes like exposure to more education or changing your seats in the classroom. Of greatest concern to parents when their child exhibits behavior consistent with a learning disability is to try and explain it through a variety of motivational attributions (e.g., child is lazy) or by blaming the school (e.g., poor instruction)—both of which are untrue and inaccurate, in these cases. Neuroscience can provide educators with a clear view to what processes may be involved in learning difficulties.

Despite how a learning disability is treated, parents, teachers, and children need a frame of reference in which to understand *why* the student cannot read, or do some other specific academic tasks, as well as other children. Explaining to a parent their child has difficulty reading because they read 20 words per minute does not provide a suitable explanation, nor does misattributing the problem to faculty variables such as motivation or intelligence. Unfortunately, making attributions to internal variables is not easy. Neuroscience helps clarify how the brain works, how information is processed in the brain, and how behavioral responses emerge from the interaction of brain mechanisms. Neuroscience provides an explanatory basis with more than just explanatory power. It is also instrumental in describing the problem. Better descriptions of the problem, and more predictive causal models, lead to more focused assessment and treatment methodologies. Additionally, and rarely appreciated, such models help focus attention on what not to do and what interventions are unlikely to work.

HOW DO YOU RECONCILE RTI AS A MEANS OF DIAGNOSIS OF LD WITH KNOWLEDGE FROM THE CLINICAL NEUROSCIENCES?

RTI is not a methodology that should be used to diagnose or to categorize. Nor should RTI data, such as curriculum-based measures, be reported as a "psychological evaluation." RTI serves as a means to help children in general education and possibly reduce the number of children referred for special education who do not have a disability. RTI may only be referred to as a diagnostic process when discussed as a tiered model in which one of the tiers includes a comprehensive evaluation.

RTI, when referred to as a method of monitoring a child's curriculum progress, primarily supports general education. Schools within the United States have a substantial number of students who are struggling to succeed academically. These students require some degree of individual assistance within the school setting. However, resources within our schools are limited and most assistance that is available is often provided too late (Wright, n.d.). With implementation of early intervention services through the RTI model, school stakeholders will be able to share their problem-solving resources to attain positive outcomes for the greatest number of students (Wright, n.d.).

RTI calls for the grouping of intervention resources into tiers, which will provide schools with the ability to act quickly once a student is identified as a struggling learner. However, the question still remains as to when the struggling learner is having a sufficient amount of difficulty to be identified as learning disabled through the RTI model. Fuchs (2003) suggested that a two-part *Dual Discrepancy* formula be adapted by the schools (as cited by Wright, n.d.). The first discrepancy occurs when the struggling learner fails to achieve at the same rate as his or her grade or age peers. The second discrepancy is a gap in the rate of learning as compared to peers within the classroom. A gap in the rate of learning is identified if a student fails to close the achievement gap even after various evidence-based interventions are implemented. However, would this formula be sufficient in identifying learning disabilities or would there be an increase in the rate of false positives?

Instead of attempting to identify learning disabilities solely through the proposed Dual Discrepancy model, we propose combining evidence gleaned from RTI with traditional neuropsychological tests. Neuropsychological tests serve to answer the questions that RTI is attempting to answer. Such questions serve to determine what intervention should be used, how we monitor intervention progress, and how we know if an intervention worked or not. Despite the attempt to address these questions, RTI does not sufficiently provide answers to all of these questions.

RTI should not be viewed, or accepted, as a process that excludes the use of testing to uncover answers to what may be the cause of a student's underlying difficulty. Just as the model of RTI is viewed as incorporating consultation throughout each step, testing to get more concrete and specific hypotheses of the underlying problem and the most appropriate secondary intervention for a student, or group of students, is more likely to provide beneficial results. As the field of neuropsychology has gained in sophistication, so has the ability to prove that there are neurological explanations for learning difficulties (Berninger & Richards, 2002). The neurological findings, such as those that are seen when the brains of "good readers" and "bad readers" are compared, provide educators with important information about the learning process (Berninger & Richards, 2002).

Neuropsychological tests can also provide answers as to why students are underachieving. According to Feifer (in press), the primary goal of cognitive neuropsychological assessment is to understand the underlying processes associated with student difficulties and not to establish a discrepancy between IQ and achievement. In addition, oftentimes learning disorders occur co-morbidly with other conditions such as Attention-Deficit/Hyperactivity Disorder (ADHD); (Kronenberger & Meyer, 2001). Neuropsychological testing can serve to identify such conditions. With this knowledge, various interventions can be administered that target the true root of the student's problem.

WHAT ROLE DOES NEUROPSYCHOLOGY HAVE TO PLAY IN THE DIAGNOSIS OF LD?

By utilizing neuropsychology in the diagnosis of learning disabilities (LDs), practitioners are able to obtain an in-depth analysis of how students with learning difficulties are functioning. It also provides teachers with instructional hints as to how different students learn within their classrooms by providing evidence of how effectively they use cues to learn (Berninger & Richards, 2002). According to Berninger and Richards (2002), the functional brain-system approach to learning is compatible with Vygotsky's social constructivist model. Learning can be studied by looking at a student's development, social interaction, and the zone of proximal development. Both genetic and environmental factors can be viewed in terms of student development.

While genetic variables play a role in neural development, effective teacher instruction can improve a student's functioning in various academic areas. Berninger and Richards (2002) have suggested that, "although the sensory and motor systems may peak during preschool years, the developmental window for cortical activity is wide open during middle childhood and adolescence, the peak period for formal education" (p. 8). Such findings should give educators hope in that what they are doing for students can produce long-lasting effects. Additionally, neuroscience has the unique ability to show psychologists the functions of the brain, and the processes that are involved in learning to do many of the tasks that are required of growing brains. In the aspiration of viewing students in a more holistic manner, it seems only natural that another helpful way of understanding a student's world would be embraced.

Although neuropsychology provides a complete assessment of learning (Feifer, in press) and can play a vital role in the diagnosis of LD, there have been many legitimate criticisms of testing. For example, Ysseldyke,

Alzozzine, Richey, and Graden (1982) have suggested that LD is a socially invented concept used to remove bothersome children from the educational mainstream. Additionally, Ysseldyke et al. (1982) concluded that LD was an "oversophistication" of low achievement because the differences between LD and Low Achievement students are indistinguishable. A reevaluation of the data has been conducted along with a synthesis of other studies, all of which have disproven these conclusions (Kavale & Forness, 1994). Subsequent longitudinal studies have also reliably distinguished these two groups (Short et al., Feagans, McKinney, & Appelbaum, 1986), and the Learning Disabilities Roundtable (2005) concluded that the concept of Specific Learning Disabilities is valid and neurologically based. A meta-analysis conducted by Fuchs and Fuchs (2002) leaves "no doubt" that such groups can be distinguished. Problems with assessment practice are exaggerated to support particular researcher's own preference of how school psychology should be practiced (Kavale, Holdnack, & Mostert, 2005).

The value of assessment, the reality of clinical disorders, and the utility of neuropsychological research continues to be discounted by many in the field of school psychology (Gresham & Witt, 1997; Reschly & Ysseldyke, 2002). This obstinate disregard can possibly be explained as being politically based to promote an alternative practice, such as the RTI approach, to provide additional support for the Regular Education Initiative (REI), and to redistribute funding from special education to low-income children (Fuchs & Fuchs, 2002; Fuchs & Young, 2006). Regardless, when interpreting recent changes to federal guidelines in identifying disabilities and how school psychology is being practiced in the school, it is important to take note of and consider this historical context.

In the same light, questions have been raised around positive outcomes attributed to problem-solving models (Telzrow, McNamara, & Hollinger, 2000). Empirically validated benefits have been found to be lacking in multiple studies (Fuchs et al., 2003). Fuchs et al.. (2003), while reviewing these studies, concludes that the evidence for RTI approaches is lacking and insufficient and that the argument that such models are scientifically based is also unproven. The continued widespread implementation of RTI approaches, even though the questions around the empirical data persist, has triggered alarms and raised some concerns (Hale et al., Naglieri, Kaufman, & Kavale, 2004; Naglieri & Crockett, 2005). Similar conclusions have been reached in other professions (Graner & Faggella-Luby, 2005) and, with RTI pilot programs, some of which are over 2 decades old, have still not provided the necessary empirically defensible evidence to support the RTI advocates' claims (Naglieri & Crockett, 2005). Support and enthusiasm for RTI continues to exist within the field, however it is difficult to overlook the blaring contradiction of RTI's own philosophical standards. RTI standards are built around scientifically based practices, of which many have a clear lack of scientific-based evidence that support the RTI approach. By providing empirical data to explain patterns of behavior described as a learning disability, neuropsychology helps moderate politically based discussions involving educational policy. Additionally, such data provides the core basis for why psychologists in the school should continue to be concerned by children who exhibit learning disabilities.

WHAT ROLE DOES NEUROPSYCHOLOGY HAVE TO PLAY IN DESIGNING INTERVENTIONS IN THE CONTEXT OF RTI?

Evidence-based interventions are the cornerstone of the RTI process. The purpose of this type of intervention model is to provide a rationale for an intervention's use. While utilizing evidence-based interventions within the field is considered good practice, recent legislative mandates require the use of *scientifically based research* (Walcott & Riley-Tillman, 2007) within education. The No Child Left Behind Act of 2001 (NCLB) is one such mandate that requires schools to be accountable and provide evidence toward student progress.

Of fundamental importance in the RTI model is data collection for the purpose of determining the effectiveness of an intervention. Data collection within this model utilizes methods, such as curriculum-based measurement (CBM) probes, in order to track student progress. CBM probes in the areas of mathematics, reading, spelling, and written expression are being utilized in low-stakes classroom and screening type decisions. However, CBM should not be used as the sole determinant of a child's progress in high-stakes eligibility decisions. Best practices indicate that it is useful to combine it in a multi-method process (Christ, Davie, & Berman, 2006). According to Feifer (in press), the use of cognitive neuropsychological assessment can be used in data collection. Therefore, it seems likely that a compilation of CBM and cognitive neuropsychological assessment would be the best way to collect data in all areas of student functioning.

Neuropsychology can be used throughout the RTI process as interventions are decided, developed, and assessed. In the new age of evidence-based interventions, neuropsychology could be utilized to provide evidence that may not be visible through a systematic behavior observation, which is essentially the basis of analysis with RTI. Neuropsychology provides school psychologist as practitioners as well as researchers with a new tool that uncovers the multiple aspects of learning (such as reading and writing) that were once believed to be more similar than they may be in reality. Additionally, neuropsychological assessment can be used to help guide intervention development or to help modify an intervention that has proven unsuccessful.

The holistic view of education that is represented by the RTI model would do education a disservice by excluding the importance of a student's brain functioning when determining ability to learn and preparing strategies to improve. For example, not all reading problems are phonetic, and testing to identify the area of difficulty may lead to earlier, more accurate, interventions. Neuropsychological methodology provides the essential tools that help explain and specify particular learning problems that may elude even the best teachers and most observant parents.

REFERENCES

Berninger, V. W., & Richards, T. L. (2002). *Brain literacy for educators and psychologists*. San Diego: Academic Press.

Brown-Chidsey, R., & Steege, M. W. (2005). *Response to intervention*. New York: Guilford.

Christ, T. J., Davie, J., & Berman, S. (2006). CBM data and decision making in RTI contexts: Addressing performance variability. *Communique, 35*(2). Retrieved September 2, 2007, from http://www.nasponline.org/publications/cq/mocq352cbmdata.aspx.

Feifer, S. G. (in press). Integrating RTI with Neuropsychology: A scientific approach to reading. In a special edition of *Psychology in the Schools: Applications of Neuropsychology*.

Fuchs, D., & Fuchs, L. S. (2002). Is "Learning Disability" just a fancy term for low achievement? A meta-analysis of reading differences between low achievers with and without the label. *Learning Disabilities Summit: Building a Foundation for the Future White Papers:* National Research Center on Learning Disabilities.

Fuchs, D., Mock, D., Morgan, P. L., & Young, C. L. (2003). Responsiveness-to-Intervention: Definitions, evidence and implications for the learning disabilities construct. *Learning and Disability Research & Practice, 18,* 157–171.

Fuchs, D., & Young, C. L. (2006). On the irrelevance of intelligence in predicting responsiveness to reading instruction. *Exceptional Children, 73,* 8–30.

Gottlieb, J., Alter, M., Gottlieb, B. W., & Wishner, J. (1994). Special education in urban America: It's not justifiable for many. *The Journal of Special Education, 27,* 453–465.

Graner, P. S., & Faggella-Luby, M. N. (2005). An overview of responsiveness to intervention: What practioners ought to know. *Topics in Language Disorders, 25,* 93–105.

Gresham, F. M., & Witt, J. C. (1997). Utility of intelligence tests for treatment planning, classification, and placement decisions: Recent empirical findings and future directions. *School Psychology Quarterly, 12,* 249–267.

Hale, J. B., Naglieri, J. A., Kaufman, A. S., & Kavale, K. A. (2004). Specific learning disability classification in the new Individuals with Disabilities Education Act: The danger of a good idea. *The School Psychologist, 58,* 6–13.

Individuals with Disabilities Education Improvement Act of 2004 (IDEA), P. L. N., 118 Stat 2647. (2004).

Kavale, K. A., & Forness, S. R. (1994). Learning disabilities and intelligence: An uneasy alliance. In T. E. Scruggs & M. A. Mastropieri (Eds.), *Advances in learning and behavioral disabilities.* (Vol. 8, pp. 1–63). Greenwich, CT: JAI Press.

Kavale, K. A., Holdnack, J. A., & Mostert, M. P. (2005). Responsiveness to intervention and the identification of specific learning disability: A critique and alternative proposal. *Learning Disability Quarterly, 28*(1), 2–16.

Kronenberger, W. G., & Meyer, R. G. (2001). *The child clinician's handbook* (2nd ed.). Needham Heights, MA: Pearson Education.

Naglicri, J. A., & Crockett, D. P. (2005). Response to intervention (RTI): Is it a scientifically proven method? *Communiqué, 34,* 38–39.

Reid, R., & Lienemann, T. O. (2006). *Strategy instruction for students with learning disabilities.* New York: Guilford.

Reschly, D. J., & Ysseldyke, J. E. (2002). Paradigm shift: The past is not the future. In A. Thomas & J. Grimes (Eds.), *Best practices in school psychology* (3rd ed., pp. 3–36). Washington DC: National Association of School Psychologists.

Roundtable, L. D. (2005). *Comments and recommendations on regulatory issues under the Individuals with Disabilities Education Improvement Act of 2004, Public Law 108-446.* Retrieved September 14, 2005, from http://www.ncld.org/content/view/278/398/

Schmitt, A. J., & Wodrich, D. L. (in press). Reasons and rationale for neuropsychological tests in a multi-tier system of school services. In a special edition of *Psychology in the Schools: Applications of Neuropsychology.*

Short, E. J., Feagans, L., McKinney, J. D., & Appelbaum, M. I. (1986). Longitudinal stability of LD subtypes based on age-and IQ-achievement discrepancies. *Learning Disability Quarterly, 9,* 214–225.

Telzrow, C. F., McNamara, K., & Hollinger, C. L. (2000). Fidelity of problem-solving implementation and relationship to student performance. *School Psychology Review, 29,* 443–461.

Walcott, C. M., & Riley-Tillman, C. (2007). Evidence-based intervention from research to practice. NASP *Communiqué, 35*(6). Retrieved September 1, 2007, from http://www.nasponline.org/publications/cq/mocq356research.aspx.

Wright, J. (n.d.). *RTI_wire.* Retrieved January 4, 2007, from http://www.jimwright online.com/php/rti/rti_wire.php.

Ysseldyke, J., Alzozzine, B., Richey, L., & Graden, J. (1982). Declaring students eligible for disability services: Why bother with the data? *Learning Disability Quarterly, 5,* 37–43.

14

Neuropsychological Aspects of Learning Disabilities Determination: Scientific and Cultural Considerations

Sangeeta Dey, Psy.D.

WHAT DO YOU THINK NEUROSCIENCE HAS TO OFFER THE ASSESSMENT AND IDENTIFICATION OF LEARNING DISABILITIES?

Since all learning and behavior originates in the brain and individual differences in behavior are due to individual differences in the brain's functioning, assessing biological abnormality of the brain when learning disabilities (LDs) are suspected is important. It is imperative that assessment procedures consider genetic, structural, physiological, and other complex factors involved in brain functioning. Disregard for such important brain-based mechanisms will preclude our understanding of the link between critical neurological anomalies and LD.

Although we are still far away from establishing one-to-one correspondence between specific brain areas and LDs, the advent of noninvasive neuroimaging tools has led to some groundbreaking findings. In particular, these sophisticated imaging techniques have permitted researchers to look closely into the brains of children with LD in *real time*. For instance, the extensive study of functional brain systems in children with dyslexia provides overwhelming support for neuroscience's contribution in understanding this complex phenomenon and validates the need for continuation of investigation in this area (Shaywitz et al., 2002). Furthermore, it is due to neuroscience's efforts that phonological-processing difficulties have been identified as a primary deficit in dyslexia (Temple et al., 2001). These findings, in turn, have led to the development of assessment instruments that specifically evaluate phonological skills in children who are at risk of LD.

Besides the development of valid assessment tools, findings from neuroscience are also offering hope for early identification for LD, particularly dyslexia. For example, it has long been acknowledged that children who present with delays in their language development likely experience difficulties in learning to read (e.g., Catts et al., 2002). Several studies have attributed these early language vulnerabilities to difficulties in acquiring phonological-processing skills (e.g., Tallal & Gaab, 2006). Research also indicates that both language learning impairment (e.g., Tallal & Piercy, 1973) and reading disabilities can be caused by phonological-processing deficits (e.g., Shaywitz, 1998). Interestingly, scholars have discovered significant differences in the brain's electrical activity between infants who later demonstrate a language learning impairment and those who do not by measuring their responses to different sounds (Benasich et al., 2006). Putting it all together, it makes us wonder if indeed brain differences observed at such an early age are indicative of language learning impairment and if this could be considered a warning sign for dyslexia. Studies are currently being conducted to test this hypothesis with variable levels of success (e.g., Lyytinen et al., 2005).

Routine screening of preschoolers using high-tech instruments for diagnostic purposes might seem too far fetched, but so was the concept of having advanced technologies that would permit us to look inside a functional brain. Given the tremendous progress that neuroscience has made in the past few decades in identification of brain mechanisms, there are reasons to feel optimistic that the discipline will evolve to a point where neurological findings will be routinely used to determine or validate diagnoses of LD. In the interim, with the help of knowledge acquired from brain-based studies, researchers should continue to develop psychometrically sound assessment tools for early evaluation and identification.

HOW WILL FUTURE DEVELOPMENTS IN NEUROSCIENCE AFFECT HOW WE CLASSIFY AND INTERVENE WITH LEARNING DISABILITIES?

The diagnostic issues related to LDs have undergone tremendous changes and multiple studies in various disciplines are continuing their efforts to offer reliable definition and classification of LD. The *Diagnostic and Statistical Manual* (DSM) and succeeding versions have adopted a menu approach for clustering constellations of observable behavioral expressions of pathology. It is not at all surprising that the DSM has received criticism for overlooking the underlying neurological apparatus and physiological processes that are far more complexly integrated and are not entirely captured in the labels. Further, although the verbal labels used to categorize LD in our nosology are useful for communication purposes, verbal labels disregard the complexity of individual differences within the context of developmental expectations.

Just as with genetics, neuroscience is now offering new possibilities in our quest to understand and classify learning disabilities. Neuroimaging techniques have identified the brain as infinitely more complex than previously thought. For example, research has indicated that language is not confined to a single area in the brain; instead, the language network covers a wider region in the brain. This helps delineate that, while a more prominent phenotypic presentation of LD might be indicative of aberrant functioning in a certain area of the brain, anomalies in the brain of an individual with LD are complex and probably not focused in a single area. Toward that end, a broader classification offered by Rourke, van der Vlugt, and Rourke (2002) corroborates this complexity as it describes specific patterns of strengths and weaknesses in a child's learning, academic, and social functioning. In particular, electrophysiological studies have identified differences in brain activity between nonverbal learning disabilities (NLDs) and basic phonological-processing disabilities (BPPDs).

Further, as the arrival of sophisticated techniques has allowed researchers to examine the brain in action, it also has provided valuable insight about brain functions when it is not working normally. As is evident, one of the most robust and consistent findings has been that the brains of individuals with learning disabilities are indeed different from nonimpaired brains. For example, neuroimaging techniques have linked reading deficiencies with defective wiring in the area of the brain responsible for decoding. Taken together, these findings suggest that if brain functions in individuals with dyslexia are indeed unique and consistently exhibit characteristic differences, with time, a distinct profile of neurological anomaly should emerge and aid in a more precise classification of dyslexia.

In practice, however, classifications based solely on neuroscience have been criticized due to the nonspecific nature of the brain anomalies as well as discrepant findings amongst researchers. While this drawback corresponds to the challenges related to complex functioning of the brain itself, to some extent this difficulty is also due to neuroscience's reliance on definitions/classifications of LD that have been offered by professionals from the field of education and psychology. In other words, neuroscientists are attempting to investigate *LD classifications* that are based on *supposed* behavioral presentations. Paradoxically, these existing classifications have themselves been criticized for discounting heterogeneity within children with LDs. Several studies have reported significant overlap between Attention-Deficit/Hyperactivity Disorder (ADHD) and language-based LD (Dykman & Ackerman, 1991; Semrud-Clikeman et al., 1992). Studies have also indicated how children with learning issues, attentional difficulties, or both are at risk for social and emotional difficulties (e.g., Kavale and Forness, 1996). These co-morbidities further challenge the current classification system, which tends to pigeon-hole children under specific exclusive labels. Therefore, future development in neuroscience will also depend on our understanding and conceptualization of LD.

Notwithstanding, current advances in technology are opening new avenues and offering possibilities to learn about LD in infancy by measuring the brain's electrical activity in infants in response to different sounds (Benasich et al., 2006). This obviously is a shift from the traditional approach of going from phenotype to brain; instead, researchers are now aiming to go first to the underlying neurological mechanisms to delineate anomalies in brain functioning. The final goal is to avert LD or, at minimum, to develop targeted interventions. As neuroscience has also demonstrated that brains of people with dyslexia normalize after receiving appropriate educational interventions, neuroimaging techniques will assist in designing remediative instructional materials.

In summary, it is hoped that advancement in neuroscience will help us become proficient in identifying children as early as possible. In the years to come, while more sophisticated technology might help in a more precise classification of LD, the ultimate goal is to prevent painful social and emotional experiences for children with LDs.

WHAT ROLE DOES NEUROPSYCHOLOGY HAVE TO PLAY IN THE DIAGNOSIS OF LD?

The field of neuropsychology constantly strives to design and use empirical assessment tools to identify neurological correlates of LD. It furthers our understanding and ability to reliably identify and classify LD by establishing consistency in neuropsychological profiles for children who experience difficulties in learning.

One of the goals of neuropsychological evaluation is to provide clarification regarding a child's diagnostic status, but the scope of such an evaluation goes far beyond an exclusive diagnosis. To see it as such would fall short of understanding the scope and repercussions of a child's presenting learning problems. A thorough neuropsychological assessment offers an estimate of a child's developmental functioning and provides recommendations for management and educational planning. The assessment also identifies the child's learning strengths and weaknesses in a manner that goes beyond the presenting isolated learning difficulties. Specifically, a neuropsychological evaluation maps a child's learning profile and provides a framework that explains specific learning issues with which a child presents, such as reading or math, and how the brain regions that correlate with these areas might affect other aspects of a child's functioning. These hypotheses have become possible through accumulated methodical measurement, data-collection and analysis, and the careful inductive reasoning methods of scientist-practitioners that draw inferences about the relationship between neuropsychological phenotype and etiology. For instance, numerous studies have identified a neuropsychological profile associated with nonverbal learning disability (e.g., Rourke et al., 2002), thereby helping parents and educators appreciate a child's profile and anticipate difficulties in areas such as executive functioning, motor skills, and social adjustment. Although considerable variability within neuropsychological phenotypes is reported, which is expected given the brain's complex organization, such variability helps to account for possible comorbid conditions, such as co-occurrence of ADHD and dyslexia. Further, such variability also helps to identify the potential of the brain's intact collateral cognitive systems that can be harnessed and productively engineered.

Neuropsychological evaluations have been criticized for their constraints in assessing children from nontraditional backgrounds (e.g., children from an impoverished environment or children who have been adopted from other countries). The following case study demonstrates how a comprehensive neuropsychological assessment for children from nontraditional backgrounds could prove to be a valuable resource for identifying underlying cognitive processes and hypothesizing possibility of learning deficits. Notably, this case describes a child who might not be considered an appropriate candidate for standardized assessments. Nonetheless, the case highlights the importance of diagnostic conceptualizations based on existing empirical knowledge of the brain's functioning.

Jane is an 11-year, 11-month-old girl who was adopted from India. Jane's parents noted that she is experiencing considerable difficulties in her acquisition of academic skills. Although academic problems are commonly observed in children identified as English Language Learners (ELLs), Jane's parents reported concerns about several aspects of her learning and development that fell outside the realm of ELL. For instance, the child was unable to learn and follow the basic two-step directions even with the provision of modeling and reminders. While the parents intensively worked with the child at home to teach her basic daily living skills, the school diligently offered academic instructions based on her ELL standing. However, even with such collaborative efforts the child's progress was reported to be modest at best. At this point, the parents requested special education support; nonetheless, the educators maintained that Jane's profile reflects challenges to be expected from ELLs and the aftereffects of impoverished upbringing, and that her current environment will be helpful in reducing deficits presently observed in her functioning across domains.

Jane's parents finally decided to get a neuropsychological evaluation to assess Jane's neurocognitive and developmental functioning, to assist with the diagnostic picture, and to obtain recommendations for her educational programming. Given Jane's background, a variety of nonverbal assessment tools were used to bypass the cultural and language demands inherent to the general assessment tools used for measuring the intellectual functioning of typical English-speaking children. In the following paragraphs, a neuropsychological analysis of Jane's performance on selected instruments is discussed.

Results of cognitive testing using Leiter International Performance Scale–Revised (Roid & Miller, 1997) generated scores that fell approximately in two categories: The first cluster of scores fell within average expectations and was on two of the tasks that were primarily perceptual in nature. The scores on the second grouping fell in the borderline range and were typically on tests demanding reasoning skills. Of note, this categorization should not be perceived in absolute terms as most of the tasks demand a combination of both reasoning and perceptual capacity; however, the degree of involvement of such skills varies depending on the nature of the task. Jane's difficulties were further evident on her rendition of the Rey-Osterrieth Complex Figure Test, on which she was asked to copy a geometric form and then to recall it, as well as on the test of Visual-Motor Integration–Fifth Edition (Beery, Buktenica, & Beery, 2004), a more structured measure of design copying. In both cases, she was noted to experience difficulties in managing and integrating details, even while she was able to retain and recall the overall gestalt of the figure with greater ease.

Neuropsychologically, Jane presented with a pattern of functioning that displayed an approach typically described in children with left-hemispheric inefficiency, the side of the brain that neuroscience research has typically implicated in the processing of language-related functioning. Neuropsychological phenotypes of individuals with language-based learning disabilities indicate that they often process information in a distinctive fashion, which is evident on nonverbal tasks as well. In particular, they often exhibit difficulties with managing details, regardless of their proficiency in processing and comprehending the "big picture." This association is attributed to the shared function of the left hemisphere of the brain in language development, as well as in detail-oriented information processing and sequential reasoning. This characteristic style of information processing was evident in Jane's performance on the nonverbal cognitive battery and on tests assessing her nonverbal processing. Furthermore, assuming the contralateral organization of the brain system, Jane's deficits in the rapid execution of fine motor tasks were pronounced in her right-dominant hand, once again implicating her weaker left side of the brain.

During the feedback session with the family and follow-up conversations with her educators, it was acknowledged that, despite neuropsychological insinuation of a specific learning disability (SLD), specifically a language-based learning disability, given paucity of standardized assessment tools available for comprehensive evaluation for children with Jane's background and other psychometric constraints relevant to norms, it remains very difficult to discern specific diagnoses that would accurately capture the unique pattern of vulnerabilities and strengths in her profile at this time. It was also conveyed that there still might be the possibility that the current deficits in Jane's profile simply represent aftereffects of impoverished upbringing, and that her current environment may be helpful in reducing some of the deficits presently observed in her functioning across domains. However, based on her present neuropsychological profile, and her lack of progress at both home and school, Jane's challenges seem to be more representative of a neurological dysfunction in her cognitive profile than of a temporary difficulty resulting from a lack of exposure to English or absence of opportunity.

It was also communicated to the family and the educators that Jane would indeed derive benefits from her current supportive environment and will continue to make gains in her overall functioning. However, as evident from her neuropsychological profile, and despite the benefit of her current social and learning environment that she is being afforded, Jane's eventual presentation will always be of a child who has an innate learning style that highly favors reasoning through nonverbal versus verbal means. Further, it was conveyed that such a learning style will significantly impact Jane's functioning in the academic domain, potentially requiring compensatory strategies, specialized supports, and at minimum a thorough understanding of her cognitive profile.

While the school personnel were still debating the validity of SLD versus ELL issues, a magnetic resonance imaging (MRI) study was recommended by Jane's neurologist to rule out any organic bases for her difficulties. Jane's MRI revealed brain abnormalities on the left hemisphere that were described as being indicative of injury to this region, thereby corroborating the neuropsychological findings. While follow-up neurological examinations were still being conducted to determine the precise nature and implication of Jane's brain abnormality, this finding substantiated the hypothesis that was exclusively based on qualitative analysis of her neuropsychological profile.

As evident from the aforementioned case, while the field of neuropsychology is still developing, it offers an impressive framework for understanding of LD. Due to response-to-intervention's (RTI's) exclusive focus on treatment failure as a method for diagnosis, it fails to offer comprehensive interventions that would remediate other potential challenges secondary to shared localization of the brain with areas responsible for other key cognitive or emotional functioning. While focusing on and aiming to remediate children's individual challenges is indeed helpful, targeted interventions in isolated areas fail to adequately see the child as a whole and, in turn, do not appropriately foster or challenge the *intact* cognitive processing skills. In comparison, neuropsychological assessment offer a precise and comprehensive diagnostic classification that attempts to account for all aspects of a child's cognitive and psychological profile for the valuable guidance it will provide to the intervention process and the child's future achievements and social-emotional adjustment.

WHAT ROLE DOES NEUROPSYCHOLOGY HAVE TO PLAY IN DESIGNING INTERVENTIONS IN THE CONTEXT OF RTI?

Similar to other fields where advances in basic science need to be translated into applied methods of practice, the most vexing challenge that has always plagued neuropsychology is transferring brain-behavior related dysfunctions from evidence to effective interventions. Critics argue that neuropsychology has focused on assessment and diagnosis rather than intervention. By comparison, the supporters of RTI claim to prevent overdiagnosis of SLD by emphasizing interventions.

While offering interventions via scientifically based classroom instructions is the final goal for both neuropsychology and RTI, the first step to any intervention planning ought to be a comprehensive assessment of the child's strengths and weaknesses to identify the root cause of the problem. Delaying the precise delineation of the problem by using unfocussed and "hit-or-miss" approaches may lead to undesirable consequences. In some cases, by the time an evaluation is considered, the child already has amassed a solid record of repeated failures resulting in entrenched shoddy problem-solving approaches and learning habits, negative outcomes that are difficult to unlearn. Furthermore, social stigma, labeling, and the emotional problems caused by such ingrained defeatism, performance failure, and demoralization will compound the best belated efforts and will then make it extremely difficult to tease out actual cognitive limitations from myriad social, emotional, and motivational issues. Given the developmental nature of some learning issues, the cumulative damages incurred might even be irreversible.

RTI's approach of providing early identification and intervention yields positive results for children with subtle learning difficulties; however, a neuropsychological evaluation should be conducted as early as possible in the intervention process to provide a blueprint for areas that should be precisely targeted for intervention. As is well established by researchers, a child's deficits in an area of learning could have different underlying causes. For example, reading difficulties in children could be due to varying combinations of contributing factors, such as attentional issues, language-processing vulnerabilities, and anxiety. Neuropsychology's comprehensive approach to assessment, that includes intellectual, cognitive, social-emotional, and achievement, helps identify the underlying cause of the observable problem (e.g., reading). This more comprehensive approach to evaluation allows for far more accurate differential diagnosis. The precise identification of strengths and weaknesses permits the design of targeted intervention plans to also help schools direct their efforts and allocate precious limited resources in the right direction.

In contrast to a scientific and empirically based and targeted approach in the modern field of neuropsychology, RTI is a mysterious process of interventions using unspecifiable methods of effective action for undefined problems. By comparison to sound neuropsychology by competent practitioners, RTI is akin to peoples of ancient Rome giving prayers and offerings to Sentia, the Goddess of child mental development, blindly petitioning the grace of the gods for divine intervention to produce favorable outcomes, with just as much confidence in prospects for success.

Lastly, given developmental changes in the neuropsychological presentation of children, a neuropsychologist can work collaboratively with the school's team to follow the child over time to monitor progress and determine with empirical certainty if and how cognitive deficits, academic issues, or emotional difficulties resolve. This has two advantages: First, it will help educators understand if the intervention offered to a child with a particular presentation was helpful, which will facilitate educators continually refining their intervention techniques. Second, follow-up assessments of a child's developmental functioning and progress will assist in fine-tuning the child's services as the needs change over time and as natural maturation of cognitive functions unfold.

REFERENCES

Beery, K. E., Buktenica, N. A., & Beery, N. A. (2004). The Beery-Buktenica Developmental Test of Visual-Motor Integration: Beery VMI Administration, Scoring, and Teaching Manual (5th ed.). Minneapolis: NCS Pearson.

Benasich, A. A., Choudhury, N., Friedman, J. T., Realpe-Bonilla, T., Chojnowska, C., & Gou, Z. (2006). The infant as a prelinguistic model for language learning impairments: Predicting from event-related potentials to behavior. Neuropsychologia, 44, 396–411.

Catts, H. W., Fey, M. E., Tomblin, J. B., & Zhang, X. (2002). A longitudinal investigation of reading outcomes in children with language impairments. Journal of Speech Language & Hearing Research, 45, 1142–1157.

Dykman, R. A., & Ackerman, P. T. (1991). Attention deficit disorder and specific reading disability: Separate but often overlapping disorders. Journal of Learning Disabilities, 24, 95–103.

Kavale, K. A., & Forness, S. R. (1996). Social skill deficits and learning disabilities: A meta analysis. Journal of Learning Disabilities, 29, 226–237.

Lyytinen, H., Guttorm, T. K., Huttunen, T., Hämäläinen, J., Leppänen, P. H. T., & Vesterinen, M. (2005). Psychophysiology of developmental dyslexia: A review of findings including studies of children at risk for dyslexia. Journal of Neurolinguistics, 18, 167–195.

Roid, G. H., & Miller, L. J. (1997). Leiter International Performance Scale-Revised. Wood Dale, IL: Stoelting.

Rourke, B. P., van der Vlugt, H., & Rourke, S. B. (2002). Practice of child-clinical neuropsychology: An introduction. Lisse, The Netherlands: Swets & Zeitlinger.

Semrud-Clikeman, M., Biederman, J., Sprich-Buckminster, S., Lehman, B. K., Faraone, S. V., & Norman, D. (1992). Comorbidity between ADHD and learning disability: A review and report in a clinically referred sample. Journal of the American Academy of Child and Adolescent Psychiatry, 31, 439–448.

Shaywitz, S. E. (1998). Dyslexia. New England Journal of Medicine, 338, 307–312.

Shaywitz, B., Shaywitz, S., Pugh, K. R., Mencl, W. E., Fulbright, R. K., Constable, R. T., Skudlarski, P., Jenner, A., Fletcher, J. M., Marchione, K. E., Shankweiler, D., Katz, L., Lacadie, C., Lyon, G. R., & Gore, J. C. (2002). Disruption of the neural circuitry for reading in children with developmental dyslexia. Biological Psychiatry, 52, 101–110.

Tallal, P., & Piercy, M. (1973). Developmental aphasia: Impaired rate of non-verbal processing as a function of sensory modality. Neuropsychologia, 11, 389–398.

Tallal, P., & Gaab, N. (2006). Dynamic auditory processing, musical experience and language development. Trends in Neurosciences, 29, 382–390.

Temple, E., Poldrack, R. A., Salidis, J., Deutsch, G. K., Tallal, P., Merzenich, M. M., & Gabrieli, J. D. (2001). Disrupted neural responses to phonological and orthographic processing in dyslexic children: An fMRI study. Neuroreport, 12(2), 299–307.

15

Identifying a Learning Disability: Not Just Product, but Process

Colin D. Elliott

What has been will be again,
what has been done will be done again;
there is nothing new under the sun.
Is there anything of which one can say,
"Look! This is something new"?
It was here already, long ago;
it was here before our time.

Thus the writer of Ecclesiastes (Chapter 1, vv. 9–10; Holy Bible, New International Version) made his observation of the essential nature of human activity. There is nothing new about response to intervention (RTI). It has been around from time immemorial. What teacher down the ages has not encountered a student who finds difficulty in learning something? What physician or psychologist down the ages has not had a patient or client who needed treatment? It is always possible, of course, to decide to give no special treatment in the hope that improvement will take place spontaneously. In most cases, however, the professional makes a decision to try some intervention to see whether it works. If it is successful, the professional has a grateful client. If it is not, then something else is tried to see if that works. And that is the process of RTI. It is only recently that this very basic principle of applying an intervention and observing its effect has received the accolade of an acronym that has swept through school psychology like wildfire; but we have always used it.

In medicine, it is very clear that if a physician tries a few interventions without success (perhaps drugs of different kinds and in different dosages), the patient is considered to have a problem that needs further investigation as to its cause. Therefore, more diagnostic work is specified. The problem that everyone is facing in school psychology is that it is being suggested that, if a number of children (for example, poor readers) fail to respond to RTI, they should then be all categorized with the same learning disability (LD in reading) and be provided with the same teaching resources.

WHAT DO YOU THINK NEUROSCIENCE HAS TO OFFER IN THE ASSESSMENT AND IDENTIFICATION OF LEARNING DISABILITIES?

In this response, I take the term *neuroscience* to include insights from the fields of cognitive psychology and the science of measurement of individual differences. All three fields have major overlaps of theoretical constructs.

Definition of Learning Disabilities

There appears to be considerable professional agreement on the definition of the nature of LD. The well-known definition of *specific learning disability* (SLD) in IDEA 2004 states: "Specific learning disability means a disorder in one or more of the basic psychological processes involved in understanding or in using language, spoken or written . . ." The definition gives a list of the ways in which SLD may be manifested, then gives a list of inclusionary conditions (essentially within-person features concerned with brain structure and functioning), and finishes with a list of exclusionary conditions (sensory impairments, Mental Retardation, emotional disturbance, and environmental disadvantage). The definition thereby emphasizes that dysfunction in basic cognitive or neuropsychological processes is the primary cause of LD. The recent position statement of the National Association of School Psychologists (NASP, 2007) confirms the Association's alignment with that definition:

> There is general agreement that:
>
> - Specific learning disabilities are endogenous in nature, and are characterized by neurologically-based deficits in cognitive processes;
> - These deficits are specific, that is, they impact particular cognitive processes that interfere with the acquisition of formal learning skills;
> - Specific learning disabilities are heterogeneous—there are various types of learning disabilities, and there is no single defining characteristic common to all learning disabilities;
> - Specific learning disabilities may co-exist with other disabling conditions (e.g., sensory deficits, language impairment, behavior problems), but are not due to these conditions . . . (NASP, 2007).

Neuroscience lies at the heart of the assessment and identification of LD. Former operational definitions of LD in terms of a severe discrepancy between achievement and ability are deeply flawed. Whether the discrepancy is defined as that between an ability score and an *obtained* achievement score, or between an obtained achievement score and the achievement score *predicted* on the basis of the individual's ability score, the method takes no account of within-child causal factors. The use of severe discrepancy criteria resulted in an inability to differentiate between individuals with neurocognitive-processing difficulties and those whose poor achievements are environmentally caused: All were identified as LD, regardless of causality.

An Example of LD Subgroups

Let's consider the possible causal factors in specific reading disability. As an example of the range of possible strengths and weaknesses found in children with this disability, I analyzed the patterns of cluster scores of a sample of 161 students, all with Word Reading scores below 85, who had been assessed by a number of school psychologists on the Differential Ability Scales (DAS; Elliott, 1990) and who had been identified as having either dyslexia or LD. Only differences between the three cluster scores were analyzed—the clusters are Verbal (a measure of crystallized ability: *Gc*), Nonverbal Reasoning (NVR—a measure of fluid reasoning: *Gf*), and Spatial (a measure of visual-spatial ability: *Gv*). Differences between subtest scores were ignored for the purpose of this analysis. Students were assigned to groups based upon the following criteria:

1. Flat profile: No significant differences between any cluster scores.
2. Low Spatial, High Verbal: Spatial score significantly lower than Verbal.
3. Low Verbal, High Spatial: Verbal score significantly lower than Spatial.
4. High NVR: Nonverbal Reasoning score higher than both Verbal and Spatial, and significantly higher than at least one of them.
5. Low NVR: Nonverbal Reasoning score lower than both Verbal and Spatial, and significantly lower than at least one of them.

Note first of all that we always expect a number of students who are poor readers to have flat cognitive profiles: They may be having difficulties learning to read, but these difficulties are not the result of deficits in cognitive processing. Note secondly that students were assigned to groups 2 through 5 only if they had a significant difference (16 standard score points; $p < .05$) between two or more clusters. Such differences are reliable and not subject to the criticism that they capitalize on chance. The number of LD students with

Table 15.1   Number of Students Identified as Having Dyslexia or LDs with Various Profiles.

Type of Profile	Number of Students with Profile	Percentage with Profile	Expected Base Rate
Flat	56	34.8	50.1
High Spatial, Low Verbal	10	6.2	10.7
High Verbal, Low Spatial	20	12.4	10.0
High NVR	9	5.6	14.8
Low NVR	66	41.0	14.4
Sample Size	*161*		

various profiles is given in Table 15.1, together with the expected base rate (that is, the percentage in the standardization sample with such a profile).

As an example of the mean differences between scores, see Figure 15.1, which shows the cluster score profile of the Low NVR subgroup. Here, mean differences between the NVR score and the Verbal and Spatial clusters amounts to 17 to 20 standard score points. These results are presented in somewhat greater detail by Elliott (2001, 2005).

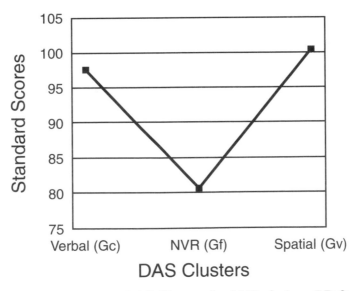

Figure 15.1. Mean Scores on DAS Clusters for 66 Dyslexic or LD Students in the Low NVR subgroup.
Note: All students had Word Reading standard scores below 85.

In evaluating this evidence, it is important to remember first that these analyses were done solely on the basis of three cluster scores and, second, that the subgroups were identified on the basis of statistically significant differences between scores. The use of a larger number of clusters, such as are found in the DAS-II (Elliott, 2007a) and the range of possible statistically significant differences between subtest scores would add hugely to the complexity of the analyses. A far larger number of LD subgroups may therefore be expected in real life.

What Does All This Mean?

Neuroscience, and its associated field of cognitive ability assessment, is clearly able to differentiate between subgroups of children with LD who have significant and very different cognitive processing deficits.

There are two major groups of causes of a child's failure to learn at school. On the one hand, there are various possible environmental causes—home conditions, quality of school and teachers, cultural factors, or illness. On the other hand, there are various possible endogenous, constitutional causes— genetic endowment probably accounts for many individual differences in the way information is processed, and injuries or changes to the brain through life events account for others. Individuals differ hugely in such cognitive processing areas as general cognitive ability, verbal development, visual-spatial discrimination, integration of verbal and visual information, higher-order reasoning and planning, memory factors (short-term, intermediate-term, working memory, visual-verbal memory), cognitive processing speed, the development of phonological awareness, and so on. The task for the clinician is to identify the characteristics of the individual and sift the evidence in coming to an understanding of the causes of that person's cognitive strengths and weaknesses.

According to the IDEA 2004 definition and the NASP (2007) position statement, an individual should only be identified as having LD if there were evidence of specific cognitive processing difficulties with *an endogenous cause*. This is not to say that a child with major sensory impairments, who shows significant evidence of Mental Retardation, who has had an adverse upbringing should not receive services. Far from it! But such children require *different* services to those provided for individuals with SLDs. Different causes require different solutions. And neuroscience is the discipline that provides the methods and techniques to do the job of assessment and identification.

Observing a child's response to a teacher's intervention may help to clarify the nature of some of his or her difficulties. It can establish that the child is failing to learn. However, it can never result in the detailed analysis of specific dysfunction in basic cognitive or neuropsychological processes that is necessary in identifying and understanding the reason for the failure.

HOW WILL FUTURE DEVELOPMENTS IN NEUROSCIENCE AFFECT HOW WE CLASSIFY AND INTERVENE WITH LEARNING DISABILITIES?

In the early years of the neurosciences, most work seems to have been done on simplifying the complexity of observed human behavior through generating broad constructs that have general application, whether in terms of brain structures or factor-analytic structures of human ability. It seems most likely that future developments will lead to greater detail and complexity in our understanding of the nature of learning disabilities.

The instruments we will need to do this work have already been growing in complexity. Starting with the original Stanford-Binet Intelligence Scale, with its single variable of mental age or IQ, we have seen the Wechsler scales (which grow in complexity with each revision), followed by such test batteries as the Woodcock-Johnson and the DAS, both of which have become more detailed with each successive revision. As we know from the field of medicine, it is only as diagnostic procedures become more refined that treatments can become more differentiated. So it must be in the field of learning disabilities. Treatments and interventions in the area of learning and behavior are notoriously difficult to implement, and no doubt our diagnostic/analytic procedures are well ahead of our ability to intervene effectively. But that is no reason to abandon the enterprise of developing any further understanding of disabilities.

Many clinicians will know of the tremendous relief experienced by students when they understand something about why they are having difficulties. It is a blessing to know you are not stupid. If that were the only reason for pressing on with future development, we should still do it.

HOW DO YOU RECONCILE RTI AS A MEANS OF DIAGNOSIS OF LD WITH KNOWLEDGE FROM THE CLINICAL NEUROSCIENCES?

To my knowledge, most psychologists who have been involved for much of their professional lives with individual assessment have no problem with integrating RTI with psychometric and neuropsychological assessment methods. The problem that has arisen is the suggestion that RTI can and should be used in order to diagnose and identify LD (e.g., NASDSE, 2005). At that time Reynolds (2005) aptly pointed out that "as an approach to pre-referral intervention, RTI is highly appropriate and shows great promise in promoting problem solving and the improvement of instructional practices overall. As a method or process of diagnosis of individual children, it fails."

The NASP position statement on the identification of children with SLD seems to have come to a more balanced conclusion about the need to balance the information obtained from an RTI approach with the more detailed diagnostic information obtainable from using a comprehensive clinical evaluation. The statement reads: "When a learning disability is suspected, and instruction and intervention within general education [*i.e., RTI*] fail to meet a child's educational needs, a comprehensive assessment by qualified professionals is an essential step in the identification of a specific learning disability." NASP, however, manages to suggest that this comprehensive evaluation, which is at Tier 3 in a three-tier system of staged interventions, should include curriculum-based measurement (CBM) and procedures for monitoring RTI as well as norm-referenced measures that assess basic psychological processes.

The problem here is that behavioral assessment methods such as CBM may most readily be applied to hierarchies of basic skills. Although such methods are linked to the school curriculum (e.g., measures of reading fluency) and can be argued to be necessary for developing appropriate instructional programs, they are not in themselves sufficient for capturing cognitive deficits that may underlie poor performance. Behavioral assessment methods such as CBM do not take into account cognitive deficits that may cause the child not to learn specific academic skills. The behavioral approach focuses primarily on the assessment of specific skills and abilities taught in the classroom. By definition, *curriculum-based measurement* is not an appropriate means of diagnosing strengths and weaknesses in psychological processes. The use of CBM alone could never produce results such as the DAS profiles described previously, in which distinctive subgroups of LD students are identified, based on strongly contrasting characteristics of information processing. Each of these contrasting patterns of strengths and weaknesses leads to the same outcome: unexpectedly poor achievement that is resistant to teaching using conventional methods. This is because classroom instructional methods are based on the assumption that students all have similar learning characteristics, thereby enabling students to be generally taught in relatively large groups. And it is also why students with significant strengths and weaknesses in basic cognitive processes have difficulty learning in normal classroom environments.

To repeat, CBM assesses the *outcome,* or the product, of learning— what the child has fluently learned in the classroom—and not the *process.* Although some authors suggest that the behavioral and cognitive approaches are mutually exclusive, or at least that one can use CBM to the exclusion of psychometric approaches, a mixture of the two approaches is arguably the best possible form of practice (Elliott, 2007b).

To summarize my position, I support the use of RTI at the first two levels of the three-tier assessment and intervention model. As I stated at the beginning of this chapter, RTI has always been used, and will always be used whenever teachers have a problem in getting a child to learn something. When they get to the third-tier stage of shaking their heads and wondering why this child is still not learning despite their best efforts, assessments based on a detailed analysis of basic psychological and neuropsychological constructs is needed to yield a better understanding of the nature of the child's underlying difficulties.

WHAT ROLE DOES NEUROPSYCHOLOGY HAVE TO PLAY IN THE DIAGNOSIS OF LD?

Neuroimaging and neuropsychological research has demonstrated over the years that the cognitive processing difficulties shown by LD children have likely structural or functional correlates in the brain (for recent research, see, for example, Badzakova-Trajkov, Hamm, & Wladie, 2005; Cao et al., 2006; Collins & Rourke, 2003; Semrud-Clikeman, 2005; Semrud-Clikeman & Pliszka, 2005; Shaywitz, Lyon, & Shaywitz, 2006; and Zadina et al., 2006).

As previously stated, the nature of LD is a dysfunction in basic cognitive or neuropsychological processes. Cognitive psychology and neuropsychology have much to tell us about the information-processing structures that undergird learning and that often account for difficulty in learning or even outright failure. There is a general consensus among researchers that the structure of cognitive abilities described by CHC theory, based on the pioneering work of Cattell, Horn, and Carroll (see, for example, McGrew, 2005; and Alfonso, Flanagan, & Radwan, 2005), is robust across populations, samples, and instruments, and represents the best current knowledge on the factor structure of human abilities. Elliott (2007b, Chapter 2) takes some steps in mapping this structure, based on the factor analyses of data sets, onto what is known about the structure of processing systems of the brain. Our knowledge of neuropsychological structures is converging with that of the structure of abilities from psychometric research. This is hardly surprising, because if the factors derived from factor analysis have any underlying reality, this must be based on brain function. The two disciplines of factor-analytic research and neuropsychology have a pivotal role to play in our understanding of the causes of LD.

REFERENCES

Alfonso, V. C., Flanagan, D. P., & Radwan, S. (2005). The impact of Cattell-Horn-Carroll theory on test development and interpretation of cognitive and academic abilities. In D. P. Flanagan & P. L. Harrison (Eds.), *Contemporary intellectual assessment: Theories, tests, and issues* (pp. 185–202). New York: Guilford.

Badzakova-Trajkov, G., Hamm, J. P., & Wladie, K. E. (2005). The effects of redundant stimuli on visuospatial processing in developmental dyslexia. *Neuropsychologia, 43,* 473–478.

Cao, F., Bitan, T., Chou, T.-L., Burman, D. D., & Booth, J. R. (2006). Deficient orthographic and phonological representations in children with dyslexia revealed by brain activation patterns. *Journal of Child Psychology and Psychiatry, 47,* 1041–1050.

Collins, D. W., & Rourke, B. P. (2003). Learning-disabled brains: A review of the literature. *Journal of Clinical and Experimental Neuropsychology, 25,* 1011–1034.

Elliott, C. D. (1990). *Differential ability scales.* San Antonio, TX: The Psychological Corporation.

Elliott, C. D. (2001). Application of the Differential Ability Scales and the British Ability Scales: Second Edition for the assessment of learning disabilities. In A. S. Kaufman & N. L. Kaufman (Eds.), *Specific learning disabilities and difficulties in children and adolescents: Psychological assessment and evaluation* (pp. 178–217). New York: Cambridge University Press.

Elliott, C. D. (2005). The Differential Ability Scales. In D. P. Flanagan & P. L. Harrison (Eds.), *Contemporary intellectual assessment: Theories, tests, and issues* (pp. 402–424). New York: Guilford.

Elliott, C. D. (2007a). *Differential ability scales* (2nd ed.). San Antonio, TX: The Psychological Corporation.

Elliott, C. D. (2007b). *Differential Ability Scales: Introductory and technical handbook.* San Antonio, TX: The Psychological Corporation.

McGrew, K. S. (2005). The Cattell-Horn-Carroll theory of cognitive abilities: Past, present, and future. In D. P. Flanagan & P. L. Harrison (Eds.), *Contemporary intellectual assessment: Theories, tests, and issues* (pp. 136–181). New York: Guilford.

National Association of School Psychologists. (2007). NASP position statement on identification of children with specific learning difficulties. http://www.nasponline .org/about_nasp/positionpapers/SLDPosition_2007.pdf.

National Association of State Directors of Special Education. (2005). *Response to intervention: Policy considerations and implementation.* Alexandria, VA: NASDSE.

Reynolds, C. R. (August, 2005). Considerations in RTI as a method of diagnosis of learning disabilities. Paper presented to the Annual Institute for Psychology in the Schools of the American Psychological Association, Washington DC.

Semrud-Clikeman, M. (2005). Neuropsychological aspects for evaluating learning disabilities. *Journal of Learning Disabilities, 38,* 563–568.

Semrud-Clikeman, M., & Pliszka, S. R. (2005). Neuroimaging and psychopharmacology. *School Psychology Quarterly, 20,* 172–186.

Shaywitz, B. A., Lyon, G. R., & Shaywitz, S. E. (2006). The role of functional magnetic resonance imaging in understanding reading and dyslexia. *Developmental Neuropsychology, 30,* 613–632.

Zadina, J. N., Corey, D. M., Casbergue, R. M., Lemen, L. C., Rouse, J. C., Knaus, T. A., & Foundas, A. L. (2006). Lobar asymmetries in dyslexic and control subjects. *Journal of Child Neurology, 21,* 922–931.

16

Integrating RTI with Cognitive Neuroscience in the Assessment of Learning Disabilities

Steven G. Feifer

WHAT DO YOU THINK NEUROSCIENCE HAS TO OFFER IN THE ASSESSMENT AND IDENTIFICATION OF LEARNING DISABILITIES?

According to the U.S. Department of Education (2006), approximately 2.9 million children in the United States receive special education services due to a specific learning disability. This staggering figure represents more than 5.5% of the entire school-aged population and virtually half of all children receiving special education services under the Individual with Disabilities Education Act (IDEA). Furthermore, annual U.S. Department of Education spending on elementary and secondary education has increased from $27.3 billion in 2001 to $38 billion in 2006, up by nearly 40%. In 2007, the department will spend 59% more on special education programs than it did in 2001. While the money saturates into education at record amounts, the sobering truth remains that student achievement has remained relatively stagnant or, in some cases, actually declined. For instance, according to the National Center for Educational Statistics (2005), the primary federal agency responsible for collecting and analyzing a variety of educational data in the United States and other nations, the results from the most recent Trends in International Mathematics and Science Study (TIMSS, 2004) revealed that American eighth-grade students rank 15th in an international study of math achievement. By the time these same students graduate high school, they score near the bottom when compared to most industrialized nations. As political pundits wrestle with the mounting pressure of increased funding for educational purposes, perhaps a different course of action fueled by a scientific understanding of the learning process may be required. In other words, solving the conundrum known as *lackluster student achievement* may not be tied to a particular dollar amount, but instead resonates in the study of brain-behavioral relationships with respect to learning. Perhaps if educators had a better understanding of the cerebral organization of the brain, the mystery of literacy, number acquisition skills, written expression, and the like would be unveiled for all to see.

Most prudent educators, psychologists, school administrators, and parents yearn for a greater insight into the neurobiological building blocks necessary for children to acquire many academic learning skills, especially literacy. According to the U.S. Department of Education (2006), approximately 80% of students identified as having a specific learning disability primarily have difficulty with reading skills. This begs the question of how exactly does the typical preliterate kindergarten child with a vocabulary of some 3,000 to 4,000 words upon entering school develop a working vocabulary of better than 50,000 words upon graduating high school (Pinker, 2000)? Furthermore, what are the neurobiological mechanisms that allow students to rapidly and automatically recognize a given word in a mere 200msec? The cognitive machinery necessary for the average child to acquire some 10 new words per day over the next 12 years of their academic career begins with an exploration of the neural pathways mediating the reading process. As Moats (2004) succinctly observed, conceptions of reading instruction, reading development, and ultimately reading disabilities should take their lead from the neurosciences in order to provide a scientific rationale for the selection, implementation, and monitoring of reading programs designed to meet the needs of children who manifest early reading difficulty. It is critical that educators become aware of the neural underpinnings of learning in order to create a more *brain-friendly* academic environment consistent with evidenced-based instruction. As Goldberg (2005) noted:

> I have always been dumbfounded by academic psychology being dominated by individuals who are not only ignorant about the brain, but were proud of being ignorant. An infatuation exists with the bogus notion that it is somehow possible to study cognition in its Platonic isolation.

Current research in neuroscience has revealed a number of important insights with respect to the neural underpinnings of literacy. Clearly, despite the language or culture, there are certain universal truths in how the human brain acquires linguistic codes pertaining to reading. First, in all word languages studied to date, children with developmental reading disorders (dyslexia) primarily have difficulties in both recognizing and manipulating phonological units at all linguistic levels (Goswami, 2007). Second, children in all languages initially become aware of larger acoustical units within the words themselves such as syllable, onset, and rhyme. However, in a complex language such as English, when one letter may map to as many as five distinct phonemes or sounds, English-speaking children tend to develop phonemic awareness more slowly than children in more phonologically consistent languages such as Spanish or Italian (Goswami, 2007). Third, specific neuro-imaging techniques have demonstrated that phonological processing is a by-product of the functional integrity of the *temporal-parietal* junctures in the left hemisphere (Rumsey, 1996; Paulesu et al., 1996). A further explanation of the relationship between the temporal and parietal lobes may be in order. The temporal lobes in the left hemisphere have long been associated with a multitude of functions involving linguistic skills, and the parietal lobes have long been associated with modulating spatial activity. Hence, the interface of the temporal and parietal lobes in the left hemisphere represent a natural symbiosis in the brain involving the spatial arrangement of acoustical codes (Goldberg, 1989). Neuroimaging studies have noted a decreased activation in the left temporal-parietal regions and the superior temporal gyrus (plana temporale) during phonological processing tasks such as rhyming or segmenting various sounds in words (Pugh et al., 2000; Sandak et al., 2004). Additionally, *Diffuse Tensor Imaging (DTI),* which involves the functional organization of white matter tracts, have also implicated microstructural anomalies of perisylvian white matter in the left hemisphere of both children and adults with reading deficits (Noble & McCandliss, 2005). As Temple (2002) observed, most dyslexics have difficulty with phonological processing, which may indeed stem from disorganization of white matter tracts connecting the temporal-parietal regions with other cortical regions involved in the reading process.

As Temple (2002) observed, most dyslexics have difficulty with phonological processing, which may indeed stem from disorganization of white matter tracts connecting the temporal-parietal regions with other cortical regions involved in the reading process (See Figure 16.1).

The aforementioned neuroscientific findings clearly have direct implications with respect to the development of reading curricula in our schools. For instance, there is a certain hierarchical structure in the teaching of phonemic awareness based upon brain development that should be helpful in facilitating and cultivating the *phonological processor* of the brain (see Table 16.1). Furthermore, a neuroscientific understanding of the literacy process can also have profound implications on the assessment and identification of a specific learning disability in a child. For instance, there appears to be compelling evidence that skilled readers activate the quicker, more rapid, and automatic neural pathways to decipher words in print (Pugh et al., 2000; McCandliss & Noble, 2003; Shaywitz, 2004; Owen, Borowsky, & Sarty, 2004). Conversely, dyslexics do not activate these self-same pathways, but instead rely

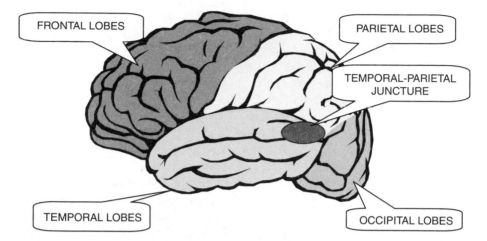

Figure 16.1 Temporal-Parietal Juncture of the Cerebral Cortex

on different pathways, forged in part by compensatory mechanisms, which are slower and less efficient to assist with word-recognition skills (Shaywitz & Shaywitz, 2005). Therefore, it is critical for educators to begin recording reading fluency and speed at early ages using curriculum-based measurement techniques to gauge the number of words a student can read correctly in a minute. These rapid fluency measures will enable teachers to closely monitor reading proficiency and, from a neuropsychological standpoint, measure the extent with which these quicker neural pathways have become acclimated to taking over the reading process from the slower paced ones. Students who show early signs of phonemic-awareness difficulties and demonstrate poor reading-fluency skills should be targeted as being *at risk,* and be provided with intense levels of services at early ages to bolster these critical reading skills. Unfortunately, most school districts continue to rely on the flawed *discrepancy model,* highlighting variances between a student's purported level of intelligence and scores from a nationally norm-referenced achievement test as the sole criteria for an educational disability. Utilizing the discrepancy model is tantamount to a *"wait-and-fail"* policy where interventions are often implemented far too late in the learning acquisition process. In summary, the field of school psychology has come a long way since the term *learning disability* was first coined by Samual Kirk. The profession is finally at a point where we have reached a veritable pinnacle in our scientifically based understanding of brain-behavior relationships, and our assessment technology needs to rapidly advance to reflect this progress.

Table 16.1 Developmental Sequence of Phonological Processing (Feifer & Della Toffalo, 2007)

Activity	Ages	Purpose	Brain Development
1. Response to Rhymes	3–4	Three and four year old children can memorize nursery rhymes, rhyming songs, and provide the final word in rhyming text.	The myelination of the auditory cortex in the temporal lobes allows children at approximately age three to more closely discriminate speech sounds (Berninger & Richards, 2002).
2. Classifying Phonemes	4–5	Children at this age begin to match similar sounds together and can pick the sound that does not belong (*e.g., book, look, took, cat*).	Brain development tends to progress from the right hemisphere to the left. By age four children can begin to take sound discriminations from the right hemisphere and classify them in the left, as the brain now allows for crosstalk between the hemispheres (Berninger & Richards, 2002).
3. Segmenting Words	5–6	Five year olds can isolate sounds in the beginning and end of words and capable of inventive spelling (*e.g., KT for cat*).	Crossmodal associations now become more automatic allowing for visual or orthographic representation of words (*parietal lobes*) being stored in an auditory manner (*temporal lobes*).
4. Phoneme Segmentation	6–7	By first grade, children can tap out the number of phonemes in a word, and can often represent all the sounds in a word by inventive spelling.	Brain development and myelination also proceeds from back to front, especially in language zones. Posterior regions code the sounds while anterior structures arrange them sequentially (Berninger & Richards, 2002).
5. Phoneme Deletion	6–8	Depending upon the complexity of the word, children can delete or can substitute the sound of one word to create another word (*e.g., "say the 'sting' without the 't'"*).	The instructional environment is crucial in sculpting the tertiary regions of the brain for higher-level thinking and the manipulation of phonemes.

HOW DO YOU RECONCILE RTI AS A MEANS OF DIAGNOSIS OF LD WITH KNOWLEDGE FROM THE CLINICAL NEUROSCIENCES?

Response-to-intervention (RTI) is a phrase that has captivated a national movement, redefined educational policy, and, most importantly, has come to represent a long-awaited alternative method in determining a student's eligibility for special education services. Subsequent to the 2004 reauthorization of IDEA, states are no longer allowed to *require* school districts to consider a discrepancy between IQ and achievement as being a necessary condition to identify students as having a learning disability. Among the many provisions in this bill, school districts may opt-out of using a *discrepancy model* to identify a specific learning disability, and replace it by using an RTI model. In other words, rather than comparing a student's level of academic achievement with scores from intelligence test measures, school districts now have the flexibility to craft a policy whereby students who do not respond to evidence-based intervention programs may be considered eligible for special education services. RTI is not new. What is new, however, is RTI's explicit support in federal special education law as a viable alternative to less effective traditional models of determining student eligibility for special education services. In short, RTI refers to an expansive array of procedures that can be used to determine eligibility and need for special education services within a problem-solving model that emphasizes scientifically validated instructional approaches.

Nevertheless, there can be inherent weaknesses when overrelying upon an RTI approach, the discrepancy model, or any other singular methodology when determining an educational disability in a child. From a statistical point of view, in order to minimize the chances of committing a Type I error (mistakenly classifying a child as being disabled) or a Type II error (failing to classify a child as being disabled when indeed he or she is), the relative merits of combining multiple methods of data collection within a multilayered framework should be adhered to (Hale et al., 2006). It is interesting to note that neither RTI nor the *discrepancy model* addresses the core elements in the current definition of a learning disability. According to the U.S. Department of Education Learning Disabilities Roundtable (2002), *"The identification of a core cognitive deficit, or a disorder in one or more psychological processes that is predictive of an imperfect ability to learn, is a marker for a specific learning disability."* (p. 5)

Certainly, RTI can identify children with low achievement, but RTI alone cannot diagnose a core psychological learning deficit, which clearly is the centerpiece in the definition of an educational learning disability. At best, RTI can make the assumption that a child did not respond to an evidence-based

Table 16.2   Proposed 4-Factor Model of Defining a Reading Disability (Feifer & Della Toffalo, 2007)

1. There should be data to document that a student's *rate* of learning in one or more aspects of reading skill development is substantially slower than grade-level peers over a specified period of time.

2. There should be data to document that the student has not responded to evidence-based interventions when compared to grade-level peers over a specified period of time.

3. There should be data from cognitive neuropsychological assessment indicating the presence or absence of specific processing deficits that are directly related to the reading process. This should include measures of phonemic awareness, phonological processing, language skills, working memory skills, executive functioning skills, and rapid and automatic retrieval skills.

4. There should be data ruling out other major sources of constraints upon school success such as emotional, cultural, medical, or environmental factors.

intervention due to either an inherent disability or implementation errors in the delivery of the intervention. Similarly, an aptitude-achievement discrepancy model can make the assumption that a child who is not achieving at a level commensurate with his or her cognitive ability may be underachieving due to a learning disability, though it cannot prove that one exists. According to Semrud-Clikeman (2005), only direct school-based neuropsychological evaluations examining core psychological processes can determine the presence of specific cognitive markers such as working memory deficits, executive dysfunction, poor retrieval fluency, and phonological processing deficits that may be the root cause for a learning disability. Therefore, the first step in fusing together the tenets of RTI within a cognitive neuroscience framework is a comprehensive definition of a learning disability taking into account both extrinsic and intrinsic factors that may hinder the learning process. In the case of reading, the following 4-factor criteria outlined in Table 16.2 may be helpful to capture the essence of both RTI and cognitive neuropsychology.

The criteria proposed in the aforementioned 4-factor model virtually demands that a combination of both RTI procedures and cognitive neuropsychological assessment be used to determine the presence of a reading disability. Furthermore, the definition remains consistent with IDEA 2004, the U.S. Department of Education Learning Disabilities Roundtable (2002), and the International Dyslexia Association (2003). In essence, the first factor consists of a more *standardized* RTI approach implemented by classroom teachers using evidence-based instructional materials within a standardized core curriculum. Most RTI models specifically identify three *tiers* of intervention corresponding to increasing levels of support and assistance for students manifesting learning or behavioral problems. Therefore, data collection in Tier I should be used to assess a student's rate of learning in multiple aspects of the reading process. A fundamental component of Tier I is utilizing periodic curriculum-based measurement probes to frequently monitor the rate of student progress over time. School psychologists and other educational staff should assist with data interpretation, help ensure the fidelity of instructional approaches, and weed out other environmental variables that may encumber the learning process.

The second component of this 4-factor definition of a reading disability can be readily addressed in Tier 2 of an RTI model. Tier 2 is designed for those students who fail to respond or maintain appropriate educational progress in Tier 1. One advantage of Tier 2 is to provide a specific intervention for a child at early grade levels without necessarily labeling the child as having an educational disability. Often times, a more *individualized* problem-solving approach based upon the intrinsic characteristics of the learner is undertaken to select an appropriate intervention, as opposed to the lock-step standardized approach that characterizes Tier 1. There should be an emphasis on identifying the learning problem more specifically in Tier 2 by using a variety of data-gathering techniques. These may include curriculum-based measurement reading probes, informal reading inventories, and reading readiness measures such as DIBELS.

Lastly, the fundamental tenet within any RTI model is data collection. This can be done through processes already discussed, or include the use of cognitive neuropsychological assessment, especially when addressing the third and fourth factors highlighted in Table 16.2. The primary goal of a cognitive neuropsychological assessment is to acquire data relevant to the integrity of core cognitive constructs associated with the learning process, and not to establish a discrepancy between a student's intellectual ability and academic achievement. For a reading assessment, this may include measures of phonemic awareness, phonological processing, language skills, working memory skills, executive functioning skills, attentional capacity, reading fluency skills, and intellectual ability. It is vital for school psychologists to become familiar with specific core psychological processes involved with reading, as well as various subtypes of different reading disabilities. Furthermore, a working knowledge of remedial reading programs is also needed so psychologists and educators can more readily determine the types of intervention programs that offer a child the best chance for success. In addition, other comorbid conditions may need to be identified and treated as part of the intervention process. Table 16.3 lists the relative strengths and weaknesses of both RTI and cognitive neuropsychology in the identification of a specific reading disability.

Table 16.3   Relative Strengths and Weaknesses of RTI and Cognitive Neuropsychology (Feifer & Della Toffalo, 2007)

RTI Strengths	RTI Weaknesses
• Enhanced ecological validity	• Assesses limited aspects of academics
• Quicker and cheaper	• Not a diagnostic approach
• Specifically measures an area of academics	• Does not answer the WHY question
• Measures curricular learning	• Difficult to implement across grades
• Linked to a problem solving model	• Poor differential diagnosis
• Allows for more efficient progress monitoring	• Does not delineate a firm time line for a student to respond
• Data can easily be linked to curricular decisions	• Difficult to apply to other academic endeavors besides reading
• Encourages scientific interventions be used	• Limited guidelines on how long to stay within each tier
• Allows students to receive help at earlier grades	• Discounts neurocognitive factors
• Deemphasizes labeling kids	• Does not address lack of evidence-based instructional techniques in math and written language
• More collaborative decisions made	
• Reduces "curriculum casualties"	
• A proactive and not reactive model	
• Eliminates the overemphasis on IQ scores which can lead to a disproportionate number of minorities in special education	

Neuropsychology Strengths	Neuropsychology Weaknesses
• A thorough and complete assessment of learning	• Can be costly and time consuming
• Provides diagnostic information	• Most psychologists trained in IQ testing and not cognitive neuropsychology
• Allows for differential diagnosis	• Reports too long and technical
• Answers the WHY question pertaining to student underachievement	• Difficult for school systems to interpret the results
• Constructs are scientifically based	• Often completed by outside psychologists with little insight on school cultural and climate
• Measures the National Reading Panel's five core constructs pertaining to reading (and not just fluency measures)	• Recommendations often not practical
• Can explain what functions can be remediated versus what functions need accommodations	• Most effective only when students have not responded to earlier interventions; not a proactive method
• Most likely assessment to hold up in due process hearing	
• Not useful for progress monitoring	

WHAT ROLE DOES NEUROPSYCHOLOGY HAVE TO PLAY IN THE DIAGNOSIS OF LD?

School psychology is currently undergoing a paradigm shift, due in part to the onslaught of data illustrating the irrelevance of IQ in the identification of students with learning disabilities (Fletcher et al., 2004). The profession of school psychology, which has been inextricably linked to the assessment of intelligence, has traditionally defined most educational disabilities as stemming from a significant discrepancy between a student's ability (IQ) and academic achievement. Throughout the years, there have been numerous shortcomings inherent within the *discrepancy model,* including the statistical impreciseness of using cut-off scores from two different normative samples (i.e., Wechsler Intelligence tests versus Woodcock-Johnson Tests of Academic Achievement), the overreliance upon a Full-Scale IQ score in an attempt to capture the dynamic properties of one's reasoning skills (Hale & Fiorello, 2004), and the lack of agreement on the magnitude of the discrepancy at various ages and grades (Feifer & DeFina, 2000). Perhaps the most notable shortcoming of the *discrepancy model* is that it often results in a wait-to-fail scenario in which a student must display a certain level of failure in order to qualify for special educational services. This was especially at odds with the National Reading Panel's (2000) conclusion highlighting the importance of early interventions services for children with reading difficulties.

Driven by new regulations as stipulated in IDEA 2004, a greater number of practitioners are favoring a more pragmatic assessment approach, based upon how a student responds to a particular intervention, as the basis for a learning disorder. Many proponents of an RTI model discount the use of nationally norm-referenced tests, and favor a *curriculum-based measurement* approach directly linking assessments with interventions (Shinn, 2002; Rechsly, 2003). Such an approach forces practitioners to concentrate on targeting and monitoring interventions aimed at improving academic performance. Curriculum-based measurement (CBM) has become the measurement technique of choice within most RTI models, and provides educators with a quicker, more cost-effective, and more ecologically valid means of identifying reading deficits at much younger ages in children. While CBM can quickly assess *where* a student lies in relation to the curriculum, it yields little data indicating *why.* In other words, CBM is not a diagnostic procedure designed to determine the underlying cognitive culprits for poor academic performance. Hence, the National Joint Commission on Learning Disabilities (2005) concluded that RTI alone is not sufficient to identify a specific learning disability, and that a multidimensional model of assessment utilizing multiple instruments should be employed.

Cognitive neuropsychological assessment attempts to pinpoint specific processing deficits hindering the learning process in order to better explain why a student may have difficulty acquiring a particular academic skill. According to Grigorenko (2007), neuroscientists have made great strides in understanding the cognitive machinery involved with literacy. The ability of neuropsychology to pinpoint specific processing deficits emanating from specific neural connections in the brain clearly lays the foundation for a better understanding of what constitutes a true *learning disability*. Furthermore, a classification system based upon various subtypes of reading, writing, or math disorders can be invaluable to educators by allowing them to target interventions in a more systematic manner. Perhaps nowhere is this more self-evident than in the case of reading.

To date, there is converging evidence that successful oral reading involves three distinct brain systems. The first involves the dorsal (top) regions of the brain in the temporal-parietal cortices that modulate phonology (Shaywitz, 2004). The temporal-parietal system is associated with rule-based analysis and learning, and tends to be critical in the initial mapping of graphemes with phonemes (Pugh, et al., 2000). This system relies on relatively slower paced pathways, and tends to be used for beginning readers to learn how to sound out words (Shaywitz, 2004). A specific reading disability stemming from deficits in the phonological system is often termed *dysphonetic dyslexia* (Feifer & Della Toffalo, 2007). The hallmark feature of dysphonetic dyslexia is an inability to utilize a phonological route to successfully bridge letters and sounds. Instead, there tends to be an overreliance on visual and orthographic cues to identify words in print. Since there is little reliance on letter-to-sound conversions, these readers frequently guess on words based upon the initial letter observed. Hence, students with dysphonetic dyslexia have tremendous difficulty incorporating strategies to allow them to crash through words in a sound-based manner, tend to be relatively inaccurate, and often approach reading by simply memorizing whole words. According to Noble and McCandliss (2005), poor phonological processing in the early years leads to inefficient neural mappings between letters and sounds. Failure to develop these critical skills in the reading process may lead to a host of academic deficiencies including poor spelling skills, slower paced reading fluency skills, and ultimately difficulty with passage comprehension skills.

The second critical brain system involved with the reading process is the occipital-temporal region (fusiform gyrus), which is primarily involved with reading speed and fluency (Pugh et al., 2000). The occipital-temporal pathways are highly interconnected neural systems that respond in just 200ms to the visual features of a word to allow for automatic and rapid word-recognition skills. Hence, during CBM and fluency types of tests, the integrity of the occipital-temporal stream, or what some refer to as the *visual-form word area*, is really being measured. Specific reading deficits stemming from inefficient mapping of the visual-word form area is often termed *surface dyslexia* (Feifer & Della Toffalo, 2007). Surface dyslexia is basically a lack of reading fluency skills due in part by difficulty rapidly and automatically recognizing the orthography of print. Slower reading speed can also stem from difficulty processing visual information in a rapid fashion or due to difficulties in recognizing the linguistic value of the word itself, irrespective of the child's visual processing skills. Therefore, the occipital-temporal region of the left hemisphere is primarily responsible for the rapid and automatic recognition of words and, to a certain extent, is very much dependent upon the work of the temporal-parietal region (Schatschneider & Torgeson, 2004). In other words, effective phonological mapping of sounds greatly enables the *visual word form area* to perform its job.

A third brain system involved in the reading process is located in the frontal lobes and represents the endpoint of the inner articulation system that fine-tunes the ability to orally sound out words. The frontal regions of the brain also have critical importance with respect to reading comprehension. It has been estimated that some 10% of all school-aged children have good decoding skills, though continue to have persistent difficulties with reading comprehension skills (Nation & Snowling, 1997). A cognitive processing model can be extremely beneficial in dissecting the critical components necessary for effective reading comprehension. These include constructs such as: *executive functioning,* which involves the strategies students use to organize incoming information with previously read material; *working memory,* which is the amount of memory needed to perform a given cognitive task; and *language foundation skills,* which represent the fund of words with which a student is familiar. Executive functions represent a compilation of numerous cognitive constructs that directs the learning process including task initiation, maintaining a persistent pattern of effort, resistance to distractions, and plotting a general strategy or course of action when actively engaged in a problem-solving task. Children with reading comprehension difficulties often display marked deficits on selected aspects of executive functioning skills, especially working memory skills (Reiter, Tucha, & Lange, 2004). Working memory involves the ability to hold representational knowledge of the world around us in mind, coupled with the mental flexibility to manipulate this knowledge in whatever manner we choose to facilitate retrieval (Levine & Reed, 1999). Therefore, specifying the underlying linguistic and cognitive factors associated with poor reading comprehension skills can be helpful toward developing more effective intervention strategies to assist children throughout their learning journey. Figure 16.2 depicts three major brain circuits involved with reading.

In conclusion, even if there was complete understanding of every neural pathway with respect to the literacy process, this would most likely account for just half the variance involved in the acquisition of reading skills (Grigorenko, 2007). According to Grigorenko (2007), there are three additional

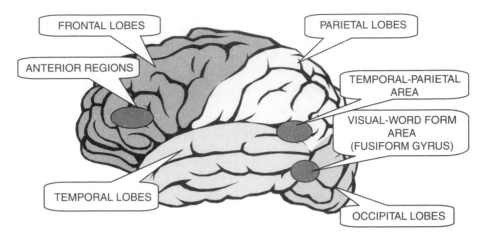

Figure 16.2   Major Neural Circuits Involved with Reading

factors accounting for as much as 50% of the variance in the development of reading, all of which are driven by environmental factors. The first involves the socioeconomic status of the child, which often entails access and opportunity to a quality literacy environment. The second involves the actual pedagogical style of the teacher. And the third factor is the extent to which a student's home environment values literacy (Grigorenko, 2007). Still, cognitive neuropsychology can be an invaluable diagnostic tool to assist educators in moving beyond nonspecific terms such as a *learning disability* and allow for a better understanding of the reading process by identifying specific reading subtypes that can derail successful learning. These subtypes begin to emerge by an examination of reading through the multidimensional lenses of brain-based learning.

WHAT ROLE DOES NEUROPSYCHOLOGY HAVE TO PLAY IN DESIGNING INTERVENTIONS IN THE CONTEXT OF RTI?

The *No Child Left Behind Act of 2001*, in addition to *IDEA 2004*, as well as most federally funded grants all require educational practitioners to use *scientifically based research* to guide not only curricular development in our schools, but also as a foundation for implementing interventions for unsuccessful learners. Why? Between 1977 and 1994, students with disabilities increased from 3.7 million students to 5.3 million students, despite the fact that overall public school enrollment remained relatively constant during this period (Fuchs et al., 2003). Clearly, specific interventions designed for both regular education and special education students had not proven successful during this period as evidenced by the escalation of students needing services. Often times, the daunting task of sorting through the myriad of educational quick fixes, latest trends, unconventional gadgets, and disproven techniques falls upon the shoulders of most school administrators. Despite the necessity to use interventions with a proven track record of success, the fact remains that most educational interventions are not *scientifically based*. At best, educational interventions tend to be *evidenced based,* as there is evidence to suggest an academic remediation program may be successful for some students in certain grades. Simply put, there is a dearth of literature that actually links the cognitive profile and academic needs of an individual learner in a specific grade with a specific remediation program. According to Feifer and Della Toffalo (2007), most educational research clearly lacks the scientific rigor and stringent methodology needed to demonstrate an association between a practice, strategy, curriculum, or program and student achievement.

Currently, IDEA 2004 allows school districts to designate up to 15% of their federal IDEA Part B funds for Early Intervening Services (EIS) to students in kindergarten through grade 12. The intent of this EIS funding is to allow districts to proactively address students who have not been identified as needing special education or related services but who need additional academic and behavioral support to succeed in general education. EIS activities often include professional development activities to enable educators to deliver scientific-based instruction as well as direct service interventions. Most RTI service delivery models have stressed the need for more data-based decision making and the necessity for utilizing *evidence-based* interventions. In short, RTI should be viewed as a *process,* not a panacea or a flawless diagnostic tool, that educators can use in a systematic fashion to ensure that educational resources are applied in the most judicious and prudent manner possible using multiple tiers of instruction.

However, effective remediation of academic skills should also require that interventions be tailored to the individual learning needs of the child. Should RTI simply rely upon standard protocol interventions irrespective of the learning strengths and weaknesses of the child, then educators may find themselves reverting back to a *one-size-fits-all* mentality that simply cannot meet the needs of any diverse student population. The overarching philosophy of incorporating a school-based neuropsychological assessment within an RTI service delivery model is to determine the underlying causes hindering a child's academic performance. In other words, what are the critical cognitive constructs responsible for modulating skills such as reading, writing, and mathematics? Furthermore, can these constructs be isolated, measured, and analyzed in order to determine why a student has not responded to a previous intervention and more importantly, to help determine what intervention a student may have more success with?

With respect to reading, the National Reading Panel (2000) found overwhelming evidence that supports using an explicit phonics program as the primary remediation strategy for younger students, though not necessarily older ones. Torgeson et al. (1999) also concluded that younger learners who have not developed the executive functioning capacities or abstract thinking abilities to sufficiently organize incoming information respond best to a highly structured and explicit type of phonological training. Therefore, more *implicit* phonological approaches used to teach reading at younger ages were somewhat ineffective, despite the intensiveness of the training (Torgeson et al., 1999). Further support for using explicit phonological instruction for younger students was ascertained by Shaywitz and Shaywitz (2005). In a novel study, these researchers (Shaywitz & Shaywitz, 2005) recruited a group of second- and third-grade children, all of whom had reading impairments, to receive two specific types of reading interventions. The *community intervention group* received a variety of school-based interventions for 50 minutes per day for 8 months. The *experimental intervention group* received solely an explicit phonics program, very systematic in nature, and based primarily upon the alphabetic principle. The results indicated that children in the *experimental group* (explicit phonics instruction) made significantly greater gains in reading accuracy, reading fluency, and reading comprehension than did children in the *community intervention* group. This study was also one of the first to illustrate how brain chemistry and brain-activation patterns can be changed through educational remediation. Hence, the use of *evidence-based* interventions involving explicit teaching of phonology can facilitate the development of specific neural systems that underlie reading (Shaywitz & Shaywitz, 2005).

However, there still remains the question as to why older children do not respond nearly as well to explicit, phonologically based instruction as younger children? Ratey (2001) suggested that perhaps the reason older children were less responsive to certain types of instruction may be due to a type of *Neural Darwinism* characteristic of brain development. In other words, the old corollary "Use it or lose it" is very apropos when referring to the need for certain critical pathways to be explicitly stimulated, in this case with direct phonological instruction, for adequate reading to commence. Ratey (2001) used another adage, "Neurons that fire together wire together," to explain that neural connections begin very early, and tend to stay intact and strengthen with continued and repeated exposure to a particular sensory stimulus. Therefore, early environmental experience is critical in the development of literacy in children, so neural connections can be given the opportunity to form permanent synaptic connections. Consequently, students who are not offered explicit phonological instruction at early stages in the neural formation of literacy skills may have greater difficulty acquiring these self-same skills

Table 16.4: Four Reading Intervention Rules (Feifer & Della-Toffalo, 2007)

1. *Balanced Literacy*—the key to developing reading success with any student is to incorporate a balanced literacy approach. This is especially critical with students possessing deficits including poor phonological processing skills, poor fluency skills, poor comprehension skills, poor verbal short-term memory skills, and poor language processing skills.

2. *Top-Down Strategies*—most students with severe forms of dyslexia do not respond to conventional remediation programs due to atypical development in various regions of the brain responsible for modulating the phonological aspect of reading and mapping these sounds to the visual word-form association areas (Temple, 2002; Noble & McCandliss, 2005). Rather than increasing the intensity and level of phonological instruction, educators should *change* the type of instruction from a *bottom-up* approach, to more of a *top-down* methodology.

3. *Socioeconomic Status*—students who come from poor environmental backgrounds are certainly at risk for developing more significant reading problems. According to Noble and McCandliss (2005), socioeconomic status (SES) is a very strong predictor of reading skills due primarily to the home literacy environment. Therefore, every opportunity should be made to provide these children with more opportunities to read.

4. *Motivation and Confidence*—every effort should be made to keep the reading process as enjoyable and entertaining as possible. Practicing reading and literacy exposure are the only ways to develop skill mastery.

at later ages due to inefficient preestablished neural connections. Therefore, phonological instruction at the later grades has the daunting task of not only forging new neural connections, but also disassembling previous ones.

In summary, there is a crucial need for educators to fathom a basic understanding of brain-behavioral relationships, especially with respect to coinciding interventions with brain development. Clearly, younger readers tend to be more successful with more *bottom-up* strategies to learn the basic tenets of reading as highlighted by the success of explicit phonological reading programs. On the other hand, utilizing more *top-down* methods, such as teaching morphology, latin roots, prefixes, suffixes, and utilizing word meaning cues, may be more effective for older elementary school children when learning basic phoneme segmentation. For instance, in a study by Richards et al. (2006), older students in a morphological treatment group improved *significantly more* than students in a phonological treatment group on direct measures of phonological decoding. What could explain such a juxtaposition? The answer most likely lies in the brain's ability to engage in a cross-over effect of mapping phonemes to morphemes, as children actually create mental maps based upon a complex webbing of phonology (sound units), orthography (letter shapes), and morphology (meaning) over time. Table 16.4 details four rules of thumb to keep in mind when working with students with significant reading deficits.

REFERENCES

Feifer, S. G., & DeFina, P. D. (2000). *The neuropsychology of reading disorders: Diagnosis and intervention.* Middletown, MD: School Neuropsych Press.

Feifer, S. G., & Della Toffalo, D. (2007). *Integrating RTI with cognitive neuropsychology: A scientific approach to reading.* Middletown, MD: School Neuropsych Press.

Fletcher, J. M., Coulter, W. A., Reschly, D. J., & Vaughn, S. (2004) . Alternative approaches to the definition and identification of learning disabilities: some questions and answers. *Annals of Dyslexia, 54*(2), 173–177.

Fuchs, D., Mock, D., Morgan, P. L., & Young, C. L. (2003). Responsiveness-to-intervention: Implications for the learning disabilities construct. *Learning Disabilities Research & Practice, 18*(3), 157–171.

Goldberg, E. (1989). Gradient approach to neocortical functional organization. *Journal of Clinical and Experimental Neuropsychology, 11*(4), 489–517.

Goldberg, E. (2005). The *wisdom paradox.* New York: Gotham Books.

Goswami, U. (2007). Typical reading development and developmental dyslexia across languages. In D. Coch, G. Dawson, & K. W. Fischer (Eds.), *Human behavior, learning and the developing brain* (p.145–167). New York: Guilford.

Grigorenko, E. L. (2007). Triangulating developmental dyslexia. In D. Coch, G. Dawson, & K. W. Fischer (Eds.), *Human behavior, learning and the developing brain* (p. 117–144). New York: Guilford.

Hale, J. B., & Fiorello, C. A. (2004). *School neuropsychology.* New York: Guilford.

Hale, J. B., Kaufman, A., Naglieri, J. A., & Kavale, K. A. (2006). Implementation of IDEA: Integrating response to intervention and cognitive assessment methods. *Psychology in the Schools, 43*(7), 753–770.

International Dyslexia Association (IDA). (2003). *Finding the answers (pamphlet).* Baltimore: Author.

LD Roundtable (2002). *Specific learning disabilities: Finding common ground.* Washington DC: Office of Special Education Programs. Retrieved August 28th, 2007 from the NASP website: http://www.nasponline.org/advocacy/SLD_OSEP .pdf.

Levine, M. D., & Reed, M. (1999). Developmental *variation and learning disorders.* Cambridge, MA: Educators Publishing Services, Inc.

McCandliss, B. D., & Noble, K. G. (2003). The development of reading impairment: A cognitive neuroscience model. *Mental Retardation and Developmental Disabilities, 9,* 196–205.

Moats, L. (2004) . Relevance of neuroscience to effective education for students with reading and other learning disabilities. *Journal of Child Neurology, 19*(10), 840–845.

Nation, K., & Snowling, M. (1997) . Assessing reading difficulties: The validity and utility of current measures of reading skill. *British Journal of Educational Psychology, 67,* 359–370.

National Joint Committee on Learning Disabilities. (2005). Responsiveness to intervention and learning disabilities. Retrieved August 30, 2007 from http://www .ldonline.org/njcld.

National Reading Panel. (2000). *Teaching children to read: An evidenced based assessment of the scientific research literature on reading and its implications for reading instruction*. Washington, DC: National Institutes of Child Health and Human Development.

Noble, K. G., & McCandliss, B. D. (2005). Reading development and impairment: Behavioral, social, and neurobiological factors. *Developmental and Behavioral Pediatrics, 26*(5), 370–376.

Owen, W. J., Borowsky, R., & Sarty, G. E. (2004). FMRI of two measures of phonological processing in visual word recognition: Ecological validity matters. *Brain and Language, 90,* 40–46.

Paulesu, E., Frith, U., Snowling, M., Gallagher, A., Morton, J., Frackowiak, R. S. J., & Frith, C. (1996). Is developmental dyslexia a disconnection syndrome? *Brain, 119,* 143–157.

Pinker, S. (2000). *The language instinct*. New York: Harper-Collins.

Pugh, K. R., Mencl, W. E., Jenner, A. R., Katz, L., Frost, S. J., Lee, J. R., Shaywitz, S. E., & Shaywitz, B. A. (2000). Functional neuroimaging studies of reading and reading disability (developmental dyslexia). *Mental Retardation and Developmental Disabilities Research Reviews, 6,* 207–213.

Ratey, J. J. (2001). *A user's guide to the brain: Perception, attention, and the four theatres of the brain*. New York: Pantheon Books.

Rechsly, R. J. (2003). *What if LD identification changed to reflect research findings?* Paper presented at the National Research Center on Learning Disabilities Responsiveness-to-Intervention Symposium, Kansas City, MO.

Reiter, A., Tucha, O., & Lange, K. W. (2004). Executive functions in children with dyslexia. *Dyslexia, 11,* 116–131.

Richards, T. L., Aylward, E. H., Field, K. M., Grimme, A. C., Raskind, W., Richards, A., Nagy, W., Eckert, M., Leonard, C., Abbott, R . D., & Berninger, V. W. (2006). Converging evidence for triple word form theory in children with dyslexia. *Developmental Neuropsychology, 30*(1), 547–589.

Rumsey, J. M. (1996). *Neuroimaging in developmental dyslexia*. In G. R. Lyon & J. M. Rumsey (Eds.), *Neuroimaging: A window to the neurological foundations of learning and behavior in children*. (p. 57–77). Baltimore: Paul H. Brookes.

Sandak, R., Mencl, W. E., Frost, S., Rueckl, J. G., Katz, L., Moore, D. L., Mason, S. A., Fulbright, R. K., Constable, R. T., & Pugh, K. R. (2004). The neurobiology of adaptive learning in reading: A contrast of different training conditions. *Cognitive, Affective, & Behavioral Neuroscience, 4*(1), 67–88.

Semrud-Clikeman, M. (2005). Neuropsychological aspects for evaluating learning disabilities. *Journal of Learning Disabilities, 38,* 563–568.

Schatschneider, C., & Torgeson, J. K. (2004). Using our current understanding of dyslexia to support early identification and intervention. *Journal of Child Neurology, 19,* 759–765.

Shaywitz, S. (2004). *Overcoming dyslexia*. New York: Random House.

Shaywitz, S., & Shaywitz, B. (2005). Dyslexia: Specific reading disability. *Biological Psychiatry, 57,* 1301–1309.

Shinn, M. R. (2002). Best practices in using curriculum-based measurement in a problem-solving model. In A. Thomas & J. Grimes (Eds.), *Best practices in school psychology IV*. Bethesda, Maryland : National Association of School Psychologists.

Temple, E. (2002). Brain mechanisms in normal and dyslexic readers. *Current Opinion in Neurobiology, 12,* 178–193.

Torgeson, J., Wagner, R., Rashotte, C., Rose, E., Lindamood, P., Conway, T., & Garvan, C. (1999). Preventing reading failure in young children with phonological processing disabilities: Group and individual responses to instruction. *Journal of Educational Psychology, 91,* 579–593.

U. S. Department of Education (2005). *The nation's report card: Mathematics 2005.* Washington DC: National Center for Educational Statistics.

U. S. Department of Education, Office of Special Education and Rehabilitative Services (2006). Twenty-sixth annual report to Congress on the implementation of the Individuals with Disabilities Education Act. Washington, DC: Author.

17

Neuropsychology and RTI: LD Policy, Diagnosis, and Interventions

Lisa A. Pass and Raymond S. Dean

WHAT DO YOU THINK NEUROSCIENCE HAS TO OFFER LAWS AND POLICIES ASSOCIATED WITH LEARNING DISABILITY DETERMINATION?

Learning disabilities have long been a focus of study in neurology and neuropsychology. In fact, the etiology of a variety of learning disorders has been shown to be secondary to a number of neurological disorders (e.g., Gilger & Kaplan, 2001). The notion of *specific learning disabilities* (SLDs), such as impaired math, reading, written expression, and language, has existed for some time. Clearly, the construct of a *learning disability* (LD) as articulated in the Individuals with Disabilities Education Act (IDEA) has had a substantial influence in the diagnosis and treatment of learning disabilities in both clinical and school settings. However, the way that LD is currently understood and diagnosed may be in fact limited by the current legal description. Because the definition of LD has been historically tied to neurobiology, the fields of neuroscience and neuropsychology may influence current laws and policies associated with LD determination by providing information and practices that can inform the creation of more accurate definitions of learning disabilities.

Since the early 1960s, the symptoms associated with LDs have been described in neurological terms. Early on, the characteristic pattern of LD was recognized in learners with above average IQ concurrent with notable learning and behavioral problems and was described in terms of *minimal brain dysfunction*. This language solidified the connection between particular academic difficulties and an underlying neurological disorder (Fletcher et al., 2007). The more recent federal definitions of LDs—codified through inclusion in the 1969 Learning Disabilities Act, and again in the All Handicapped Children Act of 1975 (Public Law 9-142), and currently included in the language of IDEA 2004—have continued to imply the inclusion of such an aberration in underlying *processing functions*. Further, recent federal limitations of *specific learning disabilities* explicitly exclude learning problems that are secondary to a sensory disorder, mental deficiency, emotional disturbance, economic disadvantage, and linguistic diversity. By excluding these particular characteristics, the definition emphasizes that LDs are constitutional factors intrinsic to the learner. This point of view indicates that a learner who has symptoms stemming from sensory disorders, mental deficiency, and emotional disturbance is thought to meet diagnostic criteria of a learning dysfunction that is secondary to a neurological and/or medical disorder. Thus, children with learning difficulties could be more accurately characterized as having *Idiopathic Learning Disabilities*. Like other idiopathic disorders, this descriptor suggests only that the direct cause of the symptomology cannot be identified, not necessarily that an etiology is not neurobiological in nature.

How these exclusionary factors rule out genetic and/or congenital abnormalities that may be responsible for learning impairment is not clear from the present policy emphasizing the use of the *Response-to-Intervention* (RTI) approach. Such a conclusion is not distant from data showing somewhat greater than 60% comorbidity between LD and other treatable medical and psychological disorders. Moreover, these disorders would likely not be discovered without a greater evaluation than that proposed by RTI proponents. In other words, how are other potentially treatable disorders to be ruled out prior to the treatment begun following the application of RTI?

For some time, psychologists have relied upon the *medical model* or the *diagnostic-prescriptive* approach when diagnosing LD. The efficaciousness of this approach has been variable. It is of particular concern that the RTI model seems to be poised to encounter the same types of problems, but only on a larger scale. The policy of using discrepancy data from an unknown, classroom-focused test, and then judging success in treatment as the primary criterion for LD identification and treatment effectiveness, is likely to create considerable confusion and further misclassifications. This confusion stems not only from concerns about the psychometric properties of the individual tests administered to gauge student progress, but also from perhaps the most critical component, the teaching approach used in the instruction of the material. We have yet to read research in any instructional area as to an agreed-upon standard approach in the teaching of any specific academic discipline. In fact, although educational reform of late has targeted improving school-based achievement, the accumulation of research on how children learn has gained little.

In sum, the legal definition of LD excludes a number of learning disorders, such as those primarily caused by physical disability, Mental Retardation, emotional problems, or disadvantage (U. S. Office of Education, 1968). While the definition has survived primarily unchanged despite repeated policy reauthorization, there are salient shortcomings in thinking about LD in these terms for both research and practice. Since this definition hints at the complex and heterogeneous nature of the dysfunctional cognitive processes associated with LD, by explicitly enumerating those disorders that fall within the exclusionary conditions, it notably neglects outlining inclusionary criteria for any of the specific LDs beyond the use of IQ-achievement discrepancy. Contemporary policy, as noted by Fletcher et al. (2007), tends to define LD not by what it is, but by what it is not.

HOW WILL FUTURE DEVELOPMENTS IN NEUROSCIENCE AFFECT HOW WE CLASSIFY AND INTERVENE WITH LEARNING DISABILITIES?

Recently an approach to the identification and treatment of children's learning disorders has received a good deal of attention by professionals of various stripes. Although the educational practice has been known by various names throughout the years, it is most often referred to as *Response to Intervention* (RTI). This approach is presented by most proponents as "a process of remedial interventions that can help generate data, to guide instruction, and identify students with learning disabilities (LD) who may require special education and related services" (NJCLD, 2005, p. 13). In coordination with NJCLD, core concepts include "the systematic (1) application of scientific, research-based interventions in general education; (2) measurement of student responses to the interventions; and (3) use of the response data to change the intensity or type of subsequent intervention" (NJCLD, 2005, p. 13).

Historically, public education has long been asked to go beyond its original mission—the transmission of basic knowledge. Responsibilities of public education have ranged from sex education and countering racial intolerance, to the inculcation of prosocial values. *Progressive Education* stressed the teaching of all children, including those with learning impairments secondary to genetic, social, cognitive, neurological, and emotional disorders. As a people, we expect a basic level of academic knowledge for all of our children. This rather egalitarian view runs counter to the capitalistic competition we find in other realms of our society. Regardless, the educator has long been asked to provide an undefined minimum knowledge base for all children. Facing the demands of growing responsibility and ever more stringent standards over the past 40 years, educators have been vulnerable to the temptation to search for a cure-all educational *panacea*—a mandate that must have seemed an overwhelming task.

RTI, one of our most current and popular panaceas, is in actuality an outgrowth of past educational approaches, such as *peripheral intervention* and *teacher and curriculum-based assessment*. Indeed the search for *the way* of teaching children is not a new endeavor. Similar expectations were seen during the behavioral zeitgeist of the 1960s to 1970s. At that time, the proposed remedy, known as the *individualized learning approach,* was wed to the idea of *Mastery Learning*. The notion was to establish a learner's level of knowledge in a specific area and parse new information in just enough small increments that the learner would not produce errors in his or her response (i.e., errorless learning). The approach was considered promising based on its characteristics of being data driven and its capacity to provide the instructor with feedback on the rate of learning in response to changes in the intensity or type of subsequent intervention. However, while data supported it, the method was complex and labor intensive for the teacher in the creation of an individual approach for each student. Even with the *learning machine* (see basement storage) the approach proved terminal.

With the paradigm shift to more cognitive research and practice beginning in the middle-to-late 1970s, there has come a twin interest in neuropsychology. Over the past few decades, neuropsychology has evolved from a method of localizing lesions to a more efficacious focus on a functional neuropsychological approach of diagnosis and treatment planning (e.g., Dean-Woodcock Neuropsychological System—DWNS; Dean & Woodcock, 2003). Indeed, recent data have shown the DWNS to provide high utility in the diagnosis and treatment of learning disorders, without the psychometric difficulties pointed out by Fletcher et al. (2005). In fact, assessment results on the DWNS provides all the features suggested by Fletcher, Lyon, Fuchs, and Barnes (2007) in their recommendations for the implementation of the RTI approach. However, the DWNS clinician must be weary of the feasibility of RTI as *the* approach in meeting the needs of >10% of the school-age population. Moreover, when considered from a clinical point of view, RTI does more in describing what the child does not have than what he or she does have.

HOW DO YOU RECONCILE RTI AS A MEANS OF DIAGNOSIS OF LD WITH KNOWLEDGE FROM THE CLINICAL NEUROSCIENCES?

RTI is a framework for working with students who fail to learn at the same pace as other students in general classrooms. Traditionally, students who consistently fail to perform as well as expected are identified by teachers or parents as possible candidates for testing and identification through formal assessment. RTI was developed as an alternative to the traditional referral method (as was the individualized learning approach) to try to reduce overidentification of children as LD by implementing a multitier system of research-based intervention trials before the formal referral process begins.

In this way, children who are simply lacking in appropriate instruction will not be misidentified as learning disabled. According to IDEA, these interventions must be supported by research that proves their effectiveness.

RTI, with its use of research-based instruction, regular monitoring of student progress, and empirical decision making, seems to differ little from the mastery/errorless learning approaches of the 1950s to 1970s. If it is consistently and accurately used as it was designed, RTI may lend itself to the remediation of academic difficulties and underachievement in children (Lyon et al., 2001; Speece, 2005). Catching problems early and applying preventative techniques for children at risk for academic difficulties may help children who might otherwise experience debilitating problems if intervention is delayed (Fuchs et al., 2003).

However, by itself, RTI is not designed as a diagnostic approach to SLDs, but instead to remediate students who have difficulty learning specific material at pace with their classmates. There is much support for the notion of the heterogeneous nature of LDs, which is due primarily to a deficit in some, but not all, of the basic psychological processes that leads to unexpected underachievement. Failure to learn, in itself, is not sufficient for diagnosis of LD. If RTI is used as the sole criterion for diagnosis of SLD, then the discordance between the RTI model and the SLD construct and definition will prevent accurate classification.

Although RTI seems to hold some promise for helping schools move away from the simple IQ-achievement discrepancy model for diagnosis and identification, critics have noted that, in its current form, it has a limited ability to correctly identify students with LD (e.g., Fletcher et al., 2007; Semrud-Clikeman, 2005; Hale et al., 2006). In addition, its attempts to remediate symptoms of learning problems are rather grandiose, with time- and resource-intensive methods. In addition, there seems to be little support provided to the teachers in the schools to help them carry out the RTI process. There are many factors that contribute to or hinder the learning and academic performance in children, including emotional disability, teacher-student interaction patterns, anxiety, depression, and other environmental factors. These factors may be easily overlooked as teachers choose interventions for their struggling learners (Hale et al., 2006). Further, as with the individualized learning approach, even with moderately successful outcomes, the amount of resources necessary to apply RTI to learning problems becomes more unrealistic with time and as the child experiences years of failure.

WHAT ROLE DOES NEUROPSYCHOLOGY HAVE TO PLAY IN THE DIAGNOSIS OF LD?

Neuropsychology has much the same role to play in the diagnosis of learning disabilities as it does in the diagnosis of a complaint of a memory loss. If one is to diagnosis a "disorder," it should, in fact, exist. Indeed, little convincing data exist that learning impairments are not but a symptom of a number of possible underlying factors. Based on the longstanding observation that children with learning disabilities tend to have an uneven profile of ability, demonstrating strengths in some areas of performance and difficulty in others, LD has become synonymous in the schools with ability-achievement discrepancy. Despite decades of research criticizing the practice of using a single discrepancy score for diagnosis and identification as inadequate and misleading (e.g., Berninger, 2001; Flowers et al., 2000; Kavale, Kaufman, Naglieri, & Hal, 2005), many school systems have continued to adhere to this policy. It is commonly recognized that basing a diagnosis of LD solely on a discrepancy between ability and aptitude results in overidentification (Kavale, Holdnack, & Mostert, 2005) and increased confusion about the best practices associated with diagnosing and intervening for children and adults with LD (Kavale & Forness, 2003).

Although RTI seems to hold some promise of helping schools move from the simple IQ-achievement discrepancy model for identification, critics have noted that, in its current form, it has a limited ability to correctly identify students with LD. Although RTI is designed to ensure that children who are struggling with learning are receiving the appropriate instruction for their individual needs, it rarely strives to pinpoint the underlying cause of the achievement gap. Factors outside of instruction that can impede learning and performance, such as emotional disability, teacher-student interaction patterns, anxiety, depression, and other environmental factors, may be overlooked as teachers choose interventions for their struggling learners.

Neuropsychologists are specialists of the relationship between brain and behavior. With such training and expertise, neuropsychologists are well trained in the diagnosis of LD—not solely by identifying the surface symptoms expressed in the classroom, but through multidimensional assessment techniques designed to explain the underlying cause of the learning problems (Mathes & Gregg, 2006). By collecting, analyzing, and interpreting data from multiple sources—including results of formal neuropsychological testing, parent and teacher report, informal classroom portfolio, and results from RTI intervention techniques—neuropsychologists can differentiate between the intrinsic and extrinsic factors that may be affecting learning.

Although the use of formally assessed IQ-achievement discrepancies as the sole evidence for special education placement has numerous problems, the utility of formal assessment and neuropsychological tools in the identification of children with LD is still viable (Dean & Woodcock, 2003). To abandon formal assessment techniques would be shortsighted and tantamount to "throwing out the baby with the bath water." For example, it has been proposed that the patterns of intraindividual cognitive strengths and weaknesses that are common in children and adults with LD can be used to determine the underlying cause of academic problems (Woodcock, 1984). Identification of specific strengths and weaknesses offers a direct link between cognitive assessment and intervention (Mather & Wendling, 2005), resulting in the opportunity to apply those research-based interventions that are most closely designed for the individual's particular dysfunction.

Even discounting the potential logistical difficulties associated with a policy of RTI, a complete neuropsychological examination would provide a more accurate description of the underlying dysfunctions that gives rise to a sequela of symptoms useful in the diagnosis and treatment of learning disorders secondary to treatable disorders. For example, over the last decade, researchers have been able to identify structural differences between clinically deficient readers and normal readers (Grigorenko, 2001) and have found evidence that suggest that children with learning disabilities process information differently from those children without learning problems (Schlaggar et al., 2002; Semrud-Clikeman, 2005). In sum, while the future does not look very hopeful for RTI, the efficacy of the approach would be improved with the inclusion of a neuropsychological examination to the RTI process to rule out treatable disorders and those that would exclude the child from the RTI approach.

Although RTI is designed to ensure that children who are struggling with learning are receiving the appropriate instruction for their individual needs, it rarely strives to pinpoint the underlying cause of the achievement gap. Factors outside of instruction that can impede learning and performance, such as emotional disability, teacher-student interaction patterns, anxiety, depression, and other environmental factors, may be overlooked as teachers choose interventions for their struggling learners. By collecting, analyzing, and interpreting data from a variety of sources, including formal assessment, informal assessments (including CBM screeners and other assessments given during the RTI process), teacher and parent report, medical records, prenatal and early developmental factors, and classroom portfolios, neuropsychologists can help student-based teams make informed decisions about which interventions hold the greatest promise for the individual student. Interventions have been found most effective when they are linked directly to the pattern of disability (Fletcher et al., 2007). Applying the most appropriate intervention early in the RTI process should result in fewer intervention trials and less instructional time away from the general classroom curriculum.

REFERENCES

Berninger, V. W. (2001). Understanding the "lexia" in dyslexia: A multidisciplinary team approach to learning disabilities. *Annals of Dyslexia, 51,* 23–48.

Dean, R. S., & Woodcock, W. (2003). *The Dean-Woodcock Neuropsychological System.* Itasca, IL: Riverside.

Fletcher, J. M., Francis, D. J., Morris, R. D., & Lyon, G. R. (2005). Evidence-based assessment of learning disabilities in children and adolescents. *Journal of Clinical Child & Adolescent Psychology, 34,* 506–522.

Fletcher, J. M., Lyon, G. R., Fuchs, L. S., & Barnes, M. A. (2007). *Learning disabilities: From identification to intervention*. New York: Guilford.

Flowers, L., Meyer, M., Lovato, J., Wood, F., & Felton, R. (2000). Does third grade discrepancy status predict the course of reading development? *Annals of Dyslexia, 50,* 49–71.

Fuchs, D., Mock, D., Morgan, P. L., & Young, C. L. (2003). Responsiveness-to-Intervention: Definitions, evidence, and implications for the learning disabilities construct. *Learning Disabilities Research and Practice, 18,* 157–171.

Gilger, J. W., & Kaplan, B. J. (2001). Atypical brain development: A conceptual framework for understanding learning disabilities. *Developmental Neuropsychology, 20,* 465–481.

Grigorenko, E. L. (2001). Developmental dyslexia: An update on genes, brains, and environments. *Journal of Child Psychology and Psychiatry, 42,* 91–125.

Hale, J. B., Kaufman, A., Naglieri, J. A., & Kavale, K. A. (2006). Implementation of IDEA: Integrating response to intervention and cognitive assessment methods. *Psychology in the Schools, 43*(7), 2006.

Kavale, K. A., & Forness, S. R. (2003). Learning disabilities as a discipline. In H. L. Swanson, K. R. Harris, & S. Graham (Eds.), *Handbook of learning disabilities* (pp. 76–93). New York: Guilford.

Kavale, K. A., Holdnack, J. A., & Mostert, M. P. (2005). Responsiveness to intervention and the identification of specific learning disability: A critique and alternative proposal. *Learning Disability Quarterly, 28,* 2–16.

Kavale, K. A., Kaufman, A. S., Naglieri, J. A., & Hale, J. (2005). Changing procedures for identifying learning disabilities: The danger of poorly supported ideas. *School Psychologist, 59,* 16–25.

Lyon, G. R., Fletcher, J. M., Shaywitz, S. E., Shaywitz, B. A., Torgesen, J. K., Wood, F., et al. (2001). Rethinking learning disabilities. In C. E. Finn, Jr., A. J. Rotherham, & C. R. Hokanson, Jr. (Eds.), *Rethinking special education for a new century* (pp. 259–287). Washington, DC: Thomas B. Fordham Foundation. Retrieved from http://www.excellence.net/library/special ed/index.html

Mather, N., & Gregg, N. (2006). Specific learning disabilities: Clarifying, not eliminating, a construct. *Professional Psychology: Research and Practice, 37,* 99–106.

Mather, N., & Wendling, B. (2005). Linking cognitive assessment results to academic interventions for students with learning disabilities. In D. P. Flanagan & P. L. Harrison (Eds.), *Contemporary intellectual assessment: Theories, tests, and issues* (2nd ed., pp. 269–294). New York: Guilford.

National Joint Committee on Learning Disabilities. (2005). *Responsiveness to intervention and learning disabilities: Concepts, benefits and questions*. [Report] Alexandria, VA: Author.

Schlaggar, B. L., Brown, T. T., Lugar, H. M., Visscher, K. M., Miezin, F. M., & Peterson, S. E. (2002). Functional neuroanatomical differences between adults and school age children in processing of single words. *Science, 296,* 1476.

Semrud-Clikeman, M. (2005). Neuropsychological aspects for evaluating learning disabilities. *Communication Disorders Quarterly, 26*(4), 242–247.

Speece, D. L. (2005). Hitting the moving target known as reading development: Some thoughts on screening children for secondary interventions. *Journal of Learning Disabilities, 38,* 487–93.

U. S. Office of Education. (1968). First *annual report of the National Advisory Committee on Handicapped Children*. Washington, DC: U. S. Department of Health, Education, and Welfare.

Woodcock, R. W. (1984). A response to some questions raised about the Woodcock-Johnson. *School Psychology Review, 13*, 355–362.

18

Neuroscience, Neuropsychology, and Education: Learning to Work and Play Well with Each Other

Michael D. Franzen, Ph.D.

WHAT DO YOU THINK NEUROSCIENCE HAS TO OFFER IN THE ASSESSMENT AND IDENTIFICATION OF LEARNING DISABILITIES?

Neuroscience, in its relation to the assessment and identification of learning disorders, has a checkered history of promise and unfulfilled expectations. From early times, when children who exhibited the symptom patterns later known as Attention-Deficit/Hyperactivity Disorder (ADHD) but who were earlier said to have a condition known as *minimal brain dysfunction* (MBD), neuroscience has been called upon to offer explanations in the form of diagnoses, if not actual explanatory mechanisms and definitive treatments. The concept of MBD was hypothetical and was given because environmental and psychological explanations were insufficient to account for the symptoms. However, assuming the mantle of neuroscience in the adoption of the term MBD did little to advance understanding or treatment of the condition. Fortunately, neuroscience has more to offer in the contemporary world.

Currently, basic neuroscience has limited application to the clinical identification of learning disabilities. There is no laboratory test, no chemical assay, no neuroimaging scan that has both sensitivity and specificity in the diagnosis of learning disabilities. However, research has indicated the obverse of that question namely, that individuals with learning disabilities demonstrate anomalies of neurochemistry or neurofunction. Further examination of those anomalies may help us to understand the conditions and may eventually assist in the more precise diagnosis of different learning disabilities.

Currently, neuroimaging can assist in the diagnosis of certain disorders such as autism or Williams' syndrome (Samango-Sprouse, 2007), but even there the diagnosis is still largely a clinical diagnosis.

Learning disabilities involve a rich mixture of independent and dependent variables across behavior, brain physiology, environment, emotional functioning, and academic achievement. Similarly, the neurosciences frequently involve multifactorial investigations of phenomena. There are the lab studies that investigate simple levels of single neurochemicals, but the neuroscience investigations of clinical phenomena frequently attempt to integrate the variables from a wider array of systems levels. Therefore, the heuristic models utilized by the neurosciences may be helpful in investigating the complexities of learning disabilities. Learning disabilities include genetic factors as well as environmental exposures, settings, and events. Grigorenko (2007) offers a model for understanding developmental dyslexia in such a matrix of systems and variables. Hopefully, by accounting for, or at least by considering, a wider array of variables, a greater understanding of the condition may be reached.

HOW WILL FUTURE DEVELOPMENTS IN NEUROSCIENCE AFFECT HOW WE CLASSIFY AND INTERVENE WITH LEARNING DISABILITIES?

The future of neuroscience can be seen to progress along at least two avenues. The first is in advances in technology that will allow greater understanding of the brain structures and functions involved in learning and greater precision in evaluating the effects of interventions. The second is in advances in a theoretical understanding of how learning and skill development proceed in order to describe a more detailed schemata of the actual processes of "normal" learning as well as the more common paths of disordered learning. The exact nature of these developments is difficult to state with any precision at this point, so perhaps this chapter can be best seen as a hopeful scenario.

The past decade has seen an explosion of technology and knowledge related to neuroimaging. Static imaging allows us to understand the differences in volume in normal and disordered skills. Functional imaging such as the PET scan and fMRI provide a window on what brain structures are utilized in the performance of tasks. For example, recent research has indicated that training in deductive reasoning results in changes in activation and use of the right ventromedial prefrontal area of the brain (Houde et al., 2001). Presumably, other training tasks may have underlying brain areas that show changes with experience. In that way imaging technology now limited to the lab may be transferred to the education clinic as a way of checking the effectiveness of training or educational interventions. For example, in a more direct application to education, Delazer et al. (2003) report on the use of fMRI to elucidate the brain structures activated in complex arithmetic tasks. Subjects who received training in the completion of the arithmetic tasks showed a differential pattern of brain activation. Similarly, there are both event-related potential and fMRI evidence that different brain areas are implicated in processing accurate versus erroneous mathematical equations (Menon et al., 2002).

Knowledge of the difference between how adult brains reflect learning and how child brains reflect learning can help us develop educational methods that more directly reflect the actual brain processes underlying the acquisition of skills and knowledge (Byrnes, 2007). Knowledge about the neurobiological changes that occur during adolescence (Yurgelun-Todd, 2007) can help us develop more effective educational strategies for teenagers. Advances in developmental neuroscience can help fuel advances in educational effectiveness.

One of the most exciting and productive areas of new developments in neuroscience is in the understanding of executive functions and the brain areas that largely subserve those functions, namely the frontal lobes. Recent research has helped to provide a greater understanding of the neurochemical processes of the frontal lobes including serotonin (Robert, Benoit, & Caci, 2007), acetylcholine (Amici & Boxer, 2007), and dopamine (Bonci & Jones, 2007). It is not that simple pharmacology can ever replace experience and practice in education, but instead that knowing about the chemical processes implicated in various learning activities can help direct medical complements to educational interventions. The simplest example is the already common use of stimulant medication to activate the frontal lobes and improve attentional processes in children with ADHD. Future developments may include identification of the optimal neurochemical environments for remediation of other forms of learning disorders. Medication will never replace education, but pharmacology may complement pedagogy.

WHAT ROLE DOES NEUROPSYCHOLOGY HAVE TO PLAY IN THE DIAGNOSIS OF LD?

It is useful here to consider the distinction between learning disorders and learning disability. A *learning disability* is a state and school district defined legal category. The categorization is specific but exclusive. Frequently the requirements include average, near average, or above average intellectual capacity in conjunction with low levels of academic achievement in the context of adequate educational efforts. There may be specific psychometric criteria such as a difference between an IQ score and an achievement score being more than 1.5 standard deviations or the achievement score being at least 2 years below actual grade placement based upon age and achievement in other academic areas. These definitions are precise.

On the other hand, *learning disorder* is a clinical entity. There are even limited DSM-IV clinical criteria. There must be lesser than expected academic achievement. If there is psychological distress or disorder, it must be an effect of the learning disorder and not a cause of it. There cannot be a medical or neurological etiology, unlike learning disability, where a history of closed-head injury or a seizure disorder may be an etiological event. These definitions are vague and permeable. The definition of *less than expected academic achievement* is not given an operational definition.

Yet another distinction between the two concepts is in who can make the determination. State law or educational district regulation may require that a certified school psychologist make the determination. State licensing laws may allow a licensed psychologist, including a neuropsychologist, or a physician-psychiatrist to make the diagnosis of a learning disorder.

Aside from the diagnosis, what does a clinical neuropsychologist bring to the table? Perhaps it is not so much the person as the activity. A comprehensive neuropsychological evaluation provides a profile of strengths and weaknesses. This allows for interventions that capitalize on strengths to compensate for weaknesses. The results can be generalized to individualized intervention plans for all individuals. The question the evaluation seeks to answer is: What is the optimal teaching/learning strategies for a given individual? Theoretically, all individual students could benefit from such an evaluation. However, it is the nonaverage student who is not benefiting from the average instruction who stands to gain more from having an educational plan tied to a specific pattern of cognitive ability and disability.

Clinical neuropsychology does not have a specific role in the diagnosis of learning disorders. It is, however, able to play a unique role in the identification and specification of such disorders. Psychiatrists are able by their licenses and training to diagnose learning disorders. School psychologists are able by their licenses and scope of practice to identify and assess learning disorders, are able by regulation to certify that a child has a learning disability, and are able to determine that a child is eligible for specialized services in the school system. The clinical neuropsychologist can by virtue of training and expertise determine whether a child meets criteria for a learning disability. However, in many regions, the body politic has specified that only a certified school psychologist can make that determination. The clinical neuropsychologist can still play a vital role in this endeavor by providing assessments that identify the cognitive profile of a child and by providing an explication of the underlying physiological/neurological substrate of the difficulties. The clinical neuropsychologist can help rule out the potential role of emotional dysfunction or medical diagnosis in producing the difficulties that the child presents.

For example, a child may present with declining achievement over the second through third grades. The observed problems include anxiety in the classroom, poor performance in mathematics, behavioral acting out including expression of anger and irritability in the classroom and at home especially during homework, and poor peer relationships. Even before a detailed history is taken, there are multiple differential diagnoses that can be considered and each would involve a different intervention or treatment. If the underlying problem is ADHD or an Anxiety Disorder, it is unlikely that the additional educational services that would be suggested by RTI would be effective. Instead, a pattern of academic failure with increased dysphoric mood and further behavioral difficulties may result.

An extreme example would be of a child with developmental brain dysfunction or a medical disorder (Silver et al., 2006). If a nonverbal learning disorder or a complex partial seizure disorder existed, implementing additional but nonspecific educational interventions such as under the RTI model could not possibly remediate the difficulty. Of course not all children who exhibit less than optimal academic performance will eventually be found to have a developmental brain dysfunction. But the clinical neuropsychological evaluation would be much more likely to identify such children and then refer them to the most appropriate treatment. In a more subtle example, a child with a phonologically based reading difficulty would not benefit from an educational intervention that stressed morpheme-phoneme relations.

The clinical neuropsychologist, by providing a comprehensive evaluation of a child, can describe individual strengths and weaknesses. In an ideal world, all children would then be given comprehensive neuropsychological evaluations and the results of each assessment would be used to develop an (actual) individualized education plan. Unfortunately, such a system is expensive and unwieldy. Instead, all children are assumed to be equal in ability, aptitude, and additionally have equal strengths in all component areas of cognitive operation. The definition of disability or need for services in RTI is attractive at first blush. There is no need for stigmatization of the child by referring them to individualized testing and taking them out of the classroom. There is a smooth progression from classroom instruction to the provision of scientifically based interventions. If some particular intervention does not work, another intervention is put in place. This continues until an intervention that works is utilized. However, as is so often the case of love at first sight, closer examination indicates undesirable features. There are no criteria for when it can be decided that an intervention is not working. There is no procedure for identifying what alternate intervention is likely to be helpful and should be tried first (or next).

Even though it has its own drawbacks, the alternative of using clinical neuropsychological or diagnostic academic testing to first identify problematic areas for intervention is preferable on several levels. First, it allows interventions to be tailored to the specific identified problem area. Under RTI, a child might be identified as having a reading problem on the basis of poor classroom performance (lack of response to typical instruction). In fact, that is usually how children are now identified for referral for neuropsychological testing. However, under RTI, the child would then be referred for some unidentified, nonspecific reading intervention that is more intense than the typical instruction. The method and criteria under which this would happen are not specified. Under the neuropsychological model, a comprehensive neuropsychological evaluation would be used to determine if the poor reading performance is due to a generalized attention problem, a visual attention problem, a visual-perceptual (orthographic recognition) deficit, a decoding deficit, or a verbal comprehension deficit. The intervention is then planned to address the specific deficit uncovered utilizing the identified strengths. Under RTI, the child would continue to be treated with seemingly random interventions until one worked.

WHAT ROLE DOES NEUROPSYCHOLOGY PLAY IN DESIGNING INTERVENTIONS IN THE CONTEXT OF RTI?

Of all the questions posed in this volume, this is perhaps the thorniest. The design of an intervention program by a clinical neuropsychologist is predicated upon a comprehensive evaluation. The neuropsychologist identifies the strengths and weaknesses of the individual child and designs a program of interventions that capitalize on strengths and attempt to remediate weaknesses: Neurobiological, cognitive, emotional, social, and psychological are considered and utilized or addressed. However, the RTI system eschews comprehensive and instead offers remediation when achievement is not up to certain standards. It would seem that the clinical neuropsychologist has little to offer, or at least little that is valued, in the RTI system.

There are areas where a clinical neuropsychologist can provide substantial contribution to the RTI system. The first is in the area of designing remediation treatments. Although there is not an individual assessment, the clinical neuropsychologist typically knows the empirical literature better than the average teacher. The clinical neuropsychologist can bring that information to bear on the design of the second- or third-level interventions that are being implemented. Although the exact nature of the reading difficulty is not known in a given child who is not responding to typical classroom instruction, the clinical neuropsychologist may be more familiar with the literature indicating that children who are encouraged to write are more likely to practice reading skills. This information can be used to build a brief, daily journal program into a reading intervention. Alternately, the program can pair reading students into pairs for pen pals or email buddies.

The clinical neuropsychologist may be more familiar with the literature on executive functioning and remediation. This information can be folded into reading interventions such as in the model presented by Gaskins, Satlow, and Pressley (2007). The clinical neuropsychologist would know about the relative prevalence of visual-based versus phonologically based reading impairment and could design a second and third level of interventions that reflects the relative prevalence. Finally, because the neuropsychologist knows about measurement and experimental design, he or she can make large contributions to the design of an adequate system to evaluate the effectiveness of programs put in place.

REFERENCES

Amici, S. (2007). Oiling the gears of the mind: Roles for acetylcholine in the modulation of attention. In B. L. Miller and J. L. Cummings (Eds.), *The human frontal lobes functions and disorders* (pp. 135–144). New York: Guilford.

Bonci, A., & Jones, S. (2007). The mesocortical dopaminergic system. In B. L. Miller & J. L. Cummings (Eds.), *The human frontal lobes functions and disorders* (pp. 145–162). New York: Guilford.

Byrnes, J. P. (2007). Some ways in which neuroscientific research can be relevant to education. In D. Coch, K. W. Fisher, & G. Dawson (Eds.), *Human behavior, learning and the developing brain: Typical developments* (pp. 30–49). New York: Guilford.

Delazer, M., Donahs, F., Bartha, L., Brenneis, C., Lochy, A., Treib, T., & Benke, T. (2003). Learning complex arithmetic–an fMRI study. *Cognition and Brain Research, 18,* 76–88.

Gaskins, I. W., Satlow, E., & Pressley, M. (2007). Executive control of reading comprehension in the elementary school. In L. Meltzer (Ed.), *Executive function in education* (pp.194–215). New York: Guilford.

Grigorenko, E. L. (2007). Triangulating developmental dyslexia: Behavior, brain, and genes. In D. Coch, G. Dawson, & K. W. Fisher (Eds.), *Human behavior, learning and the developing brain: Atypical development* (pp. 117–144). New York: Guilford.

Houde, O., Zago, L., Crivello, F., Moutier, S., Pineau, A., Mazoyer, Tzourio-Mazoyer, N. (2001). Access to deductive logic depends on a right ventromedial area devoted to emotion and feeling: Evidence from a training paradigm. *Neuroimage, 14,* 1486–1492.

Menon, V., MacKenzie, K., Rivera, S. M., & Reiss, A. L. (2002). Prefrontal cortex involvement in processing incorrect arithmetic equation: Evidence from event-related fMRI. *Human Brain Mapping, 16,* 119–130.

Robert, P. H., Benoit, M., & Caci, H. (2007). Serotonin and the frontal lobes. In B. L. Miller & J. L. Cummings (Eds.), *The human frontal lobes functions and disorders* (pp. 121–134). New York: Guilford.

Samango-Sprouse, C. (2007). Frontal lobe development in childhood. In B. L. Miller & J. L. Cummings (Eds.), *The human frontal lobes: Functions and disorders* (pp. 576–593). New York: Guilford.

Silver, C. H., Blackburn, L. B., Arffa, S., Barth, J. T., Bush, S. S., Troster, A. I,
    Moser, R. S., Elliott, R. W. NAN Policy and Planning Committee. (2006). The
    importance of neuropsychological assessment for the evaluation of childhood
    learning disorders. *Archives of Clinical Neuropsychology, 21,* 741–744.
Yurgelun-Todd, D. (2007). Emotional and cognitive changes during adolescence.
    Current Opinions in Neurobiology, 17, 251–257.

19

Diagnosing Learning Disabilities in Nonmajority Groups: The Challenges and Problems of Applying Nonneuropsychological Approaches

Javier Gontier and Antonio E. Puente

WHAT ROLE DOES NEUROPSYCHOLOGY HAVE TO PLAY IN THE DIAGNOSIS OF LEARNING DISABILITIES?

There are well-known federal statutes that bar discrimination against persons with any kinds of disabilities, including those in learning (Pullin, 2002). Thus, individuals with learning disabilities have the right to access education and its derived services. They also have equal opportunity to obtain similar results as and reach the same level of academic achievement as individuals with no or limited disabilities. To assure individuals with disabilities equal opportunity of academic success, appropriate intervention, rehabilitation programs, and accommodations need to be determined. These strategies seek to assure the right to access opportunities to achieve skills, knowledge, and socialization by being integrated at school and, subsequently, in vocational and personal endeavors. The level of academic achievement will determine also the quantity and quality of job opportunities, income, and finally their quality of life. As a result, the early selection of the appropriate rehabilitation processes, interventions, and accommodations for any learning disability is crucial in facilitating students with learning disabilities to get equal opportunity. The strategies selected for each individual must be based on scientific, reliable, and accurate assessment procedures addressing all the issues that are related to the disability in its origin, daily functioning manifestation, the future expected performance, and contextual and idiosyncratic expression. To do otherwise increases the possibility of bias and discrimination, both of certain types of disabilities and of groups who historically have been over-represented within learning disabled groups.

The Individuals with Disabilities Education Improvement Act (IDEIA) defines *learning disability* as a disorder in which one or more imperfections are manifested in psychological processes of using language or doing mathematical calculations (IDEA, 2004). As a consequence, the measurement of psychological processes should be measured with appropriate instruments. The psychological processes related to using language and performing mathematical calculations are regulated by brain functions that have been studied for decades within the specialty of clinical psychology. For example, Spreen (2000) offers a review in which identified areas of the brain are involved as components of processes of reading and arithmetic. The article also discusses the evolution of learning disabilities and the persistence of different subtypes from childhood to adulthood. Measurements and, hence, understanding of the relationship between cognitive and language processes and brain functioning are possible by using neuropsychological assessment procedures. The quality and reliability of these procedures have been evidenced by the extended research available in studies of validity, reliability, and fairness in scientific literature (Mitrushina, Boone, & D'Elia, 1999; Goldstein & Beers, 2004) and in databases such as PsycINFO. These studies are presented in a variety of scientific forums such as the National Academy of Neuropsychology, International Neuropsychological Society, and the Division of Clinical Neuropsychology of the American Psychological Association. These studies are published in journals such as *Archives of Clinical Neuropsychology, Applied Neuropsychology, Child Neuropsychology, International Journal of Neuropsychology, Journal of Experimental and Clinical Neuropsychology, Neuropsychology, Neuropsychology Review,* and *The Clinical Neuropsychologist.*

The provision of reliable and valid instruments to assess individuals with learning disabilities is one of the most important contributions of clinical neuropsychology in the assessment of learning disabilities. Clinical neuropsychology is both a science and a profession centrally involved in providing legal and professional regulations associated with the assessment process of learning disabilities. Regulations state standards of competence for technicians that perform the testing, for the testing situation and context, and for the interpretation of expected results of the assessment process (Puente et al., 2006). Protection for the public and their rights are also provided by the American Psychological Association (APA) and the ethical principles that state that any testing service provided must be guided by nonmaleficence and be based in the best available scientific evidence (American Psychological Association, 2002). Additional direction for the use of tests, assessments, and their outcomes is also provided by the testing guidelines developed by the APA in conjunction with related professional organizations (American Educational Research Association, American Psychological Association, & National Council on Measurement in Education, 1985). In summary, neuropsychology provides the best and most robust foundation to date for scientifically developed and, hence unbiased, approaches for the determination of deficits in the acquisition of information and knowledge.

One important issue in the application of neuropsychology in the diagnosis of learning disabilities is the scarce availability of neuropsychologists. According to Puente (2006), there are probably less than 5,000 neuropsychologists in the United States and only a small part of them work in the school systems or provide learning disabilities services as part of their clinical protocols. In contrast, the number of school-aged children with learning disabilities appears to exceed 5% of the total school-aged child population (D'Amato et al., 2005). With this critical discrepancy in mind, one alternative is what D'Amato et al. (2005) consider an *evolving model*. They suggest that more standard psychological evaluations are typically carried out by school psychologists within the school system, whereas the more difficult or severe cases tend to be evaluated by neuropsychologists. One possible solution, such as the one implied with the RTI system, is that, to reach a greater number of children and to do so more quickly, a system focused on assessment by teachers using observational strategies will increase, and do so quickly, the number of children that would be evaluated. Thus, the majority of the students who have some type of learning disability or who are suspected of having some type of learning disability will probably be assessed using curriculum-based assessment, and in more difficult cases the child will be evaluated by a school psychologist.

The possibility exists that a reduction of scientifically based assessment practices completed by trained personnel will correlate with an increase of nonscientifically based assessment completed primarily by bachelor's-level educators untrained and unappreciative of the complexities associated with brain dysfunction and the acquisition, retention, and retrieval of information and knowledge. This situation will be particularly problematic with children associated with nonmajority groups resulting in an increase of false positives in children of ethnic-minority groups and false negatives in children affiliated with majority groups. Hence, the crisis facing this particular situation is how to integrate neuropsychological assessment more readily and quickly, and not in the integration of responsive and dynamic yet nonscientifically based approaches to assessment.

WHAT ROLE DOES NEUROPSYCHOLOGY HAVE TO PLAY IN DESIGNING INTERVENTIONS IN THE CONTEXT OF RTI?

RTI has been defined as a preventive model based on the fact that response to intervention is introduced to children during the early stages of learning such as the stages of reading development (Justice, 2006). This approach has several strengths that can be extracted from the review that Justice published. First, RTI is a model that is applied in the earliest stages that children start formal education. Early reading instructions are used as examples and they are given to children in preschool to assess skills that are supposed to be related to the development of reading skills. The way in which children respond to these instructions and their performance in the tasks are observed and measured by their teachers. According to their behavior and performance, children may be classified as having a learning disability and they are assigned to receive some compensatory training or rehabilitation. However, what is causing this behavior or performance in each task will be very different from one child to another. Motivation or low tolerance to frustration might produce the same behavior that a learning disability is causally related to, such as any disability to process numbers and to answer mathematical problems. Hence, no matter which issues surfaces first (i.e., disability or motivational problem), the eventual outcome or behavior needs to be addressed.

Second, RTI is a group of actions that runs in a continuum process during a period of time in which reading is expected to be developing. This methodology with a process approach allows a continued monitoring of changes that are happening in children during different ages. Monitoring and assessment are provided not only in one single event, but in a fluid and evolving situation. This continuity in an assessment-intervention process makes possible the development of a potentially more reliable picture of how change happens, and also what are the possible factors intervening in change: family, social environment, nutrition, education, social interaction, and learning methods issues.

Third, there is an important variability in speed and strategies that children use to learn. A continued process of monitoring facilitates detection of reading difficulties that are expected but are part of the normal process of learning and that do not require any special intervention to get the expected reading achievements levels.

In contrast, RTI has several features that can be addressed from a neuropsychological view. First, genetically caused learning disabilities have been identified in school-aged children such as Velo-Cardio-Facial syndrome (De Smedt et al., 2007). These children do not need to undergo the difficult and long process of assessments, interventions, and monitoring to be identified and *only then* receive the appropriate treatments or rehabilitation. These children would benefit from early educative assessments and monitoring that the RTI process provides. There are some unusual caveats that come with this approach, however. Measurements of intellectual ability are rejected by the RTI model as sources of information for the decision-making process.

Nevertheless, the rights of individuals with disabilities, by design, allow and encourage the right to access all resources that make it possible to have equal opportunities to be academically successful. The RTI process may inherently be incomplete and provide little, if any information about its etiology, development, and trajectory. Knowledge about cognitive, genetic, and neurological issues must be gathered to develop a more complete and scientifically based educative and rehabilitation plan. It is at this point in which neuropsychology has an important role to play in gathering available updated scientific data of the relation between cognition, behavior, and brain function for a particular type of syndrome. Neuropsychological functioning measures have an extended scientific base and they are able to provide comparative data that help to clarify the relation between individual psychological functioning and the expected functioning for age groups. In summary, neuropsychology provides a scientifically based understanding of the problems at hand and, as a consequence, provides a more solid foundation to a responsive intervention program.

The Ecological Neuropsychological Model, as described by D'Amato, Crepeau-Hobson, Huang, and Geil (2005), provides an interesting approach to integrate in a comprehensive and dynamic way information from the different systems in which an individual with a learning disability is involved and interacting. This approach not only develops a method to gather the information related to an individual with learning disability but also it gives guidelines of how compensatory resources, rehabilitation, or interventions must be planned. This approach captures the dynamic, early, and integrated approach associated with RTI while encapsulating the scientific, reliable, and valid measurement of neuropsychological assessment.

The RTI approach appears silent on issues of diversity and cultural dissimilarity. The validity of RTI is based on its specificity in detecting children who have a learning disability and by avoiding that diagnosis in children and do not (Geisinger, Boodoo, & Noble, 2002). The assumption is that RTI is silent on cultural issues largely because they avoid this *confound* by addressing the fundamental issue in question—whether a child has a learning disability. However, in the United States, there are a disproportionate number of culturally diverse students in special education (Harris-Murri, King, & Rostenberg, 2006). Further, the U.S. Census Bureau statistics suggest that specific groups, such as Hispanics, are now the fastest growing segments of the school-aged population (2000). At the same time, they are becoming the fastest growing segment of the special education population as well. This potential crossing of silence on addressing diversity combined with increased number of actual students from diverse backgrounds and diverse students who have learning disabilities poses major complications for the RTI process. Thus, a larger number of incorrectly placed students and inappropriately developed intervention programs would ensue.

Crosscultural neuropsychology has been scientifically addressing the problem of assessing culturally diverse populations (Ardila, 2005; Evans et al., 2000; Nell, 2000; Perez-Arce & Puente, 1996; Puente & Perez-Garcia, 2000; Puente & Agranovich, 2003; Puente & Ardila, 2000; Wong et al., 2000). Many issues related to the assessment in culturally diverse populations in learning disabled individuals can be extracted from that literature. For instance, as Harris-Murri, King, and Rostenberg point out, instructions given to students during an RTI procedure can be perceived differently depending on the ethnicity of students. Relationships between students and protective figures or authorities in classrooms are different depending on the culture and ethnicity of students. Latino children have family in which values of respecting authority and adults are predominant and the transgressions of those rules are severely punished. Furthermore, there are special and culturally specific ways to perceive relationships that are named with Spanish words that cannot be translated to English, such as *simpatía*. Simpatía is related to the social ability to share feelings, to maintain a certain level of conformity, and to behave with dignity, emphasizing positive aspects and avoiding negative aspects in one situation (Triandis et al., 1984). Simpatía has high social worth among Latin Americans and it might result in avoidance of conflict and confrontation. Triandis et al. (1984) explored the perceived value of social behaviors in Hispanics and non-Hispanics. They found that Hispanics tend to expect more associative positive behaviors from others than non-Hispanics in social interactions. Hispanics expect to find more *simpatía* and to behave with more *simpatía* in social contexts and they tend to reject criticizing and competing behaviors. This expectation changes when there is a higher status individual in that social context. For high-status individuals, Hispanics do not reject and they tend to expect them to perform nonsympathetic behaviors, such as giving orders and disciplining. Consequently, in that context Hispanics are less likely to expect a high-status person to reveal intimate thoughts or personal problems. In the same way, Hispanics are more likely to talk with friends even if that makes them late for another engagement. Also, Latinos are more easily offended than White Americans and Black Americans by comments that carry a personal meaning. Furthermore, they prefer a service that a friend provides no matter if there are other professionals providing the same service with higher quality. These characteristics make Latin Americans more collective oriented and more centered in others' values, needs, goals, and points of view. Traditional Anglo-American culture is more individualistic oriented, emphasizing values such as competition, pleasure, a comfortable life, and social recognition (Triandis et al., 1985).

Individual and cultural differences need to be considered when an assessment and/or an intervention is planned. Specifically, neuropsychology needs to integrate and to compare findings of studies from other countries and cultures as a foundation for addressing the increasing diversity of the American population as well as the generalizability of the application of neuropsychological principles of learning disabilities in a globlalization context. The database PsycINFO is able to provide 11,359 articles from journals written in English and that have the words *neuropsychology* or *neurosciences* in their names. However, the same database is capable of finding only 46 articles that are published in journals that have the word *neuropsicologia*— the Spanish and French word for neuropsychology—in their names. This is a very restricted knowledge base as it applies to Hispanic populations. In contrast, there are a wide range of journals publishing neuropsychology in Latin America: *Revista Brasileira de Neuropsicologia, Revista Chilena de Neuropsicología, Revista Española de Psicología, Revista Argentina de Neuropsicología, y Revista Neuropsicología, Neuropsiquiatría y Neurociencias de Colombia*. However, review of that literature still indicates a critical paucity of information relative to the application of neuropsychological assessment in general and, specifically, to Spanish-speaking populations.

Differences in social interaction and social perceptions among cultures will impact the answers that children with diverse cultural backgrounds and ethnicities will give to assessment procedures such as RTI (Harris-Murri et al., 2006). Questions about studies of validity and fairness of the instruments used in RTI in culturally diverse populations arise because there is some evidence of students who are misplaced either in special or in normal academic programs. Psychology, knowledge of psychometrics, and crosscultural neuropsychology would contribute to the study of reliability, validity, and fairness of instruments in culturally and ethnically diverse populations that are been using in RTI procedures. In response, valid and correct assessments would then provide for appropriate and responsive intervention programs for learning disabled children of all types.

HOW WILL FUTURE DEVELOPMENTS IN NEUROSCIENCES AFFECT HOW WE CLASSIFY AND INTERVENE WITH LEARNING DISABILITIES?

An historical definition of learning disabilities was made a by the National Joint Committee for Learning Disabilities (NJCLD) in 1981 (Hynd et al., 1986). This definition states that learning disabilities have a presumed cause in a central nervous system dysfunction. Later definitions have become more focused in the academic impairments that are not due to sensorial, motor emotional, environmental, or economical factors (Zillmer, Spiers, & Culbertson, 2008). Common subtypes of identified learning disabilities are dyslexia, dyscalculia, and dysgraphia. Even tough definitions of learning disabilities will change; there is a large amount of research and evidence of brain dysfunctions for variations of the theme. Although theories about what specific neural substrates of each subtype are not yet fully tested, the initial applications appear fruitful and robust. Future developments in neurosciences should address this issue by using the contributions of advanced technological devices. Technology such as magnetic resonance scanner, positron emission tomography, and advanced genetic assessment and their integration with neuropsychology appear to be the wave of the future. Complexity, interregional activity in the brain, and relationships between each subtype and other emotional and behavioral disorders challenge theories and definitions in neurosciences. However, there are findings that have well-established important improvements in defining neural function and localization and evolving changes of one specific skill as well as the correct testing procedure to assess it (Wolf, Bowers, & Biddle, 2000). These findings also have implications for any educational intervention. Clinical and educational research must address topics not only related to neuropsychological assessment but also to the correct and specific rehabilitation techniques and educational interventions for each subtype of learning disability.

WHAT DO YOU THINK NEUROSCIENCE HAS TO OFFER THE ASSESSMENT AND IDENTIFICATION OF LEARNING DISABILITIES?

The neurosciences have progressed enormously during the last 20 years due to the use of neuroimaging techniques such as magnetic resonance imaging, positron emission tomography, and advanced genetic testing. Since the definition of learning disabilities includes the idea that learning disabilities should be related to some anatomically identified brain dysfunction, it has increased the importance of all the evidence showing how the functioning of different systems in the brain is related to a particular learning disability and is not present in a child with no learning disabilities. Dmitrova, Dubrovinskaya, Lukashevich, Machinskaya, and Shklovskii (2005) analyzed neuropsychological performance and electroencephalographic activity (EEG) of "normal" children and children with dysgraphia and dyslexia. They found that, in comparison with children with no learning disabilities, children with dysgraphia and dyslexia have a brain intercentral interaction with predominant low-frequency EEG components. As in children with no learning disabilities, this intercentral brain interaction is predominantly high-frequency rhythms. A review of neuroimaging studies by Semrud-Clikeman and Pliszka (2005) summarized findings showing that several brain areas are related to learning disabilities. For instance, the Perisylvian region was found to be associated in children with a language disability other than dyslexia and several publications noticed changes in structural and functional brain activity after intervention in language processing in children with difficulties in auditory processing. Findings such as these as well as evidence from other areas of neurosciences provide critical foundation for the understanding of learning disabilities. There are evidence that come from the genetic field identifying chromosomes 6, 15, 16, 18, and 19 to be associated with learning disabilities using linkage analysis (Plomin & Walker, 2003). However, additional work is necessary to develop a theory of how these genes mutate and how they affect the development of the central nervous system.

Neuropsychology without neuroscience is like learning disability without neuropsychology.

REFERENCES

American Educational Research Association, American Psychological Association & National Council on Measurement in Education. (1985). *Standards for Educational and Psychological Testing.* Washington, DC: American psychological Association.

American Psychological Association. (2002). *Ethical principles of psychologists and code of conduct.* Washington, DC: American Psychological Association.

Ardila, A. (2005). Cultural values underlying psychometric cognitive testing. *Neuropsychology Review, 4,* 185–195.

Camara, W. J., Nathan, J. S., & Puente, A. E. (2000). Psychological test usage: Implications in professional psychology. *Professional Psychology: Research and Practice,* 31(2), 141–154.

Evans, J. D., Millar, S. W., Byrd, D. A., & Heaton, R. K. (2000). Cross-cultural applications of the Halstead-Reitan Battery. In E. Fletcher-Janzen, T. L. Strickland, & C. R. Reynolds (Eds.), *Handbook of cross-cultural neuropsychology* (pp. 287–303). New York: Kluwer Academic/Plenum.

D'Amato, R. C., Crepeau-Hobson, F., Huang, L. V., & Geil, M. (2005). Ecological Neuropsychology: An alternative to the deficit model for conceptualizing and serving students with learning disabilities. *Neuropsychology Review,* 15(2), 97–103.

De Smedt, B., Swillen, A., Devriendt, K., Fryns, J. P., Verschaffel, L., & Ghesquiere, P. (2007). Mathematical disabilities in children with velo-cardio-facial syndrome. *Neuropsychologia, 45,* 885–895.

Dmitrova, E. D., Dubrovinskaya, N. V., Lukashevich, I. P., Machinskaya, R. I., & Shklovskii, V. M. (2005). Features of cerebral support of verbal processes in children with dysgraphia and dyslexia. *Human Physiology,* 31(2), 5–12.

Geisinger, K. F., Boodoo, G., & Noble, J. P. (2002). The psychometrics of testing individuals with disabilities. In Ekstrom, R. B. & Smith, D K. (Eds.), *Assessing individuals with disabilities* (pp. 33–42). Washington, DC: American Psychological Association.

Goldstein, G., & Beers, S. R. (2004). Intellectual and neuropsychological assessment. In G. Goldstein, S. R. Beers, & M. Hersen (Eds.), *Comprehensive handbook of psychological assessment* (pp. 101–104). Hoboken, NJ: Wiley.

Harris-Murri, N., King, K., & Rostenberg, D. (2006). Reducing disproportionate minority representation in special education programs for students with emotional disturbances: Toward a culturally responsive response to intervention model. *Education and treatment of children, 29*(4), 779–799.

Hynd, G. W., Orbzut, J. E., Hayes, F., & Becker, M. G. (1986). Neuropsychology of childhood learning disabilities. In D. Wedding, A. M. Horton, & J. Webster (Eds.), *The neuropsychology handbook.* (pp. 456–485). New York: Springer.

Individuals with Disabilities Education Improvement Act. Conference Report. (2004). Washington, D.C.

Justice, L. M. (2006). Evidence-based practice, response to intervention, and prevention of reading difficulties. *Language, Speech, and Hearing Services in Schools, 37,* 284–297.

Mitrushina, M. N., Boone, K. B., & D'Elia, L. (1999) *Handbook of normative data for neuropsychological testing.* New York: Oxford University Press.

Nell, V. (2000). *Cross-cultural neuropsychological assessment: Theory and practice.* Mahwah, NJ: Erlbaum.

Perez-Arce, P. & Puente, A. E. (1996). Neuropsychological assessment of ethnic-minorities: The case of assessing Hispanics living in North America. In R. J. Sbordone, & C. J. Long (Eds.), *Ecological validity of neuropsychological testing* (pp. 283–300). Delray Beach, FL: Gr Press/St Lucie Press.

Plomin, R., & Walker, S. O. (2003). Genetics and educational psychology. *British Journal of Educational Psychology, 73,* 3–14.

Puente, A. E. (2006). Cómo se relaciona la cultura con la neuropsicología clínica? La construcción de una neuropsicología global desde una perspectiva personal. In *Avances en neuropsicología clínica* (pp. 6–9). Madrid, Spain: Fundación Mafre.

Puente, A. E., Adams, R., Barr, W. B, Bush, S. S., and NAN Policy and Planning Committee, Muff, R. M., Barth, J. T., Broshek, D., Koffler, S. P., Reynolds, C., Silver, C. H., & Trostel, A. I. (2006). The use, education training and supervision of neuropsychological test technicians (psychometrists) in clinician practice. Official Statement of the National Academy of Neuropsychology. *Archives of Clinical Neuropsychology, 21*(8), 837–839.

Puente, A. E., & Perez-Garcia, M. (2000). Psychological assessment of ethnic minorities. In G. Goldstein & M. Hersen (Eds.), *Handbook of psychological assessment.* Kidlington, Oxford: Elsevier Science.

Puente, A. E., & Agranovich, A.V. (2003). The cultural in cross-cultural neuropsychology. G. Goldstein, S. R. Beers, & M. Hersen (Ed.) *Comprehensive handbook of psychological assessment* (pp. 321–332). Hoboken, NJ: Wiley.

Puente, A. E., & Ardila, A. (2000). Neuropsychological assessment of Hispanics. In E. Fletcher-Janzen, T. L. Strickland, & C. R. Reynolds (Eds.) *Handbook of cross-cultural neuropsychology* (pp.87–104). New York: Kluwer Academic/Plenum.

Pullin, D. (2002). Testing individuals with disabilities: reconciling social science and social policy. In R. B. Ekstrom, & D. K. Smith (Eds.), *Assessing individuals with disabilities* (pp. 11–32). Washington, DC: American Psychological Association.

Semrud-Clikeman, M., & Pliszka, S. R. (2005). Neuroimaging and psychopharmacology. *School Psychology Quarterly, 20*(2), 172–186.

Spreen, O. (2000). The neuropsychology of learning disabilities. *Zeitschrift fur Neuropsychologie, 11*(3), 168–193.

Triandis, H. C., Marín, G., Lisansky, J., & Betancourt, H. (1984). Simpatía as a cultural script for Hispanics. *Journal of Personality and Social Psychology, 47*(6), 1363–1375.

Triandis, H. C., Leung, K, Villareal, M. J., & Clack, F. L. (1985). Allocentric versus idiocentric tendencies: Convergent and discriminant validation. *Journal of Research in Personality, 4,* 395–415.

U. S. Census Bureau. (2000). United States: 2000, *Summary Population and Housing Characteristics,* PHC-1-1, United States Washington, DC, 2002.

Wolf, M., Bowers, P. G., & Biddle, K. (2000). Naming-speed process, timing, and reading: A conceptual review. *Journal of Learning Disabilities, 33*(4), 387–407.

Wong, T. M., Strickland, T. L., Fletcher-Janzen, E., Ardila, A., & Reynolds, C. R. (2000). Theoretical and practical issues in the neuropsychological assessment and treatment of culturally dissimilar patients. In E. Fletcher-Janzen, T. L. Strickland, & C. R. Reynolds (Eds.), *Handbook of cross-cultural neuropsychology* (pp. 3–18). Dordrecht, Netherlands: Kluwer Academic.

Zillmer, E. A., Spiers, M V., & Culbertson, W. C. (2008). *Principles of neuropsychology.* Belmont, CA: Thomson Wadsworth.

20

The Role of Neuroscience and Neuropsychology in the Diagnosis of Learning Differences and the RTI Paradigm

Sally L. Kemp, Ph.D. and Marit Korkman, Ph.D.

HOW DO YOU RECONCILE RTI AS A MEANS OF DIAGNOSIS WITH KNOWLEDGE FROM CLINICAL NEUROSCIENCE?

Helping a child learn through response to intervention is the desire of every dedicated teacher; therefore, this is a concept that few with teaching experience would reject, and, certainly, parents and other professionals would see this as a laudable goal. Many teachers are accomplishing interventions and assessing progress informally in a very successful way. Others are not, however; so including accountability for appropriate intervention in the reauthorized Individuals with Disabilities Education Improvement Act (IDEA) is welcomed by many in the field (Hale et al., 2006). For many, implementing RTI in its present form with curriculum-based measurement (CBM) based on "generally effective" instruction by the classroom teacher (Fuchs et al., 2003) as the initial diagnostic step (Tier 1) is problematical.

The problem occurs not with the concept of RTI but with the realistic constraints of the classroom and the lack of standardization of curriculum-based measurement as diagnostic tools. Who is going to be responsible for being sure that CBM is valid and reliable from one school to another, from one classroom to another, and for that matter from one student to another? How are the costs of standardizing instruction to be covered? Gerber (2005) has stated that extraordinary expenditures will be incurred by school districts on such standardization costs. Without standardization of training, instruction, curricula, and CBM, however, the district would be unable to show that it was not the teacher or system who failed the child, but, rather, it was the child who failed to respond to intervention.

Research-based interventions based on the individual child's needs with adjustments as needed and the repeated monitoring of progress comprise Tier 2. The plan for specific interventions and repeated monitoring is very desirable, but from a practical point of view, how are the individualized interventions to be chosen on the basis of CBM that is neither valid nor reliable statistically? Who is to choose them?

Because the students who have not responded to intervention may qualify for special education in Tier 3, is it not essential that the diagnostic process on which the interventions are based be valid and reliable statistically? The alternative at Tier 3 is that the child receives a special education evaluation (Fuchs et al., 2003) to determine placement. Would this not be the place to start, before interventions are chosen? What is the capacity of teachers, no matter how gifted, to access, implement, and document this type of individualized three-tier approach while dealing with 25 to 30 students with different needs? Dr. Kemp, who enjoyed 20 years as a classroom teacher before entering psychology, observes that veterans in the teaching field have seen many fine plans on paper and have taken part in numerous classroom iterations addressing the broad spectrum of special needs students. Some of these plans have had great merit, but have failed to succeed in many cases due to constraints of time, money, teacher skills/style, and/or the cooperation of the administration.

With CBM of dubious reliability and validity as the initial point of diagnosis is there not a danger that inappropriate interventions will be chosen? When progress is monitored and the child has not overcome deficits, what guarantee is there that another intervention will be any more appropriate than the initial one was, if the diagnostic information is not reliable or valid? How much time will be wasted during the Tier 2 stage when the child could be receiving very specific interventions based on a valid and reliable standardized assessment?

It is also possible that a child will never be evaluated with valid and reliable diagnostic instruments before being placed in special education since Tier 3 provides an "either/or" approach to special education placement on the basis of lack of response to intervention or on an evaluation. It will be very tempting for administrators in financially strapped school districts to opt for failure to respond to intervention as a means to place the child in special education, rather than to opt for an evaluation. There is no provision in RTI for attempting to determine the child's cognitive/neuropsychological profile as a guide to the selection of interventions. How many children will fail to respond just because the appropriate intervention was not implemented or an otherwise able teacher could not implement 10 different individualized plans in a class of 30 youngsters?

The answer to these queries would appear to be that there already exists a research-based means of diagnosing children's processing strengths and weaknesses in a standardized manner so that the information can be supplied to the teacher complete with interventions based on the child's neuropsychological functioning. The significant knowledge base of pediatric neuroscience is expanding daily due to developments in brain imaging. Valid and reliable assessment tools based on current research that yield specific neuropsychological profiles of school-aged children are available and can be used to select specific interventions that are likely to be successful. Yet it appears that all of this knowledge is being side-lined by the RTI approach based on CBMs that are not valid and reliable.

RTI may ultimately fail because the teacher does not have the valid information needed to address the child's deficits in a specific, individualized manner. Surely, all can agree that it is very appropriate to address a child's specific needs with appropriate interventions and to be held accountable for the same, but is it really the teacher's job to diagnose a child's specific deficits and to identify the appropriate research-based intervention? Are teachers trained for this role and is it fair to ask them to fulfill it? Is RTI a way for some administrators to avoid funding evaluations since statistically unreliable CBMs can be used for diagnosis?

By redesigning the tier structure, these problems could be addressed. The very positive aspects of RTI, such as specific interventions and repeated monitoring, could be retained, but the diagnostic and placement phases could be made more stringent in order to address the reliability and validity issues. Figure 20.1 illustrates this revised three-tier method.

With the initial diagnostic phase (Tier 1) being shared by the teacher, school psychologist and/or psychometrist, and therapists, core standardized testing could be initiated early and a profile of functioning could be generated quickly. The teacher or other support personnel would administer academic achievement screening, rating scales, and classroom observations. The school psychologist would administer an abbreviated cognitive measure and core neuropsychological subtests across domains when the problem is unclear. If there is a more specific referral question, neuropsychological tests can be selected on clinical, research, or child-specific needs. The NEPSY-II (Korkman, Kirk, & Kemp, 2007), for instance, provides eight batteries that are suggested to assist examiners in planning assessments for common referral questions. Following the initial evaluation, teacher and school psychologist/psychometrist and/or support personnel could design interventions based on the reliable and valid data from testing. As is characteristic of RTI, interventions could be initiated quickly and progress could be monitored in Tier 2 according to an established timeline.

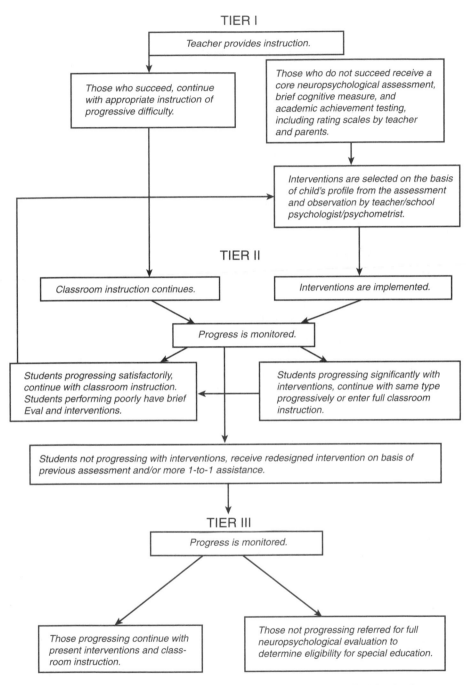

Figure 20.1   Revised Three-Tier Method. Many Aspects of RTI, Such as Specific Interventions and Repeated Monitoring, Are Retained, But the Placement Phases Include More Reliable and Valid Diagnostic Assessments.

The most important addition to the structure would be the full cognitive/neuropsychological evaluation of children who performed very poorly on the core assessment initially or who did not respond to intervention with repeated monitoring in Tier 2. According to this model, no child would be placed in special education without such an evaluation by a school psychologist trained in neuropsychology or a pediatric neuropsychologist. Determination of a specific learning disability would be based on deficits in basic psychological processes as compared to typical age-mates, as noted by Hale et al. (2006). These deficits would determine the mechanism for failure to progress in specific academic areas. They would be demonstrated by significant discrepancies present between cognitive assets and cognitive deficits within the child's own profile. A knowledge of these primary deficits would then direct the choice and even the development of means for special education.

With this revised tier structure, a teacher would not feel so "lost at sea" in trying to specify deficits and interventions and could focus instead on working on specific interventions with the child. It is likely that there will be an increased need for teacher's aides to assist with the one-to-one and small-group work. Nonetheless, the teacher load in RTI is great and it will take time, skill, and patience to make it work for both teacher and child.

WHAT DO YOU THINK NEUROSCIENCE HAS TO OFFER THE ASSESSMENT AND IDENTIFICATION OF LEARNING DISABILITIES?

Neuroscience has much to offer the assessment and identification of learning disabilities in children. Brain functions in children are amazingly complex when one considers that they are still developing. It is the typical development of the young brain over time that neuroscience has been able to address where pure educational research was not always yielding useful, specific answers. The study of developmental disorders and pediatric head trauma has provided useful human models for the study of brain function in children (Broman & Michel, 1995). Neuroimaging, however, has opened a window onto the brain and its functions that could not be dreamed of 25 years ago.

Neuroimaging is expanding our knowledge of brain function in children at a very rapid rate. In 1992, Chugani observed that the expanding PET scan technology was providing a new approach that held great promise in the diagnosis and management of brain disorders in children. Fifteen years later, Jung and Haier (2007) reported that modern neuroimaging techniques are beginning to articulate a biology of intelligence. They are finding that variations in a distributed network predict individual differences found on intelligence and reasoning tasks in adults (parieto-frontal integrative theory).

Rodriguez and Poussaint (2007) has found that neuroimaging of children with developmental delays can contribute to more effective treatment plans as measured by progress in reaching developmental milestones. In other words, knowledge of the cortical areas that are activated, or not, can allow teachers and therapists to tailor the treatment plan more specifically to the child's needs. In an fMRI study, Piercel and colleagues (2001) found that activation of aberrant and individual-specific neural sites (e.g., frontal cortex, primary visual cortex) occurred when autistic children engaged in a facial recognition task. In typical controls there was 100% consistency of maximal activation in the fusiform gyrus face area. Therefore, neuroimaging has allowed us to understand that autistic children "see" faces with a different system than their typical peers. These findings have led to the development of tools for assessing facial recognition in children with autism (e.g., NEPSY-II Facial Recognition Test; Korkman, Kirk, & Kemp, 2007), as well as studies that are investigating whether the FFG can be activated with training in order to improve facial recognition.

Simos et al. (2000) have demonstrated that right-handed children with dyslexia that had severe phonological decoding problems showed activation profiles during a printed word-recognition task that consistently featured activation of the left basal temporal cortices followed by activation of the right temporoparietal areas (including the angular gyrus). Nonimpaired readers showed predominant activation of left basal followed by left temporoparietal activation. In addition, this investigative team was able to rule out the hypothesis that hypoactivation of left temporoparietal areas in children with dyslexia was due to a more general cerebral dysfunction in these areas. Reading difficulties in developmental dyslexia appeared to be associated with an aberrant pattern of functional connectivity between brain areas normally involved in reading (ventral visual association cortex and temporoparietal areas in the left hemisphere). The authors proposed that the interindividual consistency of activation profiles characteristic of children with dyslexia underlines the potential utility of this technique for examining neurophysiological changes in response to specific educational intervention approaches. Studies such as this help us understand the brain-based learning disability that is dyslexia, separate from other developmental reading disorders. Also, training effects can be studied and evaluated using brain-imaging techniques. In one such study, Pihko et al. (2007) demonstrated that magnetic brain responses to speech sounds that were difficult to distinguish became enhanced after an 8-week training period in a group of children with developmental language impairment.

The previously mentioned studies are just a few examples of how neuroscience is contributing to our knowledge of brain function in learning disorders. Such findings are making it possible to target assessments to reveal more specific underlying problems in brain function when identifying learning disabilities and then to be able to select appropriate interventions to address the dysfunction. The ability to integrate what we see through neuroimaging with our expanding knowledge of pediatric brain function is opening up new frontiers in neuroscience daily.

A caveat, however, is that physiological techniques such as functional magnetic resonance imaging are difficult to interpret without excellent cognitive neuroscience and statistical methodology (Denckla, 1995), so it is important for all three areas to move ahead together. There are many questions still to be asked; but, ultimately, through neuroscience, we will have a much greater knowledge than we have at present of the processing deficits that lead to learning disabilities. This, in turn, will make it possible to develop more specific assessment tools and remediation techniques.

WHAT ROLE DOES NEUROPSYCHOLOGY HAVE TO PLAY IN DESIGNING INTERVENTIONS IN THE CONTEXT OF RTI?

Concerns about RTI arise from the vague explanation about how interventions will be selected, on the basis of what data they will be selected, and who will do the selecting. Further, Vaughn and Wanzek (2007) acknowledge that there is no progress-monitoring measure recommended for Tier 1 or Tier 2 that is highly reliable and valid. The emphasis seems to be on quick administration rather than reliable data. It is acknowledged that many school personnel use reading fluency as an indicator of reading comprehension, because oral reading fluency is highly related to reading comprehension. It is also notable that reading fluency, in contrast to reading comprehension, can be tested very quickly.

What about the child who is a "word caller" or hyperlexic? Reading fluency is usually good in such children, but most of them do not comprehend well what they are reading. Because parents and teachers tend to be impressed by the ease with which these children read, they do not realize that there is a comprehension problem that will become more problematical as the material becomes more abstract. In such a case, it is possible that no intervention would be suggested.

Appropriate interventions depend upon isolating the primary and secondary deficits that need to be addressed and in what sequential order. How is this to happen in the present model of RTI where students, according to Fuchs and colleagues (2003), are provided "generally effective" instruction? Progress is then monitored by either CBMs that are neither valid nor reliable or by brief screening measures that are not highly reliable, such as using oral reading fluency to measure comprehension as discussed previously.

According to Vaughn and Wanzek (2007), students can be provided interventions in a range of group sizes, including whole class, small group, pairs, and one-on-one. For the school administrator who is wishing to save money, whole-group interventions would certainly be the way to go. How effective this approach to intervention would be might not be ascertained for quite a period of time. There are no set parameters for frequency of monitoring. Further, interventions delivered within the three-tier structure may vary in the frequency and amount of time for delivery. Some schools may set a reasonable time frame for seeing progress and others may just recycle children through whole-group interventions.

While using RTI in the best of all possible worlds, a child would receive specific, effective interventions for his or her primary and secondary deficits. The latter would be determined through valid and reliable measures with standardized monitoring to assess progress at set time intervals. However, the present RTI structure appears far too vague to provide that. Fuchs et al. (2003) note that after progress is monitored "those who do not respond get something else, or something more, from their teacher or someone else" (p. 159).

Vaughn and Wanzek (2007) acknowledge that the least research has been conducted at the Tier 3 level, where students most need help and where it is likely to be assumed that, because the child has not responded to intervention, he or she should be placed in special education. They note candidly, "We have an inadequate research base about alternative interventions for students who have not responded to those interventions that are effective for the vast majority of struggling students" (p. 10). Why is a method being implemented in U.S. schools when there are still so many questions about interventions and placements for the most vulnerable students to be served?

If the goal of RTI is to provide early intervention and/or early prereferral services to students who exhibit academic difficulties (Vaughn and Wanzek, 2007), then would it not be beneficial to look to the neuropsychological model for help in designing interventions, as it is used to design rehabilitation treatment plans? Interventions would thus be based on brief, valid, and reliable neuropsychological, cognitive, behavioral/psychological, and academic screening measures to reduce inappropriate referral and identification. Testing would be administered by teachers, support personnel (speech language therapist, occupational therapist), and a school psychologist with neuropsychological training, or by a pediatric neuropsychologist.

By spreading the administration of the brief initial screening over several qualified professionals, it could be completed quickly. A profile and summary could be produced, rather than a full neuropsychological report. This team could then meet to analyze the profile and select interventions, as well as follow-up measures. This process would relieve the teacher of having the sole responsibility for initial testing and selecting interventions.

By taking this approach at the outset of Tier 1, a little more time would be invested by personnel, but there would be fewer instances of children not responding to interventions. When primary and secondary deficits are identified it is much easier to select and even to invent appropriate interventions. In other words, with this approach fewer children would be diagnosed with learning disabilities due to treatment failure. Processing disorders would be identified so appropriate interventions could be tailored to the child's needs. Problems such as Attention-Deficit/Hyperactivity Disorder (ADHD) and/ or emotional disturbance would not go undetected, because the screening would address these issues. Otherwise these children will be programmed for failure. Children with mental health issues, very poor performance on initial screening, or learning differences that did not respond to intervention would receive a full neuropsychological evaluation before any further intervention and/or placement decisions were made.

Thus, we agree with Reynolds (2007) who, in a paper presented to the convention of the American Psychological Association, discussed Fuchs and colleagues' (2003) review of the empirical literature on RTI with special attention to its effectiveness and feasibility. According to Reynolds, they concluded "more needs to be understood before RTI may be viewed as a valid means of identifying students with LD" (p. 157).

WHAT ROLE DOES NEUROPSYCHOLOGY PLAY IN THE DIAGNOSIS OF LD?

One of the roles of a neuropsychologist is to engage in hypothesis testing concerning the primary and secondary deficits that may be affecting a child's learning. These hypotheses are based on evidence that is constantly accumulating on at least two fronts: concerning the types of deficits that have been found in basic psychological processes that participate in the complex processes of learning; and concerning the brain processes that form the concrete, neuronal side of these processes. Sometimes the mechanisms of a learning disorder are very complex: What appears to be a single educational deficit in reading decoding may be the result of the interplay of a number of neuropsychological deficits, such as those in frontal executive functioning, phonological processing, speed of processing, sometimes even a mildly but nonsignificantly compromised general cognitive capacity. It is the interplay of the brain function and dysfunction in a child's profile that results in the learning differences.

The hypothesis testing carried out by the neuropsychologist involves both the administration of standardized, valid, and reliable tests yielding quantitative data as well as observations of the child's problem-solving strategies and performance that provide qualitative information concerning the *way* in which the child learns. Further, important data are collected from the teachers and parents concerning the child's development and presenting problem(s). It is also essential for the neuropsychologist to elucidate strengths the child may have that provide a means for remediation.

The neuropsychologist takes into account the child's development and learning across time, while educational evaluation is apt to focus on the child's performance at one point in time. The latter approach does not address contributions to the child's learning profile over time. For instance, in a hypothetical case, if a 12-year-old male, Andrew, were assessed with CBMs, they might reveal a reading comprehension deficit and written language problems. The teacher might select interventions in finding the main idea, highlighting details in a reading passage, and summarizing the passage, as well as practice in written expression.

If a neuropsychologist were to assess this child, the first step would be to obtain a comprehensive developmental, medical, and educational history from the parent(s). This would afford the opportunity for the parent(s) to recall that the child had bacterial meningitis at 3 years of age, for example. Often, parents and teachers do not make the connection between early traumatic events and later learning problems. What's more, a follow-up oral interview to the written history might reveal that the child had lost his extensive oral vocabulary at the time of his illness and had received occupational, physical, and speech therapy in order to learn to speak, handle small items, and walk again. The neuropsychologist would learn that, by the time Andrew entered school, his doctor felt that he would be fine. Therefore, the parents might not have pursued further therapy.

Because the neuropsychologist has a background in brain-behavior relationships, he or she would understand the importance of surveying all neuropsychological domains in this child in order to determine any residual effects on Andrew's academic functioning as a result of the bacterial meningitis. Thus, through neuropsychological assessment, it would become apparent that the youngster had a mild residual aphasia that affected subtly all aspects of language. Not only would he be having trouble understanding and expressing himself in written language, but he might well have residual dysgraphia that would make it difficult for him to execute handwriting. Finally, part of his problem in reading comprehension and written expression would likely be due to executive dysfunction. Andrew might show difficulty in formulating concepts and reasoning in the abstract. For a child with such deficits, as the reading comprehension questions became more abstract, Andrew would likely have difficulty answering them because he could not formulate abstract concepts and organize them in writing. Further, his handwriting might well be slow and labored. Before Andrew could move successfully into focusing more specifically on reading comprehension, intervention would need to focus on work with a language therapist in order to address his mild aphasia and difficulty formulating and organizing abstract concepts. Because the writing load in his class would be considerable by 12 years of age, the occupational therapist might work with Andrew on learning to use a NEO (alphasmart.com at $250). This is a two-pound word processor for students who have a full keyboard that runs on batteries and is mastered very quickly.

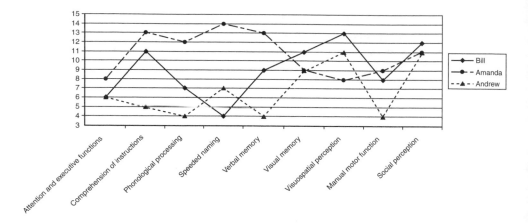

Figure 20.2   An Illustration of Three Different Test Profiles of Scaled Scores Found on Neuropsychological Assessments: Bill, Amanda and Andrew

The fine motor skills needed to use the keyboard are less demanding than those required for handwriting. With this compensation for handwriting in the classroom and his work with the language therapist, Andrew's reading comprehension and written expression would likely begin to improve, as would his confidence. In evaluating the effects of the intervention for Andrew, it must be clarified that quick progress is not to be expected in his case. The test profile of Andrew is illustrated in Figure 20.2 with a summary of his tests findings. The importance of neuropsychological assessments in the diagnosis of LD can be clarified by comparing the case of Andrew with two other cases, Bill and Amanda. Bill's test profile (Fig. 20.2) reveals a quite common pattern of strengths and weaknesses. His general cognitive level (not in the profile) is comfortably average as are his comprehension of verbal instructions and his memory for new verbal and visual material per se (Fig. 20.2). Yet, the NEPSY-II (Korkman, Kirk, & Kemp, 2007) profile suggests difficulty with analyzing the speech-sound structure in speech (Phonological Processing Test) and in the rapid retrieval of verbal names and codes (Speeded Naming). Both types of problems, especially the first one, are well documented as being primary deficits in relation to reading acquisition. If Bill, in addition, had problems with attention and executive functions and with manual motor acitivities, this could complicate the situation in school in a way that is not uncommon either. Such impairments also need to be considered in designing an intervention plan.

The third hypothetical case, Amanda, is a girl whose progress in mathematics, science, and history and also second-language acquisition has became increasingly problematic. In her case a neuropsychological examination does not reveal a pattern compatible with specific learning disorder. Rather, many domains of cognitive performance are basically quite strong but attention and attention-demanding tasks (visuoperceptual and visual memory tasks) are not well performed. A closer study of Amanda's entire situation, including parent and teacher checklists of anxiety, depression, parenting, and behavior, may reveal a difficult family situation, where the parents' divorce is causing anxiety and depression in Amanda and hence explaining her difficulty paying attention and her lack of effort in school. It is clear that in these three cases very different interventions are required.

The focus of a neuropsychological assessment is to consider a child's neurocognitive development and entire situation comprehensively; to identify the child's impairments as well as his or her strengths; and to analyze presenting problems in detail (Korkman, Kirk, & Kemp, 1998). The profile of the child's functioning can thus be analyzed for primary deficits underlying learning differences, as well as secondary consequences of those deficits. This is all accomplished against a background of knowledge of brain-behavior relationships. The more neuroscience helps us to understand function and dysfunction in a child's brain, the more specific neuropsychologists can be in identifying primary deficits underlying complex cognitive capacities—further, the more accurate they will be in detecting and distinguishing primary and secondary deficits, thus making it possible to diagnose a child's learning difficulty very specifically.

REFERENCES

Baron, I. (2004). *Neuropsychological evaluation of the child*. New York: Oxford University Press.

Denckla, M. (1995). Foreword. In S. Broman & M. Michel (Eds.), *Traumatic brain injury in children* (p. x). New York: Oxford University Press.

Fuchs, D., Mock, D., Morgan, P., & Young, C. (2003). Responsiveness to intervention: Definitions, evidence, and implications for the learning disabilities construct. *Learning Disabilities Research and Practice, 18*(3), 157–171.

Fuchs, D., Fuchs, L., & Compton, D. (2004). Identifying reading disabilities by responsiveness-to-instruction: Specifying measures and criteria. *Learning Disability Quarterly, 27*, 216–227.

Gilger, J. & Kaplan, B. (2001). Atypical brain development: A conceptual framework for understanding developmental learning disabilities. *Developmental Neuropsychology, 20*(2), 465–481.

Hale, J., Kaufman, A., Naglieri, J., & Kavale, K. (2006). Implementation of IDEA: Integrating response to intervention and cognitive assessment methods. *Psychology in the Schools, 43*(7), 753–769.

Hartlage, L., & Long, C. (1997). The development of neuropsychology as a professional psychological specialty: History, training, and credentialing. In C. Reynolds & E. Fletcher-Janzen (Eds.), *Handbook of clinical child neuropsychology* (2nd ed.). New York: Plenum.

Korkman, M., Kirk, U., & Kemp, S. (1998) *A Developmental Neuropsychological Assessment*. San Antonio, TX: The Psychological Corporation.

National Association of School Psychologists. (2007). *NASP Position Statement on Identification of Students with Specific Learning Disabilities*. Approved by NASP Delegate Assembly, July 2007.

Pihko, E., Mickos, A., Kujala, T., Pihlgren, A., Westman, M., Alku, P., Byring, R., & Korkman, M. (2007). Group intervention changes brain activity in bilingual language impaired children. *Cerebral Cortex, 17,* 849–858.

Piercel, K., Müller, R-A., Ambrose, J., Allen, G., & Courchesne, E. (2001). Face processing occurs outside the fusiform "face area" in autism: Evidence from functional MRI. *Brain, 124*(10), 2059–2073.

Reynolds, C. (August, 2005). *Considerations in RTI as a method of diagnosis in learning disabilities*. Paper presented to the Annual Institute for Psychology in the Schools of the American Psychological Association, Washington, DC.

Rodriguez, D. P., & Poussaint, T. Y. (2007). Neuroimaging of the child with developmental delay. *Topics in Magnetic Resonance Imaging, 18,* 75–92.

Simos, P., Breier, J., Fletcher, J., Bergman, E., & Papanicolaou, A (2000). Cerebral mechanisms involved in word reading in dyslexic children: a magnetic source imaging approach. *Cerebral Cortex, 10*(8), 809–816.

Vaughn, S., & Wanzek, J. (April, 2007) LD Talk: Reading and RTI. *National Council of Learning Disabilities*. Retrieved September 5, 2007 from the NCLD website: http//www.ncld.org/content/view/1226.

21

Q & A about the Role of Neuroscience and Neuropsychology in the Assessment and Treatment of Learning Disorders

Rosemarie Scolaro Moser, Ph.D.

WHAT DO YOU THINK NEUROSCIENCE HAS TO OFFER THE ASSESSMENT AND IDENTIFICATION OF LEARNING DISABILITIES?

As a culture and society, we are no longer residing in the Dark Ages: Our continued scientific development provides us with knowledge and tools to more effectively function and live. Over the past century, our understanding of learning disabilities has evolved from one of nonexistence to one of brain-behavior knowledge and expertise. Neuroscience, and the application of neuroscience by the field of neuropsychology, has provided that expertise, which has manifested itself in more sensitive testing tools, comprehensive evaluation of cognitive processes, and updated techniques and strategies to address cognitive weaknesses. In a society that has graduated from rotary, to touch tone, to cell phones with cameras, is it not time that we routinely implement that expertise and utilize that knowledge base in the evaluation of our youth who experience learning disabilities?

Unfortunately, at a time when we possess sensitive, sophisticated assessment tools that can better diagnose learning disabilities and that can offer tailored educational interventions at all levels, there appears to be a movement in our educational system to more heavily rely on shorter, cursory skill assessments by individuals who are not trained in brain-behavior relationships. This state of affairs increases the risk of misdiagnosis and decreases the accuracy of targeted interventions. This is especially the case in students who may exhibit mild learning difficulties or who function within the normal limits, but who are otherwise intellectually capable of above average or superior functioning if provided the proper assistance. They are missed by the RTI radar. These are the students for whom time may be lost because they do not fall below "expected levels" of academic functioning, or because the current RTI framework does not identify them as particularly in need of intervention, or because the referral for a comprehensive evaluation is stalled risking lost time in academic intervention years.

When I first began evaluating students, I was a psychology graduate student placed in a school psychology practicum in the public school system. My experience was fairly straightforward. I learned how to administer a battery of intellectual and achievement tests, behavioral checklists and drawings, as well as a Bender-Gestalt Visual-Motor Test (which was a standard part of the test battery at the time). I was a member of a child study team that usually included a social worker and a learning specialist. We each evaluated the children who had been identified with learning difficulties and then met to discuss their learning profiles and to create individualized educational or learning plans. We worked together to match specific educational tasks or interventions to the child's weaknesses we had identified. We also documented any strengths that could be utilized to compensate for the weaknesses and that could help promote the child's educational growth.

However, there was a missing link. In my graduate school classes, my course work focused on cognitive processes, understanding the dysfunctional brain, and the applications of neuroscience. Although I had learned that functional brain mechanisms are key in learning—in the acquisition of new knowledge—my school psychology practicum experience, and the child study team evaluations in which I participated, did not provide an appreciation of that link. In other words, the evaluations did not identify the underlying brain mechanisms that were associated with the learning difficulties and thus did not use that understanding to better prescribe a plan of educational intervention. There was no clear link between our students' brain processes and their school difficulties.

The situation seemed analogous to that of a physician diagnosing a headache, treating it with painkiller/analgesics, but ignoring what caused the headache in the first place. Could the headache be due to a sinus inflammation, tension, brain tumor, or stroke? Could it be the omen of encephalitis? Lyme Disease? By just providing symptomatic relief, the pain might go away entirely, it might be reduced temporarily and later return, or the painkiller might not work at all. Without knowing the cause, the effectiveness of the treatment is a gamble. And if the condition is not properly treated early, complications may occur, recovery can be prolonged, and damage may be done.

As a school psychologist, obtaining training and experience in neuropsychology provided me with the framework for the missing link between brain processes and learning behavior. Such training permitted me to under-stand not only *what* was going on, but also *why* it was happening. This link improved the rationale and efficacy of my recommendations. However, the trend now in schools to postpone or circumvent psychological or neuro-psychological evaluations, in favor of waiting to see a response to interven-tion, seems both disarming and regressive in the context of our advances in neuroscience and neuropsychology.

HOW DO YOU RECONCILE RTI AS A MEANS OF DIAGNOSIS OF LD WITH KNOWLEDGE FROM THE CLINICAL NEUROSCIENCES?

The current RTI initiative has been described by Vaughn & Wanzek (April, 2007), where the "critical feature . . . is the early implementation of appropri-ate interventions for students demonstrating learning difficulties or risk for learning difficulties" (p. 4). In theory, this appears to be a very admirable objective. However, the assessment of students to determine the need for early intervention and the appropriateness of the intervention has been prob-lematic. Students may not receive comprehensive evaluations that are based on neuroscience applications and may be rushed into interventions aimed more at making them look "normal" in their reading scores rather than opti-mizing their learning experiences and allowing them to demonstrate their full potentials. If a student is first placed in an educationally tiered intervention program, it unfortunately may be months or years later before the student will receive the proper comprehensive evaluation and tailored intervention.

Optimally, learning disabilities should be first identified in school, at the beginning of a child's academic career. In particular, a student presents with a significant discrepancy between his or her intellectual ability and his or her actual school achievement. A common presentation of a learning disorder occurs when a child who appears to have been performing well in the early school grades begins to lag behind and struggle when the academic pace increases or when reading skills do not seem to progress as expected given the child's intellectual ability.

Another common presentation occurs in the transition to middle school or high school, when a seemingly very intellectually bright student experiences an unexpected decline in school performance. In the latter presentation, these students are bright enough to compensate for their unidentified weak-nesses up until the critical point when the academic course load becomes too demanding to maintain and manage any longer. Their weaknesses begin to dramatically surface in the form of poor school grades. To properly deter-mine discrepancies between ability and achievement and to diagnose learn-ing disability, comprehensive testing should be administered.

Consider the following case example: A school has described a student as average in skills and abilities, performing well within normal limits, but the parents believe the student is performing below her or his potential and should be more academically capable. The child is frustrated and bored in the classroom and is on the verge of becoming a behavioral problem. This is the case of a third-grade student whose parents believed he was very bright, but he was performing only within the average range in school. The school saw no reason for an evaluation referral. However, after much insistence by the parents, a child study team evaluation indicated that his general intellectual level was in the average range and that overall achievement was also in the average range. The school thus concluded that the child was indeed performing up to potential and that his parents simply overestimated their child's ability. There was no learning disorder identified by the school.

The parents subsequently sought a private neuropsychological evaluation that provided a clearer picture of this child's learning profile. First, a review of the testing performed by the school revealed much scatter, or uneven areas of intellectual ability. Even though his overall intellectual ability was within the average range, there were areas of significant deficiency as well as superior functioning. Second, neuropsychological testing indicated superior auditory or listening memory, but very poor visual memory, and impaired performance on visual discrimination and visual tracking tasks. Third, neuropsychological testing also provided evidence to rule out visual attention difficulties, so that the problem would not be mistaken for an attention disorder. Thus, the child exhibited impaired visual processing that was compensated for by superior range listening and auditory ability in the early school grades when knowledge acquisition is less dependent on reading skills. However, this child's visual discrimination skills, which impact reading and visual learning, were not as strong as expected and were holding him back from expressing his full potential. As a result, his academic performance was about average, even though his parents sensed greater potential. Furthermore, this is the type of child whose academic performance would have been more difficult to maintain as he progressed through school, because of greater demands on his relatively weak visual processing/reading skills for knowledge acquisition in the upper grades.

The previous case is just one example of how a child's learning needs could be missed if a comprehensive neuropsychological evaluation has not been performed.

WHAT ROLE DOES NEUROPSYCHOLOGY HAVE TO PLAY IN THE DIAGNOSIS OF LD?

The educational and health services we provide our youth are an investment in their and our futures. Proper early identification and treatment of learning disabilities results in the most successful outcomes. If our ultimate goal is to provide our children with the most effective, comprehensive educational services available, then we must commit ourselves to employing the techniques and tools that will achieve that goal.

Neuropsychology is the study of brain-behavior relationships and as such is the science that provides the tools that can assist in diagnosis and treatment/management of a variety of conditions that are related to cognition or thinking processes. The American Psychological Association Council of Representatives (1996) has defined *clinical neuropsychology* as the application of "principles of assessment and intervention based upon the scientific study of human behavior as it relates to normal and abnormal functioning of the central nervous system. The specialty is dedicated to enhancing the understanding of brain-behavior relationships and the application of such knowledge to human problems" (p. 149). The definition also elaborates on the populations served by this specialty, one of which is the population of "[c]hildren with learning disabilities of developmental or organic basis . . ." (p. 149).

Neuropsychological evaluation provides a comprehensive assessment of the student's abilities, skills, and cognitive processes, beyond what is typically provided by a learning or school evaluation. Neuropsychological evaluations assess processes such as memory, language skills, sensory/perceptual/motor skills, visual/spatial abilities, mental speed/efficiency/flexibility, physical/mental coordination, executive functioning, listening skills, auditory processing, attention and concentration, problem-solving skills, reasoning, general intellectual abilities, and achievement skills. Such an assessment identifies the child's strengths and weaknesses, and any specific brain dysfunction, so that an educational intervention can be tailored to the child's learning profile. This is especially helpful when standard instructional interventions do not appear to be successful.

Learning disorders are disorders of cognition, in which an individual's cognitive processes are not performing as expected given the individual's intellectual abilities. The *Diagnostic and Statistical Manual–Fourth Edition* (American Psychiatric Association, 2000) describes learning disorders of reading, mathematics, and written expression in which the particular ability, "as measured by individually administered standardized tests, is substantially below that expected given the person's chronological age, measured intelligence, and age appropriate education" (p. 53). In particular, the "disturbance . . . significantly interferes with academic achievement or activities of daily living that require (the specific) ability" (p. 53). Furthermore, when the learning disorder is more generalized, rather than specific to one ability, a Learning Disorder Not Otherwise Specified (NOS) is diagnosed.

School and learning evaluations assess intellectual abilities, both verbal and nonverbal, as well as different areas of achievement, such as reading, writing, spelling, math calculations, and academic skills. Such evaluations are usually the first step in identifying a learning disability. The assessment of ability and achievement is important in order to identify discrepancies that would help explain the student's weak academic performance or problem areas. However, such evaluations alone have limited capacity to explain the source or reason for the difficulties identified. In other words, we can identify the student's level of performance in a number of intellectual and achievement areas, but such evaluations are limited in understanding the cognitive processes that result in that level of performance.

Consider the case of a student for whom an undiagnosed learning disability was suspected as the culprit of her academic difficulties. The student had been achieving A/B grades until entering a very academically competitive high school. Her grades plummeted to the below average range and she complained of attention and concentration difficulties. The school believed that the student had a possible learning disorder and Attention Deficit Disorder that had gone unidentified. Indeed, in the second grade, the student had been referred for evaluation of attentional difficulties, although none had been clearly identified and she never received any educational interventions. The parents did not believe that she was experiencing any learning or attentional disorders but thought that she was undergoing a significant emotional/social adjustment in response to her new, overly challenging school environment that required her to be more independent and self-organized, at a time when she was more interested in boys.

In this case, a comprehensive neuropsychological examination diagnosed a post-concussion syndrome that had been ignored. Through thorough interview, it was determined that the student had sustained two mild concussions, 1 month apart, with no loss of consciousness, during the field hockey season, in the fall, when she began her new school. Other factors, such as social/emotional adjustment were indeed issues, but could not totally account for the significant decline in school performance in a student who had previously been an honors student. Personality/emotional test results were within normal limits. The student's achievement scores prior to entrance to the new school were very superior. Thus, the dramatic decline in school performance could not be easily attributed to a learning or attentional disorder, nor to a more demanding academic program. Neuropsychological testing revealed very deficient reaction time, processing speed, and memory scores, which were significantly inconsistent with previous school performance and achievement test scores. These weak areas were consistent with the profile of an unresolved concussion. Also, the timing of the decline was consistent with the onset of the concussions. Although memory scores were depressed and lower than expected, attention testing did not support an attentional disorder, thus ruling out the possibility of an early childhood undiagnosed Attention Deficit Disorder. Retaining new information was a main problem for her and resulted in the significant decline in academic performance that was inconsistent with previous school records, achievement scores, and grades. Appropriate recommendations were offered with regard to classroom accommodations, rest, physical exertional testing by an athletic trainer, return to play decisions, and follow-up/retesting to determine recovery and need for further future interventions/accommodations. It was expected that this student would improve over time as her brain healed. Thus, it was important not to misdiagnose her as having a learning disability.

The critical point made here is that, by not using neuropsychological assessment, we are likely to miss the reasons or causes for the learning disability or other learning problems we observe, and, worse yet, we may misdiagnose those problems. Thus, when we try to move forward as an educational team in the best interests of the student, to create an educational plan or to treat the disorder, we may not be very effective. Such a situation can result in (a) a waste of precious time in the student's formative academic career; (b) a reduction in the student's self-esteem, with increased feelings of self-doubt, as limited academic progress is achieved; (c) very frustrated and angry parents who believe that their child's needs are not being met; and (d) poor utilization of services that can presumably waste taxpayers' dollars.

This is in no way meant to devalue or be critical of the important services provided by teachers, special education specialists, school psychologists, or school personnel. Rather, we should communicate to all those who interface with students who experience learning problems that there are limitations in the diagnosis and treatment of those learning problems when the evaluations that are used to identify them are limited in scope. Neuropsychological evaluation provides the broader scope.

WHAT ROLE DOES NEUROPSYCHOLOGY HAVE TO PLAY IN DESIGNING INTERVENTIONS IN THE CONTEXT OF RTI?

In a position paper by the National Academy of Neuropsychology, Silver et al. (2006) describe the added value of a neuropsychological evaluation:

> For example, teachers may change how they present verbal or visual material to a child depending on the strengths and weaknesses in the child's memory profile. Is it also helpful for teachers to know how "flexible" the child's brain is. Can the child "shift" or change quickly from one idea to another? Can the child learn a new task and then reapply it or "generalize" it to a new situation? The answers to these and other brain-related questions help teachers design educational programs that can be tailored to the child's ability profile. Without this kind of information, a child's progress is slowed, and frustration mounts for teachers and parents, as well as the child. (p. 742)

Consider the case of a student who had been identified as experiencing a learning disorder but, after years of participating in a prescribed individualized educational plan, the student still struggled well below expected achievement levels. The student seemed to be falling further behind over the years, widening the gap between the student and her classmates. This middle school student's parents sought neuropsychological evaluation to better understand their child's learning profile and to determine if there were weaknesses that the school had not identified, which could account for the lack of progress. A neuropsychological evaluation identified mild neuropsychological impairment, with auditory processing and sensory difficulties that had not been diagnosed. In essence, the child had been receiving intense tutoring in all subjects, but the tutoring had not taken into account that she was primarily a visual learner and would benefit from auditory/sensory training. Adjustments were made in her educational plan.

It is hoped that educators, learning specialists, child study team members, parents, third-party payors, and legislators will be able to appreciate the added value of neuropsychological evaluation in accurately diagnosing learning disabilities and in properly creating effective educational plans that can best meet the needs of our youth who struggle with learning problems. It is important that, in our public enthusiasm to quickly improve the academic skills of our youth, and to improve the educational report cards of our schools, we do not ignore the contributions of neuroscience and neuropsychology in the identification and treatment of learning disabilities.

REFERENCES

American Psychiatric Association. (2000). *Diagnostic and statistical manual–Fourth Edition*. Washington, DC: American Psychological Association.

American Psychological Association Council of Representatives. (1996). Archival description of the specialty of clinical neuropsychology. *Appendix K XVI.3.* Washington, DC: American Psychological Association.

Silver, C. H., Blackburn, L. B., Arffa, S., Barth, J. T., Bush, S. S., Koffler, S. P., Pliskin, N., Reynolds, C. R., Ruff, R. M., Troster, A. I., Moser, R. S., & Elliott, R. W. (2006). The importance of neuropsychological assessment for the evaluation of childhood learning disorders. *Archives of Clinical Neuropsychology, 21,* 741–744.

Vaughn, S., & Wanzek, J. (April, 2007). LD Talk: Reading and RTI. http://www.ncld.org/content/view/1226.

22

RTI and Neuropsychology: Antithesis or Synthesis

Andrew L. Schmitt, Ronald B. Livingston, and Owen Carr

WHAT DO YOU THINK NEUROSCIENCE HAS TO OFFER LAWS AND POLICIES ASSOCIATED WITH LEARNING DISABILITY DETERMINATION?

While lawmakers and educational leaders are forging forward to define and implement changes in the identification and treatment of children with learning disabilities, the vast and rapidly developing field of neuroscience has largely been ignored. This is a rather perplexing situation given that historically most definitions of learning disabilities involve a disruption of one or more of the basic cognitive processes involved in learning and academic achievement. Primarily driven by recent changes in IDEA 2004, the proposed model generally described as *response to intervention* (RTI) may significantly alter current approaches toward the identification of learning disabilities.

While neuropsychological techniques have not been routinely applied in most educational settings (at least not as often as we believe is warranted), the current climate of change may provide an opportunity for the introduction of some of the exciting new advances in the field of basic and applied neuroscience. On the other hand, there is a persistent danger that neuroscience may be relegated to an even less significant role than in the past. It is our opinion that some educational professionals who have for decades opposed the use of practically all standardized assessments have seized on the RTI movement as a way of reducing the use of standardized tests in the identification of children with disabilities. This includes intelligence and other tests of cognitive abilities (including neuropsychological procedures). The basis of their opposition likely varies depending on the individual, but the systematic avoidance of psychological assessment procedures largely disregards over 100 years of research on the merits of psychometric methods.

Most researchers and clinicians now agree that the IQ-achievement discrepancy approach is not effective in identifying children with LD. Accordingly, most researchers agree that a model based on RTI holds promise. However, the RTI model has been evaluated primarily in the context of reading disabilities with children in the early grades. Its extension to other learning disabilities and with older children requires further research (Feifer & Toffalo, 2007; Reynolds, 2005). Nevertheless, some proponents of RTI appear quite comfortable in their ability to generalize this approach to other disabilities and other age ranges. Additionally, some proponents of RTI appear to support it as the *only* process necessary or appropriate for identifying children with SLD (and possibly a number of other disabilities). We are always apprehensive when someone suggests "their way is the only way." This frequently seems to be the case with RTI as espoused by some. At the same time, all of the neuropsychologists we know acknowledge that RTI has something to contribute to the identification of students with SLD and welcome its inclusion in a comprehensive SLD assessment paradigm. However, most neuropsychologists do not see RTI as the *only* assessment technique needed to identify children with SLD. Seemingly consistent with this perspective, the Office of Special Education Programs stated:

> . . . an RTI process does not replace the need for a comprehensive evaluation. A public agency must use a variety of data gathering tools and strategies even if an RTI process is used. The results of an RTI process may be one component of the information reviewed as part of the evaluation procedures required under 34 CFR §§300.304 and 330.305. As required under 34 CFR §§300.304(b), consistent with section 614(b)(2) of the Act, an evaluation must include a variety of assessment tools and strategies and cannot rely on any single procedure as the sole criterion for determining eligibility for special education and related services. (OSEP, p. 9, 2007)

In the ideal world, lawmakers, educators, psychologists, and neuroscientists would collaborate to develop an operational definition of learning disabilities that results in a comprehensive, objective approach to identifying children with these disabilities. This assessment process should include multiple techniques that have been empirically shown to provide valid information in identifying students with disabilities and tailoring interventions to meet their specific needs. In the identification and treatment of children with SLD, there is ample room for both RTI and neuropsychology. They can and should be used in a complementary manner. We are all in agreement that the ultimate goal is to promote the welfare and education of children with disabilities, not winning turf battles over expertise or ideology.

WHAT DO YOU THINK NEUROSCIENCE HAS TO OFFER THE ASSESSMENT AND IDENTIFICATION OF LEARNING DISABILITIES?

Definitions of learning disabilities have been extremely varied, and, consequently, the construct has been elusive since the first attempt at a definition in the 1890s by W. Pringle Morgan and John Hinshelwood (Fuchs et al., 2003). However, amongst diagnoses, this problem is not unique to learning disabilities, and does not release psychologists, neuroscientists, and educators from the responsibility of developing a consensus regarding an operational definition of LD. Laws and policies that do not include an operational definition of LD based on advances in neuroscience and sound psychometric principles will ultimately result in determination by subjective judgment or overly simplistic mechanistic procedures (e.g., untested discrepancy models). Although the general paradigm of diagnosis preceding treatment is considered standard practice in both general medical and psychological treatment models, most of the current interpretations of RTI appear to eschew this most important aspect of diagnosis. Some have argued that *diagnosis* may not or should not play a central role in the process of providing needed services to children in school settings. However, this position does not mitigate the need to obtain as much reliable and valid information as possible regarding the extent, nature, and possible etiology of each child's particular learning problem. In fact, it is incumbent on us as researchers, clinicians, and educators to apply the best available science to determining causal factors in any given child's struggle.

We believe that RTI holds promise and has an important role to play in the identification and treatment of SLD. However, based on existing research, it is not evident that RTI by itself is a panacea. It is likely part of the answer to properly identifying and helping children with learning disabilities, but it is not the whole answer. Accordingly, advances in the field of neuroscience certainly do not provide the sole answer to this complex and multidetermined problem. Neuroscience has the capacity to provide some of the major tools needed to develop objective, testable hypotheses regarding the factors that relate to any child's inability to learn as expected. Interventions based on these hypotheses may inform the treatment process as it is implemented.

The current IDEA definition of LD includes the expectation that each child with the disability must display a *"disorder in the basic psychological processes."* Despite the seemingly obvious importance of gaining information about these basic psychological processes, no methodology is specified under current law or incorporated in most RTI models. Neuroscience is entering a stage whereby it can now provide detailed information of the basic underpinnings of cognitive domains to include memory, attention, executive function, reasoning, motor function, visual and auditory processing, and phonological awareness. As policy is further delineated, recognition of the contribution and importance of the various cognitive abilities can contribute immensely to the diagnostic process. Lawmakers can improve upon current methodology by including neuropsychological techniques within the identification procedures as an integral part of the RTI model. By so doing, interventions can be designed with the child's unique cognitive characteristics in mind. Additionally, as various models are tested, research regarding the relationship between cognitive characteristics and interventions can further inform the educational process.

HOW WILL FUTURE DEVELOPMENTS IN NEUROSCIENCE AFFECT HOW WE CLASSIFY AND INTERVENE WITH LEARNING DISABILITIES?

The role of neuroscience has been paramount in aiding the understanding of how brain functionality affects the learning process. Information regarding specific structures and neural circuitry provides great insight not only into the integrity of function, but also the localization and complexity of processes involved in specific learning tasks. Future developments in the area of neuroscience have the unique potential of contributing to both the identification of those with learning disabilities and the implementation of effective intervention. As the process of assessment advances in the coming years, refinements of the assessment process will provide an important tool in understanding and identifying underlying cognitive processes. With an increase in the understanding of not only *how* but *when* certain neurological processes develop, measures will gain validity to the extent that they are incorporated at the time of measurable development. Future developments in neuroimaging techniques and neurological assessment will likely also advance the understanding of when optimum assessment should occur. Ideally, this could result in reducing the requirement of achievement failures for identification while maintaining the employment of a valid method of evaluation.

The other piece of the overall puzzle of learning disabilities, with the first being identification, is that of intervention. As with any puzzle, the altered shape of one piece necessitates accommodations by the other piece in order to create a proper fit. As the understanding of neurological processes involved with learning disabilities progresses, advancements in intervention will follow. What role might neuroscience play in this evolution? Further knowledge about the function of structures and neural circuitry during specific learning activities and developmental stages can greatly assist in developing both targeted and comprehensive intervention approaches. An increased understanding of the integration of academic and social functions could lead to interventions capable of maximizing the potential of each. Updated age-appropriate interventions could be developed using new information on developmental processes gained through future studies, and these interventions could provide unique stimulation during targeted stages of development. In addition to concerns with stages of development, the existence of comorbid conditions will require further evaluation.

Rapid advances in neuroimaging may provide unique opportunities for investigating the underlying structural and functional causes of learning disabilities. Research opportunities may flourish as changes in the child's academic environment may be found to produce correlated changes in neurological function. As the child begins to experience academic success resulting from targeted interventions, neuroimaging can begin the process of uncovering the neurological substrates of the evidenced improvements. For example, in a recent study, Simos et al. (2007) used magnetoencephalography to obtain spatiotemporal brain-activation profiles with 15 children with reading disabilites during the performance of an oral sight-word reading task. Interventions involved the targeting of deficient phonological and decoding skills and the development of reading fluency skills. Normalizing changes were found in the posterior part of the middle temporal gyrus, the lateral occipitotemporal region, and the premotor cortex. Although this research may not generalize to all children with reading deficits or other types of SLD, it provides an exciting framework for the potential relationships between structural and functional aspects of brain changes and educational interventions. These explorations may lead to a better understanding of the underlying elements of learning disabilities and provide data for future intervention. Again, it is our position that RTI and neuropsychological assessment should be viewed as complementary processes, not competing ones. Several authors have elaborated on how an RTI process and neuropsychological assessment can be appropriately combined into a comprehensive model (e.g., Feifer & Toffalo, 2007; Semrud-Clikeman, 2005).

Additionally, neuropsychological assessment procedures may assist in identifying the role of comorbid conditions such as Attention-Deficit/ Hyperactivity Disorder (ADHD), anxiety, and depression and provide assistance in more accurate classification and treatment. Advanced understanding of the complexity involved with these comorbid conditions and their effects on the developing brain may provide vital information when developing and implementing effective treatment plans for students with SLD.

HOW DO YOU RECONCILE RTI AS A MEANS OF DIAGNOSIS OF LD WITH KNOWLEDGE FROM THE CLINICAL NEUROSCIENCES?

Reconciliation requires some common goals between neuroscience and RTI. This remains a vexing problem, since RTI implementation policies have progressed thus far without the inclusion of many applicable features of clinical neuroscience. Although many definitions of RTI exist, the essential elements generally incorporated in the RTI process have been used for many years as a prereferral option. However, in recent years it has taken on a more central role in making LD eligibility decisions. As with any emerging model, potential problems are evident in the RTI approach. One such problem is the lack of agreement in exactly what the RTI process involves and what role it plays in the identification of students with disabilities. For example, according to some current interpretations of RTI, the individual responsible for making the diagnostic decision may choose to completely abandon the use of any scientifically valid psychometric procedures. Simply stated, if it is shown that an individual has not displayed academic improvements after being introduced to increasingly intense interventions, a learning disability may be diagnosed. In using this model, identification may be based purely on student achievement (possibly measured with instruments with unknown reliability and validity) without incorporating methodologically sound approaches that consider causal factors, etiology, and competing explanations and/or disorders.

One of the most common arguments against complete reliance on an RTI approach is that there is an underutilization of standardized assessments. Some are concerned that RTI will create an ability-tracking system whereby students with IQs below 90 will be disproportionately identified as having an SLD (Reynolds, 2005). If one relies exclusively on RTI, there is no objective way to differentiate between individuals with specific cognitive processing deficits and/or SLD and those that may be considered "slow learners" (i.e., students with borderline intellectual functioning and commensurate achievement). Accordingly, if one shuns the use of standardized IQ tests, how is Mental Retardation ruled out as a differential diagnosis? Some have suggested that Mental Retardation can be ruled out by examining achievement scores and measures of adaptive behavior; however, this is not consistent with contemporary psychological assessment practice. If the goal of the RTI movement is to classify every student with achievement below grade level (i.e., defined as a standard score of 80) as having a learning disability, then this should be explicitly stated so it can be debated on its own merits.

Semrud-Clikeman (e.g., 2005) notes that RTI is skill focused and does not assess the child's ability to generalize learning to other contexts or engage in more abstract problem solving. She also notes that RTI is not able to detect subtle differences in learning problems. For example, two children with reading problems may have completely different underlying processing problems (e.g., one attentional problems, one decoding problems). Without the central component of assessment, RTI will also be plagued by significant diagnostic confounds that impact academic performance, yet may be only tangentially related to LD, such as emotional and behavioral disturbances. A timely assessment can inform appropriate treatment of these separate conditions, one that has a well-founded history in psychology and psychiatry. Remember, as currently envisioned by the OSEP, RTI should be used in conjunction with, not in place of, a comprehensive evaluation. We agree that RTI can become an integral component in the development of hypotheses regarding a child's primary educational problems. Assessment of cognitive abilities can be integrated at several tiers within the RTI process. Through an understanding of the child's cognitive profile (including general ability, relative and normative strengths and weaknesses, and underlying psychological processes), neuroscience can play a significant role in implementation of RTI in accordance with current law and with the use of scientifically valid approaches.

WHAT ROLE DOES NEUROPSYCHOLOGY HAVE TO PLAY IN THE DIAGNOSIS OF LD?

Clinical neuropsychology is an applied science concerned with brain-behavior relationships. It involves the application of principles from neuroscience, coupled with validated psychometric techniques, in a clinical setting. The goal of the assessment typically involves an effort toward diagnostic clarification as well as recommendations regarding client care and treatment planning. As a profession, neuropsychology has decades of research, practice, and specialized procedures used to gain insight into an individual's unique capacities, strengths, and weaknesses. As a specialty, it is heavily steeped in the *scientist-practitioner* model of clinical psychology. Only through a scientific approach can one obtain accurate and unbiased information regarding an individual's present level of functioning and the possible etiology of dysfunction. By gaining a thorough understanding of the levels of function in various neurocognitive domains, one can make reasoned inferences and testable hypotheses regarding the reasons for the possible functional difficulties or deficits. Is it truly possible to accurately make intervention decisions, much less diagnostic decisions, without obtaining detailed information regarding an individual's level of functioning in a wide variety of neurocognitive behavioral manifestations?

One of the major early roles of neuropsychology involved the diagnosis of various types of brain damage and psychiatric conditions. With increased sophistication in brain-imaging techniques, diagnosis has become less central to the general practice of neuropsychology. Nevertheless, neuropsychology continues to play an important contributory role in making determinations regarding an individual's cognitive strengths and weaknesses in both psychiatric and nonpsychiatric populations. Understanding an individual's cognitive profile enables one to make reasoned predictions based on sound psychometric theories and neuropsychological techniques. Considering neuropsychology's traditional contributions to diagnosis, coupled with an understanding of neuroscience and psychometric theory, it seems inconceivable to broadly reach diagnostic decisions on learning disabilities without significant and regular consultation from this science and profession.

All school psychologists are trained to provide assessments and recommendations for some diagnostic considerations; however, only those with additional neuropsychological training and experience are uniquely qualified for a more detailed neuropsychological analysis when deemed necessary. Although it may be unnecessary and impractical to employ the services of a child neuropsychologist at the initial stage of inquiry regarding every child's academic struggle, the inclusion of neuropsychological assessments as a part of the diagnostic and treatment team is essential at some point within the RTI process for many children. If the neuropsychologist's unique skill set is used for no other purposes, his or her expertise in ruling out various conditions and neurological adjuncts to LD (brain injury, subtle neurological deficits, and developmental delays) may make them an invaluable component of a comprehensive evaluative process. Although numerous models of inclusion can be envisioned, one example may be to rely on a neuropsychological evaluation subsequent to the initial stages of RTI. If, for example, initial interventions using the RTI approach are deemed unsuccessful, a referral to a school psychologist may be appropriate for an initial level of assessment and recommendations. If the problems persist, a neuropsychologist can provide additional information to the process such as a detailed analysis of the child's function in various cognitive domains including memory, attention, problem solving, processing, reasoning, and so on. The neuropsychologist's approach begins with a careful analysis of the specific referral question. A detailed clinical interview, coupled with behavioral observations and reliable, valid, psychometric measures, provides the neuropsychologist with a wealth of information that informs reasonable hypotheses for the child's academic difficulties. Although educators are more qualified to directly observe academic performance in vivo, the neuropsychologist has the tools to make valuable inferences based on current neuroscience regarding the child's unique strengths and weaknesses in any given cognitive domain. The neuropsychologist can attend to elements in the LD definition regarding *processing deficits* that have been relegated to insignificance, despite the clinical need to assess this important element of learning. Again, we support a model where both RTI and neuropsychological techniques are included in a comprehensive and complimentary process (e.g., see Feifer & Toffalo, 2007; Semrud-Clikeman, 2005).

WHAT ROLE DOES NEUROPSYCHOLOGY HAVE TO PLAY IN DESIGNING INTERVENTIONS IN THE CONTEXT OF RTI?

Considering the rapid rate of advances in neuroscience and the relatively low level of application of neuropsychological procedures in school settings, there are limitations to our understanding of the relationship between neuropsychologically based interventions and measurable improvements in children with learning disabilities. While we support the inclusion of neuro-psychological assessments in the identification of SLD and believe they provide useful information in treatment planning, we acknowledge that the validation of neuropsychologically based interventions needs further exploration.

Given these limitations, there are neuropsychological models that may hold promise in treating children with learning disabilities. Teeter and Semrud-Clikeman (1997) describe several models, including an early model developed by Rourke (1994). Rourke's system, the Developmental Neuro-psychological Remediation/Rehabilitation Model (DNRR), was specifically designed for LD children and represents an early attempt at using both cog-nitive and metacognitive strategies for remediation. The model proceeds with a seven-step strategy that begins with assessment geared at obtaining a detailed neurocognitive profile. This initial strategy, informed by a foun-dation of underlying neurocognitive processes, is followed by a series of steps that involve gaining an understanding of the demands of the child's environmental milieu; making behavioral predictions based on the relation-ship between the environmental demands and the child's neurocognitive profile; monitoring and modifying intervention strategies; continuous data collection and analysis; and periodic reevaluation of remediation plans. The Rourke model provides adequate structure to develop a practical and useable template, and yet remains open to the incorporation of new advances in our understanding of the neuroscientific correlates of learning disabilities. This type of model can be adapted and incorporated into an RTI process as a compliment to the process, rather than serving as a competing paradigm.

Teeter and Semrud-Clikeman (1997) outline several other programs that also offer promise for inclusion within an RTI strategy. The Reitan Evalua-tion of Hemispheric Abilities and Brain Improvement Training (REHABIT) (Reitan & Wolfson, 1992), although not specific to LD, also approaches remediation with an understanding of the child's unique neurocognitive profile. Reitan and Wolfson use a three-step strategy involving assessment, training, and rehabilitation. This model, like the Rourke model, requires continuous monitoring and evaluation, with concomitant changes to the intervention strategies. In essence, this reflects the scientific method of developing testable hypotheses and gradually refining these hypotheses to reflect the introduction of new information.

As research is considered a continuous process within the rapidly growing field of neuropsychology, research designs pertaining to the evaluation of neuropsychologically based remedial interventions are highly encouraged within the RTI model. It is clearly unreasonable to expect that each child with an SLD undergo brain imaging. However, it seems prudent to offer carefully designed research opportunities to children with intractable LD—designs that may explore the neurological underpinnings of LD and the degree of brain plasticity in such disorders. Through such explorations psychologists, educators, and other researchers can benefit from a growing understanding of the underlying neurological correlates of learning disabilities.

We are also aware that there is a substantial cost inherent in the creation of a comprehensive neuropsychological evaluation as an integral component of RTI. It is acknowledged that schools have limited resources with which to finance complex and comprehensive assessment and intervention strategies. However, despite these limitations, we believe the inclusion of neuropsychological procedures is desirable and necessary in order to adequately address the needs of children with learning disabilities.

REFERENCES

Feifer, S. G., & Toffalo, D. A. (2007). *Integrating RTI with cognitive neuropsychology: A scientific approach to reading.* Middleton, MD: School Neuropsych Press, LLC.

Fuchs, D., Mock, D., Morgan, P. L., & Young, C. L. (2003). Responsiveness-to-intervention: Definitions, evidence, and implications for the learning disabilities construct. *Learning Disabilities Research & Practice, 18*(3), 157–171.

Individuals with Disabilities Improvement Act of 2004, Publication 108-446, 602, 30 (A).

Reitan R. M., & Wolfson, D. (1992). *Neuropsychological evaluation of older children.* Tucson, AZ: Neuropsychology Press.

Reynolds, C. R. (August, 2005). Considerations in RTI as a method of diagnosis of learning disabilities. Paper presented to the Annual Institute for Psychology in the Schools of the American Psychological Association. Washington, DC.

Rourke, B. (1994). Neuropsychological assessment of children with learning disabilities: Measurement issues. In C. R. Lyon (Ed.), *Frames of reference for the assessment of learning disabilities: New views on measurement issues* (pp. 475–514). Baltimore: Paul H. Brooks.

Semrud-Clikeman, M. (2005). Neuropsychological aspects for evaluating learning disabilities. *Journal of Learning Disabilities, 38*(6), 563–568.

Simos, P. G., Fletcher, J. M., Sarkari, S., Billingsley-Marshall, R., Denton, C. A., & Papanicolaou, A. C. (2007). Intensive instruction affects brain magnetic activity associated with oral word reading in children with persistent reading disabilities. *Journal of Learning Disabilities, 40*, 37–48.

Teeter, P. A., & Semrud-Clikeman, M. (1997). *Child neuropsychology: Assessment and interventions for neurodevelopmental disorders.* Needham Heights, MA: Allyn & Bacon.

U. S. Department of Education. Office of Special Education and Rehabilitation Services (OSERS). (2007). Questions and answers on response to intervention (RTI) and early intervening services (EIS). Retrieved September 10, 2007, from http://idea.ed.gov/explore/view/p/%2Croot%2Cdynamic%2CQaCorner%2C8%2C.

23

Utilizing RTI As an Opportunity to Identify and Plan More Effective Educational Interventions for Children with Learning Disabilities

Amy Nilson Connery

WHAT ROLE DOES NEUROPSYCHOLOGY HAVE TO PLAY IN THE DIAGNOSIS OF LD?

The discrepancy model restricted the scope of identification of children with learning disabilities to those failing to make academic progress and who also met strict IQ-achievement test score criteria. Many children who required intervention were not identified under this system. As many school districts move away from this model, neuropsychologists can assist in creating a definition of learning disabilities that is expanded in important ways. An understanding of the impact of neurocognitive functional deficits on successful academic performance, as well as knowledge of neurodevelopment and the complexity of the academic environment, can help to more appropriately identify children with learning disabilities to plan for targeted intervention and accommodation.

Fawcett and Nicolson (2007) note that in the practice of medicine it is not sufficient to define the symptom, but one must search for the cause of the symptom in order to identify an adequate treatment strategy. So, while failure to make academic progress remains the presenting symptom of a learning disability, the functional deficits impeding this progress must be identified so that attempts can be made to intervene in a timely fashion.

An important step in this process is identification of neurocognitive deficits, which were not considered under the LD discrepancy model, but are known to have a profound impact on learning efficiency. This includes such things as executive function, attention, memory, and processing speed. Often, the subskills of a more complex academic skill are intact, but a deficit in an area of neurocognitive function is what impedes adequate educational progress. Other times, a neurocognitive weakness exacerbates a deficit in a subskill. Because of the detrimental impact on learning, children identified as having a weakness in an area of neurocognitive function can be classified as *learning disabled* and provided with appropriate interventions and accommodations.

Previous methods of diagnosing learning disabilities have not adequately identified, and therefore not appropriately accommodated, children with known constellations of learning difficulties, such as nonverbal learning disorders. An understanding of problems in academic functioning as more than just poor performance in math and reading, and consideration of the contribution of other neurocognitive functions as stated previously, can help to more appropriately intervene with these children. While in the former system these children may have been identified for difficulties with math, deficits in executive functions are frequently the most debilitating. Therefore, intervention to improve math skills is important; however, intervention to support the child in organization of materials, planning ahead for assignments, and navigation of the social milieu may be more essential and effective as a strategy to support academic functioning.

An expanded definition of learning disabilities can allow for early identification to alert teachers or caregivers of a potential future learning problem. An understanding of a child's specific neurocognitive strengths and weaknesses, along with knowledge of neurodevelopment and how academic demands change and cumulate, can assist in identifying those children at risk. For example, parents or teachers may not be concerned that a child is not reading by the end of kindergarten, but identification of specific deficits in phonemic awareness or letter recognition can alert educators of the need for immediate intervention. Likewise, a child with deficits noted in executive functions with poor ability for planning and organization will likely not have difficulty in early elementary school. However, identification of this difficulty is critical to support him or her in making the transition to middle school when there are greater demands on self-directed learning, organization, and planning and he or she will likely not succeed without supports in place.

While many states have moved away from the discrepancy model and strict criteria for identifying learning disabilities, this narrow definition of what learning disabilities are will likely remain in the culture for some time. Neuropsychologists can play an important role in extending the definition of learning disabilities beyond academic underachievement in reading or math to include a broader range of neurocognitive function. This expanded understanding can assist to more effectively identify and accommodate children who require specialized intervention.

WHAT ROLE DOES NEUROPSYCHOLOGY HAVE TO PLAY IN DESIGNING INTERVENTIONS IN THE CONTEXT OF RTI?

To maximize the likelihood that educational interventions in the context of RTI will be effective for a particular child, neuropsychologists should play an integral role in designing interventions. The determination of which particular research-based intervention should be utilized for a specific child is made through interpretation of qualitative test performance, assessment of the neurocognitive functions underlying the specific academic difficulty, and consideration for other important neurocognitive strengths and weaknesses essential for efficient learning. It is very important that the interventions attempted are appropriate for a particular child to both optimally intervene for academic problems and to attempt to avoid the more costly intervention of inclusion in special education or the more serious consequence of school failure.

With RTI comes an opportunity to consider test interpretation and qualitative process and performance and no longer be hindered by test scores in and of themselves as in the discrepancy model. Neuropsychologists are uniquely trained to understand and interpret qualitative test performance, such as the child's process and approach to problem solving, speed, and efficiency, as well as the significance of the pattern of test scores (Baron, 2000). Examination of the specific aspects of the qualitative performance may help to explain why the child is falling behind or the teacher has expressed concern.

Consider the following example of two 9-year-old children.

Examiner: What does boat mean?
Child 1: Huh?
Examiner: What does boat mean?
Child 1: Bored?
Examiner: Boat.
Child 1: Boat is in the water.
You ride it.
How much more minutes left?

Examiner: What does boat mean?
Child 2: A boat is a vehicle used for traveling by water.

Both children receive points for this response. However, a qualitative examination of the responses does not show equivalent performance. The first child's response may indicate concerns for auditory processing deficits, an attentional deficit, or problems organizing expressive language, which further testing will elucidate. The second child gave a good quality verbal response with no evidence of problems.

In order to adequately plan an appropriate intervention tailored to a child's specific needs, the specific neuropsychological nature of the learning problem must be determined. For example, it is not useful to state that a child has a math disorder, but rather to define the underlying neurocognitive processes that inhibit efficient math performance. Evaluation for strengths and weaknesses in such areas as visual-spatial processing, procedural memory, fact retrieval, or other language deficits is a critical component in determining which interventions will be most appropriate for a particular child.

RTI creates an opportunity for the evaluation of neurocognitive functions, such as attentional control, executive functions, and memory, which are essential for efficient learning, but are not necessarily assessed or considered in standard special education evaluations. Identification of these functions through neuropsychological evaluation becomes critical for planning effective interventions. For example, if an intervention is planned for two children who struggle with reading, with particular deficits in phonemic awareness and phonics, but one child also has deficits in sustained attention and the other child has poor verbal memory, they are not likely to benefit equally from the same intervention. While intervening or accommodating weaknesses, understanding neurocognitive strengths is also important to attempt to capitalize on what a child does well. An intervention plan must be centered on a child's strengths and on "what actually works for the individual child" (Holmes Bernstein, 2000, p. 419).

Many have criticized the discrepancy model as a "wait-to-fail" approach in which many children were not adequately identified. Some educators have praised the move to RTI as a better solution. However, the danger exists that neuropsychology will be kept out of the assessment process, the specifics of a learning problem may not be accurately identified, and again the child will have wasted precious time with an ill-suited or inappropriate educational intervention (National Joint Commission on Learning Disabilities, 2005).

HOW DO YOU RECONCILE RTI AS A MEANS OF DIAGNOSIS OF LD WITH KNOWLEDGE FROM THE CLINICAL NEUROSCIENCES?

Utilizing RTI as a means of diagnosing learning disability runs contrary to knowledge from the clinical neurosciences. Standardized interventions are promoted and a child's failure to respond to the particular interventions chosen can result in a diagnosis of learning disability. Reynolds (2005) notes that RTI promotes a "one size fits all approach to intervention and remediation," neglecting a very large literature on individual differences (p. 3).

Reynolds (2005, p. 3) describes RTI as "a model of diagnosis by treatment failure." Children can be diagnosed as learning disabled "based on what they are not, rather than what they are" (Lyon et al., 2001, p. 267). Utilizing the model in this manner determines only that these particular interventions did not work for this particular child. The specific learning issue or the severity of the learning problem is not more clearly defined.

Because individual differences will make it so that a certain program is more or less effective for a particular child, a child's failure to respond to a particular intervention should not result in a diagnosis of learning disability. If used for diagnosis in this way, RTI will likely have the same problems with misdiagnosis as did the discrepancy model. Failure to respond to intervention should lead to a more thorough examination of that individual child's characteristics that could help to elucidate why that child might have had more or less success with a particular intervention (Lyon et al., 2001).

In many models of RTI, interventions are implemented before a more in-depth assessment has occurred. This raises the possibility that a problem could be inaccurately or not thoroughly identified resulting in the application of inappropriate interventions for that child's specific difficulty. The intention of the model seems to be that a diagnosis of learning disability is made when the child does not respond to intervention. Therefore, it is very problematic if a risk exists that interventions have not been targeted at the actual problem. Additionally, this model does not take into account that the learning problem and the child's failure to respond to intervention may be related to another *nonacademic* issue, such as an emotional disturbance or environmental stressor, thereby again increasing the risk for misdiagnosis (Reynolds, 2005).

The federal definition of learning disability considers the contribution of neurobiology and excludes environmental influence. The diagnosis of learning disability through RTI appears to do the opposite and considers the environment while neglecting neurobiology. Failing to improve in response to the environment (i.e., educational intervention) can signify the presence of a learning disability in this model. Conversely, does the model imply that a child who profits from an intervention and responds well does *not* have a learning disability?

Neuroscience shows us that the educational environment can exacerbate a learning difference so that it becomes a learning disability. Likewise, a good educational environment can improve neural weaknesses and brain function (Sherman, 2004). However, processing differences seen on functional imaging studies suggest that, for some children, a learning disability is not "cured" with an intervention (Lyon et al., 2001). An effective intervention can result in "compensatory adjustments in functional brain systems" rather than "[eradication of] neurobiologic differences" (Moats, 2004, p. 4).

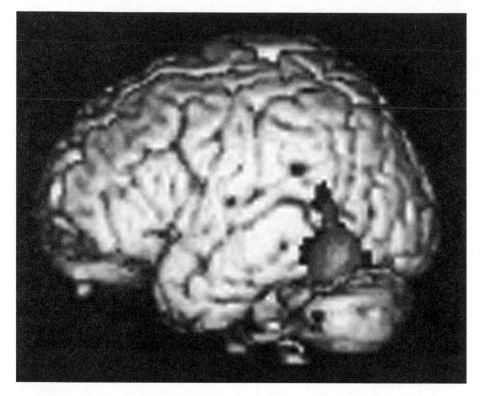

Figure 23.1   PET data shows brain regions more active in university students without a history of dyslexia than those with a history of dyslexia. The difference remains despite the high educational attainment of both groups.
E. Paulesu et al. (2001). Dyslexia: Cultural Diversity and Biological Unity. (Electronic version). *Science, 291,* 2165–2167.

Consequently, for some children, retention of the diagnosis of learning disability would be beneficial despite a good response to intervention. A child with dyslexia, for example, may no longer require specialized reading intervention, but could continue to receive essential accommodations for the neurobiological weakness, such as extended time for tests or access to books on tape (Moats, 2004). In this manner, the RTI model would recognize the contribution and interplay of both the environment and neurobiology to learning disabilities. Figure 23.1 provides a visual of the brain regions affected in those with dyslexia.

It may be important to think of RTI as an academic intervention and a step in the process of special education eligibility, but not for the purpose of diagnosis. Fuchs and Fuchs (2001) propose that, after a failure to respond to intervention, a comprehensive evaluation can occur to make a definitive diagnosis. This evaluation can be the means for diagnosing learning disabilities in the RTI model. However, Reynolds (2005) points out that, in the practice of medicine, problems must be adequately defined and described *before* a treatment is decided upon and initiated. While likely costly, consideration should be made for the comprehensive evaluation Fuchs and Fuchs propose to occur at the initial stages of RTI. Learning disabilities can be diagnosed if appropriate at this stage. Interventions can then be applied to more accurately defined target symptoms in order to improve the chances that a child will be successful with RTI interventions. Children with learning disabilities can be referred for more intensive intervention depending on their responses to these first implemented interventions.

WHAT DO YOU THINK NEUROSCIENCE HAS TO OFFER LAWS AND POLICIES ASSOCIATED WITH LD DETERMINATION?

IDEA (2004) retained the previous definition of learning disability, as well as the exclusionary criteria. *Environmental, cultural,* or *economic disadvantage* remain in special education policy as factors that preclude the diagnosis of learning disability and access to special education. Continued consideration of learning disabilities in policy definitions as attributable to the neurobiology of the child, while neglecting the impact of environmental factors on brain function, is not congruent with knowledge from the neurosciences (Lyon et al., 2001).

A child's neural circuitry is the result of both neurobiology, or genetic factors, and the impact of the particular environment in which that child functions. "Great potential for various functions is genetically prepared for the brain, and a suitable environment can stimulate healthy brain development and the proper application of brain functions" (Koizumi, 2004, p. 435). So, while an optimal learning environment can have a positive impact on brain structure and function, an inadequate or deprived environment can have a detrimental impact on the brain, placing children at increased risk for learning difficulties (Lyon et al., 2001). The environment can "exacerbate a child's learning problem to the extent that a relatively minor learning difficulty is transformed into a bona fide learning disability" (Taylor, 1989, p. 349).

While environmental deprivation can result in inadequate neural circuitry leading to learning problems, social and economic factors are also related to increased risk of exposure to other conditions. "Malnutrition, limited pre- and post-natal care, exposure to teratogens and substance abuse . . . can place children at risk for neurological dysfunction, leading to cognitive, linguistic, and academic deficits" (Lyon et al., 2001, p. 268). A deprived or poor environment can impact the developing brain and create lasting neurocognitive and neurobehavioral effects.

Research on reading is of considerable interest here because of the significant advances made in understanding the neurobiology of reading disorders. Reading research has demonstrated that approximately half of the variance in reading ability can be attributed to genetics (Moats, 2004). This leaves half of the variability explained by environmental factors. "Many of the conditions excluded as potential influences on LD are themselves factors in impeding the development of cognitive and linguistic skills that lead to the academic deficits frequently observed in RD children" (Lyon et al., 2001, p. 267). In fact, Shaywitz (2003) notes that an unfortunate result of the exclusion of environmental factors in learning disabilities has been that problems with reading are frequently underidentified in children from disadvantaged environments.

The danger of environmental exclusionary criteria is not only that children with learning disabilities arising from the detrimental impact of the environment on the child will not receive necessary educational intervention, but also that educators may attribute learning disabilities to environmental causes when this is not accurate. Anectdotally speaking, I have seen many children with language-based learning disabilities who did not receive intervention because learning problems were dismissed as related to bilingualism or inadequate exposure to English outside of school. In one tragic example, the child had reached fifth grade with profound language deficits, which had been dismissed as resulting from poor environmental exposure to English. In fact, the child was from Nigeria and English was his primary language.

Fawcett and Nicholson (2007) advocate for a new discipline called *pedagogical neuroscience*. Koizumi (2004) calls the approach *developing the brain* or *brain science and education*. These disciplines would combine neuroscientific knowledge with research in learning and education and could assist in bridging the gap between the neuroscience community and education policy. The proposed disciplines are an affirmation that neuroscience can make an important contribution to special education law. While it will always remain critical to evaluate learning difficulties in the context of the child's environment, neuroscience has given us valuable information about the environmental impact on the brain. Removing the exclusionary criteria of environmental, cultural, or economic disadvantage from the law will serve children more effectively in the educational system.

REFERENCES

Baron, I. S. (2000). Clinical implications and practical applications of child neuropsychological evaluations. In K.O. Yeates, M.D. Ris, & H.G. Taylor (Eds.), *Pediatric neuropsychology: Reseach, theory, and practice* (pp. 439–456). New York: Guilford.

Fawcett, A. J., & Nicolson, R. I. (2007). Dyslexia, learning, and pedagogical neuroscience. *Developmental Medicine and Child Neurology, 49,* 306–311.

Fuchs, D., & Fuchs, L. S. (2001). Responsiveness-to-intervention: A blueprint for practitioners, policymakers, and parents. *Teaching Exceptional Children, 38,* 57–61.

Holmes Bernstein, J. (2000). Developmental neuropsychological assessment. In K. O. Yeates, M. D. Ris, & H. G. Taylor (Eds.), *Pediatric neuropsychology: Reseach, theory, and practice* (pp. 405–438). New York: Guilford.

IDEA (2004) Individuals with Disabilities Education Improvement Act of 2004. *Public Law* 108-446.

Koizumi, H. (2004). The concept of 'developing the brain': A new natural science for learning and education. *Brain & Development, 26,* 434–441.

Lyon, G. R., Fletcher, J. M., Shaywitz, S. E., Shaywitz, B. A., Torgesen, J. K., Wood, F. B., et al. (2001). Rethinking learning disabilities (Electronic version). In C. E. Finn, A. J. Rotherham, & C. R. Hokanson, (Eds.), *Rethinking special education for a new century* (pp. 259–287). Washington, DC: Thomas Fordham Foundation.

Moats, L. (2004). Relevance of neuroscience to effective education for students with reading and other learning disabilities. *Journal of Child Neurology, 19,* 840–845.

National Joint Committee on Learning Disabilities (2005). *Responsiveness to intervention and learning disabilities.* Retrieved July, 2007, from http://www.ldonline.org.

Paulesu, E., Demonet, J. F., Fazio, F., McCrory, E., Chanoine, V., et al. (2001). Dyslexia: Cultural diversity and biological unity (Electronic version). *Science, 291,* 2165–2167.

Reynolds, C. R. (2005). Considerations in RTI as a method of diagnosis of learning disabilities. Paper presented to the Annual Institute for Psychology in the Schools of the American Psychological Association, Washington, DC.

Shaywitz, S. (2003). *Overcoming dyslexia.* New York: Alfred A. Knopf.

Sherman, G. (2004, August). *Are there structural brain differences in kids with ld?* Retrieved July, 2007, from http://www.schwablearning.org.

Taylor, H.G. (1989). Learning Disabilities. In E. J. Mash & R. Barkley (Eds.), *Behavioral Treatment of Childhood Disorders* (pp. 347–380). New York: Guilford.

24

Neuropsychology, Neuroscience, and Learning Disabilities: Brain-Behavior Relationships

Arthur MacNeill Horton, Jr.

WHAT DO YOU THINK NEUROSCIENCE HAS TO OFFER LAWS AND POLICIES ASSOCIATED WITH LEARNING DISABILITY DETERMINATION?

The first point to be made is that laws and policies associated with learning disability determination should be placed in the context of public policy and the greater good of the human race. That is to say, the reason for laws and policies concerning learning disability determination is the assumption that the determination is in the best interest of society. Laws are not happenstance but rather the crystallized political will of the majority of the population at the time the law was enacted (e.g., Prohibition, No Child Left Behind). Most people would indeed agree that it is important for society to encourage the education of children—it is so obvious that it is trite to state, but it is central to the issue of learning disabilities determination. Societies see a public good in having children educated and so ours has enacted laws and policies to ensure that all children are provided with an appropriate education. Educated adults are expected to be economically productive so they can be taxed and knowledgeable citizens so they will vote responsively and ensure that democracy works. This is why all states have compulsory school attendance laws and truant officers and school social workers, and so on.

The second point to be made is that children learning is seen as a public good and essential for successful economic competition among nations and the conduct and continuation of a democratic form of government. Societies

306

with well-educated populations are seen as better able to produce goods and services in an increasingly technological international environment, and poorly educated citizens are seen as undesirable persons who are a drag on society and thus are discriminated against in terms of immigration laws and policies, for example. Countries want well-educated persons with financial resources to immigrate into a country so they can increase a country's wealth and ability to produce more wealth. The purpose of the education of children is to provide them with the knowledge and skills that will enable them to function in society effectively, not become a burden on society, and hopefully to produce more wealth in turn.

In all forms of competition, however, there are those with natural advantages and those without. If one is playing basketball, being tall and coordinated is a great advantage. If one plays football, being big and strong and fast is ideal for success. Learning is similar. Some children have advantages over others. The simplest and most common case in American education is by academic-achievement testing, and the usual way that academic achievement is assessed in America is by standardized tests such as the Scholastic Aptitude Tests (SATs), the Medical College Admission Tests (MCATs), and the Law School Admission Tests (LSATs) and so on. Some persons have talent for taking academic-achievement standardized tests and do well in society. Others are not as able on academic-achievement standardized tests, but are they to be automatically considered dumb? In some cases yes, and in some cases no. Grossly oversimplified for effect, there are two types of persons who do not do well on standardized tests: first, those who are actually less intelligent, and second, those who for some reason do not do well on academic-achievement standardized tests but who are very intelligent. For some reason, the second type of person either has not learned the necessary academic knowledge and skills or is unable to demonstrate the learned academic knowledge and skills in the standardized-testing situation. In other words, these are people who have the ability to learn but for some reason the learning has not taken place. In a very broad sense, these are persons with learning problems. In a more narrow sense, persons with peripheral sensory deficits (e.g., blind, vision problems, hearing problems) have not been considered as having *learning disabilities* as a group but do have learning problems, in a general sense. The groups with diagnosed neurological and neurodevelopmental disorders (i.e., brain damage, acquired brain injury) clearly have learning problems and may be considered as having a *learning disability,* but a diagnosis of a neurological or neurodevelopmental disorder is not required as, historically, the concept of learning disabilities came from neurological settings where children presented who were intelligent but had difficulties in learning academic skills—but neurologists were unable to find clear and firm evidence on traditional neurodiagnostic procedures (e.g., Brain MRI, EEG, Physical Neurological Exam, Spinal Tap). On the other hand, however, comprehensive standardized neuropsychological testing has been able to differentiate validly and reliably learning disabled children from children with brain damage and also from normal children (Reitan & Wolfson, 1992). Generally, learning disabled children fall on a continuum of severity of neuropsychological dysfunction between normal children who can learn and children with neurologically diagnosed brain damage. In short, the middle is where learning disabled children stand.

The third point is that what neuropsychological testing can offer to laws and policies associated with learning disability determination is an objective means of identifying which persons have learning problems and have difficulties in neuropsychological functioning. The most important word in the last sentence is *objective* because the determination of learning disabilities has political and financial implications for school systems. If a person is identified as having a learning disability then more expensive education services would be required. While school systems may prefer methods of identifying learning disabilities rather than constraining the number identified to a percentage of the school population and/or falling under certain budget constraints. The tension in the education system is that the greater good to society is that all children are appropriately educated, even those who have had problems learning but are intelligent, but local school systems have to pay for special education services. Therefore, there is a conflict of interests as the larger society has a clear interest in ensuring that all children are appropriately educated but local school systems are concerned with managing their budgets. Laws and policies associated with the determination of learning disabilities should be based on objective scientific evidence, not political considerations. Neuroscience through neuropsychology can provide objective scientific evidence upon which to base laws and policies associated with the determination of learning disabilities.

WHAT DO YOU THINK NEUROSCIENCE HAS TO OFFER THE ASSESSMENT AND IDENTIFICATION OF LEARNING DISABILITIES?

Neuroscience through neuropsychological testing offers methods and procedures to objectively assess and identify persons with learning disabilities. In this context, the term *learning disabilities* is considered to be applying to persons with problems in learning academic knowledge and skills, who have adequate intelligence, due to neuropsychological dysfunctions but may not have a neurological diagnosis and do not have diagnosed sensory impairments (e.g., blind, deaf, vision impaired, hard of hearing). Neuropsychological testing can differentiate groups of children with learning disabilities from groups of children with normal learning histories and groups of children with neurologically diagnosed brain damage (Reitan & Wolfson, 1992). The groups of learning disabled children fall in the middle between groups of children with normal learning histories and groups with neurologically diagnosed brain damage.

Neuroscience, through neuropsychological testing, also offers methods and procedures that can aid in better characterizing the types and varieties of neuropsychological impairments found in groups of children identified as having learning disabilities. The neuropsychological approach to learning disabilities postulates that the children with learning disabilities have neuropsychologically based processing deficits that impede their learning of academic knowledge and skills. Newly developed measures of executive functioning such as the Test of Verbal Conceptualization and Fluency (TVCF) (Reynolds & Horton, 2006) and revised measures of memory in children such as the Test of Memory and Learning–Second Edition (TOMAL-2) (Reynolds & Voress, 2007) provide means and procedures for assessing the most essential abilities and skills that underlie learning abilities in children of school age. Moreover, the TVCF and TOMAL-2 are simply examples of a large number of neuropsychological instruments that can be of value in measuring neuropsychologically based processing skills and abilities.

In addition, new developments in neuroimaging are expected to increase in diagnostic sensitivity and complement neuropsychological testing in identifying and assessing children with learning disabilities. It is expected that new insights will emerge as there are new scientific developments in neuroimaging technology.

In addition, neuroscience in the form of neuropsychology has theoretical models of brain functioning that can inform the assessment and identification of learning disabilities. The brain-behavior relationships model of A. R. Luria (1970) provides a dynamic and heuristic understanding of neuropsychological processing and functioning. Luria's model of higher cortical functioning involved three major brain blocks: (a) the lower brain-stem structures; (b) cerebral cortex posterior to central sulcus; and (c) cerebral cortex anterior to the central sulcus. These major blocks make unique contributions to the human brain functioning.

Block One

The lower brain-stem structures are responsible for maintaining the tone and energy supply of the cerebral cortex. They also provide for the tone and energy level of the cerebral cortex in order for the higher level areas to subserve memory and executive functioning abilities.

Block Two

The area posterior to the central sulcus or the posterior cerebral cortex is the area where sensory stimuli of a visual auditory and tactile nature are identified, perceived, and encoded.

Block Three

The area anterior to (or in front of) the central sulcus is involved in the initiation, production, monitoring, and evaluating of motor responses. The anterior cerebral cortex received information from the posterior sensory processing and there is formulation of intention planning and production of motor behaviors and monitoring and evaluation of the effects of motor behaviors.

Neuropsychological Developmental Stages

Luria (1970) postulated a number of stages by which neuropsychological functions are developed and environmental/cultural influences interact with neurological structures to develop higher level mental abilities such as memory and executive functioning. Luria said that higher cortical functioning requires both the interaction of normal neurological development and specific environmental stimuli of a cultural, historical, and social nature. Appropriate interaction of neurological development and environmental stimuli optimize higher cortical functions of language, memory, and executive functioning (Luria, 1970).

HOW WILL FUTURE DEVELOPMENTS IN NEUROSCIENCE AFFECT HOW WE CLASSIFY AND INTERVENE WITH LEARNING DISABILITIES?

The future is always difficult to predict, but some trends are likely to continue. Further developments in neuroimaging and neuropsychological testing will increase knowledge of how the human brain works in encoding, storing, evaluating, and retrieving of information and planning and monitoring behavior. This is likely to lead to new ways of classifying and intervening with learning disabilities. The most recent developments in neuroimaging have suggested that human information processing is determined by multiple brain areas simultaneously and sequentially functioning in diverse neuronetworks that vary with the tasks, settings, experiences of the person studied, and cognitive stimuli involved. Parsing these neuronetworks can be expected to help to better understand how human learning in children proceeds and fails to proceed.

In addition, new developments in neurogenetics (i.e., genetic influences on brain functioning) are likely to increase. Understanding how genetics influences brain functioning could lead to new ways of classifying learning disabilities (Olsen & Gayan, 2001). For example, one theory is that a proportion of persons with learning disabilities are simply individuals who were genetically engineered for optimal visual-spatial and perceptual-motor functioning to the detriment of auditory-verbal and linguistic-linear processing. When persons with such a genetic loading are high performers, they do very well in simultaneous processing situations, but in repetitive performance, linear processing situations they do poorly. As traditional academic-achievement situations are biased toward repetitive performance and linear processing situations, these persons who do less well are classified as learning disabled rather than having a particular genetically determined learning style. Genetic engineering and the unleashing and suppressing of genetic expressions may prove to provide methods of turning on and off particular problems in learning. In the future, current learning disabilities may be corrected by genetic means and all would have equal abilities to learn.

For example, the incidence of language-based learning disabilities in the United States has been associated with the characteristics of the language spoken. In countries such as Italy where the characteristics of the language spoken are very different the incident of learning disabilities is very different. Similarly, the ways in which similar verbal stimuli are mentally processed in Chinese and English speakers, who have Chinese as their first language, are different as original Chinese speakers process linguistic identification of pictures as a bihemisphere process, where English speakers process similar stimuli as a left-hemisphere process. Understanding the neuroscience of language and brain functioning, therefore, will hopefully lead to new insights into the classification of learning disabilities.

HOW DO YOU RECONCILE RTI AS A MEANS OF DIAGNOSIS OF LD WITH KNOWLEDGE FROM THE NEUROSCIENCES?

Response-to-Intervention (RTI) will be discussed with respect to various aspects of treatment planning and intervention. RTI is actually treatment intervention in reading instruction from a behavioral perspective. The extant clinical child research literature suggests substantial empirical support of behavioral methods in a wide variety of settings and situations with many categories of children with problems, but not with the diagnosis of LD. A more appropriate way of understanding the relationship of RTI and neuroscience-neuropsychology is a problem-solving model that combines diagnosis of LD, neuropsychological testing, treatment planning, and various behavior-management implementation techniques.

Problem-Solving Model

In terms of developing a general approach that incorporated RTI, the problem-solving model previously developed by Lewinsohn and colleagues (Lewinsohn, Danaher, & Kikel, 1977) is of particular value. Lewinsohn and

Table 24.1   Lewinsohn's Model

1. General Assessment of Neuropsychological Functioning
2. Specific Assessment of Neuropsychological Functioning
3. Laboratory Evaluation of Intervention Technique
4. Real-World Application of Intervention Techniques

his colleagues have proposed a model of remediation strategies (Lewinsohn, Danaher, & Kikel, 1977), which has proposed to be of significant value in terms of conceptualizing treatment interventions. Lewinsohn's model is divided into a number of phases with respect to intervention and assessment. The specific phases are enumerated in Table 24.1.

In terms of the four phases, the first two are focused on the neuropsychological assessment of the person and the last two are used to evaluate RTI type interventions. The first phase deals with normative comparisons among persons—or, put in another way, how does the individual compare to other peers when assessed on standardized measures of intelligence, neuropsychological functioning, social skills, emotional status, or academic achievement (Horton & Wedding, 1984)? It is important to appreciate what the child is like compared to other children of the same age, gender, educational level, and socioeconomical background. Traditional diagnoses of the DSM-IV or ICD-10 type often emerge from this phase.

In the next phase, the second phase, the focus is upon comparison of the child within him or herself. More specifically, what is the child's internal structure of ability or abilities, what are his or her strong points and which are his or her weak points? For example, is the child particularly good in verbal or language abilities or is the child particularly good in manipulatory or visual-spatial activities? Understanding the child's internal ability structure can be very helpful in terms of understanding what tasks the child is uniquely capable of performing and where the child's personal competence/environmental stress match-up may be problematical.

In many ways, phase two, a specific assessment of neuropsychological functioning, may be seen in other contexts as a behavioral assessment (Horton & Wedding, 1984). This phase involves examining the child's actual behavioral functioning as seen in a systemized fashion relative to the child's abilities. In planning treatment interventions, it is helpful to have a baseline of specific problem-associated behaviors. This allows decisions to be made regarding what are problem behaviors that may need to be changed. Very often, it is helpful to pinpoint or target specific behaviors for either enhancement or decrements and to obtain measurements of the behaviors in question over time so that there can be a comparison of the effect of intervention strategies on the baseline of behaviors in a preintervention period.

In the third phase, specific treatment interventions are evaluated. Basically, RTI techniques would be conceptualized using a behavior paradigm (Bandura, 1969). In the behavioral model it is usually best to begin to apply treatment interventions in relatively controlled situations. In working in classroom settings, however, it is not possible always to have the same degree of experimental control that one would have in an experimental psychology laboratory. Nonetheless, many possible sources of error and variance should be accounted for or attended to when attempting to implement an intervention. Moreover, it is helpful to continue specific assessment of selected target behaviors so that it will be possible to demonstrate improvements on those target behaviors over time. Continuous assessment over time helps to provide data that allow a logical rationale for making decisions regarding initial treatment/intervention effectiveness. If initial treatment effectiveness can be demonstrated in phase three (an activity that may not always be as easily accomplished), then some serious consideration should be given to clinical application.

Clinical application, in this model, is addressed in phase four. In the early days of behavior modification, behavioral assessments and interventions would be initiated and, after an initial positive behavior change, then the behavior modifiers would pack up and leave. It takes no genius, or to use a contemporary phrase *rocket scientist*, to discern that, after the behavior modifiers leave, problem children were often able to discriminate treatment and "real-world" conditions and change their behavior accordingly. In a nutshell, the children realized that they were not going to be reinforced for various behaviors after the treatment conditions ended and would stop behaving appropriately.

Nowadays, it has been realized that it is important to work out or devise a specific system to maintain and promote further generalization of any treatment gains realized when the treatment intervention was introduced in a controlled setting (Bandura, 1982). This may require more training, specific programming of reinforcement, and additional allocation of resources, but it is crucial to devoted specific efforts to be sure treatment interventions are maintained and generalized to additional settings. Otherwise, any behavioral gains may soon prove to be illusionary and fleeting. Bandura (1982), for example, has postulated that there are different methods for the initiation of change, different methods for the maintenance of change, and different methods for the generalization of change. It is important to realize that in terms of intervening in a child's problems the techniques to initiate change may very possibly be different than the techniques necessary or most effective for the maintenance of change and these may be entirely separate from those that are most effective in promoting the generalization of positive behavior changes to different settings, persons, and behaviors. Therefore, individuals contemplating using behavior-modification techniques in a consultation relationship should appreciate that there are a number of steps and phases that have to be addressed and failure to address these issues would constitute inadequate service delivery and cause the entire enterprise to become a failure.

REFERENCES

Bandura, A. (1969). *Principles of behavior modification*. New York: Holt, Rinehart, & Winston.

Bandura, A. (1982). Self-efficiency mechanism in human agency. *American Psychologist, 37,* 122–147.

Horton, A.M., Jr., & Wedding, D. (1984). *Introduction to clinical and behavioral neuropsychology*. New York: Praeger.

Luria, A. R. (1970). *The working brain*. New York: Basic Books.

Lewinsohn, P. M., Danaher, B. G., & Kikel, S. (1974). Visual imagery as a mnemonic aiding brain damaged persons. *Journal of Consulting Clinical Psychology, 45,* 771–723.

Olsen, R. K., & Gayan, J. (2001). Brains, genes and environment in reading development. In S. B. Neuman & D. K. Dickenson (Eds.). *Handbook of early literacy*. (pp. 81–94). New York: Guilford.

Reitan, R. M., & Wolfson, D. (1992). *Neuropsychological evaluation of older children*. Tucson, AZ: Neuropsychology Press.

Reynolds, C. R., & Horton, A. M. (2006). *Test of verbal conceptualization and fluency*. Austin, TX: Pro-Ed, Inc.

Reynolds, C. R., & Voress, J. A. (2007). *Test of memory and learning, second edition*. Austin, TX: Pro-Ed, Inc.

25

Knowing Is Not Enough—
We Must Apply.
Willing Is Not Enough—
We Must Do.
—Goethe

Elaine Fletcher-Janzen

WHAT DO YOU THINK NEUROSCIENCE HAS TO OFFER THE ASSESSMENT AND IDENTIFICATION OF LEARNING DISABILITIES?

For many years, researchers and professionals in special education have looked to neuroscience as they investigate the etiology of learning problems (D'Amato & Dean, 2007; Reynolds, 2007; Edelston & Swanson, 2007, 2007). The failure of early attempts to remediate learning disabilities through perceptual-motor training and processes dimmed enthusiasm for finding neuroscientifically based curative treatments for learning problems (Hynd & Reynolds, 2005; Reynolds, 2007) but did not detract from the federal definition of learning disabilities being neurobiologically based (Applequist, 2007;Edelston & Swanson, 2007, 2007).

The National Institutes of Health (NIH) realized a few years ago that there were growing barriers between clinical and basic research. The increasing complexities involved in conducting clinical research were making it more difficult to translate new knowledge from the laboratory bench to the clinic—and back again. These challenges were limiting professional interest in the field and hampering the clinical research enterprise at a time when it should have been expanding. The National Institute of Health (2007) currently believe that:

> To improve human health, scientific discoveries must be translated into practical applications. Such discoveries typically begin at "the bench" with basic research—in which scientists study disease at a molecular or cellular level—then progress to the clinical level, or the patient's "bedside." (p. 4)

Scientists are now increasingly aware that this bench-to-bedside approach to translational research is really a two-way street. Basic scientists provide clinicians with new tools for use in patients and for assessment of their impact, and clinical researchers make novel observations about the nature and progression of disease that often stimulate basic investigations.

The federal trend toward translating scientific information into useful clinical applications is now paralleled in the field of neuroscience and learning disabilities in particular. For example, research conducted by individuals such as Sally Shaywitz (2004) and colleagues have clearly outlined three areas of the brain essential to reading that are different in children with dyslexia. Their research goes on to strategically designed remediation interventions and then evidence of changes in areas of the brain as a result of the interventions (Simos et al., 2002). Their research also extends to investigating how strategic interventions in reading can be applied in the classroom and school. These studies are groundbreaking and have set the standard for translating brain-behavior research because they hold so much promise for direct clinical and academic effects.

Another example of neuroscientific laboratory work translating into the field of learning disabilities and reading is research conducted by Posner and Rothbart (2007a, 2007b). Their research explains brain functions that include: attending to information; controlling attention through effort; regulating the interplay of emotion with cognition; and coding, organizing, and retrieving information. Posner and Rothbart then go on to relate how these aspects of brain functioning and development can support school readiness, literacy, numeracy, and academic expertise.

Neuroscience used to be isolated in the laboratory, but technological advances have progressed to the point that imaging results can translate laboratory investigations into clinically useful activities. This advancement has only just begun and it promises to continue full force (Scientific & Computing Imaging Institute, 2007). In some areas of investigation, the baton from laboratory to classroom is being held by sets of consistent researchers and not passed from one group with the hope of it translating to others who will bring it into practicality (e.g., Fletcher et al., 2007; Shaywitz, 2004). Essentially, the major research breakthroughs in learning disabilities in the past 15 years have come to us from neuroscience and have been powerful catalysts for the enhancement of clinical practice and the identification of learning disabilities. Neuroscience has shaped the field of learning disabilities for many years and has increased translational efforts to reach directly into the classroom. There is no indication that this contribution will wane in years to come; on the contrary, the federal government is leading the way and acting as a catalyst for the translation of neuroscientific research results into practice, and the bar has been set by clusters of researchers who have created seminal research programs that extend from laboratory to the individual student.

HOW WILL FUTURE DEVELOPMENTS IN NEUROSCIENCE AFFECT HOW WE CLASSIFY AND INTERVENE WITH LEARNING DISABILITIES?

There are probably two areas of growth in neuroscience that will continue to affect how we classify and intervene with learning disabilities. The first is the promise of neurogenetics that hopes to map genes expressed in the brain, as well as of brain circuitry and cell location. So far, over 99% of the neuroscience literature focuses on only 1% of the estimated 15,000 to 16,000 genes expressed in the brain and so the genetic mapping of the human brain has far to go. However, the ultimate goal is not just to map the brain but to "make connections between anatomical, genetic, and behavioral observations" (Gewin, 2007, p.12). Genes do not automatically produce certain types of behavior but they do determine the basic structure of neural networks that interact with the environment (through experience) to produce behavior. Right now, there are researchers who have begun to identify the heritability of different types of attentional neural networks and the connection to phenotypic profiles (e.g., Posner & Rothbart, 2007a). Researchers on autism spectrum disorders have isolated over 10 genes that influence autistic behaviors that unfold later on in development (NIH, 2005). With regards to learning disabilities, researchers have isolated genes that appear to be specific to phenotypes of phonological decoding, orthographic coding, single-word reading, and phonological awareness (Grigorenko, 2005). In addition, many studies of the genetic aspects of dyslexia also try to understand how the genetic risk interacts with environmental risks to produce a disability in reading (e.g., Fisher & DeFries, 2002; Fletcher et al., 2007).

The second area for future developments in neuroscience is the advances in and clinical applications of neuroimaging technology. New kinds of imaging techniques are being developed that present original and exciting ways of understanding brain processes. For example, diffusion tensor imaging (DTI) looks more at processing efficiency as opposed to localization of function. It highlights the structural integrity of the brain wiring as axonal tracts are illuminated and the strength of the flow of information from one area to another is revealed during specific cognitive activities (see Fig. 25.1 for an example of a DTI brain image). Imaging methods such as DTI are assisting researchers in the understanding of dynamic localization of processes associated with

Figure 25.1 Visualization of a DTI Measurement of a Human Brain.
Depicted are reconstructed fiber tracts that run through the mid-sagittal
plane. Especially prominent are the U-shaped fibers that connect the two
hemispheres through the corpus callosum (the fibers come out of the image
plane and consequently bend toward the top) and the fiber tracts that
descend toward the spine (blue, within the image plane).
Courtesy of Gordon Kindlmann at the Scientific Computing and Imaging
Institute, University of Utah, and Andrew Alexander, W. M. Keck Laboratory for
Functional Brain Imaging and Behavior, University of Wisconsin-Madison.

reading. For example, Beaulieu et al.'s (2005) research results suggest that diffusion tensor imaging of the brain underlines the "importance of regional connectivity in left temporo-parietal white matter for enhance reading performance in healthy children" (p. 1,270). In the future, the imaging of dynamic localization may significantly impact our understanding of what processes are involved in any given academic activity—and the areas of intervention focus. It is hard to imagine that brain imaging at this level for the individual child will be readily available and affordable in the future, but the trends are evident globally (Linden, 2006).

Another recent and significant advance in imaging is the establishment of the MRI brain-imaging database housed at McGill University. It is an international effort to create a normative comparison of brain images of children and adolescents. Researchers at six American pediatric study centers collected magnetic resonance imaging (MRI) scans of more than 500 normal children, from newborns to aged 18. Each child's brain was scanned a minimum of once every 2 years over a period of 6 years, and more often for younger, more rapidly developing children. The data will provide a point of comparison for researchers interested in observing how a healthy brain develops, as opposed to a brain affected by neurological disorders. The database cost over $30 million to create but has been made available free to the worldwide scientific community via an online website (Bourguignon, 2006).

In the future, brain imaging may also become a direct instrument of measurement for the effectiveness of any intervention. If technology and translational research continue to expand at the current rate, we could expect that imaging would have a central part in learning disabilities classification *and* remediation. This level of specificity is not possible today other than in the laboratory. However, if it can be done in the laboratory then perhaps the only remaining issue becomes the means of translation into clinical practice. One path of translation is already happening as neuroscientists have already identified some common tests that are proxies for specific brain/cognitive processes such as word-form recognition and phonemic awareness (e.g., Beaulieu et al., 2005; Shaywitz, 2004) and also broader processes such as attention or executive functions (e.g., Posner & Rothbart, 2007b). These psychometric tests have been additionally validated by imaging as well as the usual psychometric theory and methods of test validation. It is reasonable and exciting to believe that imaging and psychometrics will continue to intertwine and support a more direct assessment of the brain/cognitive processes of children with suspected learning disabilities.

In summary, ongoing research in neurogenetics, advances in brain-imaging technology, establishment of brain-imaging databases, imaging validation of psychometric instruments that measure brain functions, and measurement of processing changes through remediation are powerful scientific advances already influencing our understanding, assessment, and treatment of learning disabilities.

HOW DO YOU RECONCILE RTI AS A MEANS OF DIAGNOSIS OF LD WITH KNOWLEDGE FROM THE CLINICAL NEUROSCIENCES?

Neuroscientifically based research makes an economic statement for the efficacy of RTI identifying and remediating phonologically based reading disabilities (Fletcher et al., 2007; Shaywitz, 2004). The scientific evidence is neurobiologically based, has used brain imaging as a measure of identification and treatment efficacy, and has translated well to curriculum-based measurement techniques of assessment and progress (Fuchs & Young, 2006). Therefore, the neuroscientific support of RTI to remediate many reading problems is sound and substantial—*but only for some phonologically based reading disabilities in young children who do not have comorbid disorders and that are remediated in tightly controlled conditions for extended periods of time.*

RTI, at this point in time, has promising evidence of efficacy for a specific group of conditions (e.g., Vaughn, 2007; Fletcher et al., 2007) but it does not account for many of the confounding variables that prove to be the rule not the exception in the real world. Given that LDs are: (a) frequently present with other disorders; (b) are frequently mistaken for other disorders; (c) co-occur with other reading and learning disability subtypes (Hooper, 1996; Semrud-Clikeman, 2005); (d) developmentally timed in emergence, progression, and expression; (e) sensitive to cultural variables such as socioeconomic status (NCCREST, 2007; Sirin, 2005); and (f) should evidence consistently across schools, district, and states, it is clear (from the research evidence to date) that RTI cannot possibly be a reliable and valid method for predicting LD or meeting the federal guidelines for the diagnosis of LD. There are simply too many variables that require careful professional analyses left out of RTI procedures to transform it into a valid one-size-fits-all method of identifying learning disabilities.

This does not mean to say that RTI is not a valuable approach to the *prevention* of learning disabilities; on the contrary, neuroscience has supported the use of phonological instruction in struggling readers as an agent of actual change in brain function (e.g., Fletcher et al., 2007; Shaywitz, 2004). These are outstanding and commendable findings that will influence our understanding of reading intervention for many years to come. These findings do not, however, reflect the reality of clinical practice in the schools and the rich diversity of learning issues—they reflect the laboratory. Sometimes science translates into the reality of the classroom and many times it does not. In the case of RTI, the translation of neuroscience is substantial but it stops abruptly by imposing laboratory-controlled conditions into classrooms across the country that are anything but controlled! By emphasizing group data and treating the classroom as a controlled laboratory environment, the richness of the pupil-teacher relationship is ignored: The human element, that is many-times random and powerful, is ignored. The right to a culturally and clinically competent analysis of the child's world before being labeled is therefore denied; and, therefore, RTI as a sole method of identifying learning disabilities is insupportable.

The neuropsychological approach (Silver et al., 2006) to learning disabilities identification embraces the single case subject research design and preserves the uniqueness of the individual and complements teacher judgment. It surveys the child's environment and understands the bilateral and highly individualized relationship between genes and experience. It also "integrates etiological and performance factors, keeping in mind the effects of emotional/behavioral factors, to assist in developing effective interventions" (Silver et al., 2006, p. 4).

OSERS and NASP have recently stated that the determination of LD can only take place in the context of a comprehensive assessment and this position is well within the intent and wording of the law. This is not to say that RTI does not contribute important information to the assessment process. The most direct contribution that RTI (only when implemented with integrity and fidelity) provides to the diagnosis of LD is to eliminate environmental confounds in a single case subject designed comprehensive assessment. Considering the research base to date, it can be said that RTI is an evidence-based and economical way to determine if the student has phonologically based reading problems and if he or she has been exposed to appropriate teaching methods. If the child does not respond to well-executed interventions then RTI data provide an invaluable real-life and interactive history on which to base a comprehensive assessment. Theoretically, if a child fails to respond to well-designed interventions then we at least know that, or that there is a severe and nonremediable phonologically based reading issue or something other than a phonologically based deficit at work and creating academic difficulties. What exactly is creating the continued difficulties requires an objective, in-depth, and comprehensive assessment that involves a thorough understanding of neurobiological basis of learning on the part of the examiner, multiple sources of data, culturally competent practices, nationally norm-referenced instruments, and clinical competence with differential diagnosis.

In summary, the reconciliation of RTI and neuroscience (in the assessment and identification of learning disabilities) is complimentary. Appropriately conducted RTI provides an invaluable source of information on which to build a comprehensive assessment of a child struggling with reading or other academic areas. Again, the relationship should be complimentary and reflect a cooperative system. Posner and Rothbart (2007b) aptly conclude: "We, with many of our colleagues, see different levels of analysis in psychology as informing each other, with each level of equal scientific validity.

Bridging these levels can allow a higher level of understanding and prediction" (p. 2).

WHAT ROLE DOES NEUROPSYCHOLOGY HAVE TO PLAY IN THE DIAGNOSIS OF LD?

The role of neuropsychology in the diagnosis of LD is essentially natural and seamless. Neuropsychologists assess the same areas involved in a school-based LD comprehensive assessment but include tests that are specific to broad and localized brain processes and contribute unique perspectives about how the brain processes evidence in behavior (academic and social). Neuropsychologists also tend to have specialized knowledge about chronic illness disorders that expose the child to potential ongoing medical problems that affect brain and academic functioning such as mild brain injury, epilepsy, asthma, and diabetes.

The differential diagnosis involved in the assessment of children who exhibit LD symptoms is quite complex and requires (ethically and legally) the ruling out of comorbid conditions that are difficult to identify and treat. Children evidence psychopathology and neurodevelopmental conditions much differently than adults (e.g., brain injury sequelae, depression, anxiety), and the comprehensive assessment results benefit greatly from the brain-behavior expertise of the clinician. Many school and outpatient-based clinicians will refer to pediatric clinical neuropsychologists when they sense organic or developmental issues that need to be identified and understood (Silver et al., 2006).

As information from the neurosciences translates and evolves, aspects of brain functioning that were relegated to neuropsychology years ago (e.g., executive functions, working memory) are now routinely assessed in clinical and school settings (Hynd & Reynolds, 2005). For example, it is commonly understood that Attention-Deficit/Hyperactivity Disorder (ADHD) is frequently comorbid with LDs. It is not possible to determine the comorbid status of ADHD/LD in these settings unless some formal measures of attention, organization, planning, and impulsivity are administered and interpreted in light of the DSM criteria and differential conditions (Barkley, 2003; Fletcher-Janzen, 2005; Semrud-Clikeman, 2005). Indeed, there are multiple reasons why a child might exhibit ADHD symptoms and knowledge of brain-behavior relationships is essential to finding the etiology of the symptoms and subsequent treatment direction (Semrud-Clikeman, 2005).

Now that the discrepancy model of LD determination has been largely abandoned, it is possible to include neuropsychological principles in LD assessment in a formal way in multiple settings. As to a new model of defining and determining LDs, no single method has gained large-scale popularity as yet. However, the World Health Organization's International Classification of Functioning (WHO, 2007) has been adapted to children (Simeonsson,

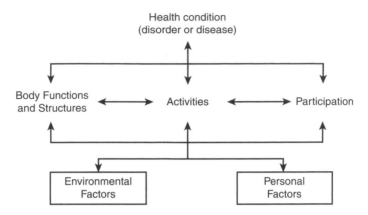

Figure 25.2   World Health Organization Model of the International Classification of Functioning.

Pereira, & Scarborough, 2003) and holds much promise for a model of disability that transcends politics, settings, and country boundaries. Figure 25.2 depicts the WHO model and its constituent elements. The reader is directed elsewhere to obtain details and research literature about the model (WHO, 2007), but a cursory glance will show that the model includes all aspects of functioning (biological [including neuropsychological], sociological, psychological, environmental, and systems) and speaks to a global effort to share a common understanding of the elements of disability from a humanistic perspective. Not only will this model standardize language about disability functioning, it will lead the way in setting a global standard of the *right of individuals to receive a comprehensive assessment of their overall functioning to determine disability and treatment.*

In summary, we live in exciting times, when the promise of neuroscience and neuropsychology is evidence based and available for translation into the clinic and classroom. As we are no longer constrained by the discrepancy model as a means for LD identification, it is paramount that policy makers and educational professionals stay open to the inclusion of neuropsychological principles into the LD identification process because the practical applications of neuroscience are growing at a very rapid rate and are being assimilated into the global model of disability that will be the standard for many years to come.

REFERENCES

Barkley, R. S. (2003). Attention-Deficit/Hyperactivity Disorder. In E. J. Mash and R. A. Barkley (Eds.), *Child pathology* (2nd ed., pp. 75–143). New York: Guilford.

Beaulieu, C., Plewes, C., Paulson, L. A., Roy, D., Snook, L., Concha, L., & Phillips, L. (2005). Imaging brain connectivity in children with diverse reading ability. *Neuroimage, 25,* 1266–1271.

Bourguignon, M. (2006). Technology takes guesswork out of data collection. *McGill Report, 38,* 1.

D'Amato, R. C., & Dean, R. S. (2007). Neuropsychology. In C. R. Reynolds & E. Fletcher-Janzen (Eds.), *Encyclopedia of special education* (pp. 1439–1440). New York: Wiley.

Edlelston, D., & Swanson, H. L. (2007). Learning disabilities. In C. R. Reynolds and E. Fletcher-Janzen (Eds.), *Encyclopedia of special education* (pp.1231–1234). New York: Wiley.

Fisher, S. E., & DeFries, J. C. (2002). Developmental dyslexia: genetic dissection of a complex cognitive trait. *National Review of Neuroscience, 3,* 767–780.

Fletcher, J. M., Lyon, G. R., Fuchs, L. S., & Barnes, M. A. (2007). *Learning disabilities: From identification to intervention.* New York: Guilford.

Fletcher-Janzen, E. (2005). The school neuropsychological assessment. In R. C. D'Amato, E. Fletcher-Janzen, & C. R. Reynolds (Eds.), *Handbook of school neuropsychology* (pp. 173–213). New York: Wiley.

Fuchs, D., & Young, C. L. (2006). On the irrelevance of intelligence in predicting responsiveness to reading instruction. *Exceptional Children, 73,* 8–30.

Gewin, V. (2007). *A golden age of brain exploration.* PloS Biology, 3, e24.

Grigorenko, E. (2005). A conservative meta-analysis of linkage and linkage-association studies of developmental dyslexia. *Scientific Studies of Reading, 9,* 285–316.

Hooper, S. R. (1999). Subtyping specific reading disabilities: Classification approaches, recent advances, and current status. *Mental Retardation and Developmental Disabilities Research Reviews, 2,* 14–20.

Hynd, G. W., & Reynolds, C. R. (2005). School neuropsychology: The evolution of a specialty in school psychology. In R. C. D'Amato, E. Fletcher-Janzen, & C. R. Reynolds (Eds.), *Handbook of school neuropsychology* (pp. 3–14). New York: Wiley.

Linden, D. E. J. (2006). How psychotherapy changes the brain–the contribution of functional neuroimaging. *Molecular Psychiatry, 11,* 528–538.

National Institutes of Health. (2005). Autism and genetic research. Retrieved August 29, 2007, from: http://www.nimh.nih.gov/healthinformation/autismmenu.cfm

NCCREST. (2007). Cultural considerations and challenges in response-to-intervention models: An NCCREST position statement. Retrieved August 20, 2007, from http://www.nccrest.org/index.html

NIH. (2007). Translational research. Retrieved August 6, 2007, from: Office of Portfolio Analysis and Strategy, National Institutes of Health http://nihroadmap.nih.gov/clinicalresearch/overview-translational.asp

Posner, M., & Rothbart, M. (2007a). *Educating the human brain.* Washington, DC: APA.

Posner, M., & Rothbart, M. (2007b). Research on attention networks as a model for the integration of psychological science. *Annual Review of Psychology, 58,* 1–23.

Reynolds, C. R. (2007). Neurological organization. In C. R. Reynolds & E. Fletcher-Janzen (Eds.), *Encyclopedia of special education* (pp. 14–39). New York: Wiley.

Scientific and Computing Imaging Institute. The golden age of imaging. Retrieved August 24, 2007, from http://www.sci.utah.edu/.

Semrud-Clikeman, M. (2005). Neuropsychological aspects for evaluating learning disabilities. *Journal of Learning Disabilities, 38,* 563–568.

Shaywitz, S. (2004). *Overcoming dyslexia.* New York: Knopf.

Silver, C. H., Blackburn, L. B., Arffa, S., Barth, J. T., Bush, S., Koffler, S. P., Pliskin, N. H., Reynolds, C. R., Ruff, R. M., Troster, A. I., Moser, R. S., & Elliot, R. W. (2006). The importance of neuropsychological assessment for the evaluation of childhood learning disorders. *Annuals of Clinical Neuropsychology, 21,* 741–744.

Simeonsson, R. J., Pereira, S., & Scarborough, A. A. (2003). Documenting delay and disability in early development with the WHO-ICF. *Psicologia, 17*(1), 31–41.

Simos, P. G., Fletcher, J. M., Bergman, E., Breier, J. I., Foorman, B. R., Castillo, E. M., Davis, R. N., Fitzgerald, M., & Papanicolaou, A.C. (2002). Dyslexia-specific brain activation profile becomes normal following successful remedial training. *Neurology, 58,* 1203–1213.

Sirin, S. R. (2005). Socioeconomic status and academic achievement: A meta-analytic review of research. *Review of Educational Research, 75,* 417–453.

Vaughn, S. (2007). LD talk: Reading and RTI. Retrieved September 2, 2007, from http://www.ncld.org/content/view/1226.

World Health Organization (2007). International classification of functioning. Retrieved September 2, 2007, from http://www.who.int/classifications/icf/en/.